3192

21-00
3

The
'Ever-Victorious
Army'

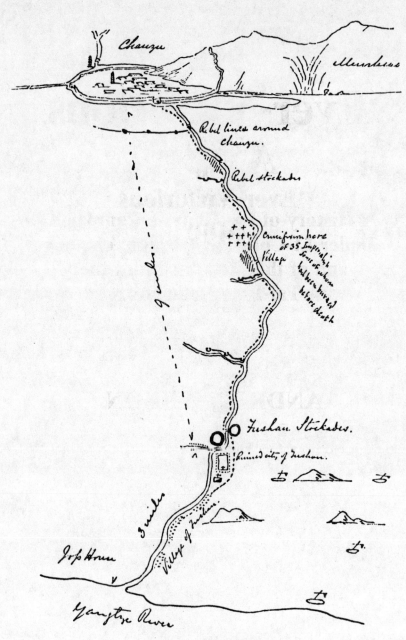

Chanzu

Mountains

Rebel lines around Chanzu.

Rebel stockades

Crucifixion here of 35 Imperialists. Some of whom had been buried before death

Village

Fushan Stockades.

Ruined city of Fushan.

Joss House

Village of Fushan

Yangtze River

FUSHAN AND CHANZU
(From Gordon's original sketch)

The 'Ever-Victorious Army'

A History of the Chinese Campaign under Lt-Col C.G. Gordon, CB, RE, and of the Suppression of the Tai-Ping Rebellion

by
ANDREW WILSON

Greenhill Books, London
Presidio Press, California

This edition of The 'Ever-Victorious Army'
first published 1991 by Greenhill Books,
Lionel Leventhal Limited, Park House,
1 Russell Gardens, London NW11 9NN
and
Presidio Press,
31 Pamaron Way, Novato, Ca.94949, U.S.A.

British Library Cataloguing in Publication Data
Wilson, Andrew
The 'Ever-Victorious Army': A History of the Chinese Campaigns
under Lt-Col C.G. Gordon, CB, RE, and of the suppression
of the Tai-Ping Rebellion.- New ed.
1. China. Tai-Ping Rebellion
I. Title   951.043

ISBN 1-85367-089-8

Publishing History
The 'Ever-Victorious Army' was first published in 1868
(William Blackwood & Sons). The text is reproduced now
exactly as the original edition, complete and unabridged.
For this addition 10 illustrations and 7 maps have been added.

In reprinting this book for a modern audience any imperfections in
the original typesetting are inevitably reproduced and the quality
falls short of the high standards normally to be expected in a modern book.

Printed in Great Britain by Antony Rowe Ltd

CONTENTS.

PART I.

THE ORIGIN OF THE REBELLION.

CHAPTER I.

THE PRINCIPLES OF THE CHINESE STATE.

Relations between the Past and Present of China—Antiquity of the Chinese Nation and Government—The doctrine of Filial Piety—Advancement of able men to official posts—Geographical isolation of China—The Chinese language politically considered—The Doctrine of Harmony—A successful ideal state—Symmetrical oneness of the Chinese state—Sages, Worthies, and Worthless—Chinese political action founded on a Christian principle—The harmony of relationships—Feeling against the employment of force in government—Respect for age and learning—Education universal in China—Position and titles of the Emperor—Mutual responsibility, . 3-21

PART II.

OUR COLLISION WITH THE REBELS.

PART III.

COLONEL GORDON'S CAMPAIGN.

CHAPTER VIII.

THE ORGANISATION OF GORDON'S FORCE.

CHAPTER IX.

GORDON'S FIRST VICTORIES.

CHAPTER X.

BURGEVINE'S HISTORY AND FATE.

CHAPTER XI.

THE FALL OF SOOCHOW, AND THE EXECUTION OF ITS WANGS.

CHAPTER XII.

GORDON'S FURTHER OPERATIONS.

CHAPTER XIII.

THE DISSOLUTION OF GORDON'S FORCE, AND A REVIEW OF ITS RESULTS.

CHAPTER XIV.

THE MEDICAL ARRANGEMENTS OF GORDON'S FORCE.

PART IV.

THE END OF THE TAI-PINGS.

CHAPTER XV.

A VISIT TO TSENG KWO-FAN—SKETCHES OF NATIVE AND ENGLISH OFFICIALS IN CHINA.

CHAPTER XVI.

THE FALL OF NANKING AND THE LAST STRUGGLES OF THE TAI-PINGS.

CHAPTER XVII.

NIEN-FEI AND MOHAMMEDAN REBELS.

CHAPTER XVIII.

THE PRESENT AND FUTURE OF CHINA.

APPENDICES.

LIST OF ILLUSTRATIONS

LIST OF MAPS

PREFACE.

THE Chinese people and Government have had to struggle during the last ten years with difficulties of no ordinary kind. In that period they have carried on a prolonged war with two of the most powerful nations of the earth, whose demands upon them, however warrantable, necessarily weakened the power of the Chinese State by lowering it from an authoritative position; they have had to adapt their long-isolated civilisation to the disintegrating influence of close contact with Foreigners*—a difficult and hazardous task, only accomplished by a ministerial *coup d'état* almost tantamount to an internal revolution; and they have suppressed a great internal movement, which had become a most formidable rebellion chiefly because a long period of isolation and of peaceful prosperity had led the authorities of the country to neglect the arts of war.

The latter feat forms the topic of this book; but it has been found impossible to treat of it in anything like a

---

* The words "Foreigner" and "Foreign," when commenced with a capital letter, refer to the Europeans and Americans in China as opposed to the people of the country. Hence "Foreign" is a proper name nearly equivalent to the term "Occidental," which some writers use in its place.

satisfactory manner without many references to the other
two difficulties just mentioned; for they not only all
existed contemporaneously, but were also closely connected, and aggravated each other in a high degree.
It was not merely that the war with Foreigners gave
opportunity to the Tai-ping Rebels, and the Rebellion
diminished the means of external defence: the Rebellion had its origin in the contact of China with Foreign
nations; it was almost suppressed in 1859, when a new
difficulty between Foreigners and the Imperial Government came to its aid; the loss of power consequent on
the Rebellion made it difficult for the Emperor to grant
Foreign demands, and the loss of prestige caused him
by Foreigners decreased his power of dealing with the
Rebellion.

Several interesting and instructive works—such as
those of Mr Meadows, Mr Oliphant, Commander Brine,
and Dr Rennie—have been published, relating to the
first half of the transition period through which China
has recently passed, and which closes with the Peking
coup d'état of 1861; but the important events which
followed, which have resulted in the complete suppression of the Tai-ping Rebellion, and the restoration of
China to a state of comparative order and peace, are
known to the British public only through an indistinct
recollection of telegrams and newspaper reports, or
through the frantic complaints of ignorant or unscrupulous Tai-ping sympathisers. In these events Foreigners
in China took an important part. Some Englishmen
and Americans fought on the side of the Rebels; while
on the other hand it will not be forgotten that almost
every mail from the Far East, during great parts of

1863 and 1864, brought home intelligence that Major (now Colonel) Gordon had taken another town from the Tai-pings and handed it over to the Imperialists. Hence this latter period has for us the double interest arising from the restoration to order of a great country with which we are commercially connected, and of the military service in it of British officers to that end.

My information on this subject has been drawn chiefly from unpublished sources. More than a year after his connection with the Chinese Government had ended, Colonel Gordon offered me his Private Journal and Correspondence relating to that connection, and other papers illustrative of Tai-ping history, with full permission to make any use of them I pleased, but expressing at the same time a strong wish that in anything published on the subject he should not be made the hero of a work in which so many other officers were engaged, who had, in his opinion, as much to do with the suppression of the Rebellion as himself, and that any relation of his services in China should be subordinated to what he considered the more important object of presenting a true account of the recent course of events in that country. He was induced to place in me this valued confidence chiefly by the perusal, after his return to England, of a pamphlet on our policy in China, which I issued at Hongkong in 1860, proposing and advocating that change of policy towards the Celestial Empire which was afterwards so ably carried out at Peking by Sir Frederick Bruce, her Majesty's Plenipotentiary; at Shanghai by Mr Hart, the head of the Imperial Maritime Customs; and by Colonel Gordon in the field.

Though I never had the slightest connection, directly

or indirectly, with the Celestial Government, or derived
any special benefit from it, yet, having lived a good deal
among the Chinese in their own Flowery Land, and being
deeply impressed with the convictions that the interests
of China and of Great Britain are at present identical,
and that a right understanding of the former country
may be of very great use in the new phase of political
matters into which we are ourselves entering, I felt
inclined to enter on the task thus committed to me.
Considering Colonel Gordon's wishes, the absence in his
Journal of all details of personal adventure, and the uninteresting nature of small military operations after the
recent great wars in America and on the Continent, it
seemed clear that the best course to pursue would be
to draw up a brief general history of the suppression
of the Tai-ping Rebellion, taking, only as a central figure,
the Foreign-officered Imperialist force officially called the
Ch'ang Sheng Ch'un or "Ever-Victorious Army," which
was originated in 1860 by Ward, an American adventurer, and which, under Colonel Gordon, did essential
service in clearing the province of Kiangsoo of Tai-pings,
and leading to the fall of Nanking, the Rebel capital.

The completion of this design has been delayed and
partially interfered with by very severe and prolonged
illness; but the delay is not a matter of regret, for no
events of great importance have very recently occurred
in China, and the lapse of time has allowed idle reports
about the continuance of the Tai-ping Rebellion to die
away. I do not plead my state of health in excuse of
any errors or defects in this short history, but only to
explain why some of the earlier chapters are more ela-
borate than may seem necessary as an introduction to

those which follow. I had planned the work on a larger scale, and with the intention of more perfect execution, but, having been reduced to writing by dictation, have been compelled to content myself with presenting matter which is either entirely new, or is of essential importance to a right understanding of recent events in China.

About a third of this volume has already appeared in the pages of 'Blackwood's Magazine;' but the remainder is entirely new matter, with the exception of a few sentences which I may have used when commenting in the 'Daily News,' or 'Pall Mall Gazette,' on passing events in the East.

I have to acknowledge my obligations for various documents and information to Major-General W. G. Brown; Staff Assistant-Surgeon A. Moffitt; Captain Roderick Dew, R.N.; Mr Dick of Tientsin; Mr James Macdonald, formerly Secretary of the Shanghai Chamber of Commerce; Dr W. Dickson, late of Canton; and especially to Colonel Gordon, with whom, however, I have had no communication in regard to matters of opinion, and who is in no way responsible for this work further than for the correctness of my account of the operations which he conducted.

My own experience in China and acquaintance with Ward when he started the Ever-Victorious Army have proved useful, as also the statements of gentlemen who had opportunities of observing some of the operations under Gordon; and I may say that all the information now available regarding the suppression of the Tai-ping Rebellion has been examined and considered, but the materials of this work have been chiefly drawn from the following sources :—

b

1. The Private Journal and Correspondence of Lieutenant-Colonel Gordon, C.B., relating to his Chinese Campaign.

2. A MS. Narrative of Gordon's Campaign, compiled under the direction of Major-General Brown, who commanded H.M.'s troops in China in 1863-64, and whose brother, Major Brown, was Gordon's A.D.C.

3. A confidential "Memorandum on the Quin-san Force," or Gordon's Contingent, printed by H.M.'s Government, but never published.

4. The Private Journal kept by Captain Roderick Dew, R.N., of his operations against the Tai-pings in the province of Chekiang.

5. Imperial Decrees and other official Chinese documents, and Tai-ping Manifestoes.

6. The Autobiographies of the Tai-ping Chiefs, the Chung Wang or Faithful King, the Kan Wang or Shield King, and the son of the Rebel Monarch, who, before being put to death by the Imperial authorities after their capture at, or shortly after, the fall of Nanking, were permitted to employ the brief remainder of their lives in writing out accounts of their history.

7. Intercepted Rebel Despatches and the Letters and Depositions of unfortunate Foreigners who served with the Tai-pings.

8. "Notes kept by" Colonel Schmidt, "an officer who served under Ward, Burgevine, Holland, and Gordon," which were published in the 'Friend of China,' a paper notorious for its Tai-ping sympathies.

9. A Medical Report on Gordon's Campaign by Staff Assistant-Surgeon A. Moffitt.

10. The Correspondence on our Relations with China

published in Parliamentary Blue-Books, and the Diplomatic Correspondence issued by the President of the United States.

11. The Chinese Classics.

12. Files of old newspapers innumerable.

In regard to several of the maps which accompany this book, I have to acknowledge my obligations, for valuable assistance rendered in the preparation of them, to Captain Sanford of the Royal Engineers, who is personally well acquainted with the country in the neighbourhood of Shanghai, having been engaged on the survey of it, and having also taken a part in the British operations against the Tai-pings. The "Sketch-map of the Operations against the Rebels in 1862-64" will be found necessary to explain Colonel Gordon's Campaign, and has been reduced from a large military plan constructed by himself and by other officers of her Majesty's army. The "Map illustrating the Operations of the Chung and Ying Wangs" is explanatory of the attempts, as described in Chap. V., of the Tai-pings to relieve Hankow. In the "Sketch-map of the Routes taken by the Rebel Forces from 1851 to 1865," advantage has been taken of the lines illustrating the early Tai-ping movements given by Mr Meadows in the map accompanying his work on the Rebellion ; but the later more important movements of the Tai-pings, up to the time of their extinction, are also shown, together with the lines established by Lí Hung-chang, in 1857, to destroy the Nien-fei. The "Sketch of Taitsan and Quinsan" may serve to explain the capture of the latter town, as described in Chap. IX. ; and the "Sketch of Country ravaged by Rebels, March 1864," illustrates Colonel Gordon's last operations. For the benefit of readers who desire to have a really good map of China on a small scale, I have given one in which (it having been prepared upon steel for another purpose by a distinguished living geographer) the spelling of the names is slightly different from that of the other maps and of the text.

The English orthography of Chinese names is at present in such an extremely unsatisfactory state that I have not thought it necessary rigidly to follow any particular system of spelling in regard to words such as "Kiangsoo" and "Soochow," which have become familiar to English eyes; and some of the names of Chinese persons and places must be incorrectly given, because they were written down, from sound, in English, by persons ignorant of Chinese, and it was not worth while to procure the proper orthography; but some of these are corrected in an appendix. In regard to little-known yet important terms, such as "Futai," I have inclined to the modification of the system of Sir William Jones, which has been adopted for Asiatic languages generally by the learned societies of Europe, and which has been followed by the American missionaries in China. The complicated system followed of late by the British Consular service in China is most misleading to English readers, and is responsible for such barbarities as "Shanghae" and "Tae-ping."

The word "Tai-ping" signifies "great peace," and is pronounced with a strong aspirate after the *T*, with the *ai* like *i* in "high" or "aisle," and with the vowel in *ping* as in "ring." It has also been written "T'hai-ping," "Tae-ping," and "Ti-ping." The first of these methods is that used by Mr Hamberg, the biographer

of Hung Sew-tsuen, and is the most correct of all; but
it is unnecessarily cumbrous for ordinary use. "Tae-
ping," the English official way of spelling the word, is
open to the fatal objection that it causes ninety-nine
Englishmen out of a hundred to pronounce the *Tae*
with a broad sound, as in "lay" or "hay," which is
very different from the Chinese. "Ti-ping" will
not do, because it suggests that the *Ti* should be
sounded as in "tippet." It may be said that "Tai-
ping" is open to a similar objection, because both in
English and French *ai* usually represents the broad
sound of *a;* but in point of fact *ai* naturally suggests
the vowel-sound in the *Tai* of Tai-ping, and has been
long used for that purpose by students of Oriental
literature. Though not perfect, it is the best representation which has been offered, and has the advantage of
being well known both in English and French literature.
The most perfectly correct spelling would be "T'hai-
p'hing."

Chinese being a monosyllabic and ideographic, not
a phonetic, language, its proper names are sometimes
separated into distinct words, as "Hong Kong" for
"Hongkong," and "Tien-tsin" for "Tientsin;" but this
is quite unnecessary in regard to the names of places,
and is even scarcely accurate, because one of the syllables
in such cases is almost always an adjective. In the names
of persons, however, a distinction should be marked between the family name and that which is conferred. To
write "Hungsewtsuen," for instance, would be like
writing in English "Smithjohn" instead of "Smith
(John)." Hung being the family name, it should stand
by itself, and the conferred name is marked by a hyphen

between the name and the adjective, so that its composite nature may be marked, thus making " Hung Sew-tsuen." * The same principle has been followed whenever practicable, as in " Tseng Kwo-fan" and " Lí Hung-chang;" but Tartar names, like " Sankolinsin," have been treated more simply, the language being alphabetic.

It is very difficult to secure perfect verbal accuracy in a work of this kind where so many minute details have to be considered and compressed, and where, to a Foreign ear, there is so little difference between the Chinese monosyllables. On looking over the work, however, now that it is in print, I observe only a few errors, and not important ones, which require correction. In p. 126, " Shensi" has slipped in instead of " Shansi ;" in one place a pamphlet of Mr Lay's has been called ' Our Policy' instead of ' Our Interests in China ;' and in a note hastily added to p. 148, " Chekiang" has, by a slip of the pen, been inserted instead of " Nganhwui," but the point referred to is more fully explained in a note to p. 298.

Perhaps it may be thought that some of the statements given in this work ought to have been supported by a fuller reference to authorities ; but to have done so in anything like a satisfactory manner I should have required to publish not one volume but at least three,

---

* Unlike ourselves, the Chinese make a practice of proceeding from generals to particulars. Hence they always put the family name first, and in addressing a letter they would write, " England, London, Piccadilly 8, Smith John." The advantages of this method are sufficiently obvious. The opposite practice could never have sprung up in a civilisation guided by intelligence ; but the most curious point about it is its want of that practicalness of which we make so much boast.

and so have ruined myself both with the publisher and the public. Besides, China is especially a country at present which stands much more in need of the general features of its recent history being pointed out to intelligent persons than of any public writer on the subject involving himself in ridiculous discusssions such as that as to whether the Tai-pings represented any national or religious movements, when to do so would be almost as bad as for a writer illustrating the great practical applications of astronomy to devote his time to combating the ignorant, the fanciful, or the interested arguments of those who still maintain that the sun goes round the earth, and that the stars are merely street lamps for the sons of men.

In conclusion, I have only to beg that readers who have been unaccustomed to see Chinese matters treated from a rational point of view, will believe that I am no Mandarin worshipper, and that I am quite alive to the great faults of the Chinese nation and Government. Their civilisation, like our own, has been in great part a failure, though perhaps not such a saddening one as ours, for it has not had such fine material to work upon ; but we must at least understand it and treat of it as it really exists, if we would avail ourselves of its experience. Mr Disraeli has well said that Europe is now passing from a feudal to a federal system. Through this stage China passed long ago ; and as we know it, its government has been committed to a body of officials chosen from all ranks of the people by a competitive examination which tests power of genius and intellect, rather than of acquirement, and which has been to some extent successful in raising the Ἄριστοι of the country to the possession of both wealth and political power. To talk of Manchu tyranny in China is about as absurd as it would be in England to speak of the tyranny of the house of Hanover. In Great Britain the power of the aristocracy, or rather say of the upper classes, has been losing ground of late years, and some barrier is necessary against the state of matters in which the power of the people can be directed by passionate demagogues, or by politicians of the American stamp who seek purely personal ends. How far the Chinese system might afford hints to this end, or supply warnings, is an important question which will soon be forced upon us by the course of events, and hence it is desirable that we should know that system as it really is, and not as it has been fancifully represented—a subject of ridicule to amuse the passing hour, or a subject of abuse to justify dubious aggressions.

MAY 1868.

LIST OF TAI-PING WANGS OR CHIEFS.

The word "Wang" properly signifies a Prince; it would be impossible to name all the Tai-ping Wangs, of whom there were about 2300 ; and among these Rebels the name did not imply any royalty by blood. In the first years of the Rebellion the title was conferred only on a select few, but latterly it was given largely by the Heavenly Monarch, and conferred by some of his adherents upon themselves. The following list of the more prominent of them may be useful in explaining the references in the text. The title is given first, then a translation of it, and afterwards the individual's name :—

1. TIEN WANG or TAI-PING WANG : the Heavenly Monarch or King of the Great Peace; Hung Sew-tsuen. This was the originator, centre, and king of the whole movement. Born 1813. Formally proclaimed his rebellion in 1850 ; established himself at Nanking in 1853, and committed suicide in June 1864.

2. TIEN WANG II. : the second Heavenly Monarch ; Hung Fu-tien. A son of Hung Sew-tsuen and of Lai, the second of the former's eighty-eight wives. Born 1848, assumed the nominal sceptre on the death of his father, and shortly after the fall of Nanking, in July 1864, was taken and executed by the Imperialists.

3. FU WANG : Hung Jen-ta. An elder half-brother of Hung Sew-tsuen, who seems to have been with the latter from the commencement, and to have had great influence. Executed after the fall of Nanking. There are also traces of another half-brother, called the Ngan Wang, Hung Jen-fu, who disappears at the fall of Nanking.

4. KAN WANG : the Shield King; Hung Jen-kan. A cousin of Hung Sew-tsuen, who joined the latter in 1859, and was made Prime Minister, being well acquainted with Foreigners, and speaking English. Some doubts have been raised as to his fate, but he seems to have been executed after the fall of Nan-

king; and the alleged Kan Wang, who appeared near Amoy in the year 1865, was probably the K'ang Wang, a chief of little note.

Then come in the five original Wangs, who alone held that title during the first years of the Rebellion.

5. NAN WANG: the Southern King; Fung Yun-san, an early friend of Hung Sew-tsuen. Killed in action in 1852.

6. TUNG WANG: the Eastern King; Yang Sew-tsin. A great fighting Chief, and organiser of the rebel movement. An incarnation of the Holy Ghost, and an aspirant for supreme power, which caused his being murdered, at the Heavenly Monarch's instigation, in August 1856.

7. PEI WANG: the Northern King; Wei Ching. Killed soon after the Eastern King at Nanking in 1856.

8. SI WANG: the Western King; Siaou Chai-kwei. A brother-in-law of Hung Sew-tsuen. Killed in action in 1852.

9. I WANG: the Assistant King; Shih Ta-kai. A great fighting Chief. Left Nanking in 1854; afterwards quarrelled with the Tai-pings, and set up for himself in the province of Szechuen. Taken prisoner by the Imperialists and executed in 1863.

To these early chiefs may be added the

10. TIEN-TE WANG: the Heavenly Virtue King; Hung Tai-tsuen. This was no relative of Hung Sew-tsuen, and the Tai-pings make no mention of his existence; but being taken by the Imperialists in 1852, he declared before his execution that he was one of the originators of the Rebellion. Probably he was an impostor.

The titles of two of the original Wangs were continued in the persons of their sons.

11. NAN WANG II. Killed when trying to escape from Nanking after its fall in 1864.

12. SI WANG II. Killed as above.

After the murder of the Eastern King in 1856, Hung Sew-tsuen created no more Wangs for some time; but when he was joined by Hung Jen-kan in 1859, and had made the latter the Kan Wang, he found it necessary to confer the title on two others of his great fighting Chiefs, viz. :—

13. CHUNG WANG: the Faithful King; Li Siu-cheng (originally called Yi Wen); a Tai-ping generalissimo, and the most distinguished leader of the latter years of the Rebellion, which he joined as a private soldier, under compulsion. Executed by the Imperialists on 7th August 1864.

14. Ying Wang : the Heroic King; Chin Y-ching; also called Sz'-yan Kow, the Four-eyed Dog. Also a noted warrior. Betrayed to the Imperialists, and executed at Showchun early in 1862.

After these so many Wangs were made that the title lost its distinctive value, but the following are the most prominent :—

15. Sie Wang : the Attendant King; Li Siu-shien. A relative of the Faithful King. Escaped from Nanking just before its fall; entered Fukien, and, pursued by the Imperialists, disappears from history at Yingling, on the Han River, in July 1865.

16. Tow Wang : the Yellow Tiger. Fought at Wuchu after the fall of Nanking, and escaped into darkness.

17. Lien Wang : the Zealous King; Li Wan-tse. Executed at Nanking in August 1864.

18. Hu Wang : the Protecting King; Chen Kuan-shu. Taken at Chanchu fu, and beheaded in April 1864. Also called "Cockeye."

19. Tso Wang ; Huang Ho-chin. Killed in defence of Chanchu in April 1864.

20. Moh Wang ; Tan Show-kuang. Assassinated at Soochow by the other Wangs in 1863.

21. Na Wang ; Kow Yuen. Beheaded at Soochow.

22. Sing Wang ; Che Wun-chai. Beheaded at Soochow. Another "Cockeye."

23. Kong Wang ; Wan Nan-tin. Beheaded at Soochow.

24. Pe Wang ; Wo Que-won. Beheaded at Soochow.

25. Tai Wang ; Sin-tin Min. Escaped at the taking of Soochow.

26. Chang Wang ; an engineer officer. Commander of the Metropolitan Force at Nanking. Spared by the Imperialists after the taking of Soochow.

27. K'ang Wang. An obscure chief who escaped with the remnant of the Tai-pings into Fukien, and was there mistaken by Foreigners for the Kan Wang or Shield King.

LIST OF LEADING EVENTS.

B.C.

2356–2254.—The age of the Emperors Yaou and Shun, when probably the earliest chapters of the Shoo King or Historical Classic were written.

2204.—Establishment of the Hea dynasty.

1621.—Commencement of the Chow dynasty, which lasted down to B.C. 249.

551.—Birth of Confucius, who gave distinct shape to Chinese political and social ideas, and also the period of Laou, the founder of Taouism, or Chinese Rationalism.

240–184 A.D.—The first Empire, which comprehended all that part of modern China which lies north of the Yang-tsze, and founded by Che Hoang-te, the builder of the Great Wall, who attempted to destroy all copies of the Classics.

A.D.

166.—Alleged Roman Embassy to China.

184–260.—The period of the three states which struggled with each other for supreme power, when the Chinese character reached its highest martial development.

260.—The second Empire, founded by the Tsin dynasty.

416.—China again divided into a northern and a southern kingdom.

420.—Nanking made the capital.

585.—The northern and southern kingdoms united.

627.—Reign of the Emperor Tai-tsung, of the Tang dynasty, who established the system of literary examinations, drew up the Celestial Code, and extended his sway into India and to the shores of the Caspian.

1260.—Peking made the capital.

1270.—Marco Polo visits Nanking and Soochow.

1281.—China conquered by Kubla Khan and the Mongol Tartars.

1368.—The expulsion of the Tartars and establishment of the Ming dynasty.

1506.—European vessels first visit China.

1616–1644.—China conquered by the Manchu Tartars, and the Ta-tsing, the reigning dynasty, established.

1637.—First English vessels visit China.

1684.—The East India Company establishes an agency at Canton.

1813.—Birth of Hung Sew-tsuen, the Tai-ping monarch.

1837.—His first trance and proclamation of himself as a heavenly prince.

1842.—The treaty of Nanking made between Great Britain and China.

1850.—Hung Sew-tsuen proclaims his temporal sovereignty.

1853.—He takes Nanking and makes it his capital.

A.D.

1856.—Murder of the Eastern King.

1858.—The Allies take the Taku forts, and obtain from the Emperor the treaty of Tientsin.

1859.—The Imperialists nearly suppress the Rebellion, and defeat the Allies at the Taku forts.

1860.—May.—The Tai-pings break out of Nanking, take Soochow, and occupy the country towards Shanghai.

June.—Ward originates the "Ever-Victorious Army."

August.—The Tai-pings attack Shanghai and are repulsed by the Allies.

September.—The Taku forts taken from the Imperialists by the Allies, an event soon after followed by the advance on Peking, the burning of the Summer Palace, and the concluding of the Convention of Peking.

December.—Allies tell the Tai-ping monarch not to attack Shanghai, and he leaves it unmolested for a year.

1861.—Hostilities suspended on the part of the Allies towards both Tai-pings and Imperialists.

August.—The Emperor Hien-fung dies.

September.—Prince Kung makes his *coup d'état*.

November. — Tai-ping attempts towards Hankow frustrated.

1862.—January.—Tai-pings again attack Shanghai, and are repulsed by the Allies.

February.—Ward again takes the field.

Allies determine to drive the Tai-pings out of the thirty-mile radius round Shanghai.

February–June.—The Allied forces co-operate with Ward and the Imperialists.

May.—Captain Dew, R.N., drives back the Tai-pings from Ningpo.

September.—Ward killed; Burgevine takes command of the E.V.A.

1863.—January.—Burgevine dismissed, and Captain Holland, R.M.I., takes command of the E.V.A.

February.—Captain Holland defeated.

The province of Chekiang is in great part restored to the Imperialists by the capture of Showshing.

March.—Colonel Gordon takes command of the E.V.A.

May.—Captures Quinsan.

August.—Burgevine joins the Tai-pings.

A.D.

1863.—September.—Gordon invests Soochow.

October.—Burgevine surrenders to Gordon.

November.—Gordon defeated before Soochow.

December.—Fall of Soochow.

Execution of the Wangs.

Gordon resigns command.

1864.—March.—Gordon resumes command and retakes the field.

Hangchow captured by the Imperialists.

Repulse of Gordon at Kintang.

May.—Chanchu fu captured.

June.—Suicide of Hung Sew-tsuen, the Tien Wang.

July 19.—Fall of Nanking.

August.—Execution of the Chung Wang.

Wuchu evacuated by the Tai-pings, who disappear from the provinces of Kiangsoo and Chekiang.

Establishment of a camp at the Fung-wang Shan, near Shanghai, for disciplining the Chinese troops.

1865.—April.—The remnants of the Tai-pings driven out of Changchow, near Amoy.

May.—Sankolinsin killed by the Nien-fei.

Tseng Kwo-fan made Generalissimo of all the Imperial Forces.

June.—Death of Burgevine.

July.—The Tai-pings finally disappear in the mountains between the provinces of Quangtung, Fukien, and Kiangsi.

The Nien-fei give much trouble in the valley of the Yellow River, and the Mohammedan rebels in Shensi.

Prince Kung made Inspector-General of all Military Camps, as a counterpoise to Tseng Kwo-fan.

1866.—Defeats of the Nien-fei and Mohammedan rebels.

A Chinese Commissioner sent to Europe, and received by her Majesty the Queen.

1867.—Improved state of China.

The Nien-fei again give trouble, and escape through the lines of Governor-General Lí, but are dispersed in the end of the year.

Discussions arise in connection with the coming revision of the Treaty of Tientsin.

1868.—Lí crushes the Nien-fei in Shantung, but some parties of them escape and unite with the Mohammedan rebels in Chili, for which Lí is degraded at Peking, but he continues to pursue the rebels and drives them before him.

LIST OF ENGAGEMENTS BETWEEN THE TAI-PINGS AND DISCIPLINED IMPERIALISTS, 1862-64.

N.B.—CHEKIANG PROVINCE............................ C.
KIANGSOO PROVINCE .... K.

K. SUNGKIANG	June 1860	Ward and 100 Foreigners.
K. QUANFULING	Feb. 10, 1862	Ward and his Force.
K. KAJOW	Feb. 21, 1862	British and French Admirals and Ward's Force.
K. TSIDONG	March 1, 1862	British and French Admirals and Ward's Force.
K. WONGKADZA	April 4, 1862	British and French Admirals and General Staveley and Force; Admiral Hope wounded.
K. SEKING	April 5, 1862	British and French Naval Forces and Ward's Force.
K. TSIPOO	April 17, 1862	General Staveley and Force, and British and French Naval Forces with Ward's Force.
K. NAIZEAN	April 27, 1862	General Staveley and Force, and British and French Naval Forces with Ward's Force.
K. KADING	May 1, 1862	General Staveley and Force, and British and French Naval Forces with Ward's Force.
C. NINGPO	May 10, 1862	Captain Dew and Encounter, &c. &c.
K. SINGPOO	May 13, 1862	British and French Forces.
K. NAJOW	May 17, 1862	British and French Forces; French Admiral Protet killed.
K. CHOLIN	May 20, 1862	British and French Forces.
K. KINSAWAI	July 17, 1862	Ward's Force.
C. YUYOW	Aug. 2, 1862	Captain Dew and Contingents.
K. SINGPOO	Aug. 17, 1862	Ward's Force.
C. TSEKI	Sept. 21, 1862	Ward killed; Captain Dew and Contingents.
C. FUNGWHA	Oct. 11, 1862	Captain Dew and Contingents.
K. KADING	Oct. 23, 1862	British and French Forces.
K. POWOKONG	Nov. 13, 1862	Burgevine and Ward's Force.
C. SHANGYU	Nov. 27, 1862	Captain Dew and Contingents.
K. TAITSAN	Feb. 14, 1863	Defeat; Holland.
C. SHOWSHING	March 18, 1863	Captain Dew and Contingents.
K. FUSHAN	April 4, 1863	Colonel Gordon and Chinese Troops.
K. TAITSAN	May 2, 1863	Colonel Gordon and Chinese Troops.
K. QUINSAN	May 31, 1863	Colonel Gordon and Chinese Troops.

K. Kahpoo	July 28, 1863	Colonel Gordon and Chinese Troops.
K. Wokong	July 29, 1863	Colonel Gordon and Chinese Troops.
K. Kahpoo	Aug. 4, 1863	Colonel Gordon and Chinese Troops.
K. Fongching	Aug. 13, 1863	Macartney and Chinese Troops.
K. Seedong	Aug. 15, 1863	Macartney and Chinese Troops.
C. Fuyang	Sept. 8, 1863	Franco-Chinese Troops.
K. Kongyin	Sept. 17, 1863	Imperialists.
K. Patachiao	Sept. 29, 1863	Colonel Gordon and Force.
K. Patachiao	Oct. 1, 1863	Repulse of Rebel attack.
K. Wokong	Oct. 13, 1863	Colonel Gordon and Force.
K. Wuliungchiao	Oct. 23, 1863	Colonel Gordon and Force.
K. Wokong	Oct. 26, 1863	Colonel Gordon and Force.
K. Leeku	Nov. 1, 1863	Colonel Gordon and Force.
K. Wanti	Nov. 11, 1863	Colonel Gordon and Force.
K. Fusaiqwan	Nov. 19, 1863	Colonel Gordon and Force.
K. Low mun Soochow	Nov. 27, 1863	Defeat; Gordon and Force.
K. Low mun Soochow	Nov. 29, 1863	Colonel Gordon and Force.
K. Soochow	Dec. 5, 1863	Surrenders.
K. Wusieh	Dec. 13, 1863	Evacuated.
C. Pinghoo	Dec. 16, 1863	Surrenders.
C. Chapoo	Dec. 20, 1863	Surrenders.
C. Haiyuen	Dec. 21, 1863	Surrenders.
C. Kanshoo	Jan. 7, 1864	Surrenders.
K. Pingwang	Jan. 9, 1864	Imperialists.
C. Haining	Jan. 25, 1864	Surrenders.
K. Yesing	March 1, 1864	Colonel Gordon and Force.
K. Tajow ku	March 3, 1864	Colonel Gordon and Force.
K. Liyang	March 9, 1864	Colonel Gordon and Force.
C. Kashing fu	March 20, 1864	Imperialists.
C. Hangchow	March 21, 1864	Franco-Chinese Troops.
K. Kintang	March 21, 1864	Repulse; Colonel Gordon and Force.
C. Yechang	March 21, 1864	Evacuated.
K. Waissoo	March 31, 1864	Defeat of Gordon's Force.
C. Semen	April 7, 1864	Evacuated.
K. Waissoo	April 11, 1864	Capture of position; Gordon & Force.
K. Chewyung	April 20, 1864	Evacuated.
K. Stockades, West Gate, Chanchu Fu	April 23, 1864	Captured; Gordon's Force and Imperialists.
C. Tezin	April 25, 1864	Evacuated.
K. Kintang	April 25, 1864	Evacuated.
K. Chanchu fu	April 27, 1864	Defeat of Gordon's Force.
K. Chanchu fu	May 11, 1864	Captured; Gordon's Force and Imperialists.
K. Tayan	May 13, 1864	Evacuated.
C. Changching	July 4, 1864	Evacuated.
K. Nanking	July 19, 1864	Captured; Imperialists.
C. Wuchu fu	Aug. 28, 1864	Evacuated.

Chinese Field Gun. *Illustrated London News*, (1860).

Dining Under Difficulty. *Illustrated London News*, (1860).

Interior of the North fort Peiho

Illustrated London News, (1860).

The King's Dragoon Guards closing with the Tatar Cavalry in the engagemen

...ear Pekin on the 21st September. *Illustrated London News*, (1860).

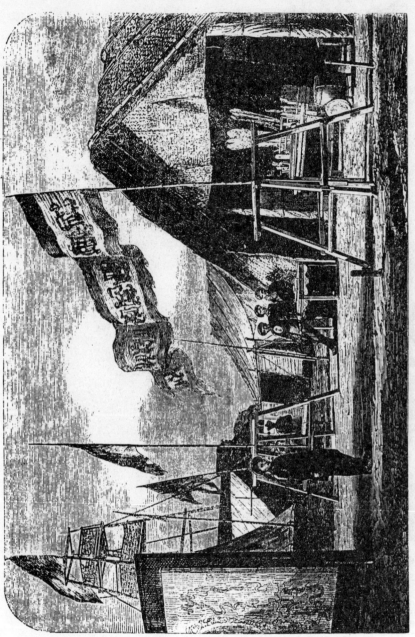

Entrance to Ching Wang's tent, Soochow. *Illustrated London News.* (1864).

Inside of the stockade at Soochow, where the Wang was beheaded. *Illustrated London News*, (1864).

Fortified bridge, Sooch

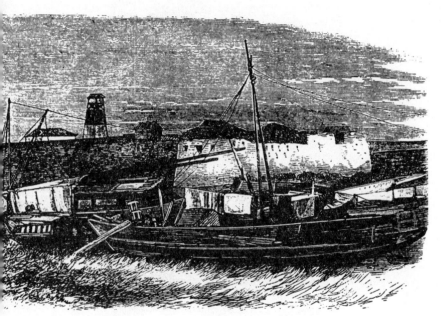

lustrated London News, (1864).

Outside of the stockade where the Wang was beheaded. *Illustrated London News*, (1864).

Interior of the walls of Soochow. *Illustrated London News*, (1864).

Troops of the Quinsan Garrison, under Major Gordon, forming square. *Illustrated London News*, (1864).

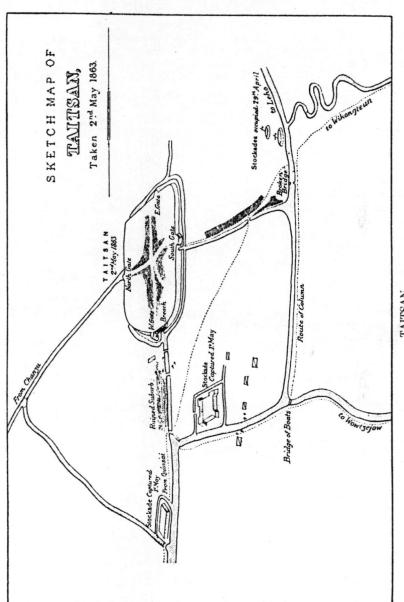

SKETCH MAP OF
TAITSAN,
Taken 2nd May 1863

TAITSAN
2nd May 1863

North Gate

E. Gate

W. Gate

South Gate

Breach

From Chanyu

Ruined Suburb

Stockade Captured 1st May

From Quinsan

Stockade Captured 1st May

Stockade Captured 1st May

Bridge of Boats

Route of Column

to Wow'sejow

Broken Bridge

Stockades occupied 29th April

to Leho

to Wikongwun

TAITSAN
(From Gordon's original sketch-plan)

SKETCH OF TAITSAN AND QUINSAN

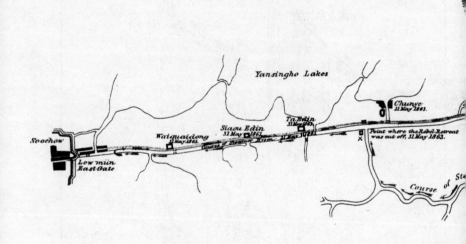

Yansingho Lakes

Soochow

Low miin
East Gate

Waiquaidong
May 1863.

Siaou Edin
31 May 1863.

Ta Edin
31 May 1863.

Quinsan
31 May 1863.

Chunye
31 May 1863.

Point where the Rebel Retreat
was cut off, 31 May 1863.

Course of Stream

Course of Stream

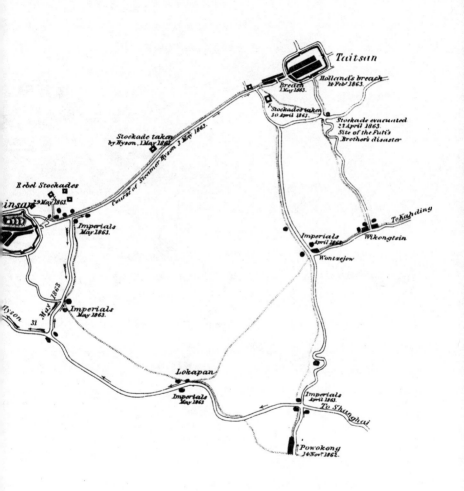

Taitsan

Holland's breach
14 Feb. 1863.

Breach
1 May 1863.

Stockades taken
10 April 1863.

Stockade evacuated
21 April 1863.
Site of the Futi's
Brother's disaster

Stockade taken
by Hyson, 1 May 1863. 3 May 1863
Course of Steamer Hyson

Rebel Stockades
29 May 1863.

insan

Imperials
May 1863.

TeKahding

Wikongtsin

Imperials
April 1863.

Wontzejow

Hyson

May 1863

31

Imperials
May 1863.

Lokapan

Imperials
May 1863

Imperials
April 1863.

To Shanghai

Powokong
14 Nov. 1862.

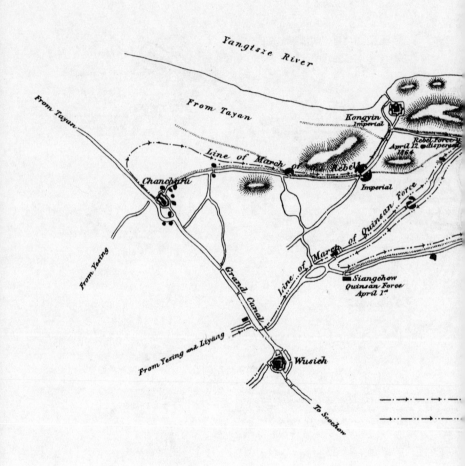

Yangtsze River

From Tayan

From Tayan

Kongyin
Imperial

Line of March Of the Rebels

Rebel Force
April 12
1864   dispersed

Chanchufu

Imperial

From Yesing

Line of March of Quinsan Force

Grand Canal

Siangchow
Quinsan Force
April 1st

From Yesing and Liyang

Wusieh

To Soochow

SKETCH OF COUNTRY RAVAGED BY REBELS – March 1864

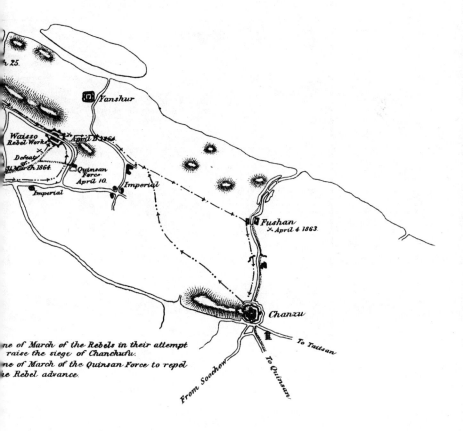

r. 25.

Yanshur

Waisso
Rebel Works

April 8 1864

Defeat
of
31 March 1864

Quinsan
Force
April 10.

Imperial

Imperial

Fushan
× April 4 1863.

Chanzu

To Taitsan

ne of March of the Rebels in their attempt
  raise the siege of Chanchufu.
ne of March of the Quinsan Force to repel
e Rebel advance.

From Soochow

To Quinsan

MAP TO ILLUSTRATE THE CAMPAIGN AGAINST THE TAIPINGS
(From the original drawn by Gordon)

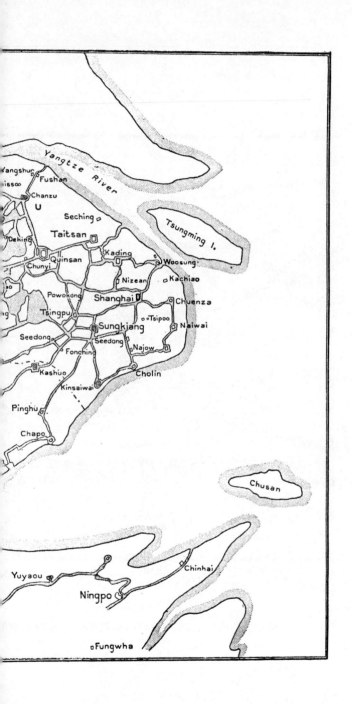

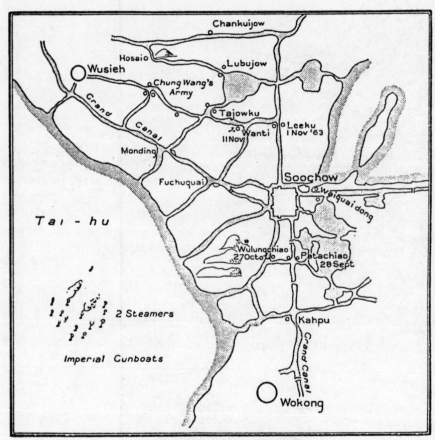

THE COUNTRY ROUND SOOCHOW
(From Gordon's original sketch-map)

The
'Ever-Victorious
Army'

CHAPTER I.

THE PRINCIPLES OF THE CHINESE STATE.

RELATIONS BETWEEN THE PAST AND PRESENT OF CHINA — ANTI-
QUITY OF THE CHINESE NATION AND GOVERNMENT — THE DOC-
TRINE OF FILIAL PIETY—ADVANCEMENT OF ABLE MEN TO OFFI-
CIAL POSTS—GEOGRAPHICAL ISOLATION OF CHINA—THE CHINESE
LANGUAGE POLITICALLY CONSIDERED — THE DOCTRINE OF HAR-
MONY—A SUCCESSFUL IDEAL STATE—SYMMETRICAL ONENESS OF
THE CHINESE STATE—SAGES, WORTHIES, AND WORTHLESS—CHI-
NESE POLITICAL ACTION FOUNDED ON A CHRISTIAN PRINCIPLE—
THE HARMONY OF RELATIONSHIPS — FEELING AGAINST THE EM-
PLOYMENT OF FORCE IN GOVERNMENT — RESPECT FOR AGE AND
LEARNING — EDUCATION UNIVERSAL IN CHINA — POSITION AND
TITLES OF THE EMPEROR—MUTUAL RESPONSIBILITY.

THE fundamental principles of the Chinese State have
never yet been fully discussed, and present in themselves, as also in their historical development, a subject
of interest and importance. Without some attention
being given to these principles, the history of China
must be tolerably unintelligible to Europeans, and so
I enter on them briefly, as necessary to a right understanding of the events relating to both the rise and the
suppression of the Tai-ping Rebellion.

It would appear very absurd to attempt to explain a
modern English political movement by a reference to
Jack Cade or the Wars of the Roses, and a French

revolution would not receive much elucidation from a history of the Carlovingian kings; but the early past of China has, for many centuries, been so closely linked to its present, that the half-fabulous Emperors, Yaou, Shun, and the Great Yu, who lived about four thousand years ago, are more really rulers of that country to-day than are its living Manchu sovereigns. Confucius, "the Master," " the Throneless King," "the Instructor of ten thousand generations," who possessed the most powerful mind that has appeared in the Far East for thirty centuries, and who is regarded by the Chinese with religious veneration, repeatedly disclaimed being more than a transmitter of moral, social, and political truth.* "I am not one," he said, "who was born in the possession of knowledge; I am only fond of antiquity, and earnest in seeking wisdom there. I do not make, but transmit, believing in and loving the ancients." One emperor of great note, Che Hoang-te, a sort of Chinese Napoleon, and builder of the Great Wall, made a most vigorous attempt to cut out this reverence for antiquity. He sought to destroy all records written previous to his reign; and, in order to accomplish this end, put nearly five hundred men of letters to death; but his efforts eventually proved futile. To this day the Chinese State is based upon an inseparable union of political, social, moral, and religious ideas, which existed in a period anterior to the birth of Abraham.

The history of the human race presents no similar phenomenon to this of China, preserving its national unity and its virtual independence for four thousand years, without any serious change in its ruling ideas, in its social civilisation, or in its theory of government.

---

* See his 'Analects,' Book vii. throughout, in Legge's edition and translation of the Chinese Classics. Hong-Kong, 1865.

Very many of its dynasties have been violently overthrown, and its external forms of government have
slightly varied from age to age ; but the principles of
its social and political organisation have remained unchanged, despite the most violent attacks upon them both
from within and from without. Mongul and Manchu
Tartars have effected nominal conquests of the Middle
Kingdom, only to adopt its ideas, manners, and institutions, to be absorbed into the mass of " the Black-haired
People," * or, when remaining distinct, to sink into despised feebleness. Elsewhere over Asia and Europe, great
empires—Assyrian, Egyptian, Persian, Grecian, Roman,
Arabian, and Teutonic—have risen in splendour, holding
sway over vast portions of the earth, only to perish in
their glory, and sometimes leave nothing but their name
behind ; while China has steadily pursued its quiet way,
enlarging its boundaries and consolidating its unity from
above twenty centuries before the Christian era to this
year of grace. Nations innumerable have risen and disappeared since the Chinese first presented themselves
with most of the marked national characteristics which
they possess at the present day. How many pantheons
of deities have been overthrown since Pwan-ku was
represented chiselling out earth and heaven ! How many
languages have found no tongues to utter them since the
Chinese monosyllables now used in the British colony of
Hong-Kong were first heard ringing on the banks of the
Yellow River ! How many characters have men invented to represent their speech since the Chinese produced their system of writing ! The more the antiquity
and continuousness of this isolated civilisation of the
Middle Kingdom is considered, the more interesting does

---

* The Chinese called themselves by this name in the earliest historical
times, having probably displaced tribes of lighter hair.

it appear, and the more forcibly does it suggest the idea, that in thus preserving a people from the earliest times, and providing for their independent development, Providence has had in view some great purpose which, as yet, we can only dimly see.

"By a long road," says a Celestial proverb, "we know a horse's strength; so length of days shows a man's heart." Judged in that way, Chinese nationality has an overpowering claim to respect, and its most intelligent students have thought much and deeply over the causes of its extraordinary longevity. Sir George Staunton (Preface to his translation of the Penal Code) and the earlier Jesuit missionaries attributed the long duration and stability of the Chinese empire to the influence of the doctrine of filial piety and parental authority, as inculcated by its sages, and universally accepted by the people. Mr Meadows, in his 'Desultory Notes,' asserts that "the long duration of the Chinese is solely and altogether owing to the operation of a principle which the policy of every successive dynasty has practically maintained in a greater or lesser degree, viz., that good government consists in the advancement of men of talents and merits only to the rank and power conferred by official posts;"—a principle which makes able demagogues rare, by opening a satisfactory path to every man of real talent. Mr R. H. Patterson, in his able essay "on the National Life of China," * lays stress on the geographical isolation of the empire, bounded as it is on the north by vast herbless and wind-swept deserts, on the west by lofty mountain-chains, and on the south and east by a tempestuous sea. To these causes, which must all be admitted as effective, there may be added, on the same level, the peculiar nature of the Chinese

* 'Essays in History and Art.'

written language, which has served as a very powerful
bond of union. The characters of that script represent
not sounds, but things and ideas, in the widest sense of
the term, and consequently it has stood in great part
superior to, and unaffected by, the fluctuations of sound
and dialect. Thus, the speech and thought of the
Chinese have been kept within certain rigid limits, all
the local streams of divergence being turned back, as it
were, into the fountain from whence they issued. Over
the spoken language, with its frequent changes and cor-
ruptions, the written language has stood supreme ; so
that while a native of Shantung may be unable to
understand the spoken words of a Cantonese, they use
identical characters in expressing the same meaning. If
the Latin races had a single character, like the Chinese
for *jen*, to denote Man, then whether pronounced Homo
in Latin, Uômo in Italian, Hombre in Spanish, Homem
in Portuguese, or Homme in French, the written word
would be the same everywhere among them, and its
being so would have a tendency to check diversity of
pronunciation, especially among the educated classes.
Out of the written language thus universal among these
races, there would arise a certain common standard for
expressions, both in speech and writing, which would
involve or evolve a certain unity, otherwise unattainable,
of thought and feeling, that would have an immense
influence in sustaining a common nationality.

But it seems to me there has been a deeper influence
at work in preserving Chinese nationality than the doctrine of filial piety, the principle of choosing able men
for official posts, or the character of the language, and
one which underlies all these secondary causes. Dr
Williams correctly states that the ' Shoo King,' or Historical Classic, " contains the seeds of all things that are

valuable in the estimation of the Chinese," and that " it is at once the foundation of their political system, their history, and their religious rites—the basis of their tactics, music, and astronomy." On examining that fragmentary but most ancient work in the light thrown upon it by the reported conversations of Confucius, and by the general practice of the Chinese in all the relations of life, there appear indications of a great and most pregnant generalisation or first principle, beyond which the mind of the Celestials has never ventured to pass, and from which arise their whole system of ideas, their social and their political organisation. It is difficult briefly to express this first principle, though it makes itself constantly felt ; but I may roughly describe it as the assertion of a Divine Harmony in the universe, which affects all existing objects, and to which the souls of men are naturally attuned. Especially in the ' Shoo King,' but through all the Classics, and in every Chinaman's principles of action, harmony is the fundamental and ruling idea. Of the Emperor Yaou, we are told in the ' Historical Classic,' * that " having become harmonious, he equalised and illumined the people of his domain." The Emperor Shun was chosen for high office, because he had been able " to harmonise " his father, his mother, and his brother, all stupid, bad relatives. The Great Yu was made Prime Minister, because he had " already equalised the land and water." When the empire is in disorder, it is said that " the people are not harmonious." When Yu advises Shun how to act, he says, " Let the elements of water, fire, metal, wood, and earth, with grain, be well regulated ; adjust the domestic virtues ; increase useful commodities, promote human existence, and cause harmony to prevail. Let these nine affairs be well adjusted ;

* Medhurst's edition and translation. Shanghae, 1846.

and, being adjusted, let them be set to music." "The announcement of T'hang" was, "Heaven has commissioned me, a single individual, to harmonise and pacify all you states and families." Of the monarch T'hai-kea, we read that "Heaven noticed his virtues, and made use of him to sustain the great decree, and soothe and tranquillise the myriad states." The intelligent prince is described as one who "harmonises with his inferiors;" but we are expressly told that "he is only a substitute (or medium): it is Heaven that works." So also in the 'Chung Yung,' or Doctrine of the Mean, a profound work attributed to the grandson of Chung-ne or Confucius, it is said of the great sage that "above, he harmonised with the times of heaven, and below, he was conformed to the water and the land." Even in the physico-theological ideas of the 'Yih King,' or Book of Changes, perhaps the most venerated of all the Classics, the Yin and the Yang, the male and female elements of creation, are considered as made in harmony, as worked on by harmonious powers, as acting harmoniously, and as moving man in the same manner when no disturbing causes interfere.

This idea of harmony underlies all the thought and institutions of the Chinese. Dimly it may be, yet most potentially they have

> " A sense sublime
> Of something far more deeply interfused,
> Whose dwelling is the light of setting suns,
> And the round ocean, and the living air,
> And the blue sky, and in the mind of man,
> A motion and a spirit that impels
> All thinking things, all objects of all thought,
> And rolls through all things."

With this Divine spirit or arrangement the Sages are in perfect accord; the Worthies seek, with ever-increasing success, to understand its dictates; and only the

Worthless stand in punished opposition to it. This is the Tien, or "Heaven," of Confucius, the Shang-te, or Deity, of the older writings. Being understood only by the Sage, it is his sacred, peculiar, and inalienable privilege to be the interpreter between Heaven and earth, Heaven and mankind. Perfectly in accord with the Divine idea, and illumined by its light, he alone knows infallibly how its harmony may manifest itself in all the affairs of human life—in the relations of prince and subject, of father and son, of husband and wife, of brother and brother, of friend and friend. Consequently he, and he alone, has a right to govern mankind. As the representative of Heaven, or the Supreme Emperor, he is by Divine right Emperor of the Great Flowery Land, of the Black-haired People, and not of these alone, but of all the nations of earth who sincerely desire to follow the ways of Heaven. And as he is Heaven to his people, so, when the Divine harmony prevails, his viceroys are Heaven to their provinces, and each father in his wide domains is Heaven to his own family. As the 'Doctrine of the Mean' has it, "All-embracing and vast, he is like Heaven. Deep and active as a fountain, he is like the abyss. He is seen, and the people all reverence him ; he speaks, and the people all believe him ; he acts, and the people all are pleased with him. Therefore his fame overspreads the Middle Kingdom, and extends to all barbarous tribes. Wherever ships and carriages work ; wherever the strength of man penetrates ; wherever the heavens overshadow, and the earth sustains ; wherever the sun and moon shine ; wherever frost and dews fall, —all who have blood and breath unfeignedly honour and love him. He is the equal of Heaven."

Rémusat, W. H. Medhurst, and other scholars by no means inclined to exaggerate in such matters, conclude

that a portion of the 'Historical Classic' was written 4000
years ago ; and, curiously enough, this view is supported
by an incidental reference in the commencement of the
work itself to the culminating of certain stars on the
evenings of the solstices and equinoxes. It is passing
strange to find thus, that in almost the earliest dawn of
time there were laid the foundations of an ideal State, so
similar in its principles, though not in all its details, to
that which Plato shadowed out in his ' Republic,' to that
which Fichte deduced in his ' Geschlossene Handelstaat,'
and to that which, less scientifically, Mr Carlyle has
made the burden of his message to his age and country.
The wonder increases when we observe that the early
Chinese sages have actually succeeded in establishing
their State so that, however it may have fallen short in
practice, yet has it always aspired towards, and theoreti-
cally been guided by, the ideas on which it was founded.
And lastly—most astounding fact of all—we find that
the State thus originated, instead of dissolving like a
dream, exists after the lapse, and despite the vicissitudes,
of forty centuries ; has extended its boundaries over the
most fertile region of Asia, and holds powerful sway
over an energetic and myriad-numbered race, which, far
beyond its own boundaries—in India, in Tartary, in
Malaya, in Australia, in California, and even in the
Atlantic-washed West India Islands—is competing not
unsuccessfully with the labour of other nations, without
losing its own ancient ideas and characteristics.

In the 'Doctrine of the Mean' it is laid down :
" While there are no stirrings of pleasure, anger, sorrow,
or joy, the mind may be said to be in a state of equilibrium. When those feelings have been stirred, and
they act in their due degree, there ensues what may be
called the state of harmony. This equilibrium is the

great root, and this harmony is the universal path. Let
the states of equilibrium and harmony exist in perfec-
tion, and a happy order will prevail throughout heaven
and earth, and all things will be nourished and flourish."
Now, not being sages, it cannot be expected that we
should enter into the essential nature of this harmony,
which bears a relation to equilibrium somewhat like that
of the being-in-action of the Buddhists to their being-in-
rest, and which reminds one of Plato's intelligible ideas,
and of that passage in the 'Timæus' where he says: Θεὸς
οὐ τω δὴ τότε πεφυκότα ταῦτα πρῶτον διεσχηματισατο
εἴδεσι τε καὶ αριθμοις—"Thus, in their first origin, God
certainly formed these things after ideas and numbers;"
but it is open to us to note the particular forms in
which this idea of harmony is envisaged, and has been
embodied in institutions. The doctrines held by the
Chinese in regard to parental authority, and the choosing of only able men as rulers, are only subdivisions of
the great idea of harmonious unity which possesses their
minds. Their notion is, that in all relationships, in all
combined action, however opposing the forces are, there
should be a symmetrical oneness. They regard all existence in its normal condition, from the lowest to the
highest, as moving sphere within sphere. Among no
other people have organisation and centralisation been
carried out to such an extent; but it must be specially
noticed that their idea is that of an organic unity, of an
organisation where the lower naturally and willingly
submits to and unites with the higher, not of an external and apparent unity produced chiefly by force.
Hence they are really a very democratic people. In
order to understand both the strength and the weakness
of Chinese civilisation, it is essential to bear in mind
that their idea of harmony manifests itself as regards

mankind, as well as in reference to everything else, in
the sub-idea of a vital organic unity, to which men
incline naturally, most usually, and for the most part.
This is the means by which the Celestials have solved,
in so far as they have done so, the problem of reconcil-
ing individual freedom with general interests, and local
with imperial government. It is an utter mistake to
suppose that, either in theory or practice, the Emperor,
or any of his subordinates, have much liberty of enforc-
ing their decrees. Confucius and all the sages of China
are at one with Plato when he said, Κακὸς μὲν ἑκὼν
οὐδείς—"No one does evil willingly"—though they
entirely shirked the question as to how evil exists at
all; and, consequently, they held that, usually at least,
good government would in itself secure willing obedience from the people. I have already noticed what the
'Historical Classic' says about a prince being able to
harmonise with his inferiors. In the 'Great Learning'
a perfect ruler is thus described : "Profound was King
Wan. With how bright and unceasing a feeling of
reverence did he regard his resting-places! As a sovereign, he rested in benevolence. As a minister, he
rested in reverence. As a son, he rested in filial piety.
As a father, he rested in kindness. In communication
with his subjects, he rested in good faith." So in the
third part of "The Great Oath," in the 'Historical
Classic,' a proverb more ancient than the book itself is
quoted : "He who soothes me is my prince ; he who
oppresses me is my foe, the abandoned of heaven and
men !" In the same work, in "The Announcement to
K'hang," the crime of a father failing "to soothe (or
harmonise) his son," is coupled with that of a son who
does not "respectfully subject himself to his father;"
and that of an elder brother becoming unfriendly to a

younger, with a younger being "unmindful of Heaven's clearly-displayed relationships." A familiar proverb in China runs: "The Emperor offending the laws is the same crime as the people doing so;" and it would be easy to quote innumerable passages from the Classics, and from the decrees of the Government itself, illustrating the great Chinese doctrine, that the harmony of all relationships is to be found in an adaptation of the higher existence to the lower, as well as in submission of the lower to the higher.

As the mystic doctrine of Harmony—fit only for Sages to discuss—becomes more definite in that of vital unity, which the Worthies may perhaps appreciate, so the latter ought to be understood and obtemperated even by the Worthless, as it manifests itself in the five relationships—of ruler to ruled, of father to son, of husband to wife, of brother to brother, and of friend to friend. On the one side the ruler must act with benevolence and in good faith; while on the other, the people must exercise reliance and submission; and it is held, so great is the confidence of the Chinese in the goodness of human nature, that if either act fitly, the other will act fitly also. When Ke K'ang asked Confucius about inflicting capital punishment, the Master replied (Analects, xii. 19): "In carrying on your government, why should you use putting to death at all? Let your desires be for what is good, and the people will be good." In book ii. 2, 3, he expressly deprecates the notion of upholding government by force, saying, "If the people be led by laws, and uniformity sought to be given them by punishments, they will try to avoid the punishment, but will have no sense of shame. If they be led by virtue, and it is sought to harmonise them by the rules of propriety, they will have a sense of shame, and moreover will become good." In the 'Great Learning,' the commentator (ch. x.) thus answers what is meant by making the empire peaceful and happy through government: "When the sovereign behaves to his aged as the aged should be behaved to, the people become filial ; when the sovereign behaves to his elders as elders should be behaved to, the people learn brotherly submission ; when the sovereign treats compassionately the young and helpless, the people do the same. Thus, the ruler has a principle with which, as with a measuring square, he may regulate his conduct. . . . . The ruler will first take pains about his own virtue. Possessing virtue will give him the people. Possessing the people will give him the territory. Possessing the territory will give him its wealth. Possessing the wealth, he will have resources for expenditure. Virtue is the root ; wealth is the result. If he make the root his secondary object, and the result his primary, he will only wrangle with his people, and teach them rapine." So likewise in family relationships, moral influence is regarded as the appropriate ruling power. Of the great Emperor Shun, we read in the 'Shoo King,' that he was elevated from the position of a husbandman because "he went forth into the fields, and daily cried and wept to the soothing heavens on account of his father and mother : he bore the blame, and drew upon himself the reproach ; while he was respectful in business, and waited on his sire Kow-Sow, penetrated with veneration and awe, until Kow also sincerely conformed to virtue." And it is recommended that this almost Christian principle should be acted upon with regard to the rebellious people of Meaou.* Similar admiration is given by the Chinese to a father for harmonising his children by moral suasion,

* The Meaoutsze or aborigines of China.

though children regardless of filial piety might perhaps be regarded as more blameworthy than fathers neglecting their parental duties. In the celebrated "Sacred Edict" of the Emperor Kang-he, the second maxim is, "Respect kindred, *in order* to display the excellence of harmony." It is a mistake to suppose, as many European writers have done, that the idea of paternal authority is that on which the Chinese State has been based. The conceptions of a certain complete harmony for all relationships, and of a graduation of authority from Heaven downwards, have determined their views, in regard both to fatherhood and to the government, to such an extent that their peculiar institutions might have sprung up had the black-haired race, by some mysterious means, been brought into existence without the aid of parents at all.

There is some difficulty in determining how far, according to the Chinese system, the employment of force is lawful and expedient in preserving the due medium of relationships. Heaven is never spoken of as vindictive, seldom even as moved to anger, but it is considered capable of terrible punitive judgment; and this prerogative, somewhat inconsistently with passages I have quoted, is spoken of as shared by its representatives, the heavenly-appointed rulers of mankind. Against unjust rulers Heaven becomes incensed, decrees their ruin, and sends down calamities on the people as a mark of its displeasure. Even so early as in the "Military Completion," in the 'Shoo King,' we read of "Heaven's exterminating decree" against an offending prince being delivered to "an insignificant one." Up to this hour the Imperial edicts conclude with the admonition, "tremblingly obey;" and it is sufficiently obvious that, constituted as men are, even among so easily-governed a race as the Chinese, authority could not be sustained, and order preserved, without a very considerable use of punishment and military force. Roughly speaking, proper relationship is sometimes so far departed from that punishment becomes a duty ; and it is worthy of note that, according to Celestial ideas, the great sign of incapacity or wickedness in a ruler is great calamities befalling the people. Heaven is then displeased beyond endurance, and all the people are in expectation that some one will arise to put in execution the exterminating decree. Hence in all Chinese political movements the declarations of both sides that they are divinely commissioned, and their frequent references to examples of the past.

To the further understanding of the system of the Chinese, it is well to note their respect for learning, their respect for age, and the universal diffusion of education among them. In the 'Great Learning' (text iv.) Confucius expresses the convictions of almost every Chinaman when he says, " The ancients who wished to illustrate illustrious virtue throughout the empire, first ordered well their own states. Wishing to order well their states, they first regulated their families. Wishing to regulate their families, they first cultivated their persons. Wishing to cultivate their persons, they first rectified their hearts. Wishing to rectify their hearts, they first sought to be sincere in their thoughts. Wishing to be sincere in their thoughts, they first extended to the utmost their knowledge." It is this relation between learning and harmony, between knowledge and the sage, that has afforded the principle of competitive examination on which governmental officers are chosen, and which has opened up the way to the very highest offices for the son of any Chinese peasant or coolie. Apart also from filial piety, this reverence for wisdom has afforded the principle of reverence for old age ; for, with their confidence in the goodness of human nature, the Celestials cannot but regard the older man, with all his past studies and experiences, as superior to the younger, and specially deserving of veneration.   The Throneless King (Confucius) himself said (Analects, ii. 4): "At fifteen, I had my mind bent on learning.   At thirty, I stood firm.   At forty, I had no doubts.   At fifty, I knew the decrees of Heaven.   At sixty, my ear was an obedient organ.   At seventy, I could follow what my heart desired without transgressing what was right."   This respect for learning and for age is fostered among the Black-haired People by their system of education.   It is expressly asserted in the Classics that a knowledge of the doctrine of the due medium may be obtained even by common persons busily occupied in the affairs of life, if their hearts are only right ; and it is obvious that a very considerable portion of the sacred writings may be understood and appreciated by persons whose minds are not very highly developed, and who have not devoted the time to study which would be required to gain what is considered a good education in European countries.   "Among the countless millions that constitute the empire," says Sir John Davis, "almost every man can read and write sufficiently for the ordinary purposes of life, and a respectable share of these acquirements goes low down in the scale of society."   And it must be observed that this education is not devoted to inflating the mind with false accounts of contemporary events, with falsifications of history, appeals to class-prejudices, and galvanic attempts at sharpness, such as constitute the intellectual pabulum offered by their newspapers to the labouring classes of America, but to the laws and other institutions of the country, the principles on which these laws are based, and to great moral and social truths, having an immediate bearing on practice, and expressed in a beautiful simple way, in sentences of which the mind cannot easily get rid. Hence the ordinary Chinaman takes an interest in the theory, as well as in the practice, of his government; and all the officials of the empire feel themselves in face of an intelligent, and sometimes exceedingly intelligent, public opinion, which they dare not disregard in the absence of a priesthood and of a standing army of any size or value. It is also obvious that this power of the people, this general information existing among them —their respect for learning, their reverence for sages, and their belief that knowledge affords a key to the harmony of relationships—are the real supports of the principle of choosing only able men for office, to which Mr Meadows attaches so much importance.

Also proceeding from their ideas in regard to harmony, we have next the Chinese ideas and practice in regard to gradations of rank, mutual responsibility, and mutual surveillance. The Emperor, representing Heaven, is Tien Tsz', Son of Heaven ; Kwa Jen, the Solitary Man ; Chin, Ourself ; Hwang Te, August Sovereign ; Hwang Shang, August Loftiness; Tieng Hwang, Celestial August One ; Shing Te, Sacred Sovereign ; and Wan Sui Ye, Father of Ten Thousand Years. But this is in virtue, not of his office, but only of the manner in which he fulfils that office. So far from his being of necessity *pater atque princeps*, Mencius boldly says : *
" The people are the most important element in a nation; the spirits of the land or grain are the next ; the sovereign is the least." Elsewhere he quotes approvingly

* Book II. part ii. chap. xiv. in the second volume of Legge's edition of the Chinese Classics.

the words of the Great Declaration in the 'Shoo King'
—"Heaven sees according as my people see; Heaven
hears according as my people hear." In the 'Historical Classic,' T'hang exclaims in his "Announcement,"
"Should any of you myriad states transgress, let the
blame rest on me, a single individual; but should I,
a single individual, offend, let it not involve you, the
multitude of states." In the "Announcement at Lo," it
is said that "the people come to meet a well-balanced
government." Confucius, who was very fond of incul-
cating subordination, counterbalanced his advice by his
repeated assertion that good government requires no
force for its support; and, as Dr Legge says, "he
allowed no *jus divinum* independent of personal virtue
and a benevolent rule." When asked (Analects, B. xii.
8) whether sufficiency of military equipment, sufficiency
of food, or the confidence of the people, was most necessary to sustaining a government, he selected the last as
most essential, and he declared that the government of a
personally correct prince would be effective without the
prince issuing orders. Thus the Emperor is properly not
so much an absolute ruler as the embodier, recorder, and
declarer of the wants and legitimate wishes of his people.

And the whole machinery of government may be
viewed not so much as a means for carrying out the
Emperor's will, as an organisation by which the wants
of the people may be met, and those of their designs
which require the exercise of supreme authority be placed
in Imperial hands. It is quite true that China, as a
nation, may be compared to a vast army under one
generalissimo, the Son of Heaven, and that this army is
elaborately divided into corps, regiments, and companies
paying, or called on to pay, implicit obedience to their
immediate leaders; but it is still more necessary to look

at the matter in a reverse light, and to consider each leader as only such in so far as he represents the natural action of those over whom he is placed. Hence a peculiarity in Chinese government which has frequently been alluded to without being properly understood. Each family, clan, village, district, department, and province, is expected to harmonise itself; and, strictly speaking, it is no part of the business of supreme authority to interfere, unless when called upon by the parties themselves, with the affairs of minor circles. If quarrels or crimes arise in a family, then the head of the family must settle these, or take the consequences, and to that end he has very great power committed to him. If a village is at war with itself, the head men have power to settle the dispute, and have practically almost unlimited power of punishing. So in the district, the department, the province. Each circle being called upon to harmonise itself, has immense power committed to it for that end, and must take equal responsibility. Hence the rationale, if not the rationality, of the Chinese system of punishing a parent for the sins of his children, and of holding a village or a district responsible for the crimes of its individual members. The whole arrangements of the nation, public as well as private, are based on a system of mutual responsibility, which of course involves a system of mutual surveillance. Even the Emperor, though nominally supreme, stands in awe of the Censorate, and of a popular revolution; the Futai, or governor of a province, has to stand well with his subjects, as well as at Peking; and the Magistrate of a district is nothing more than the recorder and executor of sentences passed by local juries.

CHAPTER II.

PREPARATIONS FOR TAI-PINGDOM.

EASTERN REVERENCE FOR ANTIQUITY—THE ASIATIC HEBREW—THE
INDO-ARYAN—CHINESE IDEAL OF HAPPY LIFE—CHINESE REBEL-
LIONS AND REVOLUTIONS — THE BALANCE OF POWER — MONGOL
AND MANCHU CONQUESTS—SECRET SOCIETIES—THE OPIUM WAR,
AND INCREASING DISORGANISATION OF CHINA.

OF course the Chinese State has fallen very far short of
the theory on which it was founded ; but I have indicated that theory, which hitherto has been overlooked by
European scholars, because some comprehension of it is
absolutely necessary to a proper understanding of Chinese
rebellions and revolutions. Every people has certain tra-
ditionary and religious ideas, sustained by spirit-stirring
stories, which underlie its institutions, and limit the working of the national mind, however despised by individuals,
and imperfectly conformed to in the national life. Despite our modern disregard of tradition, and even amid
the innumerable influences affecting modern civilisation,
each nation of Europe, of any strength, moves within a
charmed circle of its own ; and an instinctive feeling of
the limits of that circle is necessary to the great statesman, even to the great warrior. But when religious,
social, and political ideas are inextricably interwoven,
springing from one common root, as in the case of the

Chinese, and when, moreover, these are hallowed by the
history of at least four thousand years, it may easily be
believed that the influence they exercise has become
sacred, and is something quite beyond the experience
of younger and occidental nations.   Races may remain
unchanged, or nearly so ; the Copt and the Negro may
present the same features which they had when their
effigies were sculptured on the ancient tombs of Egypt ;
but of all the nations which surrounded the Chinese in
the dim morning of history, not one other remains to
tell the story of its birth.   The Hebrew race alone
preserves many of its ancient institutions, as well as its
ancient features, but its chosen place of abode knows it
no more, and its nationality was destroyed centuries
ago, while the Chinese still hold by their own ways in
their Great Flowery Land, as they did before the
Hebrews issued from the loins of Abraham.   Consequently, the old ideas on which their State was
founded, their ancient institutions, and the history of
their ancient emperors and sages, still exercise upon
them a most vital influence.

We require to go to the East in order to find races that
regard their past in a manner which largely affects their
present.   What to the modern Greek is the tale of Troy ?
or to the Roman the story of Latium ?   Thor and Odin
exercise no influence in Scandinavia, nor the Nibelun-
gen heroes in Germanic Europe ; and even the Pilgrim
Fathers are forgotten in New England.   But with the
immobile races of the East, matters in this respect are
entirely different.   The mind of the Oriental Hebrew is
still possessed by visions of his earliest forefathers wend-
ing in grey antiquity from the slopes of Ararat, holding
special communion with Jehovah, forming a chosen people,
led through the terrible wilderness by pillars of smoke

and fire, destined to rule the earth, and receiving amid the thunders of Sinai a sacred, moral, and ceremonial law of which no clause must pass away. Even at the present hour the Indo-Aryan, as he watches the red flush of morning, or sits under the palm and banian, is really dwelling in an antique ideal world of the most extraordinary kind. Accepting for his practical life, with implicit submission, the laws of Manu, and the most rigid ancient caste arrangements, his ineffable yearning for eternity and for reabsorption into deity leads him to shut his eyes on the glories of nature in India, and on all this world of outward seeming, as merely evil illusions obscuring eternal light. Aided by mystic rites and ancient hymns, he looks entranced into a vague world, at first without sky above or firmament beneath, but filled with a shoreless dazzling light of power and love, which is soon darkened by the vast shadowy forms of Varuna, and Indra, and Agni, and all the mighty gods. Ushas, the beautiful dawn, passes over the horizon; Vishnu, the preserving light, strides thrice through the universe, and the Maruts or winds sweep over; but the evil form of Shiva the destroyer appears upon the scene. Gods play with milkmaids; Rama the divine hero makes war on minor evil spirits and hideous giants; and long lines of fabulous kings enter into the vision. In the confusion which follows, the natural and supernatural, the grotesque and the sublime, become inextricably blended. The ashy devotee sitting at the roadside may be a demon, or Vishnu himself, or the Lord of Devas; but, with all its modern touches, it is the world of ancient India in which the modern Hindu daily dwells, and for him, having turned away his wearied eyes

"From earth's dull scene, Time's weary round,
To realms eternal—heavenly ground—

> Blue Krishna frolics o'er the plain,
> Varuna skims the purple main,
> Gay Indra spans the crystal air,
> And Shiva braideth Durga's hair,
> Where golden Meru rises high
> His front to fan the sapphire sky.
> And nightly in his blissful dreams
> He sits by Ganga's holy streams,
> Where Swarga's gate wide open lies,
> And Narga's smoke pollutes the skies."

Even more, perhaps, than the Hindu, the Chinaman dwells in a peculiar ideal world of his own, but it is one much less fanciful, much more definite, much more credible, and much more historical. Still it is an ideal world beyond which he can rarely pass, which constantly occupies his thoughts, and conditions his actions. Every one who has dwelt much among the Chinese, as I have done, and especially in their villages, will bear me out in saying that there is common to them all a certain simple ideal of life which they regard as constituting the highest human happiness, which they claim as their right, which they hold usually existed from the earliest times, and which is intimately connected with the doctrines of their sages, and with their historical beliefs. Unlike the Hindu, the Chinaman lives in an ordered and somewhat prosaic ideal world. He beholds, indeed, against his Turanian historical dawn the gigantic figures of Yaou and Shun, and the great Yu overshadowing the long valley of centuries ; and the great sages, such as Confucius and Mencius, correcting the errors of their times, and dropping words of invaluable wisdom ; but though all these are grand to him, they are so not so much in themselves as in their useful relationship to the knowable and the attainable—to the great primary wants of his race. The determination of the seasons, the building embankments against devastating floods, or the harmonising of

land and water, the overthrowing of unjust kings, wise,
kind action in family relationships, and the expression of
moral doctrines in an intelligible, impressive way—these
are the claims to reverence of the heroes of the Chinese
Pantheon. The (miscalled) Celestial is a narrow-minded,
but exceedingly practical, sort of being. He wants an
ordered world, but one ordered only in a certain kind of
way. Before his rapt celestial vision lie the fruitful
plains of the Great Flowery Land, lively and bright
with the normal life of China, guarded on the north
by snowy deserts, which are happily far away from him,
and on the south by stormy seas, with great winds and
waves, which he does not tempt. His ideal is a happy
family life, with age benignant, youth reverential, three
or four generations living contentedly under the same
roof; the fish-pond in front well stocked; grain abundant; tea fragrant; the village harmonised; the school
well taught; the young Confucius of the family preparing for competitive examinations; the ancestral tablets
going far back, and recording honoured names; the ancestral hall well gilded, and a fit meeting-place for the
wise elders; the spirits of deceased ancestors comforted
with offerings and loving remembrances, not left to wander friendless in the air; the holidays cheerful, with
bright silks and abundance of savoury dishes; the Emperor benevolent; the people obedient; Foreign Devils
far away or reverential; evil appearing only in the forms
of impossible demons, and hideous wicked emperors,
painted on the walls of his house as a warning to foolish
youth; no change in old customs to perplex the mind;
the sacred books reverentially read and remembered;
the present definitely arranged; the fruitage of the past
stored; behind, sages and emperors; around, happy
families; beyond, a darkness with which he little con-

cerns himself, but into which his spirit may occasionally
float a short way on some Buddhist or Tauist idea.

We may now understand the position in which a
Chinaman finds himself when he has very serious reason
to complain of the condition of his country. All the
most revered literature of that country, all the ideas
which have possessed his mind from childhood, and even
the language of the Imperial rescripts of his day, point
to the conclusion that the existing authorities rather
than the people are to blame. I have looked through
the Classics in vain for any indication of a belief that,
where great calamities befall the country, the mass of
the people may be considered as the guilty cause. The
authorities undoubtedly are in the habit of throwing
the blame off themselves, but they do so only by accus-
ing certain sections of the populace of living in guilty
opposition to the will of Heaven, and so cut off from
the rest of the people. The history of China also has
been of such a character as to sustain the notion that
the responsibility of national disaster rests chiefly with
the Government. While admitting the extraordinary
longevity of the Chinese State regarded in its essentials,
we must not leave out of view the fact that its life has
been broken, but also preserved, by innumerable rebellions and changes of dynasty. Revolution is to the
Chinaman something more even than it is to the modern
Parisian. It is, so to speak, the constitutional means of
getting rid of bad governments, and is associated in his
mind with deeds of heroic daring, of noble self-sacrifice,
and with some of the brightest periods of the national
history. De Guignes, in his 'Tableau de l'Histoire
Ancienne de la Chine,' correctly enumerates twenty-two
imperial dynasties, commencing with the Hea, founded
by the Great Yu, and ending with the Ta Tsing, the

present Manchu reigning family; and many of these
were overthrown by violence, to the great advantage of
China, or of those portions of it over which they reigned.
The 'Historical Classic' is full of "oaths" and "announce-
ments" and "chastisements" of revolutionary leaders, to
whom was delivered "Heaven's exterminating decree"
against cruel or too luxurious princes. At a later
period the famous Han, Tang, and Sung dynasties, with
many others of less note, were founded by revolutionary
violence; and the Ming, or "Bright," dynasty, which
established itself for a time against the Tartars, excited
patriotic feelings in the breasts of the Chinese. Thus,
the Tai-ping rebellion was no novel phenomenon in the
history of China, but had intimate relationship with the
national ideas and history; and Hung Sew-tsuen, its
leader, was influenced to his terrible and unsuccessful,
yet perhaps beneficial, movement, not less by the ideas
which float in the Chinese mind than by the actual
events which, as we shall presently see, led him up to
that movement, on into his terrible career, and to its
final catastrophe.

In some most important respects the present state of
China is very much what it was in the earliest recorded
times. The cities exercise but little influence, and power
lies in the balance between the Emperor with his Ministers and the country people. Bold warriors, ambitious
priests, and designing statesmen play no great part in
the national history. It is out of the country people, the
innumerable owners of the land, that the ruling power
has arisen, and it is their wants that must be attended
to. So long as they are well off they are contented
with the existing dynasty; but when they suffer greatly
then Heaven appoints some one to exterminate the
dynasty. This is the leading point in the whole history

of China. The dynasties are always established by men of lofty virtue and great force of character, perhaps aided by able and devoted Ministers ; but as generations pass away their successors deteriorate in character, and finally reach some one who combines debauchery and cruelty, so that he injures public affairs as much by his interference as by his neglect. Then comes ruin over the country ; there are signs and portents in the heavens, and there rises some patriot to say, like T'ang, who destroyed the most famous Hea dynasty, " I dread the Supreme Ruler, so I dare not refuse to destroy the wicked sovereign."

Such a period in China was that when Hung Sew-tsuen, the Tai-ping chief, arose. There were many circumstances which had tended to throw the country into a state of disorganisation, causing widespread misery ; and there were even special circumstances which tended to ascribe the evil to the ruling dynasty, and called upon a patriot to remove it from the throne. As regards the latter point, it is only necessary to note here that the Imperial family, as is well known, was Manchu. In the thirteenth century the immediate descendants of Genghis Khan conquered China in a sort of way, and established the Yuen dynasty, which ruled the country till A.D. 1368, but was then overthrown by a native line, the Ming, or " Bright." This latter reigned till the year 1664 ; but the last thirty years of their government, which had been moved from Nanking to Peking, was a continual strife with the tribes of Manchu Tartars on the frontier, and with insurrection in the interior. In 1664, a native Chinese, Le Taiching, entered Peking with his insurgent forces, and on his arrival the last Emperor of the Mings committed suicide. Le proclaimed himself emperor, but was soon driven from the capital by the Manchu Tartars, who were invited into the country by a Chinese general, Woo San-kwei, who had been defending the frontier against them, but who, looking on the usurpation of the throne by the rebel Le as intolerable, now begged their assistance against the usurper. The Manchus having entered the country had no intention of leaving it. They proclaimed Shun Chi, their chief, Emperor; and in a few years contrived to gain the government of China, and even compelled the people to shave their heads after the Tartar fashion. This was long resisted, especially in the south-east, but after a time all open defiance of the Tartar ceased, though in that part of the country secret societies were formed for the purpose of throwing off the foreign yoke, and defied the power of the Government to extinguish them. The Manchu Government, however, reigned with great moderation and justice up to the end of last century, and in fact on to about 1830; it had become quite Chinese in character, and was chiefly composed of native Chinamen, so that in the beginning of this century resistance to it had almost entirely ceased, or when it existed, was confined to those disorderly classes which, from early times, have infested the innumerable islands which fringe the southern seaboard of the Flowery Land. The Manchus as nominally ruling the country, and supplying the Imperial family at least, were always open, on account of their being Tartars, to an extra share of odium in the event of the Government failing very grossly; but up to 1830 there was no appearance of such failure, except the existence of certain illegal associations in the shape of secret societies, such as that of the Triad and of the Water Lily.

There can be no doubt that these societies had some

effect, both directly and suggestively, on the Tai-ping
movement; but, as in all such cases, it is difficult to
find out to what extent they existed, and what their real
objects were.   From the severity with which they were
pursued by the Imperial Government, we may infer that
some of them were really dangerous to the State; but
others again seem to have been harmless enough.   Thus
the "Tea Society" was suppressed in 1816, and its
leaders executed; but on turning to the Imperial edict *
on the subject, it does not seem that this association,
though illegal, was very hurtful.   Of the leaders of it,
who called themselves Wangs, the worst that is said is,
" They lyingly and presumptuously affirm that the pro-
genitor of the clan of Wang resides in heaven.   They
affirm that Mi-li-Fuh (the Buddha to come) will descend
and be born in their family, and carry all the members
of the society after death into the regions of the West,
into the palace of the immortal Sien, where they will
be safe from the dangers of war, of water, and of fire."
Other societies, however, we know, did conspire against
the Government, and sometimes openly raised the standard of rebellion; and it is interesting to notice how far
they presented characteristics common to the Tai-ping
also.   In so far as they rose above mere robber associations, or guilds for mutual protection, they seem to have
aimed either at professing a divine commission or an
intention to substitute a native Chinese for the Manchu dynasty.   The Yaou-Jin rebels, who gave so much
trouble in the provinces of Kwangtung, Kwangsi, and
Hoonan in 1832, but who had appeared so far back in
Chinese history as the Sung dynasty,† alleged that they
were descendants of Pwan-ku, a sacred legendary charac-

* ' Peking Gazette,' 27th day, 5th moon, 21st year Kia-king.
† ' Chinese Repository,' vol. i.

ter, the shaper of earth and heaven. The Pih Leen Keaou, or Water Lily Society, which has appeared at various times throughout the duration of the Ta-Tsing, the present dynasty, scarcely made a secret of their desire to overthrow the Manchus, and early in this century caused considerable trouble in the southern provinces. The San Ho Hwui, or famous Triad Society, the most formidable of all in late times, not only prepared the way for the Taipings, but also evidently gave them a number of hints. Its original title was "Tien Te Hwui"—the Celesto-terrestrial Society; and its neophytes were sworn "to recall the Ming, to exterminate the Barbarian, to cut off the Tsing, and to await the right prince." They took for their surname the word Hung. They had traditions of being directed by supernatural beings, and their head-lance took the name of Tien Hung, or Tien-yu Hung, the "Heaven-protected Hung," which is not very far from the Tai-ping Hung Tien-Wang—"Hung the Heavenly Prince," the Chinese character for Hung being in both cases the same—a point worthy of notice. There is no ground to conclude that these societies were very formidable; but their mere existence, and the claims they put forward, were sufficient to prepare the way for a wider associated movement in troublous times, and such times did speedily arrive, caused by an external series of events, and increasing incapacity in the Celestial Government.[*]

That the period of disorganisation, rapine, and war which afflicted China from 1851 to 1864 was not entirely caused by foreign import, is clear from the state of the country from 1830 to 1840, when there was a greater

* See on the Triads Dr Milne's paper in 'Transactions of the Royal Society of Great Britain and Ireland,' vol. i. part ii. (1826), and the 'Chinese Repository,' vol. xviii. p. 281.

number of rebellions, inundations, famines, and similar disasters, than it had seen for generations ; but though the people were getting discontented, and the Government weak, it is undeniable that an enormous impulse was given to these evils by the foreign relationships which ensued.   Soon after 1830 troubles began to arise with Foreigners, which caused the Peking Government considerable alarm, and induced it to take measures to maintain the isolation of the empire.   The history of the events which followed has been recorded from various points of view, and need not be repeated here ; but it may be remarked, that however desirable it was that Chinese exclusiveness should be destroyed, every writer on the subject has expressed regret that the work of doing so should have been so much an attempt on the part of Great Britain to force the objectionable opium traffic.

The British war with China of 1841-42 was most injurious to the peace of the country, because the power of the Government had for long depended greatly on prestige ; because large districts had been brought to ruin ; and because the calling out bands of local militia had taught the people their power.   It is well known that, previous to that war, the appearance of the insignia of a Mandarin, accompanied by a few lictors armed with whips, could disperse the most turbulent crowd in Canton, the most turbulent city in the empire ; and, by a long-established rule, the people were denied the possession of firearms.   But during the war arms were so generally distributed that loose characters of all kinds got possession of them, while at the same time respect for the Government had been destroyed by the manner in which its immense pretensions had been broken through by the despised Barbarian ; and, instead of ven-

C

turing on a bold course against the local riots, robber
bands, and insurrections which then arose, the Administration, conscious of its military weakness, and still
stunned by its recent defeat, began to temporise and
appeal. In 1845 at Ningpo, and in 1847 at Canton,
when serious disturbances arose from trivial causes, the
Mandarins quieted matters only by yielding. The associated banditti of the Triad increased so in many parts
of the country that life and property became exceedingly
insecure. The indemnity of 21,000,000 dollars exacted
by Britain on account of the war brought on a financial
crisis, while trade was suffering from the operations
which had taken place. Great inundations of the Yellow River and of the Yangtsze occurred inopportunely to
increase the distress and decrease the land-tax, the only
great source of revenue. In these circumstances, the
Government fell upon the fatal expedient of commuting
punishments for money, and putting civil offices to sale,
thereby increasing the number of criminals at large,
holding out inducements to crime, and exciting against
itself the animosity of the powerful literary and official
classes, who thus saw themselves defrauded of their just
privileges. Thus robbers began to increase on land, and
pirates at sea ; the local governments being powerless
to protect, the people armed and organised themselves
against banditti ; and everywhere over China, but especially in the south, troubles had gathered, and dark
times seemed at hand, when in February 1850 the
Emperor Tau-kwang " ascended on the dragon-throne to
be a guest on high," and his youthful, ill-fated son, Hien-
fung, reigned in his stead.

CHAPTER III.

THE TIEN WANG AND HIS HISTORY UP TO 1860.

HUNG SEW-TSUEN'S ORIGIN — HIS POSITION AS A HAKKA — HIS
TRANCES AND SUPERSTITIONS — THE TERRIBLE CHARACTER OF
HIS CAREER—HIS PERSONAL APPEARANCE—THE TAI-PING WANGS
—MURDER OF THE EASTERN KING — HUNG'S JEALOUSY OF HIS
CHIEFS—THE REBEL CAPITAL CONSTANTLY BESIEGED.

IT was in this troubled fermenting state of China that
there appeared one of those extraordinary men who in-
carnate in themselves the tendencies of a revolutionary
period, and who, more frequently in the East than elsewhere, gather myriads round them, and pass over their
country like a destroying but purifying tempest.

So many writers on this subject have availed themselves of the Rev. Mr Hamberg's pamphlet,* which really
contains all that is known of the early life of the Tai-
ping leader, that the facts of Hung Sew-tsuen's early
history must be quite familiar, and these have been
further substantiated by the autobiography which the
Kan Wang or Shield King wrote, prior to execution,
when in the hands of the Imperialists in 1864. But it
may be well, very briefly, to show the bearing of these
facts, to point out how far the chief's career potentially
originated in the ordinary circle of Chinese ideas, and

* 'The Visions of Hung Sew-tchuen.' Hong-Kong, 1854.

how far it was affected by his peculiar descent and by
his contact with Foreigners ; in brief, to give the rationale
of his history. No special notice seems to have been
taken of the fact, that though born within thirty miles
of Canton, he was of the Hakka, a rude race, who are
regarded as aliens by the Punti, the mass of the people
of Kwangtung.* This itself goes some way to account
for his opposition to the Imperial Government, and for
the ease with which he formed the nucleus of his insurrection. There have been hatred and feud for nearly two
centuries in Kwangtung between the Punti, or "In-
dwellers," and the Hakka, or "Strangers," who came
down on the province from the mountains of Kiangsi
and Fukien ; and the latter are regarded by the former
very much in the light of barbarians, or, say, as the Irish
of Liverpool are by the English workmen of that city.
Whether Hung Sew-tsuen's genealogy, as it was given to
Mr Hamberg, was invented after he aimed at the empire
or was literally true, is a matter of no consequence ; he
was a poor youth of a rude despised race ; and, either
from prejudice against him on that account, or from inability, never succeeded in taking a degree at Canton.
Thus his start in life was on the opposition side ; but
the Kwangtungers, generally, would scoff at the notion
of him and his *confrères* having had any special claim
to represent the native patriotic element in China. At
the same time the Hakkas are Chinese, less intelligent,
and, consequently, more indifferent to the grander ruling
ideas of the country, than are the rest of the agricultural
population, but still pretty well imbued with these ideas.
Bearing this in mind, it can easily be conceived that a

* For a description of the Hakkas, and of a residence among them, see
"Six Weeks in a Tower," by the author, in 'Blackwood's Magazine' for
June 1862.

man of Sew-tsuen's undeniable ability and wild visionary
spirit,—steeped to the lips in poverty, admired exceedingly by his immediate friends and neighbours, members
of a despised but sturdy and numerous clan, moved,
very likely, by traditions of illustrious ancestors, living
in a portion of the country becoming more unsettled
every day, hearing a rising undergrowl of discontent,
and himself denied entrance at the door of admission to
the ruling body,—would naturally cast about for some
means of asserting, and perhaps avenging, his slighted
family race and person. So far we have got circumstances and characteristics which cut him off from the
mass of his countrymen ; and to the characteristics may
be added the fact that repeated failures to take his
degree threw him, in 1837, into a state of madness,
epilepsy, trance, ecstacy, or whatever else we may like
to call it. But this disappointed youth was not an
Englishman or a Hindu. Essentially a Chinese of the
Chinese, his mind had a very wide circle of grotesque
superstitions and solemn terrible thoughts in which it
could find consolation. Was he the first in his country's
history to mourn a distracted age, or be pursued by the
demons ? Might not " Heaven's exterminating decree "
be delivered to him also, as to so many " insignificant
ones " before ? This was the result into which his visions
hardened ; but in the first of them I can recognise only
the ordinary grotesque figures which haunt the imagina-
tions of southern Chinese of a low class. The tiger, the
cock, the old woman who washed him in a river, the
taking out his heart and putting in a new one, the old
man in a black robe, whom he afterwards believed to
have been God, and the demon-exterminating sword, are
the ordinary stock-in-trade of the village geomancers
of Kwangtung. The only things which give dignity to

these visions are their connection with the old Chinese idea of the exterminating decree, and the biblical gloss he afterwards put upon them.   These visions, and their change into loftier meanings as new ideas came to him, are exactly what might have been expected from a man of very powerful imaginative mind, brought up amid the ignorance, superstition, and squalor of a Hakka village. It should be added, however, that, looking at the verses he soon began to ejaculate, at his early but as yet harmless proclamation of himself as a heavenly king, and at his whole story, there is a certain something about him —that which Goethe used to call the daimonic—which defies analysis, and even description.

The elevation of character which Sew-tsuen obtained from the conviction his trances had given that he was a chosen instrument of Heaven, sustained him in quiet up to 1843, but naturally led him to seek to extend the sphere of his influence and knowledge.   During these six years, though affairs in China were degenerating, yet they were not so bad as to afford an opening for a revolutionist ; but in 1843, when he began seriously studying Christian tracts, the opium war had opened the flood-gates.   It was natural that he should turn curiously towards the teaching of a people who had defied and so deeply injured the Government he hated ; but the whole history of his relation to Christianity shows that his was a mind which, while it might incorporate foreign ideas with its own, would never suffer itself to be ruled by them.   Neither at this time nor in 1847, when he went to Canton and put himself under the teaching of Mr Issachar Roberts, an uneducated American missionary, did he show any disposition to be a sober searcher after religious truth, but only sought that which would give force and shape to his own divine mission.   To the grossly superstitious Hakka, and to the ardent student of the more ancient Chinese classics, there was now added a third person, so to speak, imbued with certain Hebrew and Christian beliefs. It is a proof of the extraordinary power of this man's mind, and depth of his convictions, that he could blend these three individuals so completely into one under the transmuting belief in his own mission. As the poor superstitions of the Chinese peasant were elevated into this egoism, so the sublime doctrines of Christianity were degraded into it. Who could the God of the Christians be but the old man, the very God who had appeared to him in his dreams? He must have been in heaven, and the middle-aged man who instructed him how to exterminate the demons was our Lord. But then the seer himself was a Son of Heaven, so Christ became the Elder, and Hung Sew-tsuen was the Younger, Celestial Brother. There is no trace in any of the Tien Wang's productions of his having in the slightest degree appreciated the real spirit of Christianity; but the skill and completeness with which he turned some of its doctrines to his own use are really wonderful. These results were far beyond the power of a mere cunning impostor. From the hour when Hung arose from his sick-bed after his first forty days' trance, and, poor and nameless, proclaimed his avatar by fixing on his door-post the proclamation, "The noble principles of the Heavenly King, the Sovereign King Tsuen," on through success and defeat and Imperial opposition, up to the hour of his death at Nanking, when human flesh was selling in the market at so much per catty, he seems never to have wavered or abated one jot of his claim to supreme rule on earth. In ordinary times it might have been that Hung Sew-tsuen would have found an ordinary place as an able Man-

darin, a village teacher, or a literary farmer, of more
than average power and eccentricity. He might have
lived and died the admiration or the wonder of his
neighbourhood, but unknown beyond the Hwa district
where he was born ; and only his near relatives, as they
pointed proudly to the gilded letters recording his name
in the ancestral hall, or gave his departed soul kind
offerings of food, would have remembered his existence.
His bones might have been inurned in some peaceful
spot on the hills close to his home, where he used to
confer with his friend Fung Yun-san ; and when his
spirit desired to revisit earth, it might there have
had sweet repose, shaded by the pine-trees, cheered by
the singing of birds, looking down contented on the
ancestral fields still ploughed by his descendants, and
beyond these to the flowing waters of the Pearl River
and the mountains of the White Cloud. This is what,
according to all Chinese ideas, would have been a happy
and enviable fate ; but it was not decreed for him. The
son of a small peasant farmer, and himself a poor literate,
afflicted with fits of madness and trances and visions,
he was to sweep over the great Flowery Land, and, as
Tseng Kwo-fan says, cause devastation in sixteen provinces and six hundred cities. As it turned out, cruel
exterminating Wangs — not brown-haired, pot-bellied
little children — were his disciples. His ploughshare
of steel and fire drove through the great valley of the
Yangtsze, and approached the walls of Peking. No small
tawdry yamun, or village school-house, was his abode
for many years, but the ancient capital of China and the
palaces of the Ming. His visions turned into heaven-
sent edicts which decided the fate of millions, and were
pondered over in the distant capitals of Europe. At one
moment the Black-haired People seemed about to accept

his sway; and when the end came—when his earthly existence was extinguished amid the horrors of the siege of Nanking—his body was found by the Imperial conqueror "enveloped in yellow satin embroidered with dragons; his head was bald, without hair; his mustache remained, but had become grey; there was flesh on his left thigh and right shoulder; and, as soon as the examination had been concluded, the head was secured, and the remainder of the body, after being cut up, was burned"*—almost all China exclaiming, with Peking officialdom, "Words cannot convey any idea of the misery and desolation he caused: the measure of his iniquity was full, and the wrath of both gods and men was roused against him." †

There is no authentic portrait of Hung Sew-tsuen, though MM. Callery and Ivan have given what professes to be a representation of him in their lively sketch of the first years of the Rebellion. With regard to his personal appearance, however, he is known as having been of large stature, with a flowing black beard, bright eyes, and an intelligent, prepossessing countenance. Soon after establishing himself at Nanking, he entirely secluded himself within the walls of a large palace, beyond the outer court of which no male attendants were allowed to enter. In the interior the Heavenly Prince was waited upon by females alone, by his numerous wives, and still more numerous concubines, to whom accessions were made from year to year. Occasionally he held levees of the leading kings and chief men; but only his brothers and the Kan Wang, his cousin and Prime Minister, were admitted freely into his presence. Not-

---

* Tseng Kwo-fan's Memorial to the Throne with respect to the disposal of the two rebel leaders Hung Sew-tsuen and Li Sew-cheng.

† Imperial edict of 1st August 1864, in reply to Memorial announcing the taking of Nanking.

withstanding this seclusion, the Tien Wang exercised despotic power, and his edicts were usually implicitly obeyed. According to his own belief, and the profession of his followers, he was distinguished from men by being a veritable son of God, coequal with Christ, and commissioned to afford a new revelation to mankind. The Wangs, or kings, were all appointed by him on the ground of their services to the Tai-ping cause, and were described as "brethren of the same womb." Each of these Wangs had usually a distinct province and army assigned to him, but, at least in the latter years of the rebellion, the Kan Wang or Shield King, being Prime Minister, was virtually director of the movement; and, from his military skill, the Chung Wang took the lead in the field.

After the first formal proclamation of his rebellion in May 1850, and his assumption of the title of Tien Wang or Heavenly Prince in 1851, Hung Sew-tsuen selected five of his adherents as kings, and commenced that predatory march through China which enabled him to establish himself at Nanking in 1853; for in the then state of the empire as already described, his party, like an avalanche, gathered magnitude from its own movement. The armies, however, which he despatched from Nanking in the same year for the capture of Peking, were checked and destroyed after having made a long march, and the Imperialist forces which had followed him down the Yangtsze took up a position within five miles of his heavenly capital. It is a mistake to suppose that the Tai-pings were ever unopposed, or in a safe position in any place or at any moment. Nor is it less a mistake to suppose that they could in any sense be called Christians. The Blue-books on China are full of conclusive evidence as to the monstrous and blasphemous character of Tai-ping theology, and the want of reality in Tai-ping religion. They also show abundantly that the Rebels were essentially destroyers, and possessed no capabilities for reconstruction. In a sort of general way it is now very well known what the true character of this movement was, so I need only refer readers who wish more information on this part of the subject to the Blue-books, and to the volume of Commander Brine,* who is very far from being in any way prejudiced against the insurrection. The growing ferocity of Hung Sew-tsuen and of his attendant Wangs, the manner in which the exterminating decree was enforced, and the fluctuating fortunes of the Tai-pings, need only be referred to here.

The great internal difficulty which Hung Sew-tsuen had to contend with was his own aversion to guiding military operations, and the consequent danger of being superseded by one of his abler lieutenants. His cause lost much by the necessity under which he was placed in 1856, of having the Eastern King put to death; for that chief was not only his best fighting man, but also his best civil governor. Still, what else could have been done? The Eastern King, not contented with asserting that the Holy Ghost, the Comforter, was incarnated in himself, took to having trances, visions, and heavenly commands, in which he revealed that the Heavenly Father was so displeased with the Tien Wang (among other things for kicking his wives when they were *enceinte!*), that the latter was required to humble himself and receive forty lashes. Now this was going a little too far, even for Tai-pingdom. It became a question whether the Tien Wang or the Eastern King was to rule; and though the former very judiciously accepted the command for his punishment

* 'The Taeping Rebellion in China.' London, 1862.

without questioning at the moment, he soon took measures for abolishing the Eastern King and the Comforter both together ; and the massacres perpetrated by the Northern King in carrying out this order, led to that prince also being killed. This rather awkward affair made the Tien Wang very jealous of another great fighting man, the Assistant King, who, in consequence, soon after broke off allegiance, and set up for himself in the distant province of Szechuen. Thus Nanking was left for some time without any able man either to carry on the government or to conduct military affairs ; and when the latter want was afterwards supplied in the persons of the Faithful King and the Heroic King, or the Four-eyed Dog, the Heavenly Monarch was too suspicious of them to rely upon their advice, and allowed them to be foolishly interfered with and directed by his half-brothers, the Hung Jens.

Nanking, while the capital of the Tai-pings, was never free from danger from Imperialist armies, and in 1855 it was closely invested, being blockaded completely on the north-east, and partially on the south, while its river-frontage to the west was commanded by Imperialist gunboats. At the same time the important Rebel position of Nganking, some distance up the Yangtsze, was closely laid siege to by Tseng Kwo-fan ; and it was only by some very severe and fortunate fighting, that the Faithful and Heroic Kings managed to relieve these places. Even after this, at the end of 1859, the Tai-pings held only Nanking, Lowhoo, Tungching, Hochow, Nganking, Woohoo, the Two Pillars, and Taiping fu ; and the two most important places, Nanking and Nganking, were severely pressed by the Imperialists. According to the report of the governor of the province, the Imperialists had 100,000 soldiers round the former

place, besides a large fleet, and were determined to conquer the garrison by starvation. "The prospect of the
Tai-pings," says Commander Brine, "in the early spring
of 1860, had become very gloomy. Pressed by want,
the garrison of Nanking resorted to every possible means
of sustaining life short of eating human flesh. The
Imperial Government were highly elated, and the besieging force looked upon the fall of the city as a mere
matter of weeks." Out of the lower portion of the Yangtsze valley, the Tai-pings proper had no footing, though
the Assistant King was carrying on a small rebellion on
his own account in the far west of China. The movement had ceased to prosper, partly owing to the action
of Imperialist generals, who had succeeded in hemming
it within a certain limited district, and partly from its
destructive and exhausting nature, which, to continued
vitality, constantly required new districts of country to
exhaust and destroy.

PART II.

OUR COLLISION WITH THE REBELS

CHAPTER IV.

REVIVAL OF THE REBELLION, AND ITS CONFLICT WITH FOREIGNERS.

STATE OF THE REBELLION IN 1859—DESPAIR OF THE TAI-PINGS—CHANGE IN THEIR PROSPECTS CAUSED BY THE NEW DIFFICULTY BETWEEN CHINA AND GREAT BRITAIN—SANKOLINSIN—THE TAKU DISASTER OF 1859—RELIEF OF NANKING—THE TAI-PING OUT-BREAK INTO KIANGSOO — THE TAKING OF SOOCHOW — THE ADVANCE ON SHANGHAI — BRITISH NEUTRALITY — THE PEKING EXPEDITION—IMPERIAL APPLICATION FOR BRITISH ASSISTANCE—THE ALLIES DETERMINE TO DEFEND SHANGHAI—"GENERAL" FREDERICK WARD — THE CAPTURE OF SUNGKIANG — SAVAGE — REPULSE BY FOREIGNERS OF THE TAI-PING ATTACK ON SHANGHAI.

IN order to understand how much and how little British interference had to do with the suppression of the Tai-ping Rebellion, it is necessary to notice exactly how matters stood in the year 1859, which promised at one moment to see China restored to a state of order and peace. Foreign affairs had been settled apparently to the satisfaction of all parties ; and, except at Canton, where the people had got to like them and rely upon them, the Foreign forces had been withdrawn from every foot of Celestial soil. Even the Great Rebellion, now in the ninth year of its reckoning, was in a fair way of being crushed. The Faithful King says truly, in his autobiography, that at this time "Nanking was now

D

closer besieged than ever. The place was as secure as if
an iron band had encircled it. . . . . The siege of
Nanking was now progressing, and events assumed a
more threatening aspect daily." The Tai-pings lost place
after place ; their troops had neither rations nor gunpowder, and were defeated at every point ; while the
close investment of the Sacred Capital by the Imperialist generals, Chang Kwo-liang and Ho Ch'un, threatened
the very heart of the Rebellion. It is curious to notice
that in these circumstances the Heavenly Prince seems
to have remained entirely unmoved. According to the
Chung Wang, "he contented himself with merely instructing his ministers to adhere to the precepts of
Heaven, and telling them that the surrounding aspect
indicated signs of great peace." The Faithful King himself seems to have been perfectly astounded and mysti-
fied by the inexplicable way in which he and the other
Tai-pings got out of the difficulty. "Then," is all he
can say, "in those days the Heavenly Dynasty was not
doomed to be destroyed."

But instead of being content to accept the new relationship with Foreigners, and to employ all its military
power in extinguishing the still warm embers of the
Rebellion, the Imperial Government, then practically in
the hands of Su-shun, of the Prince of I, and of other re-
actionists, determined not so much to violate or discard
the Treaty of Tientsin, as by an exercise of Celestial ingenuity to make it void without departing from the letter.
The ratifications of the Treaty were to be exchanged at
Peking, but there was no special provision as to the way
in which that capital was to be reached by the British
Minister ; and the Chinese calculated that by refusing
permission to the Hon. Mr Bruce and to the vessels
accompanying him to enter the Peiho, they would bring

matters to a crisis which would relieve them from the
obligations to Foreigners which, under pressure, they had
contracted in 1858. Accordingly the forts of Taku, at
the mouth of the Peiho or White River, were repaired,
enlarged, and strengthened, but in such a way as to conceal their strength, matting being placed so as to cover
the embrasures ; and the command of these forts was
given to Sankolinsin, a man of energetic and remarkable character, but ignorant of the power of foreign
arms. Prince Seng, as he was entitled, was the leader
of Tartar cavalry who drove back the Tai-pings when they
threatened Peking in 1853. His history was a remarkable one. Being a Mongol, he was in no way connected
by blood with the ruling, the Manchu, dynasty ; and
being a poor boy, though son of a Mongol chief, he was
educated for the Lama priesthood in Peking, where he
attracted the notice of the Emperor, who took him into
his service, employed him in military expeditions, advanced him rapidly, and gave him a sister of one of the
royal wives in marriage. There was a prophecy among
the Tai-pings that their empire would be endangered by
a Buddhist priest, and this they held to have been fulfilled in Sankolinsin's Lama education. From a memorial which this Prince addressed to the Emperor in the
commencement of 1859, it would seem he fancied that
Foreign nations wished to devour China, because it had
neglected the arts of war, and had become weak. His
memorial is very interesting, as showing the feeling
entertained at that time towards Foreigners by really
well-meaning influential persons in China, and concludes
with an offer of both men and money to assist in repelling Foreign aggression. With such an instrument in
their hands, ready and eager to take the command of
the Taku forts, and looked up to by all China, the

Imperial Government felt itself strong enough to move.

Accordingly Mr Bruce, the British envoy, was refused access to the Peiho, and on the 26th June 1859 Admiral Hope attempted to force a passage through the stakes and beams which closed the entrance to the river. It was an oppressive, sultry day, with a lurid mist stretching over the muddy shores and turgid water of the Gulf of Peche-lee. The guns in the forts were concealed, and only a few ragged louts showed themselves at the gates ; but when the gunboats rushed up against the beams, suddenly the matting over the cannon of the forts rolled up, and a terrible cross-fire opened on the devoted British vessels, crashing through oak and iron, making the vessels tremble with every shot, knocking men in two, and sending splinters around. It was rather surprising for three British gunboats to be destroyed by the Chinese ; and the land attack which followed was not more suc-cessful. Men jumped out of the boats into mud and water never to rise again. The six hundred yards of mud to be crossed under a heavy fire, the two ditches, the rifles filled with mud, and the broken ladders, made the assault worse than useless. Those who crossed the second ditch had to remain under shelter of the bank until after dark, the enemy amusing them with arrows shot vertically, and with balls of blue-fire.

This disaster was, of course, not one which the wrath of Britain could endure, and its influence on the future of Tai-pingdom was very great. It not merely concen-trated the attention of the Imperialists upon the defences of the Peiho, and made them indifferent to other matters, so enabling the Rebels to recover lost ground ; it also encouraged a certain class of Foreigners at Shanghai, who saw that troublous times were coming, to devise

schemes for affording the Tai-pings what Americans
would call "aid and comfort." Further, it led to the
allied French and English expedition against Peking of
1860 ; to a temporary paralysis of the power of the
Imperial Government, which allowed the Tai-pings again
to become very formidable ; to the pressure of these last
upon Shanghai, which first caused our interference with
them, and also to that employment of British officers by
the Imperialists which, followed up as it was by Chinese
commanders, finally resulted in the extinction of the
Great Rebellion.

A detailed account of the movements by which the
Faithful King contrived to relieve Nanking for the sixth
time, would be exceedingly uninteresting. It is of more
importance to note that the rescue of the capital educed
not even an encouraging edict from the Heavenly Prince,
much less any permission for the fighting Ministers to
enter his presence. He seems in some way or other to
have held their lives pretty much in his hand, and to
have ordered them to attempt whatever he desired. Nor
is this very strange, for his life and pretensions constituted the centre of the whole revolutionary movement.
It may be well, however, as we now approach the close
of the period when Tai-pingdom had only the Imperialists to contend with, to state the positions of the opposing parties after the raising of the siege of Nanking by
Chung, the Faithful King, and Ying Wang, the Heroic
King, better known as the Four-eyed Dog.

Nanking, the Rebel capital, was not threatened by any
Imperialist force either on the north or on the south, and
in the direction of the Grand Canal and the Taiho Lake
the Tai-pings held the country as far as Liyang and
Chewying ; the Imperialist General Chang Kwoliang
having retreated to Tanyan, and Ho Ch'un to Chanchu,

both places on the Grand Canal near the estuary of the
Yangtsze. Thus a large district of rich country, lying
towards the sea, was left ill protected against the ravages
of the Tai-pings—a district which was fated to witness
their last great efforts and their final extinction. Tseng
Kwo-fan, the ablest and highest of the Imperialist generals, was at Kuanteche, a considerable way south-west of
the Taiho Lake, but he had little part in the operations
which took place at this time. His brother, Tseng Kwo-
tsun, was engaged up the Yangtsze in investing Nganking
with a large army, his covering forces being at the cities
of Soosung, Taho, Tsienchow, and in front of Tungching,
which was held by Rebels belonging to the army of the
Four-eyed Dog. In the province of Kiangsi, at Yenchow, there was also a force of Tai-pings under the command of Shí Ta-kai, the I Wang, or Assistant King; but
this was held in check, and prevented from advancing
on the provincial capital, by an Imperialist army under
the command of Paou Chiaou, stationed at Hokin, to the
south of the Poyang Lake. The Imperialist Chang Yu-
liang was advancing from Hangchow (whither he had
gone on a fruitless chase of the Faithful King) to Chanchu on the Grand Canal, where were the forces of Ho
Ch'un, and the residence of Ho Kwei-tsin, the Governor-
General of Kiangsoo. At Nanking, Yenchow, and Nganking, the Rebels had three commanding situations, of
which only the latter was invested by the enemy ; and
by pushing on their forces from the Sacred Capital towards the Taiho Lake, they kept the Imperialist troops
in Kiangsoo in a divided state.

Leaving the Four-eyed Dog to proceed to the relief of
Nganking, and at the express command of the Heavenly
Prince, but somewhat against his own inclinations, the
Faithful King advanced against Tanyan in May 1860,

and defeated Chang Kwo-liang, that general being himself drowned in a creek and 10,000 of his men being "cut up" or destroyed. This general was brave and capable. He had formerly been a Triad chief, then a leader among the Tai-pings themselves; but, as happened in many cases during this long conflict, he surrendered to the Imperialists and took service under them. The Faithful King next advanced against Chanchu, to which the remnant of the defeated army had fled, and where Chang Yu-liang (not Chang *Kwo*-liang) had assembled his force. This place was also taken, and, as the Chung Wang admits, when the Rebels entered many of the people committed suicide from fear. Ho, the Viceroy, had left it with his family before the assault; and Chang Yu-liang made another stand at Wusieh, being reinforced by an army under Liu, which came up from the Taiho Lake. Twenty-four hours' hard fighting ensued, and the Faithful King says he was just on the point of giving way when, to his unexpected delight, the enemy did so instead. This gave the Tai-pings command of the Grand Canal between the Taiho Lake and the Yangtsze and of all the neighbouring country; but southward there was still a formidable Imperialist army at Soochow, under Ho Ch'un. This general, however, was so dismayed on hearing of the death of Chang Kwo-liang that he committed suicide, and the Faithful King met with almost no resistance at one of the very wealthiest and most fashionable cities of the Flowery Land, Soochow, the capital of Kiangsoo.

"Above," says a Chinese proverb, "is paradise, but beneath are Soo and Hang." "To be happy on earth," runs another, "one must be born in Soochow;" because the people of that place are remarkable for their personal beauty. The walls of the city itself

were at this time ten miles in circumference; but outside there were four enormous suburbs, one of which,
on the west side, extended for ten miles each way, and,
besides, there was a large floating population. It was
supposed to contain about two millions of inhabitants,
and had almost a fabulous reputation throughout China
for its ancient and modern marble buildings, its elegant
tombs, granite bridges, canals, streets, gardens, quays,
intelligent men, and beautiful women. Soochow was
famous for manufactures of many kinds, but especially
for the richness and variety of its silk goods. Even after
the suicide of Ho Ch'un it might have been expected
that Ho, the fugitive Viceroy, and Chang Yu-liang would
have made some energetic efforts to save this magnificent
city from becoming the prey of the spoiler; but the Imperialist troops seem to have been thoroughly disorganised, and Ho hastened its fate by ordering the suburbs
to be fired for purposes of defence. To a large number
of the inhabitants this appeared quite as bad as falling
into the hands of the Tai-pings, and, combined with out-
rages committed by the fugitive soldiers of Chang Kwo-
liang, caused such a state of confusion and anarchy, that
when the Chung Wang advanced on the 24th May 1860
he found no opposition, and, amid the welcome of the
lower class of the population, walked in at one gate
while the Imperial troops fled at another. Shortly after
the city of Hangchow was taken by the Faithful King,
and in the province of Kiangsoo everything looked pro-
mising in the prospects of the Heavenly Empire of the
Great Peace.

Up to this period, May 1860, the Tai-pings had only
the Imperialists and the people of the country to
contend with. A few Malays and Manilamen, and,

perhaps, a crazy English sailor or two, may have found their way into the ranks on either side; but the long ten years' conflict had been entirely one of Chinese with Chinese, uninterfered with by Foreign powers and unaffected by any enlistment of Foreign auxiliaries. As I have pointed out, the Tai-ping rebellion in part originated from the opium war, and was very nearly crushed in 1859, when a new difficulty with Foreigners came to its rescue, so there was political justice in its receiving its death-blow from the hand to which it had owed so much. Had it not been for the rude shock given to the prestige of the Imperial Government by the first war with Britain, the Rebellion, so far as we can see, would not have arisen; and had it not been for the assistance given by Foreigners towards its suppression, it might, possibly, still be uselessly devastating the country. But, in the progress of events, it was quite impossible that the Tai-pings could any longer keep clear of the Foreign element which during the few preceding years had been so rapidly blending its interests with those of the Black-haired People. The hour had come when, either for weal or woe, the Tai-pings had to do with the energetic strangers from the West who had begun to swarm at the consular ports. The only question was, whether the new influence would be favourable or unfavourable to the Empire of the Great Peace.

From the autobiographical sketch of the Rebellion, written before his execution, by the Kan Wang, or Shield King, it appears that in 1860 he was made Generalissimo of the Rebel forces; and having passed four years in Hongkong, he was well acquainted with Foreigners, and knew the importance of securing them as allies. Valuable as Soochow and Hangchow were, his main object in sending the Faithful King in that

direction was to establish communications with the
open port of Shanghai, distant not 400 miles from
Nanking, and to purchase there from Foreigners about
twenty steamers, to be sent up and employed on the
Yangtsze. This would have given him the command
of that great river; and he proposed at the same time
to make other movements by land for the purpose of
relieving Nganking and thoroughly securing both banks
of the river between that place and the capital. He
saw clearly the immense importance of not allowing
Nganking to fall, and said very expressively in a letter
to the Faithful King, "Let me tell you that the great
river may be likened to a snake, the head of which
is formed by Hoopeh, the body by Kiangnan. Hoopeh
not being ours, the moment Nganking is lost the snake
is divided : and though the tail may survive, it can only
enjoy a transitory existence."

It is interesting to notice how practical were, at this
crisis, the ideas of the Shield King. The general plan
of the Imperialist authorities was to pen up the Rebels
so as to drive them into the sea, or on to the open ports,
trusting that from these latter they would be kept by
Foreigners. Thirty years before, to press the Rebels
into the sea would have been all that was required ;
but pressing them into the sea in 1860 meant thrust-
ing them upon Shanghai and other Consular ports,
where steamers and munitions of war sufficient for the
conquest of all China were to be obtained ; but the
Imperialists had good grounds to believe that we would
protect the ports, and the outbreak of the Rebels was
too sudden and unexpected to allow of effectual measures being taken to prevent their going towards the
sea.* The Tai-pings, on the other hand, saw that it was

* This point is more fully discussed in chap. xiii.

of importance to them to be in contact with Foreigners, and actually entertained the design of procuring a number of steamers for use in war. Let us bear in mind also that even at this time the opinion of Foreigners, and especially of Englishmen and Americans, in regard to the Rebels was still divided. If the delusive ideas at first entertained in regard to their Christianity and their Protestantism had entirely disappeared—and it was not alleged that they possessed any organising power—still it was held by many that they were quite as good as the Imperialists, perhaps a shade better; and that no real harm could result to China from giving them encouragement. Her Majesty's Government had directed all her representatives in Cathay to maintain a strict neutrality between the contending parties, so that the hands of the most ardent Mandarin sympathiser, if any such there were in her Majesty's diplomatic service, were effectually tied; while, on the other hand, there existed in Shanghai at that period a certain number of unscrupulous traders, and a considerable rowdy population whose interests lay, or were supposed to lie, in supporting the Rebellion, and fostering a state of anarchy and warfare in China.

To all human appearance there was even a still more cogent reason why the Tai-pings should have calculated on Foreign comfort and aid. At this moment we were really at war with Imperial China, and an allied French and English expedition was on its way to Peking to avenge the Taku disaster of 1859. Vessel after vessel was leaving Singapore and Hongkong for the Gulf of Pechelee with troops and stores. Past the desert islands of the Prata shoal, where the ribs of many a goodly ship lie bleaching under the fierce sun, in the white sand or on the pink coral; round the huge and almost unex-

plored yet lovely island of Formosa, with its great
mountains, rich tropical vegetation, and wild cannibal
tribes ; up the coast of China, broken into deep bays,
fringed with innumerable islands, and every island
fringed with boats innumerable ; through the Chusan
Archipelago, where the islands are a mass of temples ;
across the sea-like floods of the Yangtsze and the Yellow
River, pouring down into the ocean ; over the muddy
Yellow Sea, tumbling beneath the mighty crags of Shantung promontory,—a splendid English naval and military force was pursuing its way to its rendezvous under
the bare cold hills of Manchuria, with the design of advancing on the inviolate northern capital and disturbing
the Son of Heaven in his Tranquil Palace. On the
other hand, the Imperialists had braced themselves up
for one great effort against innovating foreign power ; a
large army had been collected on the Peiho ; in case of
any disaster on the seaboard, extensive fortifications had
been thrown round Tientsin ; the Taku forts had been
still more enlarged, and in their embrasures, beside the
huge English guns won in the victory of the preceding
year, might have been seen the dark firm face of the
Tartar Generalissimo, Sankolinsin,* eagerly looking sea-
ward for the first smoke of the coming fire-vessels, with
perfect confidence in his power to overcome. Looking
at all these circumstances, few could have anticipated
that any harm would have come to the Tai-pings from
their advance on the City of the Sea.

So strangely, however, do matters go in China, that,
at the very time the allies were collecting their forces at
Shanghai and elsewhere, preparatory to a march on Pe-

---

* Sankolinsin was described to Dr Rennie (' Peking and the Pekingese,'
vol. ii. chap x.) as " tall and stout, with a very energetic eye, just like Louis
Napoleon's."

king, and just at the moment they were about to start,
first the Tautai of Shanghai, and then Ho Kwei-tsin,
the Governor-General of Kiangsoo, who had come from
Chanchu fu to the consular port, applied to the British
and French authorities for assistance against the Tai-
pings. As the lives of a number of Catholic priests were
endangered, the French General offered to send 1500
men if the English would send 500 ; but Mr Bruce considered the matter too hazardous, as, should the 2000
troops be obliged to retire, a bad effect would be produced, and if they were reinforced the expedition to the
north would be crippled ; and in this view the French
Minister coincided. Still, a step was taken pregnant of
future disastrous consequences to the Tai-pings. " I decided," says Mr Bruce, in his despatch to Lord J. Russell
of the 30th May 1860,—" I decided, in concert with M.
Bourboulon, that it was expedient, both on grounds of
policy and humanity, to prevent, if possible, the scenes
of bloodshed and pillage being enacted here which took
place at Hangchow fu, when that city was lately assaulted by the insurgents ; and it appeared to me that,
without taking any part in this civil contest, or expressing any opinion on the rights of the parties, we might
protect Shanghai from attack, and assist the authorities
in preserving tranquillity within its walls, on the ground
of its being a port open to trade, and of the intimate
connection existing between the interests of the town
and of the Foreign settlement, the former of which cannot be attacked without great danger to the latter. We
accordingly issued separate proclamations to that effect
in identical terms." * This was the little cloud, no big-

* The British proclamation was as follows :—" The undersigned issues
this special proclamation to tranquillise the minds of the people.

" Shanghai is a port open to foreign trade, and the native dealers residing

ger than a man's hand, which was destined to obscure
the sun of Tai-ping success.   In a memorial sent at this
time to the Throne by Ho, that unfortunate Governor-
General, who was soon after recalled to Peking and executed for his non-success, speaks of his army as having
been annihilated in consequence of the *état de délabre-
ment* into which it was thrown by the successes of the
Faithful King, and especially by the taking of Soochow.
"Never," he wrote, "in all antiquity has there been a
state of confusion so remarkable," and, "trembling beyond measure," he begs the Emperor to make peace with
the Allies and employ all his troops against the Rebels.
When, at the risk of his head, and, as it proved, at the
cost of his head, one of the highest of Chinese officials
could write in this way, the circumstances of the Imperialist cause in Kiangnan must have been apparently
desperate indeed.

Besides the proclamation of the Allies in regard to
Shanghai, another very important, but, at the time, apparently insignificant, event was the appearance on the
stage of " General" Frederick Ward.   Before the former
had agreed to defend Shanghai, Ta Kee, and several
other wealthy merchants of that place, not relishing the
idea of its falling into the hands of the Tai-pings, had
arranged with Woo, the Tautai, to afford funds for the

therein have large transactions with the foreigners who went to their place
to carry on their business.   Were it to become the scene of an attack and of
civil war, commerce would receive a severe blow, and the interests of those,
whether foreign or native, who wish to pursue their peaceful avocations in
quiet would suffer great loss.

"The undersigned will therefore call upon the Commanders of Her
Majesty's naval and military authorities (*sic !*) to take proper measures to
prevent the inhabitants of Shanghai from being exposed to massacre and
pillage, and to lend their assistance to put down any insurrectionary movements among the ill-disposed, and to protect the city against any attack.

"Shanghai, May 26, 1860."

enlistment of Foreigners to fight against the Rebels.
He had, therefore, engaged two Americans called Ward
and Burgevine to enlist a number of Europeans and
Manilamen, and had promised these leaders a large sum
if they would retake Sungkiang, a city eighteen miles
distant from Shanghai on the river Whampoa.

Of Burgevine I shall speak afterwards. Ward was
born about 1828, at Salem in Massachusetts, and was a
man of courage and ability. Probably from poverty he
was unable, when a youth, to gratify his desire of studying at West Point; but his mind seems always to have
been occupied with military matters as affording his
proper and destined sphere in life. Like not a few of
his countrymen, he combined the life of an adventurer
with that of a sailor, and had seen a good deal of the
world before he came to China. In Central America he
had been engaged in filibustering under that celebrated
chief of filibusters, General William Walker; at Tuhu-
antepic he had been unsuccessfully engaged in trying to
found a colony from the United States; and at one time
in Mexico he had been on the point of taking military
service under President Alvarez. Ward seems to have
turned up in Shanghai some time in 1859; and his first
operation, the attack upon Sungkiang, with about 100
Foreigners, mostly seafaring men, under his command,
took place in July 1860, and resulted in a repulse with
some loss. He persevered, however, in his design; and,
having augmented his force by a company of Manilamen,
lay concealed during the day, and contrived to seize a
gate of the city just at sunset, repulsing all the Rebel
attacks till next morning, when the native Imperialist
troops coming up, were enabled to drive out the Tai-
pings. Ward then received the ransom of the city, and
Ta Kee and the other patriotic merchants were promoted

in rank. The success of this affair, together with the
high pay of 100 dollars *per mensem*, attracted more men
to the banner of the Salem adventurer, who, being
offered a further reward if he would take Singpoo, attempted to do so with 280 followers of his own, and
two six-pounder guns ; but in conjunction with 10,000
Chinese troops under General Lí Adong, and about 200
small Chinese gunboats. The Tai-pings, however, by
this time had begun to see the benefit of employing
Europeans, and at Singpoo, among others, they had an
Englishman of the name of Savage who had formerly
been a pilot. The consequence was that when Ward
attacked the city on the night of the 2d August and
succeeded in getting on the wall, his force was driven
back with very great loss, and he himself was severely
wounded in the jaw. Being an irrepressible sort of element, however, he went to Shanghai, and, despite his
wound, immediately returned to Singpoo with two eigh-
teen-pounder guns, and 100 fresh men, mostly Greeks
and Italians. But this did not avail much ; for the
Faithful King came down to the rescue of the city, surprised and outflanked Ward, took his guns, boats, and a
good many muskets, and drove him back to Sungkiang.
This latter place the Tai-ping chief soon attempted to
take by storm, but there he was repulsed, and in the
attempt Savage received a wound, from the effects of
which he soon after died at Nanking.

On the 16th of August the Faithful King advanced
upon Shanghai, leaving Sungkiang invested in his rear,
and accompanied by the Shield King, whose knowledge
of Foreigners was expected to be useful. Chung Wang
immediately sent in a proclamation to the consuls, explaining the accidental slaughter of a French priest on
the previous day, and telling them that he was about to

attack Shanghai, but that Foreigners would not be molested if they remained in their houses. No answer was sent to this communication; but the Tai-pings must have been aware of the proclamations which had been issued by the French and English authorities, and they had been warned shortly before by the Rev. Mr Edkins, and other missionaries, that the Allies would defend the city against them.

On the 18th August the Faithful advanced, burning everything before him, on a very wide front. He passed through the Jesuit establishment at Sikawai, where several Roman Catholic converts and another French priest were killed; then he attacked the Imperialists, who were intrenched about a mile from the west gate of Shanghai, occupied their camps, and drove them into the city. The Tai-pings then made an attempt to enter the gates along with these fugitives; but the walls were manned by French and British troops, who drove them back with great loss. A skirmishing fire was kept up on the walls; and the Rebels, along with whom were several Europeans, one of whom was killed, also tried to advance under cover of the Imperial flags which they had captured in the stockades. Next day the Faithful King resumed his attack, in expectation of a rising among the Cantonese and Chinchew men, who were very numerous in Shanghai, and who were only deterred from revolt by the force of the Allies. In one of the suburbs they did indeed break out, and commenced plundering and massacring the more respectable Chinese; and before that could be put a stop to, the greater part of this wealthy suburb was destroyed by fire, causing great distress among the people. On the next day, the Chung Wang again renewed his attack, and directed his efforts specially against the British settlement; but

E

he was easily repulsed, and, giving up the futile attempt, fell back with his troops on Sikawai. In his own account of this affair he says that he was induced to go to Shanghai "by some Barbarians residing there;" and, in a communication which he sent in to the Foreign authorities on the 21st August, he expressly accuses the French of having deceived him. This is rather curious, and is not quite explained away by the Hon. Mr Bruce when he remarks, in his despatch of the 4th September 1860, that the French were of all Foreigners the least likely to have made any advances to the Taipings. It is well known that the Roman Catholic priesthood in China—a very powerful body, with a system of underground communication all over the empire—were bitterly hostile to the Rebellion, and it is not at all unlikely that some of their agents may have been employed in luring the Chung Wang on to his injury by false representations of the ease and safety with which Shanghai might be occupied. Another curious point is, that in his sketch the Faithful King asserts he had prepared for a march into Shanghai, and arrangements had been made there for his reception; but a storm of wind and rain arose, which rendered the ground so slippery that neither man nor horse could obtain firm footing, and so the Foreign Devils who came out to meet him had to return without him. This is not like pure invention, and there was such a storm a day or two before the attack of the 18th August; Mr Bruce also acknowledges that the Rebel attack "took us by surprise;" so that it is far from impossible that the wealthy city of Shanghai had a narrower escape from Tai-ping occupation than it was, or is even yet, aware of.

Having inflicted an immense amount of injury upon the peasantry, the Rebels retreated on the 22d of August, and left the vicinity of Shanghai. Passing Sungkiang, which was held by Ward and his contingent, they captured Pinghoo and Kashing hien,* which caused the Imperialist general, Chang Yu-liang, to raise the siege of Kashing fu, which he was again attacking. By the capture of Shemen they managed to get in between Chang and that portion of his force which was stockaded near Kashing fu, and so to cut the latter off from Hangchow, compelling it to surrender, and the general to retreat upon Hangchow. Most of the troops thus taken in September joined the ranks of the Rebels. The Faithful King then proceeded to Soochow, where the distress of the people from famine was very great. It is to his credit that he endeavoured in every way to relieve them, and was so far successful that they erected to him an ornamental arch—a tribute of gratitude which caused them considerable trouble, when, afterwards, the city was recovered by the Imperialists, by whom it was pulled down.

* " Hien " thus used indicates the chief city of a district, and " fu " that of a department.

CHAPTER V.

TAI-PING REVERSES IN THE YANGTSZE VALLEY, AND A CHANGE OF POLICY AT PEKING.

THE TIEN WANG'S INDIFFERENCE — TAI-PING PLANS IN 1860 — FOUR ARMIES SET IN MOTION—BRITISH AGREEMENT WITH THE REBELS—NEUTRALITY STRICTLY ENFORCED—ARREST OF WARD— FAILURE OF THE REBEL MOVEMENTS—SUCCESS OF THE TAI-PINGS IN CHEKIANG—REASONS FOR KEEPING THEM FROM SHANGHAI AND NINGPO—DEATH OF THE EMPEROR HIEN-FUNG—PRINCE KUNG'S COUP D'ETAT.

THE redoubtable Tseng Kwo-fan, at this time War Commissioner against the Rebels, was now pressing the siege of Nganking ; and the Heavenly Prince, being apprehensive for its safety, ordered the Faithful King to return to Nanking, in order to oppose the Imperialists on the Yangtsze. Accordingly the latter left Soochow in charge of Chen Kuan-shu, who was afterwards called the Hu Wang, or Protecting King, but was better known by the name of " Cockeye," * one of his optics having been injured by the explosion of a percussion-cap. On the arrival of the Faithful King at the capital, he assembled the various chiefs, and, following Dugald Dalgetty's principles, recommended them to procure provisions so

* Though "Cockeye" is an English slang word, it is well known and often used by the Cantonese, Foreigners in the south having for long been in the habit of applying it to Chinamen, and Chinawomen also, who have certain peculiarities about their eyes.

long as the city was open, and not to retain money in
their hands, as that would be useless during a siege.
Upon his urging the same advice on Hung Sew-tsuen,
that Heavenly Prince only answered characteristically,
" Are you afraid of *Death*? I, the truly-appointed
Lord, can, without the aid of troops, command Great
Peace to spread its sway over the whole region." What
could Chung Wang say to this? as he himself patheti-
cally inquires. All he could do was to breathe a sigh,
and move away with a body of troops in order to raise
the siege of Nganking, that place being, in fact, the key of
the whole Rebel position in the valley of the Yangtsze.

The whole of the chiefs being assembled at Nanking
in October 1860, it was resolved that the great objects
of the coming year should be the capture of Hankow
and the raising of the siege of Nganking; and to effect
these four armies were to be put in motion. The first
army, under the Ying Wang, or the Four-eyed Dog, was
to move from Tongching to Hwangchow, along the north
bank of the Yangtsze, in rear of the covering force of
Imperialists engaged at Nganking, and thence on to
the east of Hankow. The second, under the Tu Wang,
was to cross from the north to the south bank of the
Yangtsze, in order to attack Hokeou at the entrance of
the Poyang Lake, and from thence to ascend the river on
Hankow. Another division, under the Attendant King,
was also to march on the Poyang Lake, and thence by
Nanchang, the capital of Kiangsi, on to Woochang, the
city *vis-à-vis* to Hankow, on the southern bank of the
Yangtsze. The fourth army, under the Faithful King
himself, was to march south of the Poyang Lake to
Yotchow on the Tungting Lake, and from thence to
descend the great river to Hanyang, which is only
separated from Hankow by the river Han. All these

forces were to move so as to be at or near their common
object in March or April. At the same time arrangements were made for the Rebels at Soochow to move
down on the cities of Chapu and Haiyuen, while the
Nienfei (who, without subscribing to the tenets of the
Great Peace, fought on the side of the Tai-pings when it
suited them) were to make a raid from Tongyan against
Yangchow, Kwachow, and Chinkiang. The Imperialists,
on the other hand, were thus placed :—Tseng Kwo-sun
was besieging Nganking; General Paou Chiaou and
his forces were near Hangchow; Tseng Kwo-fan, the Governor-General, was at Kimen in order to prevent any
advance on Kiangsi; and Chang Yu-liang was at Hangchow. The intended route of the Faithful King was
somewhat disturbed by General Paou, who defeated him
at Yuhain and compelled him to move into Chekiang.
In the neighbourhood of Shanghai the Rebels were pretty
quiet about this period, but they made one or two raids
against Woosung in October, and ravaged the country,
inflicting great misery on the people, and filling Shanghai
with fugitives, the latter fact affording evidence of the
terror which they inspired.

The war with the Imperialists in the north being now
ended, Admiral Sir James Hope, our naval commander-
in-chief, was able to turn his attention to the Tai-ping
question—to its effect on our trade and on our possession
of Shanghai. It was also necessary to visit the ports on
the Yangtsze which had been opened to trade by the
new treaty ; so the Admiral started up the river in
February of 1861 ; and, passing Chinkiang, which was
in a most ruinous state, anchored at Nanking. Here
he entered into correspondence with the Tien Wang
on the opening of trade in the Yangtsze, on the necessity of the Tai-pings being forbidden to interfere with

Shanghai, and on orders being given that they should not approach within 100 *li*, or 30 miles, of it ; that distance being supposed sufficient to secure it against any sudden attack. In answer to these demands the Tien Wang agreed to leave Shanghai unmolested for a year, and issued some regulations in regard to the ports on the river and its navigation. Sir J. Hope then proceeded up to Nganking, which was closely besieged by the Imperialists, Kiukiang, which was in ruins, and Hankow, establishing consulates at the two last ports. The Rebels at this time occupied the river from their Heavenly Capital to Wuhu, including the East and West Pillars. The accounts of the various officers and gentlemen who went up on this expedition agree in describing the Tai-ping cities and districts as having been in a state of great desolation, while the people who were left were in the utmost misery. On the other hand, in places which had been retaken by the Imperialists, confidence had returned ; the people were crowding back to their ruined homes, and trade and new houses were springing up.

Meanwhile at Shanghai Ward and Burgevine began again to make themselves felt, again collecting men for a third attempt on Singpoo, where they had been defeated by the Faithful King in 1860. In March and April 1861 Ward had collected a number of Foreigners and sent them up from Sungkiang to Burgevine, who was intrenched with some Imperialists near Singpoo ; but the consuls and admirals were so desirous to avoid any unnecessary embroilment with the Tai-pings, that they arrested Ward and some of his men on the 19th May, and took him to Shanghai, where he was tried as an American citizen illegally engaged in operations of war, but avoided jurisdiction by disowning his country and claiming Chinese nationality. It was arranged, however, that Ward should not then make any more attempts to enlist Europeans and Americans on the side of the Imperialists; and about the same time the Tien Wang, on demand, delivered up to Admiral Hope a number of Foreigners, some of whom were deserters from the royal navy, who had taken service with the Tai-pings, from whom they got no pay, but plenty of spirits and full permission to plunder. Thus we see that at this period a sincere attempt was made by the Foreign authorities to carry out a policy of complete non-intervention, and it was only after-events which necessitated a departure from it.

It is now expedient to turn to the movements of the Rebels in the beginning of 1861, when their various armies were put in movement for the capture of Hankow, the bold conception of the Chung Wang, who to attain this end undertook a march of not less than 500 miles. In January 1861 this chief left Shangchow, and marched without opposition through Yuchan, Quangsin, to Kianchang, which he found held by Imperialists, and which he failed to take, though he captured a force that was coming to its relief. He then pushed on to the banks of the river Kan, which runs into the Poyang Lake, but was there delayed for some time, the stream being swollen by melting snows. On crossing, he drove off the local militia, and, marching on, placed his troops in April in Ngan and Ouhning; so as far as his column was concerned it had done its part, though his failure to take Kianchang had rendered his return precarious in the event of anything unfortunate happening to the other Rebel armies advancing on Hankow. The Ying Wang, or Heroic King, advancing on his shorter line, captured Yochan and Yinchan early in March, and then attacking a camp of Amoor Tartars with great success, took all their horses. Hwangchow, a city only 50 miles from Hankow, was taken by him by surprise on the 18th March 1861, by which time he had marched a force of nearly 80,000 men 200 miles in eleven days, and had quite outflanked the Imperialists at Loosong. The column under the Assistant King, however, was not so lucky, being defeated in April at Loping, with the loss of 10,000. The Tu Wang also was checked; for after crossing the Yangtsze at the Pillars, he was met by one of Tseng Kwo-fan's generals, and completely defeated, while another portion of his army was overthrown by the Governor-General himself. When the Faithful King heard of these failures he had himself got into difficulties, for the Imperialist general, Paou, was following him up with a large force, the Governor of Hankow had despatched another to check his advance, and the people were pillaging his convoys, so he determined to turn on his tracks before it was too late; and after some narrow escapes, and a march of more than 800 miles, reached Quangsin in September 1861. The Heroic King, finding his colleagues did not approach, had also to fall back; and thus ended the grand scheme for relieving Nganking by an attack on Hankow.

Paou Chiaou followed up the Faithful King some distance, and received the Yellow Jacket from the Emperor for his services, which had saved Hankow. After retreating to Tongching the Heroic King again attempted to relieve Nganking, but his troops were sadly in want of provisions, while those of his opponent, the Governor-General, were well supplied, and assisted by a fleet of gunboats; and about this time General Ching (afterwards associated with the Ever-Victorious Army), a Rebel chief of some eminence, high in favour with the

Ying Wang, went over to the Imperialists from Ngan-king, giving up a most important post. In November 1861 Nganking fell, after having been defended heroically for three years by Yeh Yun-lai. On entering, the people were found dead in the streets by hundreds. They had been reduced to the last extremity; for human flesh had been sold as their food at 40 cash per catty, or one penny per pound; and it is worthy of note that, almost at the same time, the Imperialists besieged in Hangchow were reduced to the same dreadful extremity.

As to the movements of the Nienfei, and of the Tai-pings, from Soochow towards Chapu, of which mention has been made, it is sufficient to note that the former failed, while the latter did capture Chapu, and killed the Tartar garrison; but were told by Captain Roderick Dew, of H.M.S. Encounter, who was sent to warn them, that they were not to attack the consular port of Ningpo, to which they assented. They afterwards pushed on, and captured Haiyuen. The Faithful King, for his part, finding it impossible to relieve Nganking, determined on an invasion of the province of Chekiang, where he captured several towns, and, dividing his force, placed a portion of it under the Sho Wang. After this he continued to advance, and captured Oukiang and Tezin, north of Hangchow, and besieged Wochow, which is to the south of the Taiho Lake. Another portion of his army proceeded to the south of Hangchow. In fact, every place in the vicinity of the latter city was conquered by the Tai-pings except Ningpo, which was threatened by the She Wang, and protected chiefly by a British naval force.

It seems quite obvious that at this period the Tai-pings were in distressed circumstances, and were being driven by the Imperialists out of the valley of the

Yangtsze, down upon the seaboard lying between Shanghai and Ningpo. The fall of Nanking seemed only a
question of time, and the Imperialist theory of sweeping
them into the sea had about it some appearance of feasi-
bility. But then, on the other hand, had they been permitted to take possession of Shanghai and Ningpo, their
cause would, in all probability, have gained a new lease
of life, and caused not only China, but also Foreigners
in China, a great deal of trouble for a much longer
period than that which actually served for its final extinction. Had the Tai-pings been allowed to take Shanghai and Ningpo, they would not only have been able to
secure European arms and ammunition to an extent
before impracticable, but might also have largely reinforced their strength from the hardy maritime population of China. It would have been difficult also, in such
circumstances, to prevent European and American adventurers from taking service with them; and, once in
occupation of the cities at these consular ports, the Tai-
pings, in the event of any collision with the Foreign
authorities, would have held the residents in their power,
and would have been almost certain to apply to them
also the system of cruel intimidation which had been
continually practised throughout the Tien Wang's exterminating career. This would, of course, have directed
the arms of Foreign powers against the ruthless sectaries
of the Great Peace, but only after a most lamentable loss
of life and bloodshed had occurred. Tai-ping sympathisers have naturally felt and expressed themselves
very bitterly about this matter of our defending Shanghai and Ningpo, because it led to events which were
speedily very disastrous to the Rebel cause; but in their
zeal for the Tien Wang's Christianity and their grief at
having lost a grand opportunity for making fortunes by

the sale of bad firearms, they quite ignore not only the
necessity which the right of self-protection imposed upon
us, but also the fact that it was the distress of Tai-pingdom which drove it into the neighbourhood of the Foreign
settlements. It had the remainder of all the vast empire
of China in which to beat the Imperialists, nor up to this
period had the latter availed themselves of Foreign arms
any more than the Rebels had done. Abhorred wherever
they had been, defeated, and being slowly hemmed in
on every side, the Tai-pings in their later victories had
shown only the delusive success of despair. The Foreign
authorities had to determine whether that despair was
to end amid the plunder and burning of Shanghai and
the massacre of those they were bound to protect, or
in its congenial home amid the desolation and ruins of
Nanking.

About this time some events occurred at Peking which
had a not unimportant bearing on the future of China
and of Tai-pingdom. On the 21st August the Emperor
Hien-fung died at the Jehol, his hunting-seat in Tartary,
in the 26th year of his age and the 11th of his reign.
Unequal to the difficulties of a transition period, he had,
like many other rulers similarly placed, sought consolation in sensual indulgences, and had allowed himself to
be led by unworthy favourites. At last, as the decree
announcing his death stated, " his malady attacked him
with increasing violence, bringing him to the last extremity, and on the 17th day of the moon he sped upwards upon the dragon to be a guest on high. We tore
the earth and cried to heaven, yet reached we not to him
with our hands or voices." When the mortal shell of
this frail and unfortunate monarch was laid in its " cedar
palace," his spirit ascending on the dragon would have
many strange things to tell to the older Emperors of his

line.   He would have to speak of trouble, rebellion, and change through all the years of his reign, over all the vast plains of the Celestial Empire, from the guttural-voiced tribes of Mongolia and the blue-capped Mohammedans of Shensi, down to the innumerable pirates of Kwangtung; he might complain that, east and west, north and south, his people had been disobedient and rebellious; the administration of his empire had been set at defiance, and his sacred decrees had been imperfectly carried out by weak and corrupt viceroys, much more intent upon their own aggrandisement than upon the welfare of the people.   Year after year great bands of marauding rebels had moved across the once happy Flowery Land, marking their progress in the darkness of night by the glare of burning villages, or shadowing it in the day by the rolling smoke of consuming towns. A maniac usurper had not only sought to ascend the dragon throne, but had nearly done so, and had claimed divine honours; while invading armies of the outside barbarian had humiliated the empire, had visited the once inviolate city of Peking, and had burned the palace of the Son of Heaven.

But we, who now know more of the meaning of these events which caused the Emperor Hien-fung so much distraction, can see that they were the necessary accompaniments of a period of extraordinary, of quickening, strengthening, and, it may be hoped, purifying change. Even the death of the Emperor was a signal for a great advance.   The regency appointed to take care of the new boy-emperor consisted of Su Shu-en and the Princes of I and Ching, members of the extreme anti-Foreign party, and men who had been responsible for the cruel murders of Captain Brabazon, Mr Bowlby, and others, taken under a flag of truce in 1860.   The Supreme

Council was opposed to carrying out the distasteful conditions of the Treaty of Tientsin, and of the Convention of Peking. Prince Sankolinsin still held by the delusion that he would in time be able to resist Foreign demands at the point of the sword or the mouth of the cannon; and when a brother of the late Emperor, the more enlightened Prince of Kung, who had signed the Convention of Peking, was invited to the Jehol, there was no very sanguine expectation that he would ever come back alive, or that the invitation meant anything more than the permission, politely granted to erring members of the Imperial family, of despatching himself in private by swallowing gold-leaf, or by strangulating himself with a silken cord. Fortunately, however, as it turned out, the disposition of events was to a great extent in the hands of a woman of intelligence and strength of character. The Dowager Empress of China was the head of the regency; and she had wisdom enough to perceive that the Prince of Kung understood the interests of the country better than did her late lord's advisers, and was the statesman for the situation. So when every one expected to hear of his self-extinction, he suddenly reappeared in Peking; and though he said nothing, so far as has transpired, yet there was sufficient evidence in his countenance that he felt satisfied and secure. The result was that the entry of the youthful Emperor into Peking was accompanied by the Prince of Kung's famous *coup d'état* of the 2d Nov. 1861, which overthrew the anti-Foreign party at the capital, and led to the execution of its leaders a few days after.* This event consolidated friendly relationships between the Foreign Ministers and the Imperial Government; it gave an important impetus to the policy of strengthen-

* See Dr Rennie's 'Peking and the Pekingese,' vol. ii. chap. v.

ing the hands of that Government; and it gave security
for a healthier and more reasonable central power in
China than had existed for a long period. Many things,
as we see, were thus working together for the destruction of Tai-pingdom, and for the restoration of the
Celestial Empire to a state of comparative order and
peace.

CHAPTER VI.

ALLIED OPERATIONS ROUND SHANGHAI IN 1862.

THE TAI-PINGS WORSTED WITHOUT OUR AID — THEIR SECOND AD-
VANCE ON SHANGHAI—THE COUNTRY PEOPLE APPLY FOR PRO-
TECTION AGAINST THEM — THE ALLIES RESOLVE TO CLEAR A
THIRTY-MILE RADIUS—THE TAKING OF KADING, ETC.—DEATH OF
ADMIRAL PROTET—THE FAITHFUL KING RETRIEVES THE REBEL
CAUSE—FORRESTER'S CAPTIVITY—THE END OF THE HEROIC KING
— THE FAITHFUL KING RECALLED TO NANKING — THE ALLIES
CONFINE THEMSELVES TO SHANGHAI AND SUNGKIANG — RECEP-
TION OF THE NEWS OF WARD'S DEATH—HIS BURIAL—BURGE-
VINE APPOINTED IN HIS PLACE—LI MADE FUTAI OF KIANGSOO—
THEIR QUARREL—GENERAL STAVELEY ASKED TO APPOINT A BRIT-
ISH OFFICER—BURGEVINE ASSAULTS TA KEE—HIS DISMISSAL—
CAPTAIN HOLLAND APPOINTED TO COMMAND THE EVER-VICTORI-
OUS ARMY BY GENERAL SIR CHARLES STAVELEY.

As I have mentioned, it had been arranged between the
Tien Wang and the British authorities at Shanghai, that
in the year 1861 they were to observe strict peace towards each other; and this arrangement was kept on
both sides. It is of great importance to bear this fact
in mind, because that year was a most critical one with
the Rebels. In it they put forth all their power in order
to take Hankow and re-establish themselves in the
Yangtsze valley. When people say that the Tai-pings
were overthrown by British arms, they leave this fact
out of view. In the very turning-point of their later

history, the Rebels were allowed to fight the Imperialists without any interference on the part of Foreigners, and got by far the worst of it, though at that time the Imperial Government underwent an internal revolution, and had just had its prestige seriously injured by the advance of the Allies to Peking. The fighting which afterwards took place between Colonel Gordon and the Tai-pings in the neighbourhood of Shanghai, was not rendered necessary by any success of their cause so much as by the fact that the complete manner in which Tseng Kwo-fan had defeated the Rebels in the Yangtsze valley, forced them down again into the neighbourhood of the Consular ports of Shanghai and Ningpo.

Our interference with the Tai-pings at these ports was at first entirely in defence of our own settlements. In the end of 1861, when Sir James Hope, the Admiral commanding her Majesty's naval forces in China, went up to Nanking, in consequence of rumours that the Faithful King was about to attack Shanghai, and warned the Tien Wang against such a proceeding, he was answered impertinently, and was told whenever the year of truce had drawn to a close the Divine troops would certainly make such an attack. Accordingly, on the 11th January 1862, the Faithful King went down to Soochow, and after reducing the taxes there and alleviating the distress of the people, who had suffered much from the cruel misrule of the Hu Wang, or Protecting King, he put his forces in motion against Shanghai, capturing various towns on the way, and ravaging the country. In the proclamations which he issued he said that "Shanghai was a little place," and added, "We have nothing to fear from it; we must take it to complete our dominions." As he advanced, the horizon round the

F

Consular city was obscured for days by the smoke of burning villages, and thousands on thousands of fugitives poured into the Foreign settlements, many of them having been plunged from a prosperous condition into utter want and misery in the depth of a severe winter. This caused the Foreign community to enrol themselves into a volunteer force for the purpose of defending the city, and they and the Chinese merchants emulated with each other in relieving the distress of the fugitives. The Rebels having got down into the Pootung peninsula to the south of Shanghai, the people there petitioned the Consuls for protection in a most imploring manner, and this Admiral Hope and the French Admiral Protet were the more ready to grant because the Tai-pings had fired upon some boats under the protection of their men-of-war anchored at Woosung.

At this time General Ward had a drilled force of nearly 1000 Chinese at Sungkiang, with which the Admirals determined to act in concert; and by their combined forces, Kajow, the Rebel headquarters in the south of the peninsula, was taken on the 21st February. Several other places were also released; and both Sir John Michel, commanding her Majesty's troops in China, and Admiral Hope, having reported favourably on Ward's force, the merits of the "Ever-Victorious Army," as this infant force was now called, were very handsomely acknowledged in an Imperial decree of the 16th March 1862, and 9000 Imperial troops were ordered down to its assistance from Nganking. At this time, Sir John Michel having returned home, Brigadier-General C. W. Staveley, C.B., assumed command of her Majesty's forces in China, and determined to continue the operations against the Rebels, having just had an opportunity at Peking of consulting with the British

Minister and with Prince Kung upon the subject. Both he and Admiral Hope, who first made the suggestion, judged that the safety of Shanghai could only be secured by clearing the country round from Rebels within a radius of thirty miles; and this conclusion received the warm support of the mercantile community, with the insignificant exception of some small traders who were making a large profit by illegally selling arms to the Rebels. Had the Tai-pings been allowed to enter the native city, the inhabitants would have crowded into the Foreign settlement, which would thus have been rendered powerless to protect itself from rapine and murder. When it was once resolved to defend the place both native and foreign, it was only reasonable that care should be taken to provide it with the means of subsistence, by keeping a portion of the surrounding country free from the devastating hordes of the Rebellion. Moreover, the military authorities were of opinion that it was necessary to clear the radius in order to efficiently protect the city. This arrangement soon afterwards received the approval of Sir Frederick Bruce, on condition that the Imperial authorities should hold the places taken by the Allies.

On the 4th April the two Admirals and General Staveley, with their forces, took Wongkadza, which was strongly intrenched, the Rebels falling back on another series of stockades five miles further inland. Ward, with 500 of his disciplined Chinese, and accompanied by Admiral Hope, attempted to take this second position, but was repulsed, seven of his officers being wounded, and the Admiral receiving a ball in the leg. Next day, however, the place was attacked by a combined French and English force of about 700 seamen and marines, under Protet and Captain Borlase, R.N., assisted by Ward and 1000 of his men, when the Rebels retreated, and were pursued for some distance. A fortnight after, Tsipoo, about twelve miles above Shanghai, on the right bank of the Wompoa river, was taken by the Allies, and 300 Rebels were killed. In order to illustrate the serious character of Colonel Gordon's after operations, it is well to note that Naizean and Kading, the next places taken by the Allies (on the 27th April and 1st May), had operating against them a force under General Staveley, composed of a wing of H.M. 31st Regiment, a wing of the 67th, a company of the 99th, the 5th Bombay N.I., Bradshaw's battery of artillery, 300 British sailors and marines, 800 French sailors and Infanterie de la Marine, and 1000 of Ward's disciplined Chinese.

On the 6th May a new expedition started from Shanghai, of about the same strength, under the two Admirals and General Staveley, but with 35 guns and mortars, and took Singpoo, Najow, and Cholin. The second of these places was stormed by a party of the 31st Regiment, under a heavy fire of gingals and muskets; and Admiral Protet, who accompanied them, was shot dead,* which caused the French seamen and marines to show no mercy to the defenders.

When Kading was taken, some of the Allied troops had been left to garrison it, and they were joined by 5000 Imperialists who had come down from Nganking. These men being much elated by the success which had attended their arms in the interior, determined to attack Taitsan, a town twelve miles distant, being urged to do so by Governor Sieh, who had just learned that he was to be superseded by Lí Hung-chang, and was anxious to

---

* An Imperial decree directed high honours to be paid to him, and 100 marten-skins and 4 rolls of Imperial silk to be presented to his friends.

be able to report a victory when giving up office. The
Faithful King, however, was infuriated at this move of
the Imperialists, and went from Soochow to Taitsan with
10,000 of his picked troops. On the 15th May there
was an indecisive engagement; next morning 2000 of
his men shaved their heads, pretending to join the Imperialists; and the King, moving round so as to intercept
their retreat, attacked the latter, when the pretended
Imperialists fought on his side, and the result was a
most disastrous defeat, scarcely 2000 out of 7000 men
returning to Kading. This affair, and the manner in
which the Chung Wang began to follow up his success,
induced the Allies to return to Shanghai.

When the latter found that the Imperialists were
unable to hold the cities taken from the Rebels, they
evacuated Kading after a good deal of skirmishing, and
confined themselves to Shanghai and its more immediate
neighbourhood. Elated by his success, the Faithful
King sent out marauding parties nearly to the walls of
that city, and invested Singpoo and Sungkiang, which
were held by Ward's force. At the latter place a party
of British seamen under Lieutenant Stephens, R.N., were
introduced to assist the garrison, and fortunately in time
to resist an attack made by the Rebels to scale the walls.
During the engagements at this time it was seen that the
Tai-pings had been well supplied with arms by Foreign
traders, for nearly a third of them had muskets. The
great heat of the weather had also some effect in inducing the Allied Commanders to retain their troops
for the most part at the Consular port.

The garrison at Singpoo, commanded by Colonel Forrester, was soon closely invested by the Rebels, who
sent in a letter offering to allow the "Strange Devils
and Foreign Demons" to escape by the south gate and

return to their own country. Though the disciplined
Chinese under Forrester made many sorties against the
Rebel works, yet their position soon became desperate,
as their numbers decreased and they had fewer men to
guard the walls, which were three miles in extent, and
were liable to be escaladed at any point. Accordingly,
on the 10th June, 200 men of the 31st Regiment under
Colonel Spence, the naval brigade under Admiral Hope,
and Ward himself with two steamers and some of his
men, went up to relieve Singpoo and withdraw its garrison. Unfortunately, when evacuating this city, Ward
ordered it to be set on fire, which betrayed his intention,
and caused a great deal of confusion. The Rebels entered before the garrison had left, and taking Colonel
Forrester prisoner, drove out his force with considerable
loss, pursuing them to the spot where Admiral Hope had
halted with his naval brigade. It was a disastrous retreat, for the bridges over the innumerable creeks which
intersect the country having been previously broken
down, many of the retreating forces were drowned.

It was feared that Colonel Forrester, who had thus
been taken, would be tortured to death, but he turned
up some time after in exchange for a ransom of powder
and muskets. On being seized by the Tai-pings, his
hands and feet were bound, and he was kept in prison
without food till next morning, when he was taken before a Chief, who ordered him to be tortured, and then
decapitated. A young Tai-ping leader, however, who
admired the Foreign Devil's courageous bearing, interfered, and the sentence was not carried out. After being
kept in prison for some weeks in a state of semi-starva-
tion, he was stripped naked, was loaded like a donkey,
and in this way had to march for several days to Chapu
under a burning July sun. After that, his hardships

ceased; he was well treated, though closely guarded, and at last induced his custodians to accept a ransom. Thus, after two months' captivity, he returned to his astonished comrades with only his constitution a little shaken.

The Faithful King expatiates with considerable pleasure in his Autobiography on this victory over the "False Foreign Devils," as Ward's men were called, owing to their being dressed in European clothes. There is no doubt that at this time he might have endangered the safety of even Shanghai itself, had he not received intelligence which cut short his career in that direction, and recalled him to Nanking, which was again threatened by the Imperialists. It seems that the Ying Wang, or Four-eyed Dog, fell back on Tongching after the failure of the various expeditions to save Nanking, and that he was degraded by the Tien Wang. After some more reverses, he was deluded by an ex-Rebel, Miao Pe-ling, a subordinate of the famous General Shung Pow, to enter a city under the pretext that it would be surrendered to him; but when he did so, along with about thirty high Rebel dignitaries and leaders, the drawbridge was pulled up, and he and his friends were taken prisoners. The Four-eyed Dog, who deserved a better fate, was then executed; but his captors also came to a violent end, for Miao broke out again into rebellion in 1863, and was executed, while Shung Pow was degraded for having recommended him for service, and for that and other sins was ordered to commit suicide. The Imperialists had also advanced down the Yangtsze from Nganking, and in May 1862 had captured the West, and invested the East, Pillar— two high conical hills ten miles below Wuhu. Tseng Kwo-tsun, the brother of the Imperialist Generalissimo,

had also moved down with 40,000 men against Nanking,
had established himself at the south-west of the city, and
had extended his camps from the river to Porcelain Tower
Hill, which was still held by the Rebels, but round which
he had thrown up intrenchments. If we aided the Imperialists by defending Shanghai for them, they certainly
aided us effectually by withdrawing the most formidable
general of the Tai-pings, and a great portion of his force,
at this critical moment.

Alarmed at all this, and by the capture of some
other places both above and below his capital, the
Tien Wang ordered the Faithful King to come up to
Nanking directly, and the latter had to do so sorely
against his own judgment. His own notion was to
pour supplies into Nanking sufficient for two years,
and to allow it to be beleaguered by the Imperialists during that period, while he pursued his designs
towards the seaboard. But the Heavenly Monarch sent
a peremptory mandate to him requiring his presence, and
significantly added, "If you do not obey this decree, the
law must inevitably take effect upon you." He found
things in a bad way, and illustrates the effect of the loss
of Nganking by remarking that when a bamboo is once
split, it splits easily all the way down. Instead of lis-
tening to the wise advice of this loyal adherent, the Tien
Wang accused him of treachery, and overwhelmed him
with abuse. On reaching Nanking, the Faithful King
was ordered to take Tseng Kwo-tsun's intrenched camps,
which were defended with deep trenches and strong bastions, and with connecting drawbridges, so that a force
could be concentrated at any one point. Many weeks
were wasted in uselessly attacking this position, and his
failure in taking it was punished by severe censure, by
depriving him of his rank as a noble, and by sending

him in to Nganwhui to join the remnant of the Ying
Wang's force.

During the heats of this summer the Allied forces
remained quiet at Shanghai, round which works of
defence were completed; and Admiral Hope and General Staveley went away—the one to Chefoo to recover
from his wound, and the other to Japan to recruit his
impaired health. The only places near Shanghai from
which the Rebels were excluded was Najow, where there
was a garrison of British troops, and Sungkiang, which
was held by Ward, whose force was now 5000 strong,
well armed with percussion muskets, and supported by
artillery. This force was still paid by the Chinese merchants of Shanghai, and was only partially under the
orders of the Governor of the province. By this time
General Ward had a good position with the Chinese
authorities, and could get what money he required
without trouble. His higher officers received £70 *per
mensem*, his lieutenants £30, and the men rather more
than 1s. 6d. *per diem*, with free rations when in the
field. The non-commissioned officers and men were all
Chinese, but the other officers were Europeans with the
exception of one Chinaman named Wong Apo.* A thousand of the men were armed with Prussian rifles of the
old pattern, and the Ever-Victorious Army had by this
time assumed, chiefly owing to Ward's exertions, a
good many of the characteristics of a regular disciplined
force.

On the other side, the recall of the Faithful King
must have discouraged the Tai-pings, so on the 6th of
August Ward ventured out of Sungkiang with nearly
3000 men and retook Singpoo, leaving it to be gar-

---

* In such names as Apo, Apak, and Atai, the " A " is merely a euphonistic
aspirate, and the Chinese characters represent Po, Pak, and Tai.

risoned by the Imperialists. This event roused the Tai-pings at Soochow, and their bands again appeared in the vicinity of Shanghai, driving the peasantry before them and cramming that city with fugitives. Some good service was done in repelling these marauding bands by the mounted rangers of Shanghai, a volunteer force composed of the Foreign merchants of that place, and not a little confused skirmishing took place. Important events, which are recounted in my next chapter, had meanwhile been going on at Ningpo, and General Ward went down in September to that neighbourhood, where he unfortunately met with his death-wound. In an attack on Tseki on the 21st of September, he was shot in the stomach at the moment of attack by a stray bullet. Being carried back to Ningpo, he survived for a short time, meeting his fate with much firmness and composure, and disposing by will of the considerable fortune which he had acquired during his military career in China. Ward was a brave, energetic leader, and managed very well both with his force and with the Mandarins. When the news of his death reached Sung-kiang, he was deeply lamented both by his officers and men, and by the people of the city. When his remains entered that place for interment, all the shopkeepers at once shut their shops for the day; several officers of the British army and navy attended his funeral; the usual volleys for a general were fired over his grave, and he was buried in the Confucian University, which the Chinese considered a great honour, and which place had been closed for many years until that day in September 1862. Colonel Forrester, Ward's second in command, was now offered charge of the Ever-Victorious Army, but declined, and the command was accepted by the officer next in rank, Henry Burgevine, a young American from North Carolina, who, like Ward, had been a sea-faring man, but from an early period had cherished vague dreams of founding an empire in the East. Some weeks elapsed before the new Commander took the field, and at this time an officer of the Russian Government came to Shanghai to offer Lí Hung-chang, who was now Futai or Governor of the province, the assistance of 10,000 men. But this offer was calculated to cause the Chinese alarm rather than gratification, and was respectfully declined. The new Futai, who had served long under Tseng Kwo-fan against the Tai-pings, proved to be a man of much more ability than his predecessor, and one likely to follow a definite path of his own.

The country remained quiet till November 1862, when the Moh Wang, who had made an advance from Soochow, was attacked on one side by the forces of Lí, on the other by those of Burgevine, and so met with a severe repulse, in which his son, a young man of distin-guished bravery, was killed. Before this event there was some bad feeling between Burgevine and Governor Lí, which was now increased by the latter taking the credit of this victory to himself. · General Ching, an ex-Rebel chief who fought under the Futai, and was jealous of the disciplined Chinese, did all he could to ferment the quarrel, and Burgevine himself increased it by his peremptory manner, and by rousing suspicions in the mind of the shrewd Futai as to his ultimate intentions. There were also reports that Ward, had he lived, had intended to establish himself as an independent power in the country, and so the Chinese at this time became very distrustful of the Ever-Victorious Army, and of its Commander. One consequence of this was that the merchants at Shanghai, who had hitherto supported the force from dread of the Rebels, were now not disposed to give such large sums for its maintenance as they had formerly paid. Lí became so suspicious of the new Commander, that on 1st December he went to General Staveley, begging him to remove Burgevine and to appoint an English officer in his place. He also complained much of the enormous expenses of the force both under Ward and Burgevine; of the interference by the latter with the civil government of Sungkiang; of disputes between the disciplined Chinese and the Imperialist troops; of the way in which the former plundered the people of the country, and in general of Burgevine's independent insulting demeanour. These complaints of the Chinese were not altogether without reason, especially as regarded the expenses of the force, which had amounted to £30,000 *per mensem;* but General Staveley had no wish to interfere in the matter, and stated that he had no power to grant their request, though he would communicate on the subject with the Home Government and with the British Minister at Peking. His own idea was that, if the Chinese Government wished to organise its military forces, it should be assisted in doing so under proper conditions; but he was not prepared to give his support to the Ever-Victorious Army in its then unsatisfactory state, officered as it was by a body of men who, however brave, were not fit representatives of their respective nations, and who, on any disagreement arising, might turn against the Chinese Government itself. It occurred to him, however, that some more satisfactory arrangement might be made for placing the disciplined Chinese under the joint command of Native and Foreign officers; and accordingly he drew up a rough sketch of the terms on which, if his Government approved, the services of a British officer might be obtained for the purpose.*

The quarrel between Burgevine and the Futai soon came to an issue. For two months the troops had not been paid regularly, and when 6000 of them were ordered up to Nanking they refused to proceed until the arrears were paid. Their Commander also demanded that a number of other back claims should be cleared off before he left. The fact was, that neither the men nor the officers had much relish for being sent against the Rebel capital; for the former, being chiefly natives of the Sungkiang district, were averse, like all Chinese, to going far from home, while the latter imagined, and not without some reason, that up at Nanking both their lives and their pay would be very much at the mercy of the Imperialists. On the other hand, the Mandarins were glad to make Burgevine feel how much he was in their power, and they probably expected that this unpleasant demand might enable them to get rid of him. Ta Kee, the banker through whose hands the payments of the force were made, kept back some moneys which he had promised to advance in the commencement of January, on which Burgevine, accompanied by his body-guard, paid him a visit at Shanghai, struck him on the face in the course of the altercation which ensued, and carried off for the troops a sum of money that he found conveniently ready in the banker's house.

Of course Ta Kee reported this affair to the Futai, who determined to dismiss Burgevine; but being in fear of a revolt on the part of the Ever-Victorious Army, he went to General Staveley and the American Consul, and requested they would arrest the Commander. This the General refused to do, but he informed Burgevine that

* See Appendix IV.

the Futai had dismissed him, and recommended him to give up the force quietly, a request which was at once complied with, and Captain Holland of the Royal Marines, the Chief of Staveley's Staff, was left in temporary command.   At the same time the Futai assumed the responsibility of supporting the Sungkiang force, which had hitherto been paid by the Chinese merchants; and he quelled a great commotion which arose amongst them when they heard of the dismissal of their Commander, by the simple but effectual expedient of paying their arrears.

Again General Staveley urged that Colonel Forrester should be placed in command, so anxious was he to avoid any appearance of putting the disciplined Chinese exclusively under British management; and it was only on that officer again refusing that he agreed to place Captain Holland in temporary command, and to recommend Captain Gordon of the Royal Engineers as its permanent Chief, if his Government approved of a British officer taking such an appointment.

CHAPTER VII.

CAPTAIN DEW'S OPERATIONS IN CHEKIANG.

BRITISH NEUTRALITY AT NINGPO—HOSTILE ATTITUDE OF THE TAI-
PINGS—ADMIRAL HOPE SENDS CAPTAIN DEW, R.N., TO NINGPO—
REASONS FOR OUR INTERFERENCE THERE—APAK, THE EX-PIRATE
—CAPTAIN DEW TAKES NINGPO BY ASSAULT—DEATH OF LIEU-
TENANTS KENNEY AND CORNEWALL—ORDER RESTORED IN THE
CITY—FORMATION OF FRENCH AND ENGLISH CORPS OF DISCIP-
LINED CHINESE—DESCRIPTION OF THE SURROUNDING COUNTRY,
AND EFFECTS OF TAI-PING OCCUPATION—CLEARING A THIRTY-
MILE RADIUS—TAKING OF YUYOW AND TSEKI—DEATH OF GEN-
ERAL WARD—REPULSE AT FUNGWHA—COMMANDER JONES IN A
FIX—A BISHOP'S SPOIL—HALF OF CHEKIANG RESTORED TO IM-
PERIAL RULE—PAY OF THE ANGLO-CHINESE CONTINGENT—REBEL
DEFEAT AT PIKWAN—CAPTAIN DEW GOES BEYOND THE THIRTY-
MILE RADIUS—ADVANCE ON SHOWSHING—DEATH OF CAPTAIN LE
BRETHON DE COLIGNY—DESCRIPTION OF SHOWSHING—DEATHS
OF CAPTAIN TARDIFF AND LIEUTENANT TINLING—CAPTAIN DEW
UNDERTAKES THE SIEGE—FALL OF SHOWSHING—DASHING NATURE
OF CAPTAIN DEW'S EXPLOITS.

THE operations against the Tai-pings which were carried
on at Ningpo and in its neighbourhood by Captain
Roderick Dew of the Royal Navy afford material for a
very noteworthy chapter in the history of our relations
with China. With very scanty materials, and by as
dashing exploits as the annals of the British navy have
to record, this officer not only drove the Rebels away

from the port where he was stationed, and had to protect, but also managed, by assisting in getting up a disciplined Chinese force, and by pushing his expeditions into the interior, to restore almost the entire province of Chekiang to Imperialist rule.

For some time previous to his advent on the scene, the Rebels had had very much their own way in Chekiang, but now met there with a severe check from the hostility, which they wantonly provoked, of the naval forces of Great Britain and France. This rich province had been entered in the autumn of 1861 by an army of 100,000 Tai-pings, who established themselves in the city and at the open port of Ningpo, the city of the " Peaceful Wave." Our policy at this place was at first strictly neutral; and though Captain Corbett in H.M.S. Scout was at Ningpo, he had the most positive orders not to interfere with the Tai-pings unless they insulted our people or attempted to occupy the Foreign settlement. They took good care, however, to be on their best behaviour, and remained so till they had exhausted the supplies of guns, other arms, and ammunition, which Foreigners of nearly all nations hastened to sell them. They then began to be insolent, and had a greedy eye on the Foreign settlement, intending, no doubt, if they had not been turned out of Ningpo, to have visited the Kampo (the name of our settlement), and, with their arms, to have got back the dollars they had bartered for them. Commander Craigie of H.M.S. Ringdove, senior officer at Ningpo, writing about the middle of April to his Admiral, Sir James Hope, informed him of the hostile and alarming attitude the Tai-pings in Ningpo were assuming towards Foreigners. His ship, which lay at anchor off the British Consulate, and within pistol-shot of the walls, had been fired on several times by the lawless soldiery, and many Chinese in the British settlement had been killed by bullets from the city. Expostulations with the Chiefs having failed to prevent recurrence of such insults, Admiral Sir J. Hope instructed Captain Dew to proceed to Ningpo, to use his best endeavours to bring the Tai-ping Chiefs to reason, and to warn them that, while on the one hand we had every wish to remain neutral, such neutrality depended solely on themselves, and that the Western nations would not brook insults to their flags and people. On the 24th April this officer entered the river Yung in the Encounter, passed the walled city of Chinhai, and, after steaming six miles, anchored off Ningpo.

No proper apology was offered, and matters were in an unsatisfactory state, when Captain Dew received intelligence that the late Tautai of Ningpo, Chang, had arrived with a fleet of war-junks, under the command of one Apak, formerly a pirate, but who now, with all his followers, had received pardon, and had become a good subject of the Emperor. Commander Kenney, of the French gunboat Etoile, joined Captain Dew on board the Hardy, and they visited this Imperial force. The Mandarins requested assistance in attacking Ningpo, but this was declined ; at the same time they were informed that if shots were fired either by them or by the Tai-pings in the direction of the settlement, the Allies would return fire. The Imperialist leaders Chang and Apak then stated that it was their intention to attack Ningpo, but were requested to delay for forty-eight hours, till Captain Dew had communicated with the Tai-ping Chiefs, after which time permission would be granted or refused. The latter had built a formidable granite battery, armed with 68-pounders, which both commanded our settlement and the reach of the river up which the Imperialists would have to advance. Moreover, fresh guns had been mounted in the embrasures opposite the English vessels, masked in a crafty manner by loose bricks. Thus it was now quite evident that mischief was intended by the Tai-pings, and that if the Imperialists advanced, our own ships and the settlement would suffer from the fire of both parties. Foreseeing this, Captain Dew wrote a despatch to the Tai-ping Chiefs, in which he informed them that, if they would remove their guns form the walls and battery opposite the settlement, he would guarantee that no attack should be made by the Imperialists by the river, an offer which was positively doing the Imperialists an injustice. Captain Dew also sent a letter to the Tai-ping Chiefs on the 8th May, in which he said :—

"ENCOUNTER, NINGPO, 8*th* *May* 1862.—This is to inform you, on the part of the English and French senior naval officers, that had you agreed to their demands, and removed your guns from the battery and walls, they should have felt bound in honour to have acted up to their promise, and have prevented an attack from the river on the settlement side by the Imperialists who now advance to attack you. We inform you that we wish to maintain a perfect neutrality; but if you fire guns or musketry from the battlements or walls opposite our ships or settlement on the advancing Imperialists, thereby endangering the lives of our men and people in the Foreign settlement, we shall then feel it our duty to return the fire and bombard the city."

The Imperialists were then informed that they were at liberty to attack the city, if they did not fire upon the settlement or the ships in the river, among which were of English vessels, the Encounter, 14 guns, 175 men, Captain Dew ; Ringdove, 4 guns, 90 men, Captain

Craigie ; gunboats Kestrel and Hardy, 40 men each, commanded by Lieutenants Huxham and Bogle ; and of French (who were placed under Captain Dew's orders by Admiral Protet), the Etoile, 1 gun, 30 men, Lieutenant de Vaisseau Kenney ; and Confucius, 3 guns, 40 men, Enseigne de Vaisseau Le Brethon de Coligny.

On the morning of the 10th May, Apak's Imperialist junks shaved clear of the point below the Foreign vessels, and a heavy fire was opened on them by the Tai-ping Point Battery. At the same time a volley of musketry was poured into H.M.S. Encounter by the Rebels, and so, in mere self-defence, Captain Dew was forced to take part in the engagement. A general fire began from ships and walls. The bastions, guns, and guard-house at the Salt Gate were soon smashed up by the Moorsom shells of the Encounter, while the Ringdove silenced the guns at the North Gate. Lieutenant Bogle, in the gunboat Hardy, did good service, steaming up and down before the walls on the river face, shutting up gun after gun ; and the Etoile, Kestrel, and Confucius were smashing the Point Battery. Apak and Chang, with their Imperialist war-junks, let down their anchors at the first shot, being satisfied with the honour of opening the ball. As the running spring-tide effectually prevented them coming up the river, the Kestrel was sent to tow them up ; but this aid they steadily declined, urging paltry excuses, such as having no powder. Captain Dew felt at this moment in rather a dilemma ; he knew he had no aid to expect from the Imperialists, and it seemed almost too much to hope for success in an assault on Ningpo with the two or three hundred men he could count on, against a garrison of between 20,000 and 30,000, who had been well supplied with arms by their friends in the Foreign settlement. Experienced, however, in Chinese warfare, he thought that if he could once gain and open a gate of the city while the thunder of his bombardment was still fresh in the enemy's ears, he might count on co-operation from Apak and his gang, and that a panic would ensue among the Tai-pings. On the other hand, he felt that if he rested content with what he had done, there was great danger of the Tai-pings taking heart again, letting loose fire-rafts on his vessels, and destroying the Foreign settlement.

Having determined to attack, he landed at noon to collect scaling-ladders from the houses of the missionaries, and wrote to Lieutenant Kenney, asking him to join in an assault on the city, with what men he had available, at two o'clock. At that hour Dew landed—leaving his ship in charge of the master and the gunner, with a crew of cooks, stewards, and boys—taking with him all his available men, and being joined by about 100 white-turbaned Chinese soldiers. While waiting for Lieutenant Kenney, who could scarcely stem the tide in the Etoile, he planted five ladders against the wall of the city, but soon found he had committed a grave error, for the enemy massed themselves in a graveyard beneath the wall, hove back the ladders with their spears, and with a storm of stinkpots, fireballs, stones, and bricks, forced the British sailors on the other side to take shelter in outhouses, and made the Chinese allies take to the water. On the French Lieutenant joining him with twenty men, another attempt was made with the ladders. Kenney, the first on his, was shot through the lungs; David Davis, who was foremost on the next, was shot through the head as, revolver in mouth, he topped the wall; and so Captain Dew himself was the first to gain a position on the rampart, which was soon passed by the greater part of his force; and in less than two minutes

Lieutenant Tinling and Boatswain Cantlow had a howitzer parbuckled up and ready for action.

In this way the Salt Gate was taken, and a few volleys soon cleared the neighbouring streets; but Fang, the Tai-ping Chief, soon made a great effort to dislodge the assailants. Forming his body-guard of about 400 men at the East Gate, he led them along the wall to the attack, and they came on at the double, with their yellow turbans, gaudy silk dresses, and banners, their leader being well in advance. Hastily forming all the men he could spare, French and English, from the defence of the gate, Captain Dew advanced at the charge to meet them. When within about ten yards, Fang fired both barrels of his double gun, but at that moment the whole parapet of the wall which divided the two forces fell down, having been hit by a lucky Moorsom shell, which was fired by the crew of cooks and stewards which had been left on board the Encounter. On the Allies returning to the gate, a shot came from the houses below which almost avenged the fall of the city, as the gallant First-Lieutenant of the Encounter, William Cornewall, was pierced by it through the heart.

Meanwhile Lieutenants Craigie and Siardet had taken the North Gate, and Lieutenant Bogle cut through the bridge of boats which had presented an obstacle to vessels advancing up the river. The news of this success soon spread over the settlement, reaching Apak and his followers, who now, inspired with desire for plunder, did not wait for tide or powder, but landing, crossed over the settlement, and seizing boats opposite the city, entered it like a pack of ravenous wolves. From the mastheads of the shipping the Tai-pings were seen streaming out by the West Gate; and so great was the panic that seized them, that hundreds of their number were speared by their own people in their haste to escape. Fearing the result, if he allowed his men to enter the town and mix with the Apak crew, Captain Dew re-embarked them along with the French, making arrangements in case the Tai-pings attempted to reoccupy the city, but these latter stopped as little as possible till they found themselves within the walls of Yuyow, thirty miles distant.

On the following day the city was handed over, through Mr Harvey, the British Consul, to Chang, the ex-Tautai. "I had known," writes Captain Dew, "Ningpo in its palmy days, when it boasted itself one of the first commercial cities of the empire ; but now, on this 11th May, one might have fancied that an angel of destruction had been at work in the city as in its suburbs. All the latter, with their wealthy hongs and thousands of houses, lay levelled ; while in the city itself, once the home of half a million of people, no trace or vestige of an inhabitant could be seen. Truly it was a city of the dead. The rich and beautiful furniture of the houses had become firewood, or was removed to the walls for the use of the soldiers who had dwelt thereon. The canals were filled with dead bodies and stagnant filth. The stone work of bridges and pavements had been uplifted to strengthen walls and form barricades in the streets; and in those temples, once the pride of their Buddhist priests, the chaotic remains of gorgeous idols and war gods lay strewn about, their lopped limbs showing they had become the sport of those Christian Tai-pings, whose chief, the Tien Wang, eight years before, at Nanking, had asked Sir George Bonham if the Virgin Mary had a pretty sister for him, the King of Heaven, to marry ! It has been my good fortune since to assist at the wresting of many cities from these Tai-pings, and in them all I found, as at Ningpo, that the same devilish hands had been at work, the people expelled from their houses, and their cities ruined."

After Ningpo was thus retaken, Apak, the ex-pirate, and his fleet were dismissed, and at the urgent request of Chang, the Imperialist Tautai or Governor, Captain Dew undertook the military command of the city, including the control of 400 of Ward's disciplined Chinese, who were sent round from Shanghai, and were placed in charge of the gates. A proclamation was issued to the people, inviting them to return to their homes, and stating that the Allies would guarantee the city against another visit from the Tai-pings. Such faith had the Chinese in our promise that by tens of thousands they flocked to their old homes; and in a month houses had been refurnished, shops opened, and commercial activity began to return. Some trouble was caused by a number of rowdies, the *mauvais sujets* of all nations, who appeared in the settlement, intent on robbing what little the Rebels and Apak had left in the city. They were wont to hire gangs of Chinese, and to declare they acted on Captain Dew's authority. In this manner quantities of rice, valuable medicines, &c. &c., were lowered over the walls; and a German who was caught in the very act of carrying off a 24-pounder gun, received four dozen lashes on board the Encounter. Mr Harvey and the other Foreign Consuls issued certificates to all Foreigners pursuing lawful callings; and one night Captain Dew landed a party of his men and seized all unprovided with such a document, and sent them to Shanghai. The Chinese customhouse was opened, and numerous seizures of arms intended for the Rebels were made. When the British ship Paragon was visited by a naval officer, the master declared his cargo to be bamboo wares; but on opening the hatches, 200 iron cannons, thousands of stands of small-arms, and a large quantity of ammunition, were disclosed. The cargo was confiscated by the Chinese, and the master was fined £100 for his false manifesto. The temptation to squeeze the Chinese going in and out of the city was too great for Ward's men, and sometimes for even his officers, to resist; and at last French and English men-of-war's men were placed at the gates.

These measures had the desired effect, and confidence was soon restored. It was also arranged with the Mandarins that a Chinese disciplined force of 1000 men should be raised for the defence of the city, as it was intimated that Ward would soon require his men at Shanghai. There was no difficulty in obtaining recruits from Chusan in any number. The good treatment of the men by their European officers, and, above all, the fact that they really received weekly pay in money, and not, as frequently from Mandarins, in promises, made the disciplined force a very popular one. A dozen British marines were appointed instructors to six companies, and an artillery company of 100 men was likewise formed. The artificers of the Encounter, under the gunner and carpenter, were employed in making gun-carriages and gun-gear; and so in a month the city was brought into a creditable state of defence, with sixty guns of all sizes in position. Good guard-houses were built at each gate, and solid granite magazines were also constructed. Lieutenant de Vaisseau Le Brethon succeeded Kenney (who had died from the effects of his wound) as French senior officer, cordially aiding Captain Dew in all that concerned the defence of the city, and in subsequent operations. Not wishing that France should be unfelt, he and Monsieur Giquel, formerly a French officer, but then engaged as Commissioner of Chinese Customs, raised a

Franco-Chinese corps, with the aid of some instructors from Shanghai. Occasional trips were made up both branches of the river in gunboats ; so several skirmishes occurred with the Rebels, who were concentrated in force in the walled city of Yuyow, thirty miles from Ningpo on which they appeared to meditate another attack.

On one occasion, when the Hardy and Etoile were reconnoitring, a strange deputation of aged persons came down to the river-bank, headed by a little girl leading a venerable blind old man. Their story was that the Tai-pings had the day before burned their village, carried off their sons and daughters, and because these poor helpless people had no money to give, the fiends had cut off their ears. To prevent the Tai-pings ravaging the country after this fashion, the Ringdove was placed about twenty-five miles up the river, and she effectually kept them in check for a time.

Towards the end of July, Captain Dew moved the Encounter up the river as far as her draught would allow, within ten miles of Yuyow, under the Joss-house Hill, and made preparations for attacking the city, which was held by 20,000 Tai-pings,—his orders being to use his best exertions in carrying out the policy of the Government in clearing a thirty-mile radius. The attacking force consisted of the Hardy, with 40 men of the Encounter's crew, and towing-boats containing about 500 of Ward's men ; the French steamer Confucius, commanded by Lieutenant Le Brethon, having on her deck 400 Franco-Chinese ; and 1500 Cantonese braves in a dozen armed junks which the Chinese merchants of Ningpo had fitted out. Nothing could exceed the beauty of the scenery between Joss-house Hill and Yuyow. The river wound its tortuous course among pine-clad hills, in whose gorges, fringed with the feathery bamboos, lay villages

once teeming with life, but at this time blackened ruins
haunted by hungry dogs. The large hill in the centre
of Yuyow and all neighbouring eminences seemed like a
vast tulip-field, owing to the gaudy banners of the Rebel
host. The walls of this place, three miles in circumference, enclosed a high hill. As usual with Chinese
cities, a canal encircles it, save on the side of the river,
which is navigable for a gunboat to within 200 yards
of the walls. A bridge spanned the river, and communicated with a ruined suburb on the left bank; on the
right, and commanding the city, stood a high hill, with
a large joss-house on its summit. A line of stockades
and batteries extended along either bank of the river for
half a mile; and the stream itself, which was only ten
feet deep, had been staked.

On the 2d August the gunboats advanced up the
river, and it was arranged that, when they had shelled a
tête du pont, Ward's men and the Franco-Chinese should
advance, carrying a bridge which led to the joss-house,
which, being the key of the position, might lead to the
fall of the city. After the *tête du pont* had been shelled
until it seemed untenable, the Chinese troops advanced
gallantly, led by M. Giquel and Major Morton; but on
reaching the centre of the bridge, they were brought up
by a wooden stockade and a heavy fire from the hill-top,
as well as from a large body of men concealed in a bomb-
proof near the bridge. With heavy loss they had to
retreat, and other attempts were also failures, the fall
of 100 killed and wounded, together with heavy rains,
having dispirited the assailants. Next morning a new
plan of attack was arranged, and Yuyow was taken
without much loss, the Franco-Chinese under M. Giquel
greatly distinguishing themselves. Chang, the Tautai,
was highly delighted, not so much at the fall of the city,

as at his release from the post of honour his junk had
been made to occupy near the Hardy, where round-shot
fell rather plentifully.   A large quantity of rice and a
gigantic farmyard, the plunder of the surrounding district, was found in this place.   The peasants reclaimed
their buffaloes, but the victors feasted high on poultry
for many a day.   The Tai-pings retreated to a chain of
intrenched camps about twelve miles distant, and for a
month gave no trouble.   In that interval Yuyow was
placed in a state of defence, and a garrison of 1000
drilled Chinese, half Ward's, half French, were left in it
under command of a French artillery officer, Captain
Tardiff de Maidrey, who had done good service with an
irregular artillery force at Shanghai.

Towards the middle of September the Allies received
information that the Tai-pings had collected a large force
with the intention of descending on Ningpo on two
sides, and on carrying off, if they failed to get the city,
the magnificent rice crops now ripening on the plains.
The Rebel force first descended into the Ningpo plain
and captured from the Mandarin soldiers the walled city
of Tseki, situated between Yuyow and Ningpo.   Their
foraging-parties scattered over the plain, and the villagers
came flocking into the Foreign settlement, where volunteers were collected for defence.   General Ward arrived
at Ningpo on the 18th September, and arrangements
were made for the recapture of Tseki.   At daylight on
the 20th, he and 200 of his men were sent up in boats,
while the 400 of his force in Yuyow were brought down,
Captain Tardiff undertaking to guard that place with his
Franco-Chinese.   Round Tseki the whole plain seemed
on fire.   The terror-stricken inhabitants, many of them
swimming on logs, were crossing the river ; and for miles
the long reeds on its banks gave shelter to men, women,

and children up to the middle in water. Ward, landing
with his men, made a short cut across the country to a
bridge which he was to hold, supported by the Hardy
and by Captain Dew, who was to join next morning
with all available forces. He surprised numerous looting
parties, and soon gained the bridge, and drove the Rebels
into the city. Now and then a Tai-ping would escape
into the tall rice, and give rise to an exciting chase on
the part of the infuriated villagers. It was a service of
much danger for the Hardy to approach, as her decks
could be commanded from hillocks on the banks of the
canal, which were in possession of the enemy ; but the
last glimmer of daylight found her close up to the bridge
held by Ward.

At midnight a despatch reached Captain Dew which
made it imperative for him to give up co-operation with
Ward, and return immediately to Ningpo. The town
of Fungwha, which held the same relative position
to Ningpo on the south that Tseki did on the north,
had fallen the day before, and the Rebels were advancing
on Ningpo on that side. Weighing at daylight, he
anchored off the Salt Gate at 8 A.M., and found Ningpo
like a disturbed ant's nest, the people in their terror not
knowing where to go ; so he had the gates closed, and
landing his men, held the South and West Gates, burning the suburb outside the former. The Mandarins at
this time were in a state of great fear, sleeping at night
in the gateway, and by day asking for the British gunboat to be in twenty places at once. Advantage was
taken of this state of things to get all back pay due to
the troops, also to obtain a round sum to raise a permanent force for the defence of the Foreign settlement,
and to have the canal and defensive works properly
finished.

The Hardy returned to Ningpo that evening with news of the capture of Tseki by escalade. After the gate had been shelled by Lieutenant Bogle, Ward's bodyguard, led by Captain Cooke, advanced with ladders, and took the wall and city. Ward himself, while watching the advance from the arch of a gate 200 yards from the walls, was mortally wounded by a chance ball. He was conveyed on board the Hardy, and Dr Hogge of the Encounter extracted the ball, which had passed through the abdomen and lodged in his back. On being brought to Ningpo he was carried to Dr Parker's house, and was attended also by Dr Irwin ; but there was no hope from medical aid, and he died next day after much suffering. So passed away a man who, as the originator of the idea of disciplining the Chinese, had done good service. Surmounting all difficulties, Ward, in the outset of his adventurous career, had gained a strange ascendancy over Europeans as well as Chinese by his cool and daring courage. Ever foremost in fight, he was honourably scarred, but his ambition was unbounded; and perhaps it was well for the Imperial Government of China that he was removed at this stage of the Rebellion, and that his work was left to be completed by one who, though his equal in courage and in coolness, far surpassed him in all the higher qualities of a soldier. Ward was quite collected during his last hours, and able to give directions for the disposal of the fortune which he had amassed in China. He estimated it at about £60,000 ; but his accounts were all in confusion, and mixed up with those of the banker Ta Kee and other Chinamen, so that only about £15,000 were eventually realised.

The Allies were rather hard pressed at this time, having to garrison Yuyow and Tseki; so 500 more of Ward's men,

now commanded by Colonel Forrester, were brought from
Shanghai, and on their arrival along with the Flamer
gunboat, Dew's men were re-embarked from duty on the
city walls, and preparations were made for attacking
Fungwha, which the Rebels had garrisoned in force, and
which was a considerable walled town, in a gorge of
the mountains, on the south side of the river, and was
the key to the vast plain between it and Ningpo. On
the 8th October the marines and small-arm men of
the Encounter and Sphinx were embarked in the
Hardy and Flamer gunboats, and 1000 of the disciplined Chinese under Forrester were also on board,
or towed by the French steamers Deroulide and Confucius. On arriving at a large stone bridge about twenty
miles up the river, this force was landed. Owing
to heavy rain, the narrow road was impracticable for
the conveyance of its guns, which had to be placed in
boats ; but the rain had swollen the stream, and the
boats could not pass under the bridge. A stout hawser,
however, with 100 men on it, soon removed the massive
blocks of stone that formed the arch, and enabled the
boats to get through ; and that night the expedition
quartered in a very large deserted village four miles
from Fungwha. The rain had drenched every one, and
through the night there had been constant alarms of the
enemy and of fire, so the men were not sorry when the
morning broke fine and sunshiny. A march of four
hours through a golden plain of ripe rice brought them
under the walls of Fungwha, where Forrester advanced
with 600 of his men and two guns to attack the North
and West Gates, while Dew went to the East Gate, and
established a position with three howitzers, under Lieutenant Bosanquet, at 200 yards from the wall. A storming
party of 400 men, under Major Rhode, was held ready,

supported by the marines and small-arm men. The artillery fire having silenced the guns on the walls, and knocked down a portion of the parapet near the gateway, an advance was sounded, and Bosanquet ran his guns to within fifty yards of the walls. When the ladder party reached the bridge, they were met by a heavy fire which killed most of them; and the men following, though well led by their officers, would not face the showers of fireballs, stinkpots, and powder-bags which were hurled upon them, so they fell back. To reassure them, Commander Jones, with twenty small-arm men, went to the front, and most gallantly led on through a similar fiery ordeal, followed by Lieutenants Davis and Tinling, Mr Douglas, midshipman, and Mr Coker, master-assistant, who, clearing off the dead, carried the ladders up to the walls. Ward's troop would not return, so Jones, seeing the folly of attempting to storm with his small force, wisely placed his men in the arch of the gateway, and attempted with axes to cut through the gates, but solid stone-work behind the wood resisted all his efforts. Bosanquet and Lieutenant Rawson and half their crews having been wounded, Captain Dew ordered the remainder to seek cover behind some graves, where the marines were also placed to keep down the fire of the besieged. Commander Jones and his party had to keep in the gateway till dark, when they withdrew, having had a most unpleasant time of it. Stinkpots and powder-bags, with lighted brooms attached, had been dropped over the wall, and had half suffocated them; but this was not so bad as the continued trickle of the nastiest conceivable liquid manure, which some Tai-ping humorist had capsized on the top of the arch.

Next morning a large body of 6000 Tai-pings appeared on the plain advancing towards Fungwha, on the walls

of which there was an immense excitement and display of banners. From the leisurely manner in which
the new arrivals came up, their chiefs being carried in
sedan-chairs, it was evident they had not observed the
Allies ; so they were taken at a disadvantage, and easily
routed, leaving on the plain an immense quantity of
plunder, ammunition, and stores, which had been carried by about 1000 country people, who had nearly all
been branded on the forehead as belonging to the "Heavenly Kingdom." More powder and ammunition having
arrived from the river, preparations were made for
storming the walls at seven different places at daylight
next morning, but the Rebels evacuated the city during
the night, and it was garrisoned by Ward's troops. As
the force returned to Ningpo next morning, nothing
could exceed the gratitude of the country people who
passed, flocking back to their homes to reap the harvest
that covered the plain, for the fall of Fungwha and
Tseki saving them from starvation in the coming
winter. As ever, the Rebels left behind them evi-
dences of their brutal nature. In one spot nearly a
hundred bodies of peasant men and women lay hud-
dled together, their only crime having been refusal to
carry the plunder of their own homes. The loss had
been rather serious ; 24 British officers and men, and
about 70 Chinese, had been placed *hors de combat.*

In this way the thirty-mile radius was cleared round
Ningpo, to which city the rich merchants were flocking
back from Shanghai. A new Tautai who had been appointed was ambitious to regain the other cities in the
province, and promised the necessary funds, so Ward s
force was raised to 1400 bayonets, and the Franco-Chinese to 1000. Le Brethon de Coligny, being appointed
to the command of the latter force, received a commis-

sion as commander of 1000 men from the Emperor of China. Early in November Le Brethon advanced on Shungyu, and the Tai-pings evacuated that city. Every 50 or 100 yards along the line of the Rebel retreat lay the bodies of men, women, and children. In Shungyu itself a perfect army of old women and little children were found, cold, starving, and suffering from every imaginable disease. It was well for these poor creatures that Monseigneur de la Place, Roman Catholic Bishop of Chekiang, was with the expedition. It was to the humane and energetic measures he took that many owed their lives on this as on other occasions, when cities were taken or evacuated during the Rebellion. He was wont, when others were seeking for plunder, to search for what he called his own loot—*les misérables*, whom he gathered together in some joss-house, and for whom he established rice-kitchens. The fall of Shungyu led to the evacuation of two more cities, and the Tai-pings retired across the great river of Shungyu, thus leaving half the province in Imperialist hands.

Shortly afterwards Ward's force went back to Shanghai, and Captain Dew was not sorry to end the connection with them, because he could never fully persuade the men or officers that "soldiers should be content with their pay," and cases of "squeezing" on their part were continually complained of. On one occasion the major in command at Yuyow, formerly a sergeant in one of our line regiments, sold all he could lay hands on in the city, and was arrested as he was leaving the province with plunder sufficient for a month's pay of the troops. On arrangement with the authorities, an Anglo-Chinese contingent of about 1000 men was raised, the higher officers receiving £1800 and £1000 a-year, and the captains £700, which was an inducement to respectable

H

men, and even to English officers, to serve. Several
petty officers from the English fleet engaged in it, and
by the end of December there was a respectable force
ready to take the field. At the same time Le Brethon,
at Shungyu, by the sale of rice, wood, boats, and all that
had belonged to the Rebels, was enabled to recruit 1200
men, and to clothe and arm them fairly. An arsenal
had been established, and lead and powder found in
Rebel magazines enabled him to make a good supply
of cartridges.

In the end of December an expedition, under Dew
and Le Brethon, advanced to the town of Pikwan from
a hill near which there was a magnificent view of a
noble river winding through an immense and fertile
plain (which again was cut by innumerable canals), and
at the far end of which lay the great city of Showshing,
with walls fifteen miles in circumference, the centre
of the silk district, and the key of the province. The
Rebel banners thickly fringed the opposite banks of the
river, and strong bodies of their cavalry were patrolling
the country. The reconnoitring force was attacked by
the Rebels, whom it drove back ; but, being rather small,
set off to return to Shungyu for reinforcements. On
the way, the Tai-pings in great numbers overtook and
attacked it when it was in a small town ; but Dew and
Le Brethon suddenly turned and surprised their pursuers, who, firing a volley, turned and fled, communicating their panic to, and throwing into disorder, the dense
masses which extended for a mile behind them. As
usual, the line of the Rebel march was marked by the
smoke of burning villages and hamlets ; and now, in their
retreat, they had to pass through the still smouldering
ruins. They never turned to see by how small a
number they were pursued, but, pressing on, threw away

arms and clothing to aid their flight.   A thin coat of
snow covered the muddy rice-fields, and it was only
possible to travel on the paths between them.   The
chase lasted for four miles, and many prisoners were
taken.   Some hundred Rebels had been cut off at an
angle near the river, and being hard pressed by the
disciplined Chinese, and fearing that the death they
would undoubtedly have meted, had positions been
changed, awaited them, took to the cold and swollen
river, which soon engulfed them.   Only a few nearly
reached the opposite bank, but being weary from their
march, one by one they disappeared.   Captain Dew
asserts that during the time he was associated with the
disciplined Chinese he never knew them murder a
prisoner or commit a cruel act; but can it be wondered
at that the country people could not refrain from re-
taliation when the Tai-pings were caught knife or torch
in hand ?   This officer's instructions limited him to the
employment of his own men against the Tai-pings within
a thirty-mile radius round Ningpo ; but looking to the
spirit of these instructions, and the evident and wise
wish of the Government to give all moral support to
the cause of order, he was wont, in company with his
officers and on his own responsibility, frequently to
pass up the country and to aid and assist the Imperialist forces with advice, guns, and ammunition.
The officers of the squadron were always eager to join
in these expeditions, and as they were on leave, he was
always happy to have their company and advice.

Towards the end of January Le Brethon advanced on
Showshing with 1200 of the Franco-Chinese, the first
and only expedition they ever made without being
accompanied by the Anglo-Chinese troops.   They were
very badly off for guns, having but two 12-pounder

howitzers and a couple of old English 9-pounders. A three days' march brought them unopposed to Showshing, which Le Brethon intended to carry by a *coup de main*, and failing in that, he proposed to commence a siege and wait till he could effect a breach with four 32-pounders which Captain Dew expected from Hongkong. With this view he placed the 9-pounders in position to knock away the parapet over the gateway; but at the first discharge the gun burst, and a large portion of the breech struck Le Brethon, carrying away the whole upper part of his body and causing instantaneous death. The command was now taken by M. Cymer, formerly an officer in the French army, who unwisely determined to retreat to Shungyu.

Captain Dew was at Ningpo when the news of Le Brethon's death reached the Mandarins, and he felt that Ningpo would not be safe so long as Showshing, the key of the province, remained in possession of the Rebels. Hence he sent up some of the Anglo-Chinese contingent to retrieve matters, and procured an 8-inch howitzer with Moorsom shells from Shanghai. Being warned by Admiral Kuper that the Encounter might be wanted for service in Japan, he was anxious to have matters in a secure state before leaving; and so, when Lieutenant Tinling offered to assist in conveying fresh ammunition to Showshing, leave was allowed him to take it to Sangkow, a town ten miles from Showshing, where General Tardiff and the Franco-Chinese then were; but he was also ordered, after doing so, to return to Ningpo. A few days subsequently Dew, accompanied by several of his officers, joined Tardiff at Sangkow, and meeting Lieutenant Tinling, allowed him to remain there two or three days.

Showshing was a large city, with walls thirty-five feet

high and fifteen broad, and fifteen miles in circumference ; it was garrisoned by 40,000 Tai-pings, under the
command of the Sing Wang, commonly called "Cockeye,"
who was afterwards taken and executed at Soochow.
It stands near some hills at the head of an immense
plain of forty miles in length, unrivalled even in China
for the richness of its soil and the beauty of its scenery.
This plain is intersected by thousands of canals which
in some parts will scarcely admit the passage of a boat,
but open out at others into vast lakes of thousands of
acres in area, and dotted over with picturesque islets,
with temples embosomed among their trees. Villages
and towns by hundreds lay flourishing and peaceful
around, the Tai-pings having spared them for heavy
ransoms; but the inhabitants seemed delighted to see
the Allies, and insisted on supplying them gratis with
cattle, rice, and all other necessaries.

On the evening of the 17th February the attacking
force occupied a large untenanted suburb near the Liquo
Gate, on an island with a bridge in rear, canals on both
flanks, and the city walls and gate in front. The whole
of the suburbs within 600 yards of the walls had
been levelled, on each side of the paved road leading
to the gate only beautifully carved stone pillars, dedi-
cated to the "young widows and virgins of Showshing,"
having been left standing. The gate itself was strongly
fortified by an immense strong outer wall, loopholed,
and with six guns in position. The walls themselves
being roofed over all round the city, the defenders took
up abode on them entirely. Several hills inside the
city were also fortified, while a deep canal, thirty feet
in width, encircled the whole city. After a reconnais-
sance on the following day, it was determined to breach
the wall near an angle 200 yards from the gate, while

boats and planks were got ready to form a bridge over the canal for the assaulting columns. That night the howitzer, with muffled wheels, was placed in battery 160 yards from the walls with trifling loss, while another battery of four 12-pounder howitzers was planted 100 yards in rear for its protection. On the 19th, by 8 A.M., Tardiff had made all his preparations—the boats in a dense fog were got up and hid under the arch of a bridge under the walls—and at 9 A.M. Captain Ganghan, with his Anglo-Chinese artillerymen, who alone worked the howitzers during the day, opened fire. A few hollow shot sent into the base of the wall soon formed an opening for the 8-inch Moorsom shells, which exploding therein, soon acted like so many mines and brought the wall crumbling down. The defenders meanwhile were not idle ; about thirty guns were well served during the day, and the fusilade of small-arms never ceased. At 10 A.M. Tardiff was mortally wounded by a musket-ball fired by accident by one of his own men who was in his rear. His iron constitution enabled him to live for eight hours, though his brains were scattered over the hair of his head. He had told Dew at breakfast that morning that he had a presentiment he should not survive the day, and begged the latter to succeed him in the command, as he had no one competent to undertake it. Under these circumstances Captain Dew appointed the senior instructor, with the rank of colonel, to the command, on the understanding that he carried out Dew's directions. Shortly after Lieutenant Tinling, R.N., was wounded while watching with his opera - glass the effect of the shell on the walls. He was, as he thought, in a place of safety, but a spent ball from an angle struck the back of his head. Dr Lockhead at once extracted it, and gave it as his opinion that he would be

well in a week ; but after being sent down to Ningpo,
inflammation of the brain set in and terminated fatally,
to the great grief of his brother officers, to whom his
many fine qualities had greatly endeared him.   By
2 P.M. ninety shells had effected a magnificent breach,
though between each discharge of the howitzer the Rebels
sent streams of men with sandbags to fill up the space.
An assaulting column of 800 men then advanced, and,
in spite of a heavy fire from the walls, gained the canal,
placed a bridge of boats in position, and about twenty
men, chiefly Europeans, crossed over and made for the
breach, which they had half mounted when they found
that the boats had got adrift and they were unsupported.
The Rebels soon found this out, rallied in the retreat
they had commenced, and, swarming on the walls, repulsed the attack, those of the assailants who survived
having to swim the canal.   All attempts to bring the
Chinese again to the attack were vain, though they were
rallied by Lieutenant Holders, R.N., at half musket-shot.
The loss of the Allies was 140 *hors de combat ;* and
much credit was due to Dr Lockhead, R.A., the only
medical officer, for his attention to the wounded.

Captain Dew intended to have ordered another assault
next morning ; but during the night, in spite of the fire
on it, the breach had been so far repaired that it was
impossible for the ten remaining Moorsom shells to open
it again.   Pine-trees had been driven in as piles, the
upper ends being supported by ropes, while the space
between was filled up with debris and sandbags.   A
regular siege was now commenced, the assailants making
their own position secure by throwing up a high wall,
cutting ditches, and making batteries and approaches
with gabions.   This enabled half the force to occupy
itself in attacking and dispersing large bodies of Rebels,

who issued out of the other gates and began to burn the country in the rear.

In four days all those bands had been driven into the city, and the approaches to a third gate were occupied, and the Rebel communication with Hangchow cut off, as were all convoys that attempted to enter. Ammunition seemed plentiful with the besieged, about 300 round brass shot being daily thrown into the besieging lines and among the boats. Captain Dew was most ably assisted by Mr M'Arthur, paymaster of the Encounter, and the various measures employed soon began to damp the spirit of the besieged. Day by day their fire slackened, and the fall of the city soon became only an affair of time. Early in March, D'Aiguibelle, Lieutenant de Vaisseau, having been appointed by Admiral Jaures to succeed Tardiff in the command, Captain Dew returned to Ningpo; and on the 18th of that month Showshing was evacuated by the Rebels, who retreated by the hills to Hangchow. Thus the province of Chekiang was in great part restored to Imperialist rule. The officers who served along with Captain Dew in these operations were killed off very rapidly; but distinguished success attended his movements, and it is a wonder that he has not received the Victoria Cross, for which he was recommended. A British Admiral, under whom he once served, writing to me about the capture of Ningpo, calls it "by far the best thing of the kind done either in China or elsewhere since the peace of 1815;" and really, considering all the circumstances, this praise is not undeserved.

PART III.

COLONEL GORDON'S CAMPAIGN

CHAPTER VIII.

THE ORGANISATION OF GORDON'S FORCE.

THOUGH it had done some good service, and had received its title under Ward, yet it was not until it came
under Colonel Gordon's command that the Ever-Victorious Army became in any degree worthy of its high-
sounding name, which must be taken not in a literal
but in a transcendental and Celestial sense. The
Chinese have a fine faculty for inventing happy names
—their streams are fragrant, their mountains holy, the
poorest hamlet may call itself the place of sweet-
smelling grain, and the smallest junk be a wonder of
the deep. Nor are such titles merely hollow sounds.
Foreigners, on discovering the immense discrepancy
between the Celestial phrase and that which it re-

presents, are apt to regard the former as a mere trivial absurdity; but to the Chinaman these titles have a vital significance, and the turn of a phrase will often influence his whole conduct towards the subject designated. No principle is more constantly enforced in the Chinese Classics than that wisdom lies in the proper knowledge and use of words. When it was asked of Mencius in what he surpassed, his brief reply was, "I understand words;" and elsewhere he complains of inauspicious, hurtful words, which throw men of virtue and talent into the shade. When inquiry was made of Confucius as to what was the first thing necessary to improve the government, he answered, "What is necessary is to rectify names;" and very expressively he said, that "to have a bad name is to dwell in a low-lying situation, where all the evil of the world flows in upon one." Views such as these have sunk deep into the national mind, and every Chinaman is singularly desirous that he and all his belongings should have auspicious and honourable designations. When the people are so inclined, of course the Government is very careful in all its edicts and proclamations to use either high-sounding or beautiful phraseology, whether the reference be to the Son of Earth and Heaven sitting on the dragon throne, or to a ragged lictor who runs by the chair of some petty Mandarin. Crime and official imbecility are reprobated in the most vigorous and picturesque manner by the Emperor's vermilion pencil; but where praise is to be awarded for judicious counsel or for battles won, then

> "Strength is gigantic, valour high,
> And wisdom soars beyond the sky."

Hence it is in a Celestial and somewhat transcendental, not in an occidental or literal meaning, that this phrase,

"The Ever - Victorious Army," must be understood. "Ch'ang Sheng Chi'un," however — the high - sounding title which this army received at a very early period of its existence, and by which it will be known, in Chinese history at least—turned out to be by no means extravagantly hyperbolic, seeing what was the work that it accomplished in the suppression of a most formidable movement, which afflicted the Flowery Land for more than ten years, which at one time had threatened to subvert not only the ruling dynasty, but also the institutions of the empire, and which had caused a prodigious amount of devastation and slaughter.

It has been mentioned that in January 1863, General Staveley, now Sir Charles Staveley and second in command of the Abyssinian Expedition, but then chief of her Majesty's forces in China, being applied to by the Futai for advice and assistance, offered to place Captain Holland, the chief of his staff, in temporary command, and recommended Captain Gordon, R.E., to the permanent command, if his Government should approve of its being taken by a British officer. While under charge of Captain Holland, in February 1863, this disciplined force made an attack upon the town of Taitsan, but was defeated by the Tai-pings, with the loss of some guns and of many officers and men, though the commander made great exertions, and exposed himself throughout the engagement to a very heavy fire. Another expedition, under Major Brennan, was repulsed in an attempt to take Fushan; and these two failures, together with the insinuations of Imperialists, made the Futai very much dissatisfied and disgusted with this far from victorious army.

But on the very day of Captain Holland's defeat a despatch arrived from Sir Frederick Bruce, sanctioning the placing of a British officer in command of this disciplined force; and on receiving this permission, General Staveley decided on placing Captain and Brevet-Major Gordon of the Royal Engineers in charge whenever that officer had finished with the survey on which he was engaged of the country within the thirty-mile radius round Shanghai. Captain (now Lieutenant - Colonel) Gordon, C.B., had served before Sebastopol in the Crimean war, and been there wounded in the trenches. After peace had been made, he was employed in surveying and settling the Turkish and Russian frontier in Asia,—a work of no little danger and difficulty, owing to the wild character of the tribes of Armenia and Koordistan. Engaged in the expedition against Peking, he continued on service in China after our difficulties with the Imperial Government had been arranged ; and in the end of 1861 made a long journey from that capital to the Chotow and Kalgan Passes on the Great Wall, striking down from the latter place through Shensi, and passing Taiyuen, the capital of that province, a city before unvisited by foreigners, unless by Catholic priests in disguise. In his new position as commander of the Ever-Victorious Army, Colonel Gordon did not fail to display the judgment and tireless energy which had characterised his brief but not undistinguished career. Indeed, it very soon became apparent that the Tai-pings had to meet a more formidable opponent than any they had before encountered, and one who knew how to break their ranks, not less by his skill in the arts of war than by his personal prestige, and by the assurance which his character soon inspired, that those who gave up their arms to him would receive humane and honourable treatment.

Some curiosity may be felt in regard to the composition, arms, rates of pay, and so forth, of this disciplined

Chinese force which Colonel Gordon now undertook to command ; and, moreover, without such knowledge his operations and the state of affairs in China can hardly be understood.   Its origin under Ward has already been noticed, and as further organised by Gordon it may now be described generally.

The commissioned officers were all Foreigners—Englishmen, Americans, Germans, Frenchmen, and Spaniards, but Americans were in the majority.   Among them were to be found many seafaring men, and old soldiers of our infantry regiments who had purchased their discharge.   As a rule they were brave, reckless, very quick in adapting themselves to circumstances, and reliable in action ; but, on the other hand, they were troublesome when in garrison, very touchy as to precedence, and apt to work themselves about trifles into violent states of mind.   Excited by Rebel sympathisers at Shanghai, and being of different nationalities, one half of them were usually in a violent state of quarrel with the other ; but this, of course, was often an advantage to the commander.   The non-commissioned officers were all Chinese, selected from the ranks ; but very few of these were advanced to the higher grade, as it was found that, on such promotion, the most zealous sergeants became lazy and useless.

Up to the capture of Quinsan in May 1863, the privates were principally natives of Kiangsoo and Chekiang, inferior to Cantonese and Northerners ; but after that date the force was largely recruited from the captured Rebels, who were from all parts of China, and who, having been accustomed to very hard work and no pay, found the new service an elysium, and when taken one day, never objected to going into action against their old comrades the next.

The force varied in strength from 3000 to 5000 men, divided into from five to six infantry regiments, with four batteries siege, and two batteries field, artillery. Each infantry regiment consisted, when complete, of six companies, averaging 500 men in all, as follows :—

Foreigners.

		Per Mensem.
1 Colonel or Lieutenant-Colonel,	. .	at £75 to £85
1 Major, ...	.	„ £60 to £70
1 Captain and Adjutant, . .	.	„ £50 0 0
6 Captains, each . .	.	„ 42 0 0
6 Lieutenants, each . .	.	„ 30 0 0

Chinese.

6 Colour-Sergeants, each . .	.	„ 4 0 0
12 Sergeants, each . .	.	„ 3 0 0
24 Corporals, each . .	.	„ 2 10 0
480 Privates, each . .	.	„ 1 17 6

When in garrison, they had to find themselves out of their pay; but when in the field, each man received daily, in addition to his pay, 2 lb. rice, $\frac{3}{4}$ lb. salt pork or 2 lb. salt fish, besides vegetables and oil.

The artillery was commanded by one colonel at £70 to £75 *per mensem.* Each battery consisted usually of

Foreigners.

		Per Mensem.
1 First Captain, . .	.	at £50 0 0
1 Second Captain, . .	.	„ 45 0 0
2 Lieutenants, each . .	.	„ 35 0 0
1 Sergeant, . .	.	„ 20 0 0

Chinese.

1 Colour-Sergeant, . .	.	„ 4 10 6
6 Sergeants, each . .	.	„ 3 15 0
12 Corporals, each . .	.	„ 3 0 0
120 to 150 Gunners, each . .	.	„ 2 0 0

The whole of the men and officers were paid monthly by a Chinese official of high civil rank, Paymaster Kah, a good man of business, well educated, honest, pleasing in manner, and of venerable appearance. The payment

was made in Mexican dollars, in presence of the commander, Colonel Gordon, "whose aim," one of his officers
—a commissioned officer in H.M. service—writes, "ever
was to prevent, as far as possible, squeezing and the
misappropriation of funds." The dollars required for
these payments monthly varied from the value of
£14,000 to £26,000, and at no time were the men ever
kept more than ten days in arrears. In addition to this
rate of pay, on the dissolution of the force in 1864, the
officers received large *douceurs*, varying from £200 to
£1600 each, and the men each from £2 to £3, those
wounded receiving further donations, according to the
nature of their wounds.

In General Ward's time it had been customary for the
Ever-Victorious troops to receive from about £15,000
to £20,000 for each city they captured, the sum being
agreed upon before the assault was made; but on the
appointment of a British officer to command, this practice was discontinued, and it was agreed that the troops
should be regularly paid so much *per diem*, and receive,
for special feats, anything which the Futai might deem
it advisable to give. The high rates of pay were not
necessary latterly, for recruits offered themselves in
abundance; but no change in this respect could have
been effected without causing delay in the operations,
and perhaps danger. It would certainly have caused a
revolt, as both officers and men would have been perfectly agreed on this subject; for if the pay of either the
officers or of the men had been cut down first, the other
section would naturally have expected their turn to
come next, and would have acted accordingly. When
the force was originated by Ward, high rates of pay
were fixed, because the Chinese objected to being drilled
and disciplined by Foreign Devils in a manner totally

I

different from that to which they had been accustomed, and also because they were required to wear a motley half-European uniform which subjected them to the jeers of their own people, who used to call them " Imitation Foreign Devils." This European style of dress was adopted partly to make the Rebels imagine that they had foreign soldiers to contend with ; and Wu, the Tautai of Shanghai, paid us the compliment of buying up some thousands of European boots, in order that the very footprints of the disciplined Chinese might leave a like impression. It was not till these troops became " victorious " that their appearance was any source of pleasure to them ; but after a time they became proud of the " imitation foreign devil" uniform, and would have objected to change it for a native dress.

The staff consisted of—

	Per Mensem.
The Commander, ...	at £160
Adjutant-General, ...	„ 70
Quartermaster-General, ...	„ 70
Principal Medical Officer, . . .	„ 80
Paymaster, ...	„ 60
2 Adjutants, each	„ 60
Provost-Marshal, ...	„ 70
Commandant and Second in Command, . .	„ 80
Aide-de-Camp, ...	„ 40
Brigade-Major, ...	„ 60
Medical Officers, each	„ 60
Commissariat Officers and Assistants, each .	„ 60
Military Storekeepers and Assistants, each .	„ 60

Though these officers bore high-sounding titles, it was not office work, but practical work, which they had to do, each of them having not only to give his order, but also to see that it was obeyed. To have invented new titles for their various positions would have been very troublesome ; and so it is to be hoped that officers of H.M. army will not be displeased at the appropriation which has been made.

The infantry were for the most part armed with smooth-bored English muskets; but one regiment had Prussian rifles of the old pattern, firing conical balls, and 300 Enfields were distributed in the ranks. Their pouches carried more than fifty rounds of ammunition. The artillery armament consisted of two 8-inch howitzers, four 32-pounder guns, three 24-pounder howitzers, twelve 12-pounder howitzers, ten American 12-pounder mountain howitzers, eight $4\frac{1}{2}$-inch mountain howitzers, fourteen mortars, brass, $4\frac{1}{2}$ inches to 8 inches, and six rocket-tubes. This was a heavy force of artillery in the circumstances; it was well supplied with ammunition, each piece having from 250 to 500 rounds; and the greater portion of it was mounted on travelling-carriages. Boats, however, were the usual means of conveyance for the artillery, there being sixteen of these for the artillery armament and ammunition. This part of the force was well provided with all the usual requisites, and had also large mantlets of elm, of sufficient thickness to afford the gunners protection from the fire of muskets and gingalls. So useful did these prove, that in an engagement at Tait-san one of these mantlets was found to have caught eighteen bullets. The country being intersected with creeks, each field-battery carried planks, to make a short tramway; and the infantry had planks strapped on their bamboo ladders, so that the troops were able to pass over the country easily enough. The artillery also carried a pontoon equipment, which consisted of about 150 feet of Blanchard's infantry pontoon-bridge.

The drill of the force was according to that in use in H.M. army, and the words of command were given in English. Only the .most simple manœuvres were attempted, and more stress was laid on speed than on accurate dressing. The men were trained to come into

line quickly, irrespective of inverted order.   The Chinese
drilled well, and were very steady, their great fault being
that of talking in the ranks.   Each regiment had two
buglers, some of whom knew the calls well.   The practice of the artillery, both in breaching fortifications and
in covering storming-parties, was considered by many
persons unconnected with this army to be uncommonly
good ; and the officers and men of the artillery were
far superior to any other arm of the force.   The infantry were taught to form square ; but on the only
occasion when they were attacked by cavalry — at
Waisoo in March 1864—the two regiments engaged
broke, and lost 320 of their number in killed and
prisoners.

The punishment of flogging was inflicted by the bamboo, as is usual in the Imperial army; and the commanding officers of regiments had the power of inflicting it.
The European method of flogging was objected to both
by the men and the Mandarins, so it was thought better
to employ the Chinese mode, which consisted in giving
a certain number of blows on the back of the thighs with
a rattan, or with a small piece of bamboo, somewhat like
a ruler.   Dismissal from the force was sometimes resorted to, but only by the Commander himself.   There
was, however, very little crime, and consequently very
little punishment.   Sometimes a regiment would be a
whole month without any one in it deserving punishment, and the relationship between the men and the
officers was on the whole affectionate.   The Chinese
were as a rule very orderly; and as drunkenness was
unknown amongst them, the services of the provost-
marshal rarely came into use except after a capture, when
the desire for loot was a temptation to absence from the
ranks.   On the officers it was impossible to inflict minor

punishments, because their service was voluntary, and no engagement was ever entered into with them by the Imperial Government beyond a promise of the current month's pay. Hence the only penalty which could be held over them *in terrorem* was dismissal from the force; and it says much for them, as well as for the commanding officers, that this means proved so effectual in preserving order. It was to their commanding officer they had to look for everything, as the Chinese authorities refused to give them any direct hearing; and he allotted, on the recommendation of the principal medical officer, the various sums which were given to those who were wounded. If time had allowed, it would have been better to have entered into some arrangement with the Chinese Government which would have permitted the force to have been governed by some sort of articles of war; but the Chinese were averse to binding themselves in the matter; time and circumstances pressed, and some of the bravest officers, who were not always the best behaved, would have been soon excluded by the regulations of a more regular army. Hence it was thought best to take the material as it was found, to lose no time in turning it to use, to treat it fairly, and then dissolve it if expedient, so that it could hurt no one. This plan was followed with success at considerable risk and expense—the finale being, that the Chinese crushed the Rebellion. The officers and men of the force were all handsomely dealt with at its dissolution, which was judged necessary in order to prevent likely future trouble.

After the artillery, the most important part of the force was the flotilla which belonged to it, and which was composed of steamers and Chinese gunboats. Each of the former was quite equal to 3000 men in a country such as that where the force had to act. The number

of the steamers at one time in employ varied from one
to four, and the Hyson may be taken as a specimen of
them all. This vessel was a small iron paddle-steamer,
of about ninety feet long and twenty-four feet wide,
drawing three to four feet of water, and carrying one
32-pounder on a moving platform at her bows, while at
her stern there was a 12-pounder howitzer. A loopholed
protection of elm planking ran round the bulwarks to
the height of six feet, and the steam-chests were protected by a timber traverse. She averaged eight knots per
hour, and had a crew of one captain at £80 *per mensem*, a
mate at £40, an engineer at £50, and an artillery officer
at £30. The Chinese on board were four stokers, ten
gunners, and twenty sailors. The steamers were usually
managed by Americans, who handle river-boats of this
class better than Englishmen do; and among these
Captain Davidson, of the Hyson, specially distinguished
himself by his coolness, skill, and daring. He had served
under Ward and Burgevine before Gordon gave him a
steamer to command, but died at Shanghai as he was
about to return to his native land. Strange to say,
though the Rebels were put in possession of two steamers,
the Kajow and the Firefly, they failed to make any use
of them, to speak of. Besides the steamers, the Kiangsoo force had two large siege gunboats, four large
ammunition-boats, and eight large covered boats, each
with a gun mounted at the bows. There were also
attached to it a large flotilla of Chinese gunboats, sometimes to the number of fifty. These vessels were usually
about forty feet long, ten feet broad, and did not draw
more than two feet of water, being flat-bottomed vessels.
Each had a crew of ten men, and they were propelled
by a sweep working over the stern. They carried a
6-pounder or 9-pounder Chinese gun in the bows; and

though not much used by the force, these guns were of
great service, when in numbers, to the co-operating
Imperialists, by firing with grape. The great use of
this part of the flotilla was the means of transport which
it afforded. The country being cut up by creeks, these
boats enabled an attack to be made with great suddenness
from unexpected points. By lowering their masts and
taking down their flags they could creep unperceived
along the creeks till quite close to the position of the
Rebels. Moreover, these latter usually shut themselves
up within their camps during the night, and even during
the day knew little of what was going on beyond it,
having no out-posts or out-sentries, and receiving no
reliable information from the villagers they had ill-
treated ; otherwise the boats would have been in great
danger of falling into ambuscades.

The Imperialist forces which acted in conjunction with
the Anglo-Chinese, were generally composed of men from
other provinces, and principally from Honan. They
were fine able-bodied men, and were usually kept in a
state of very strict discipline. As is usual with the
Chinese, they were divided into camps of five hundred
men, each under a blue-button military Mandarin ; and
each of these regiments was complete in itself. No
sooner was a regiment encamped than it began to
intrench itself in a square earthwork ; and sometimes
these forts were rather formidable, though cast up in a
very short time. In a few hours, on favourable ground,
they could throw up an earthwork that would offer
a most effective obstacle to a night-attack ; and they
never encamped for the night without such a temporary
security round them. When making any longer stay
in a position, the work was surrounded with ditches and
palisades within the space of three days, and stone flags

were laid down where it was possible to get material.
At night the drawbridge was raised, and six sentinels
were placed at each angle, who kept beating bamboos or
raising a peculiar cry through the whole night, and by
these a very strict watch was kept, the penalty for sleep
being death ; whereas, in the Ever-Victorious Army, the
sentries were often caught napping, as they had only to
fear being bambooed. It has often been said that the
Chinese are not a fighting people, and have no genius
for military matters ; but the celerity with which they
raised these earthworks, the skill with which they shaped
them, the judgment they displayed in choosing positions,
the facility with which they raised large bodies of men,
and their systematic mode of working these to the best
advantage, all went to prove very considerable genius
for the art of war within the limits to which it has been
developed amongst them. The long seclusion of the
Chinese, and the primitive character of their opponents
up to within the last few years, have prevented them
from developing this art in any high degree ; but so far
as they have gone with it, they have not shown themselves inferior in courage or in military skill to any
nation of the world. Among ourselves it is only the
rivalry of the different European nations which has
developed the art of war to so monstrous a height. Had
Europe, like China, been under one rule for the last ten
centuries, our weapons would not have been better than
those of the Celestials.

The soldiers employed by the Imperialists were badly
armed, judged by European usage, but usually they were
pretty well clothed, and had inscribed upon their uniform
the names of their person, regiment, and province. The
Cantonese were considered to be the best fighters, and
after them came the men of Honan. The greater num-

ber of the military officers who commanded the Imperialist troops had risen from the ranks, and were not much
better educated than the rank and file. Ordinarily there
was one Mandarin of high rank to every twenty camps
or regiments of five hundred men each ; he had complete
control over them, and was sometimes a military Mandarin, sometimes a civil one bearing military rank. He
generally had attached to him a fleet of thirty or forty
gunboats. About twenty or so of these bodies of ten
thousand men are often placed under a still higher
official, such as the Chetai of Kiangnan, who may thus
command a force of two hundred thousand men drawn
from several provinces.

As sappers, the Chinese are equal to any Europeans.
They work well ; are quite cool, from their apathetic
nature ; and, however great their losses, do not become
restless under fire like Europeans. At Chanchu fu, the
Mandarin in command was requested by Colonel Gordon
to construct trenches of approach at night, up to the
edge of the ditch around the city ; and, fully understanding what was wanted, he immediately set one thousand men to work, who, despite their number, made the
trenches very well and quietly. At Nanking the Imperialists proved they were no contemptible engineers
by carrying on mining operations for two hundred yards.
In these engineering operations the Ever - Victorious
Army took almost no part. Its soldiers could not easily
have been made to raise earthworks, and the Foreign
officers, with their limited education, were not usually
competent to superintend such operations, consequently
this force had to remain unintrenched ; and it was a
good deal due to the inertness of the Rebels that serious
night-attacks were not made upon it in frequent circumstances when such attacks might have been very success-

ful. The success it obtained was owing to its compact-
ness, its completeness, the quickness of its movements,
its possession of steamers and good artillery, the bravery
of its officers, the confidence of its men, the inability of
the enemy to move large bodies of troops with rapidity,
the nature of the country, the almost intuitive percep-
tion with which its commanding officer understood the
nature of the country so as to adapt his operations to it,
and the untiring energy which he put forth. Colonel
Gordon seems to have acted continually on the French
principle, to which Prince Frederick Charles of Prussia
so ably called attention a few years ago *—of always
taking the initiative and acting on the offensive. In
war the party thus acting has many points in its favour;
for a force on the defensive is perplexed by looking out
for and preparing to meet a great number of schemes,
any of which its adversary may undertake against it;
while he who makes the attack has one well-defined
object in view, and his troops are in much higher spirits
than those which have to stand still and wait. If, in
the Kiangnan campaign, the Tai-pings, with their large
numbers, had pushed out in their full strength and fallen
on the Ever Victorious Army, that small force could
hardly have stood against them; but this was rendered
very difficult by the nature of the country; and when
the Rebels did attempt it at Quinsan, they were out-
manœuvred, and so nearly annihilated that they never
forgot the lesson. Moreover, the jealousy of the different chiefs was an obstacle in the way of formidable combined action, and led to their being overcome in detail.
Each Wang, however gallant, was nothing more than the
head of a lot of banditti, ignorant of almost everything

* 'L'Art de Combattre l'Armée Française.' Par le Prince Frédéric
Charles de Prusse. Paris, 1860.

pertaining to organised warfare, and thinking only of skirmishing and pillage. As such they fought well, and were capable of acts of very great bravery, but were easily panic-stricken when attacked in rear or in flank, or even when boldly assailed in front. To compare small things with great, the fighting in Kiangnan was something like that which has occurred in Bohemia between the Prussians and Austrians. There was on one side the same superiority in arms and in tactics, while on the other there was the same want of cordial co-operation among the chief officers. But the great point of resemblance is, that in both cases there was, on the one side, a bold, energetic, assailing tactic, which took no thought of defeat, and which, if it had been met by an able general, might have resulted in most complete and disastrous defeat ; while, on the other, there was a puzzled expectant attitude which dispirited the troops and paralysed the talent of the commanders.

During Ward's time the Ever-Victorious Army cost, from September 1861 to September 1862, about £360,000. In the three months Burgevine was in command, about £180,000 were expended upon it; and after that it cost about £580,000. Altogether, at the lowest computation, £1,300,000 may be debited to it. If to this be added the half-million sterling expended on the Lay-Osborn flotilla, we have a total of about £1,800,000 paid in specie to Foreigners in their employ within about two years by the Chinese Government, and that exclusive of the large expenditure on the ordinary service of the Imperial maritime customs. Let us also consider here the great and various expenses of the Imperialists besieging Nanking and in the province of Kiangsoo, which may be put down as at least half a million sterling monthly, and some idea may be formed of the military expenditure of the Chinese, at a time when they were paying two-fifths of their customs revenue to Great Britain and France. If at this period Foreign governments did give China some assistance, it cannot be denied that the Celestials paid pretty handsomely for it.

Colonel Gordon's opinions as to his position when he took command of the disciplined Chinese were as follows, as expressed in a memorandum he made on the 5th May 1863. In entering on joint command with a Mandarin, Lí Adong, it was arranged that the latter should in no way interfere with the discipline of the force or with the appointment of its officers. Lí (who must be distinguished from Lí the Futai or Governor) appeared to Gordon a man well fitted for his position, and likely to be extremely useful, because his influence with the other Mandarins was so great as to prevent the action of all petty intrigues against the force, and because his knowledge of the country, and skill in obtaining information by means of spies, were of essential service. Colonel Gordon thought that the British Government was desirous that China should have armies able to cope with its internal disorder, and that the best means of assisting it to that end would be to make the disciplined Chinese force the nucleus of a new Chinese native army. The Sungkiang, or any other force entirely irresponsible to the governor of the province, would have been in a most invidious position ; daily reports about its bad conduct, sent in by the local Mandarins, would have disgusted both the Peking Government and the Foreign Ministers, while its supplies and payment would have been uncertain. At the same time, Colonel Gordon considered that the precarious way in which this army existed from month to month was detrimental to its use-

fulness and an encouragement to plunder. Its service
was by far the most dangerous to its officers of any that
he had ever seen, and their apparently high pay was not
a dollar too much. If the policy of the British Government was merely, while putting down the Rebellion, to
keep China weak, and leave the Imperialists as they
were, then he considered that his position would be only
that of a mercenary ; but believing, in the absence of
special instructions, and being by his commanding-
officer appointed * with sanction of the British Minister
at Peking, that the object of his Government was to
strengthen China and create a national army, he held
his command with pleasure.

* This appointment was soon after approved of by her Majesty's Secretary of State for War, then Lord de Grey.

CHAPTER IX.

GORDON'S FIRST VICTORIES.

BURGEVINE, of course, was very much dissatisfied with
his supercession, and the appointment of a British officer;
and on the 20th of February started for Peking, in order
to lay his case before the Foreign Ministers and the Imperial Government. Being a man of gentlemanly and
plausible address, he was well received at the capital,
and, to some appearance, soon obtained his object. Sir
Frederick Bruce evidently was charmed with him, for
in a letter to Prince Kung, dated April 2, 1863, the
British Minister says, "I have formed a high opinion of
General Burgevine's qualifications for the post he occupies. He is brave, honest, conciliatory in his manner,
and is sincerely desirous of serving the Chinese Govern-

ment, as he looks upon this country as his home." Mr
Burlinghame, the American Minister, writes of him in
similar high terms, but very loosely as to facts, for he
speaks of him as having fought in nearly one hundred
"battles" in the Chinese service, though Burgevine had
really not been in more than five engagements. Prince
Kung, in treating this subject, very clearly said that the
restoration of Burgevine was a matter which lay in the
hands of Lí, the governor of Kiangsoo; and there does
not seem to have been any disposition on the part of the
native authorities either at Peking or at Shanghai to
restore him to command, though it has been stated that
he returned to the latter city in company of an Imperial
commissioner directed to replace him in his former
position. It is quite evident from the American Diplomatic Correspondence that neither the Prince of Kung
nor Governor Lí had the slightest thought of reinstating
him; and whether his case were a hard one or not, the
Chinese authorities knew very well what manner of man
he was, and what chance there existed of their being
able to work along with him. As to the action of the
British Minister in this matter, the truth is, he at first
considered Burgevine had been unfairly dealt with; and,
taking this view, thought further, that if a man with
such apparent claims upon the Chinese Government
could be dealt with unjustly, the same course might be
adopted in regard to any Englishmen who entered the
service of the Chinese. Moreover, as the officer to be
appointed in Burgevine's place was an Englishman, Sir
Frederick Bruce believed it would be extremely un-
gracious for the British Minister to refuse his support
to the claims of this American.

On the 24th March 1863, Colonel (then Major) Gordon
was put in orders to command the force of disciplined

Chinese in Kiangsoo, and next day went up to Sungkiang
to take over the command from Captain Holland, accompanied by Captain Stack, of her Majesty's 67th Foot, as
his Commandant ; Ensign Stevens, of her Majesty's 99th
Regiment, as Adjutant-General ; Lieutenant Ward, R.A.,
as Commandant of Field-artillery ; D. A. C. G. Cooksley
as Quartermaster-General; and Assistant-Surgeon Moffitt
of the 67th as Principal Medical Officer. It was announced that both the officers and men had determined to
obey no one but Burgevine ; but Colonel Gordon, having
assembled the officers and non-commissioned officers, told
them plainly that they need not fear sweeping changes or
anything that would injure their future prospects ; and
no outbreak took place.

The first operation requested of the new commander
was an attack upon the town of Fushan, situated a considerable way from Sungkiang, above the Tsung Ming
island, at the estuary of the Yangtsze. This place, long
a haunt of pirates, was held by the Rebels ; it threatened
Chanzu, about ten miles inland, in which an Imperialist
force was besieged ; and an unsuccessful attack had
been made upon it shortly before, by Major Tapp, commander of the disciplined artillery, with 600 men and a
few howitzers. Colonel Gordon proceeded against Fushan
in two steamers, with the 5th Regiment, a 32-pounder,
and four 12-pounders, being supported also by Major
Tapp's force, and by some ordinary Imperialist troops
that were stockaded on the beach and on some neighbouring hills. The Rebel stockades were not strong,
but there were heavy masses of Tai-pings in the rear
and on each flank. The 32-pounder, however, which
was placed in position during the night at some risk
of being taken, was too much for their guns, and soon
brought down the wall of the stockade in masses. On

the advance being sounded, the defenders left, and the place was taken with the loss of only two killed and six wounded on the Imperialist side. A slight effort was made by the Rebels to return, but they only succeeded in inflicting what eventually proved a mortal wound on Captain Belcher, of the 5th Regiment. On the road to Chanzu, Colonel Gordon passed, near a large joss-house, no less than thirty-five crucified Imperialist soldiers, who had been burned in various places before death.

The garrison of Chanzu itself had a curious story to tell. They had all been Rebels, but had suddenly trans-ferred the town and their services to the other side. Their chief, Lo Kwo-chung, had persuaded them to shave their heads and declare for the Imperialist cause early in the year, and this they did in conjunction with the garrison of Fushan; but no sooner had they done so, than, to their dismay, the Faithful King came down upon them with a large force, took Fushan, and laid siege to them, trying to overcome them by various kinds of assault and surprise. He brought against them 32-pounders which had been taken at Taitsan, and partially breached the wall. He offered any terms to the soldiers if they would come over; and, in order to show his great success, sent in the heads of three European officers who had been killed at Taitsan. Lo, in these trying circumstances, had been obliged to do a good deal of beheading in order to keep his garrison stanch; but he, and probably most of his followers, felt they had committed too unpardonable a sin ever to trust them-selves again into Tai-ping hands. For this affair Colonel Gordon was made, by decree of the Emperor, a Tsung-Ping, a title which is a grade higher than any Ward ever held, and which may best be translated by our phrase Brigadier-General. This alone, not to speak of

K

the much higher position afterwards conferred upon him, is enough to confute Mr Lay's statement* that this officer never held an Imperial commission. The following are the terms in which the conferring of this grade was announced :—

Despatch from Lí, Governor of the Province of Kiangsoo, to Major Gordon.

May 16th, 1863.

The Governor has already communicated a copy of the Memorial to the Throne, despatched on the 12th April from his camp at Shanghai, in which he solicited the issue of a decree conferring temporary rank as a Chinese *Tsung-Ping* (Brigadier-General) upon the English officer Gordon, on his taking command of the Ever-Victorious Force. He is now in receipt of an express from the Board of War, returning his Memorial with the note that a separate Decree has been issued to the Prince of Kung and the Council of State; and on the same day he received, through the Prince and Council, copy of the Decree issued to them on the 9th May in the following terms :—

" Gordon, on succeeding to the command of the Ever-Victorious Force, having displayed both valour and intelligence, and having now, with repeated energy, captured Fushan, WE ordain that he at once receive rank and office as a Chinese *Tsung-Ping*, and WE at the same time command Lí to communicate to him the expression of OUR approval. Let Gordon be further enjoined to use stringent efforts for maintaining discipline in the Ever-Victorious Force, which has fallen into a state of disorganisation, and thus to guard against the recurrence of former evils. Respect this!"

The Governor has accordingly to forward a copy of the foregoing Decree, to which the officer in question will yield respectful obedience.

Translated by

(Signed)   WM. S. T. MAYERS,
Interpreter H. M.'s Consulate.

General Staveley having now resigned his command

* In 'Our Policy in China,' a pamphlet published in 1864.

from ill-health, Major-General Brown was in command
of the British troops in China, and Burgevine reappeared
on the stage, accompanied by an Imperial commissioner
from Peking. As has been pointed out, there is no
reason for supposing that the Prince of Kung had any
wish to reinstate the American in his former position ;
and Sir Frederick Bruce writes only of the commissioner
as having been sent down "to settle the affair with the
Governor"—namely, Lí ;* and he had previously expressed his opinion on the subject, and given his authority in the following passage in an official letter to
Brigadier-General Staveley :† "As respects Ward's
corps, I regret that circumstances should have led to
a misunderstanding between Mr Burgevine and the
Governor, as the accounts I had received of the former
led me to think that he was well fitted for the post.
But as this breach has taken place, it appears to me that
the great amount of foreign property at Shanghai renders it desirable that this force should be commanded
and officered by men who are not adventurers, and who
afford a guarantee, by the position they occupy in the
military service of their own country, that they are both
competent and to be relied upon ; otherwise we should
be constituting a force which would be as dangerous to
us as the insurgents themselves."

Governor Lí, in a long letter on this subject,‡ remarks
that he does not wish at all to remove Colonel Gordon,
who had worked night and day harmoniously with the
other generals ; who had already won conspicuous success ; who had reorganised the force, and proved himself
valiant, able, and honest. "As the people and place,"
he continues, "are charmed with him, as he has already
given me returns of the organisation of the force, the

* Blue-Book, China, No. 3 (1864), p. 80.   † Ib., p. 68.   ‡ Ib., p. 82.

formation of each regiment, and the expenses, ordinary
and extraordinary, in the clearest manner, wishing to
drill our troops and save our money, it is evident that
he fully comprehends the state of affairs ; and, in the
expedition he is preparing, his men delightedly obey
him, and preserve the proper order.   I cannot, therefore,
remove him without cause."   Something very much the
opposite of this is said of poor Burgevine, whom, it is
evident, Lí, and not without some reason, would not
have at any price.

In order to understand the operations which followed,
it should be noted that the field of action was the
large peninsula formed by the river Yangtsze and the
Bay of Hangchow, an immense alluvial flat in Kiangnan,* having a superficial area of nearly 50,000 square
miles.   This district has been raised from the bed of the
sea by the vast deposits of the great muddy river
Yangtsze, and, though thickly peopled, it is for the most
part only a few feet above the level of the ocean, and in
some places is even lower than that level.   Here and
there isolated hills rise to the height of a few hundred
feet, but for the most part there is a dead level, rich
with trees, growing various kinds of cereals in great
abundance, thickly studded with villages and towns,
and intersected in every direction by rivers, creeks, and
canals.   On looking across any portion of this great
plain, boats, with their mat sails, appear to be moving
in every direction over the land, and in some places the
waters spread out into lakes of considerable size, such as
the Taiho.   Except on a few lines, there are no con-
veniences for transit by land but narrow footpaths,

* Kiangnan signifies " South of the river," and comprises great part of
Chekiang, together with that portion of Kiangsoo which lies south of the
Yangtsze.

where people can only go in Indian file ; but the net-
work of waters affords great facility for the movement
of boats and of small steamers.   In order to realise this
district as it was from 1861 to 1864, we must conceive
the Tai-pings coming down upon its peaceful villages
and rich towns, moving flags, beating gongs, destroying
images and temples, seizing valuables, occupying houses,
dealing with all disobedience according to the exterminating decree of Heaven, and being a terror unto
young women ; but still not at first destroying the crops
or many of the houses, or slaying many of the males.
Then we have the Allies driving them back, firing into
their masses of men with long-range rifles, and pounding
at their stockades with heavy guns and shells.   On the
retirement of these we have the Rebels again advancing
to the neighbourhood of Shanghai, but this time in an
infuriated demoniac state, burning and destroying everything in order that there may be a waste round the
starving city, and murdering or driving before them all
the villagers.   Lastly, the Ever-Victorious Army appears
on the scene, not by any means always victorious, but
very frequently so, and bringing European drill and
officers, with heavy artillery, to bear on a settlement of
the question.   Let this be embellished (as the scene appeared to me in 1860) with views of rich fertile plains,
where the crops are trampled down or consumed, a few
narrow bridges of the willow-plate pattern, a dilapidated
pagoda or two, broken blackened walls of village houses,
the deserted streets of towns, innumerable swollen, blackened corpses lying on the slimy banks of the muddy
streams, or rotting underneath the graceful bamboos,
red flames at night flashing up against the deep dark
sky ;—let us imagine, also, the Tai-pings throwing themselves into all sorts of postures impossible to the Euro-

pean, and uttering cries scarcely less painful or hideous than those from the ravished villages ; and we may form some conception of the great Chinese tragedy which was enacted in Kiangnan.

The next movement of the Sungkiang force was against the large town of Quinsan; and in the approach to that place good service was done by the steamer Hyson, a species of amphibious boat, which possessed the power of moving upon land as well as upon water, for she could drive over the bed of a creek upon her wheels when there was not sufficient depth of water to keep her afloat. But at this time, the end of April, the force was diverted to Taitsan by certain events which it is of importance to notice, because they had no small share in afterwards causing what has been ridiculously called " the massacre of Soochow." It is to these events that we must chiefly look for an explanation and vindication of the execution by Governor Lí of the Tai-ping kings who surrendered to him at Soochow—an alleged breach of faith, which led Colonel Gordon temporarily to resign his command, and which, misrepresented and misunderstood, gave rise to a considerable outcry both in China and in this country.

After Chanzu had yielded to the Imperialists, and Fu-shan was taken, the Tai-pings at Taitsan made pro-posals of surrender to Governor Lí, who sent up his brother with about 2000 troops to arrange the matter. Tsah, the Tai-ping chief, led the Imperialists to suppose that he was prepared to give up the place, and even accepted a large number of mandarin hats to be put on by his officers when the besiegers entered. Presents were interchanged, frequent meetings were held between the two leaders, everything seemed going on smoothly, and the 26th April was fixed for giving up the city;

but when, according to agreement, a portion of the Imperialists had entered the South Gate, a gun was fired,
the gate was closed, and 1500 of them were treacherously
attacked and seized, along with all their camp equip-
ments. Of these not less than 300 were decapitated,
their heads being sent to Soochow and Quinsan as a
general encouragement to the followers of the Great
Peace, and the remainder were of course compelled to
join the Tai-pings.

In consequence of this act of stupid treachery, Gordon
and his force, to the number of 2800, were diverted
against Taitsan. He halted about 1500 yards from
the West Gate, where the Rebels had two strong stone
forts, and captured two stockades, enclosing small stone
forts. On the 2d May the 1st Regiment was moved
at an early hour towards the North Gate, in order to
prevent a retreat from that point, and to cover the
left flank of the main body of the attacking force, which
was established in the western suburb. The troops were
so placed as to be under cover, and the guns, protected
by portable wooden mantlets, were gradually pushed
forward until they were within a hundred yards of the
walls of the city, which, by 2 P.M., were rather dilapidated, as every gun and mortar available was in action.
Two hours after this, a wide breach having been made
in the walls, the boats were ordered up, and a storming
party advanced to the assault. The resistance made,
however, was now very serious—the place being garrisoned by 10,000 men, 2000 of whom were picked braves,
and its guns being served by several English, French,
and American adventurers in Tai-ping employ. The
Rebels swarmed to the breach, manned the walls, and
poured down a tremendous fire on the attacking column
as well as on the bridge beyond. Major Bannon, how-

ever, who led the storming party, succeeded in mounting
the breach, and a hand-to-hand conflict took place, in
which the assailants were for the moment worsted and
compelled to retire, the Tai-pings being bravely headed
by the Foreigners in their service. Again the guns
played upon the breach for about twenty minutes, and
then the assault was renewed. At last the 5th Regiment, under Major Brennan, advanced, and Captain
Tchirikoff's company managed to plant the colours of
that regiment on the top of the wall. On this the
storming party crowded in while the Tai-pings fled in
every direction, trampling each other to death in their
eagerness to escape. Either during or immediately after
the attack there were killed two Americans, two Frenchmen, who begged hard for mercy, and three sepoys,
formerly of the 5th Bombay Native Infantry, all of
whom were fighting with the Tai-pings. This may be
called Imperialist cruelty, but every military man knows
that whenever a place is taken by assault under the flag
of any nation, many of the defenders are put to death
though they throw down their arms and cry for quarter.
The loss on the part of the Ever-Victorious Army was
also heavy, Major Bannon of the 4th Regiment, with
twenty rank and file, being killed, while there were
wounded Lieut. Wood, R.A., Commandant of the Field
Artillery, Major Murant, Captains Chapman, Chidwick,
Ludlam, Robinson, and Williams, with 142 privates,
out of a force of 2800 men. It is doubtful whether this
assault would have been successful had it not been for
some 8-inch howitzers which were played over the heads
of the stormers, and mowed down the Tai-pings on the
breach, from a distance of only 200 yards. The steamer
Hyson also did some service by moving in the neighbourhood, throwing heavy shells into the city; and

General Brown afforded " moral support " by moving up
a small British force of about 500 * to the village of
Waikong, about six miles off.   From the statements of
Private Hargreaves, an English deserter from H.M. 31st
Regiment, who was taken prisoner in Taitsan, it appeared that, though the Europeans in the place had
fought well, they had done so unwillingly, and had told
Tsah, the Tai-ping chief, that it was useless for him to
resist. The officers of the disciplined force who specially
distinguished themselves in this engagement were Major
Brennan, with Captains Howard and Tchirikoff of the
5th Regiment, and Captains Williams and Brooks of
the 2d.

There were some circumstances connected with this
capture of Taitsan which gave rise to a curious discussion, that did not confine itself to China, but was
taken up also in this country, and was even allowed to
occupy the attention of her Majesty's Foreign Secretary.
It was a common thing among certain persons in China
at this period to invent stories of Imperialist cruelty.
For instance, most hideous accounts were published in
the ' Times of India ' of almost unmentionable atrocities,
said to have been committed on Tai-ping women and
children by the Imperialist authorities at Shanghai, and
yet, on examination, the whole dismal story turned out
to have been a pure invention. One might have thought
that such a case, and similar ones only too abundant at
this time, would have been a warning to respectable persons not to give a ready, and much less an eager, heed to
anonymous stories of the kind ; but such does not seem
to have been the immediate result. After the capture of

* This force consisted of 60 Royal Artillery, 80 Lascars, 2 howitzers,
two 5¼-inch mortars, 80 of the 31st Regiment, 150 Belooches, and 150 5th
Bombay Native Infantry.

Taitsan, an anonymous writer in the Shanghai 'Daily Shipping and Commercial News' came forward under the specious *nom de plume* of "Justice and Mercy," and insisted that, after the capture, seven Rebel prisoners had their eyes pierced out by Imperialist soldiers, and were then roasted alive, their clothes being previously saturated with oil, and that more than one Englishman witnessed the deed, powerless to save. Behind the screen of the 'North China Herald,' of 13th June 1863, another anonymous person, under the signature of "An Eyewitness," asserted that "Justice and Mercy" had exaggerated the affair; but that he himself could say, from personal observation, that the prisoners referred to were "tortured with the most refined cruelty," that "arrows appeared to have been forcibly driven into various parts of their bodies, heads, region of heart, abdomen, &c., from whence issued copious streams of blood; that strips of flesh had been cut, or rather hacked, from various parts of their bodies;" and that "for hours these wretched beings writhed in agony" before they were led out to an inhuman death. Having had a private interview with this witness, Dr Smith, the Bishop of Victoria, thought fit to write to Earl Russell on the subject, and to express his opinion that there was no reasonable doubt as to the truth of the witness's allegations.

In an official letter to the Secretary of War,* General Brown, as commander of her Majesty's forces in China, very naturally expressed his surprise that the Bishop had not communicated with him upon this subject, and had not inquired whether he, the General, could supply any reliable information regarding it. From reports made by Lieutenant Cane, R.A., and other English officers who were witnesses of the affair, and who did not speak of it

* Blue-Book, China, No. 3 (1864), p. 117.

from behind a screen, General Brown had, almost at the
time, been put in possession of the facts of the case, and
had taken all the action which it demanded. Colonel
Gordon and his force had nothing to do with the seven
prisoners who were taken by Imperialist soldiers after
they had escaped from Taitsan, and were condemned
near Waikong, where a British force was, to the punishment of the " Ling-che," or slow and ignominious death.
As the Tai-pings of Taitsan had been guilty of an act of
bloody treachery, they had no claim to be treated as ordinary prisoners of war ; and it was, moreover, alleged by
the Mandarins that these particular prisoners were special
offenders. As it was, according to the testimony of several
British officers, the sentence upon them was carried out
only in a very modified form. They were tied up and
exposed to view for about five hours, each with a piece of
skin cut from one arm and hanging down, and with an
arrow or two pushed through the skin in various places.
They did not seem to suffer pain, and were afterwards
beheaded in the ordinary way. Even this, of course, was
objectionable ; and General Brown, careful of the honour
of a British officer, at once told the Futai, Lí, that if any
similar cases were reported to him he should withdraw
his troops, and cease to act along with the Imperialists.
This was quite right ; but it should be noticed also, that
we are apt to attach an exaggerated importance to the
cruelty of Chinese punishments from our own superior
sensitiveness to pain. What might be exquisite torture
to the nervous vascular European is something much less
to the obtuse-nerved Turanian ; and it may be safely
affirmed that the Chinese penal code,* as actually carried
out, is, considering the nature of the people, not a whit

---

* The 'Edinburgh Review,' in an article on Sir George Staunton's translation of that code, said, " We scarcely know a European code that is at

more severe than that of any European country. Every
doctor who has had to perform operations on Chinamen,
knows how little they suffer in comparison with more
sensitive races. As to the conduct in such matters of
the Ever-Victorious Army, Colonel Gordon wrote to the
Shanghai 'Shipping News:'—

June 15th, 1863.

I am of belief that the Chinese of this force are quite as
merciful in action as the soldiers of any Christian nation could
be; and in proof of this can point to over 700 prisoners, taken
in the last engagement, who are now in our employ; some even
have entered our ranks and done service against the Rebels since
their capture. But one life has been taken out of this number,
and that one was a Rebel who tried to induce his comrades to
fall on the guard, and who was shot on the spot. It is a great
mistake to imagine that the men of this force are worthless; they
will, in the heat of action, put their enemies to death, as the
troops of any nation would do, but when the fight is over they
will associate as freely together as if they had never fought.
. . . If " Observer" and " Eyewitness," with their friend "Justice and Mercy," would come forward and communicate what
they know, it would be far more satisfactory than writing statements of the nature of those alluded to by the Bishop of Victoria. And if any one is under the impression that the inhabitants of the Rebel districts like their Rebel masters, he has only
to come up here to be disabused of his idea. I do not exaggerate when I say, that upwards of 1500 Rebels were killed in
their retreat from Quinsan by the villagers, who rose *en masse*.

The plunder it obtained at Taitsan had somewhat
demoralised the Ever-Victorious Army, which of course
could hardly be kept in a state of strict discipline; and
so its commander moved it back to Sungkiang, in order
that it might be reorganised. Previous to this the force
had been accustomed to dissolve after the capture of
any place, in order that the men might dispose of their

once so copious and so consistent, or is nearly so freed from intricacy,
bigotry, and fiction."

loot ; and though the practice was eminently unsoldierly, the abolition of it by Colonel Gordon was not at all appreciated by these soldiers of fortune, who had no desire to peril their lives without compensating gratifications, and whose pay was not high considering the risks they ran. General Ward had even allowed them coolies to clean their arms ; and the idea of carrying their own rations was thought quite derogatory to their dignity.   Many of the officers themselves did not show an example of discipline to the troops, and the commander was glad to have an opportunity of filling the places of some of those who had been killed, and of others who had resigned, by privates and non-commissioned officers of H.M. 99th and other regiments, who had volunteered for the service. Finding it necessary also to have some officer of rank over the commissariat and military stores, he selected Deputy-Assistant Commissary-General Cooksley, an excellent officer, for that duty, and gave him the rank of lieutenant-colonel in order that he might speak with authority to the majors commanding the different regiments, who were apt to be troublesome when rations were issued.

These efforts to improve the discipline of this rather anomalous force were not allowed to pass without violent opposition, threatening at one time to pass into open mutiny.   When Lieut.-Colonel Cooksley's appointment was made known, and just when the force was ordered to march against Quinsan, all the majors requested an interview with the commander, at which they complained of an officer of the English army being placed over them, and demanded for themselves the same rank and pay as the new lieutenant-colonel. This was at once refused, on which they retired, and soon after sent in their resignations, with the cool request that these should be accepted

at once, but that they should be allowed to serve on the
approaching expedition.   In answer to this Colonel Gordon at once accepted their resignations, and refused to
allow them to serve on the expedition ; but the position
in which he was placed was a very critical one.   The
force had been ordered to march at daybreak next morning, the 24th May, but at 8 A.M. only the commander's
body-guard had fallen in ; and the officers who had been
placed in command came to report that none of the
other men would do so.

After this matter had been settled by the officers submitting to be content with their position as majors,
Colonel Gordon left Sungkiang with 600 artillery and
2300 infantry in order to attack Quinsan, in conjunction with an Imperialist force under General Ching,
which he had left stockaded before that place, and which,
on his return, he found in some peril.   The operations
which now ensued were rather peculiar, and most destructive to the Tai-pings, who numbered about 12,000
men.   In a strategical point of view, Quinsan was a place
of immense importance, being the key to Soochow, and a
point the possession of which would completely protect
both Sungkiang and Taitsan.   No place could have better
suited the requirements of the Ever-Victorious Army
than Quinsan, or enabled them at this time to hold so
large a district of country safe from the inroads of the
Tai-pings ; but there were, to all appearance, serious difficulties in the way of gaining possession of it.   A very
large Rebel force was encamped within its walls, which
have a circumference of about five miles—and stone forts
in its neighbourhood were also held by the Rebels.   Its
ditch was more than forty yards wide ; the high hill enclosed within its walls enabled every movement in the
neighbourhood to be seen, and two or three guns placed

on the spurs of this hill would have formed a very citadel.
Altogether the position was one which afforded fine scope
for the skill of a scientific assailing commander.

Colonel Gordon, judging from his official report,* and
from other sources of information, seems to have detected
the weak point of this position. The only road between
Quinsan and Soochow is so situated between the Yansing
Lake and large creeks widening out here and there into
small lakes or sheets of water, that it seemed possible to
cut off entirely the communication between these two
cities ; and this road, though in the main good, crosses
very long bridges and follows narrow causeways, sometimes only three or four feet wide, for the space of twenty
or thirty yards, while on the inner side the creeks are
very deep. Accordingly, the steamer Hyson, with its
guns protected by iron mantlets, was employed to cut
this line of communication.   Ching, the Imperialist general acting in concert, was very anxious that the disciplined force should attack the east gate, that on the
side of Taitsan ; but this Colonel Gordon declined until
he had reconnoitred the country on the other side ; and
the result of his investigations was a determination to
attack two stockades and a very strong stone fort which
he found on the road, and on the banks of the canal
between Quinsan and Soochow, eight miles from the
former and twelve from the latter city, at the village of
Chunye.

At dawn of the 30th May, Colonel Gordon started on
this adventure in the Hyson, accompanied by the 4th
Regiment, 350 strong, with field-artillery in boats, and
by about fifty small Imperial gunboats, the whole flotilla
amounting to about eighty boats, with large white sails,
and decorated with various-coloured flags.   Some stakes,

* Blue-Book, China, No. 3 (1864), p. 111.

separating the creek which they came up from the canal
between Quinsan and Soochow, were pulled up by the
Imperialist boats, and a general advance with the steamer
and troops was made.   Immediately that the Tai-pings,
who were in great force, saw this, they vacated the
stockades, and, splitting right and left, fled along the
causeway, some to Quinsan and the remainder towards
Soochow, the 4th Regiment being despatched in pursuit
of the former, and the Hyson following up the latter.
It was understood, however, that some bad feeling between the commander at Chunye and the Tai-ping chief
at Quinsan was the chief cause of their defending the
stockades so badly.

The events which followed sufficiently proved that the
Tai-pings were taken by surprise, and completely confused by the novel mode of warfare which they had to
encounter.   The Hyson steamed slowly up the canal
towards Soochow, somewhat impeded by the numerous
boats, abandoned by their owners, which were drifting
about, and occupied, as it advanced, in firing on the clus-
ters of Rebels marching before it along the causeway.
At Taedin a fine stone fort appeared, but this also was
immediately abandoned on a shell from the steamer happening to go through one of the embrasures.   Though
this boat had on board only about half-a-dozen Europeans
and thirty Chinese gunners, six men were landed to prevent the fort being reoccupied by any of the parties of
Rebels that were coming up behind.   Continuing its
course, and always harassing the fleeing troops in front,
the Hyson passed at Siaouedin another stone fort which
had been evacuated ; and then, having headed a party of
about 400 Tai-pings, Captain Davidson had the almost
incredible audacity to take 150 of them prisoners on
board his small craft.   Soon after this, four Rebel horse-

men rode past the steamer, in the direction of Soochow, amid a shower of bullets; and when one of them was struck off his steed, the others waited for him and carried him off—a fine instance of Chinese courage and fidelity. The steamer got within a mile of Soochow, and did not turn till 6 P.M., being very uncertain as to what sort of reception it might meet with on the way back. The extraordinary good fortune which had attended this movement continued to befriend it. On the way down, a large force at Siaouedin opened a sharp fire of rifles upon the Hyson, but they were enfiladed from their position by a charge of grape, and some of them were made prisoners. Even the boat's steam-whistle seems to have done good service in frightening the Tai-pings, most of whom had heard nothing of the kind before; and it may be imagined how great must have been the effect on their untutored minds of this fiery dragon coming shrieking down in the darkness, with the glaring eyes of its green and blue lights, and its horrible discharges of grape and shells.

On returning to Chunye, tremendous firing and cheering were heard, the Imperial gunboats being found engaged with the stone fort, which in the darkness was literally sparkling with musketry. It was most fortunate that the steamer came up at this moment, for as it got to the scene of action a confused mass of men, but dimly discerned, were seen on the causeway. This was the garrison of Quinsan, amounting to about 8000 men, attempting to escape to Soochow. On the steamer blowing its whistle, this dark mass wavered, yelled, and turned back. Then followed one of those terrible scenes which are so useful in war, and may be on the whole so beneficial, but which are often so painful to witness and to read of. The number of

L

Tai-pings was so great, and their state of desperation such, that they could easily have swept Colonel Gordon's small force away ; and the Imperialists, being surrounded by the enemy, were so panic-stricken that they had commenced to abandon their gunboats when the Hyson arrived.   Hence it was necessary to fire into the Quinsan garrison, which the steamer accordingly did, driving back the dense yelling masses, step by step, with great slaughter, and pursuing them up to the walls of the city.   The shelling went on till half-past two in the morning, when as many of the garrison surrendered as could safely be made prisoners of ; and, at a later hour, an Imperialist and disciplined force, which had been left at the East Gate, entered Quinsan, and took possession of that place unopposed.

In this engagement the loss of the Tai-pings was very great indeed.   It was evident that between 3000 and 4000 men must have been killed, drowned, or taken prisoners ; but it is impossible to say how many more of the 12,000 or 15,000 in Quinsan, or on the fatal causeway, failed to reach Soochow, and perished miserably — drowned in creeks, choked in mud, and killed by the villagers, who, to show their appreciation of Tai-ping rule, rose *en masse* against the fugitives. About 800 prisoners were taken, most of whom entered the ranks of the Ever-Victorious Army ; and 8000 might have been secured, had there been troops to collect them.   In fact, almost the entire garrison of Quinsan must have been lost to the Rebels, while the casualties in Colonel Gordon's force, exclusive of the Imperialists with whom he acted, were only two killed, and five drowned.

This almost unparalleled disproportion between the two losses may readily suggest the idea of a mere

massacre, where superiority of arms on one side rendered the defence on the other a perfect farce; but
such was not the case. It was the selection of the
causeway as the weak point of the enemy, together with
the hazardous, desperate, and totally unlooked-for character of the attack, which made it so wonderful a success; and at almost any point up to the occupation
of Quinsan, the state of matters might easily have been
reversed. Had the Rebels stood to their stockades
and forts; had they returned to stone forts which the
Hyson had to leave unoccupied, or held by only a few
men; had they attacked the steamer on its return to
Taedin, where it had a narrow escape from being taken;
and had the Quinsan garrison not wavered in its fugitive attack when the steam-whistle began to sound,—
then there might have been a very different conclusion
to this bold adventure. This was one of those occasions
which occur pre-eminently in Asiatic warfare, when a
little hesitation on the part of the commander, and a
little suspension of confidence on the part of the troops,
might easily have led to a disaster on the side of the
assailants quite as great as that which, as it turned out,
befell the assailed.

The importance of Quinsan to the Rebel cause could
not easily be over-estimated. It contained a manufac-
tory for ordnance, shot, and shell, which was conducted
by two Englishmen, whose fate I cannot discover; and
it afforded a central point communicating by water
with Soochow, Sungkiang, Taitsan, and Chanzu. The
boldness of the attack and the completeness of its
success paralysed the Tai-pings and gave confidence to
the country-people. Moreover, Quinsan afforded an
excellent place for the headquarters of the Ever-Victorious, and one where the reins of discipline could be

drawn tighter than at Sungkiang, where many Chinese
resided who had been demoralised when serving under
the lax system of General Ward.   It can easily be conceived that this anomalous Chinese force was "disciplined"
only to a very limited extent.   Not a few of the officers
were what are usually called "rowdies," yet exceedingly
jealous of their position and presumed privileges ; while
the Chinese rank-and-file expected to be humoured, and,
though brave enough at times, would, in the matter
of plunder, have outgeneralled Bardolph and Ancient
Pistol.   These worthies did not at all like being quartered at Quinsan instead of being restored to their old
location at Sungkiang.   When this change of residence
was communicated to the troops, the artillery refused to
fall in, and threatened to blow the European officers to
pieces with the big guns, and the Chinese authorities
with the small ones.   This intimation of serious mutiny
was conveyed to Colonel Gordon in a written proclamation.   He ordered up the non-commissioned officers,
being convinced that they were at the bottom of the
affair, and inquired of them who wrote the proclamation, and why the men would not fall in.   They
professed ignorance on these points, and were then told
that one out of every five of them would be shot—a
piece of information which they received with groans.
As it was absolutely necessary to restore discipline, the
commander ordered a corporal, one of the most prominent of the groaners, to be dragged out and shot, which
was immediately done by two of the infantry who were
standing by.   The remaining non-commissioned officers
were then put in confinement for an hour, with the
assurance that if the men did not fall in, and if the
name of the writer of the proclamation were not given
up by the time that period elapsed, the arrangement of

shooting every fifth man would be carried out ; and this energetic measure brought them to their senses, the men falling in and the writer's name being disclosed.

At the time this fracas occurred, another serious dispute was going on between Colonel Gordon, whose hands must have been pretty full, and General Ching. This Imperialist leader had been annoyed at Gordon's method of taking Quinsan, because he had previously written to the Futai, stating that he himself only required guns to make a breach at the East Gate in order to get in ; and he was also opposed to the disciplined force being estabr lished at that place. Whether purposely or accidentally, but most probably the former, some of his gunboats opened fire with grape and round-shot on 150 men of the Ever-Victorious under Majors Kirkham and Lowden, who were co-operating with another Imperialist force under General Lí. Ching at first affected to treat this *contretemps* as a joke ; and on being rather forcibly informed it was nothing of the kind, he affected ignorance of the unmistakable green-and-red flag on which his troops had fired. Gordon wrote to the Futai about this matter, and then, with a larger force, started for the neighbourhood where the event had occurred, determined to fight Ching as well as the Rebels, if that general showed a disposition to make any more such mistakes. Mr Macartney, however, formerly surgeon in H.M. 99th Regiment, who was then, as now, in the employ of the Chinese Government, and had undertaken charge of the Futai's arsenal at Sungkiang, was sent up to arrange matters, and the affair ended in a humble apology.

CHAPTER X.

BURGEVINE'S HISTORY AND FATE.

A THIRD MUTINY—SITUATION OF SOOCHOW—GORDON'S TROUBLES —BURGEVINE'S PREVIOUS CAREER—HE JOINS THE TAI-PINGS— ALARM CAUSED IN SHANGHAI—GORDON'S PROVIDENTIAL ESCAPE —THE FOREIGN ALLIES DESERT THE REBELS—POLITE INTER- CHANGES BETWEEN BURGEVINE AND JONES — BURGEVINE AT- TEMPTS AGAIN TO JOIN THE TAI-PINGS — HIS SEIZURE BY THE CHINESE AUTHORITIES — HIS REPORTED ACCIDENTAL DEATH— THE DOUBT WHICH RESTS OVER HIS FATE.

No sooner was the fracas with General Ching settled than another and more serious danger began to manifest itself in alarming reports concerning the intentions of Burgevine, formerly commander of the disciplined Chi- nese. It was known that he was enlisting loose charac- ters at Shanghai, and was also in close communication with Foreigners who had originally been in the force, but who had left it. Burgevine, however, wrote to Colonel Gordon, with whom he was on good terms, on the 21st July, in the following words :—" You may hear a great many rumours concerning me, but do not believe any of them. I shall come up and have a long talk with you. Until then adieu." This was not very explicit or reassuring, but on the strength of it Gordon wrote to the Futai and became surety that Burgevine would not make any attempt in favour of the Tai-pings.

The rumours about their old commander had an unsettling effect on the minds of the officers ; and just before an expedition was about to start for Wokong, there was a mutiny of the artillery officers, who were annoyed at a change being made in their commander.   On the 26th July they all joined in a round-robin, refusing to serve under the new commander, Major Tapp, or to accompany the expedition.   In this case, though Colonel Gordon, as he afterwards told them, had all the inclination to shoot one or two of the leaders, he had not the power, as all the officers of the force would have resented such a proceeding ; so the course he pursued was to exercise all his personal influence in collecting any men who would offer to serve the guns, and in getting these latter started without the artillery officers.   The guns were fortunately in the boats, and the common artillerymen were quite willing to go, so the expedition started without the officers.   At dusk, however, a letter came from these now penitent gentlemen, begging that their conduct might be overlooked for that one time.   Considering all the circumstances, this had to be done, the more especially as their place could not effectively be supplied. Though given to imaginary grievances, the officers of the force were gallant men, who evinced much ingenuity and quickness, and were wonderfully sharp in acquiring a knowledge of the country.   One cause of their uneasiness was a dread of their places being supplied by officers from the British army; but of this there was little likelihood at the time, owing to the General Order, which condemned officers so acting to half-pay.   They would have had less suspicion of their commander had they known that at this very time he was being urged in influential quarters, and by well-wishers to China, to retire from his position and allow the Rebels a chance of advance, in order to force the Chinese authorities to grant terms to the force such as would induce British officers to serve.[*]

In order to explain the expeditions which now followed, it must be borne in mind that at this period the great object of the Imperial Government was the reduction of Soochow, the capital of the province, situated on the Grand Canal. Looking at the nature of the country and its system of water-communication, Colonel Gordon deemed it best to approach it gradually from all sides and cut its communications, rather than advance to an immediate attack. Soochow is peculiarly situated with regard to water-communication, for it stands on the Grand Canal, and is pretty close to the Taho or Taiho Lake,[†] a sheet of shallow water fifty miles from north to south, and nearly as many in breadth. From the Grand Canal to this lake there are four entrances open to steamers. One of these is at Kahpoo, a place ten miles south of Soochow, and there the Rebels had two strong stone forts which it was of special importance to take, not only because they secured a good communication between the lake and the canal, but because they commanded the direct road from Soochow to the Tai-ping cities in the south. The city of Wokong, three miles south of Kahpoo, was also in possession of the Rebels, and it was thought best to attack it first.

The force employed consisted of about 2200 men, infantry and artillery, in boats, with the armed steamers Firefly and Cricket, who captured Kahpoo on the 27th July. The most exciting part of the affair occurred early on the 28th July, at a Rebel fort only a few

---

[*] Private correspondence.

[†] As *Tai* means "Great" and *Ho* "Lake" or "Water," to speak of the Tai-ho Lake reminds one of the Indian griffin's "Boy, bring some *ag low;*" but the phrase has become too familiar to be changed in a work of this kind.

hundred yards from Wokong, which had been left un-occupied. As soon as the Tai-pings, however, saw the advance of the Ever-Victorious Army, they rushed out to occupy this fort; and Colonel Gordon pushed out the 4th and 6th Regiments to cut them off and endea-vour to get in before them. An exciting race ensued, and the Tai-pings managed to get in first; but the 6th Regiment was so little behind that they had immediately to run out again, with some loss. Leaving this regiment in occupation, Gordon took other stockades which com-manded the town, so that every exit from the city was closed by 10 A.M. After a vain attempt to force a pas-sage, the garrison surrendered, and about 4000 prisoners were taken, among whom were many chiefs, including the second in command—the leader, Yang Wang, a rela-tive of Chung Wang, having escaped the night before. Among those captured were a theatrical company who had just come up from Hangchow, and were sorely troubled at such a termination of their mimic fights. The Imperialist general Ching soon arrived, and was very anxious to get hold of the prisoners; but only 1500, including none of the chiefs, were given him, to be made soldiers, under a promise that they should re-ceive good treatment, and these had the option of going with the disciplined force. However, Gordon soon heard that five of these prisoners had been beheaded by Ching; and this, together with his determination to quit the command on account of the non-payment of claims which the force had necessarily incurred, determined him to leave for Shanghai.

At this time the commander of the Ever-Victorious Army must have had what many people would think the most pressing inducements to give up the command, and his army, and its victories. The service he was on was not only one of incessant toil, but of more than ordinary exposure to danger, as he had often himself to lead assaults, and, seizing reluctant officers, to march them into the thick of the fire. Some of these officers were disaffected towards him, and he was even looked upon unfavourably by a portion of his own troops. The Imperialist authorities, especially the redoubtable Ching, were a constant source of trouble, and the Futai took no steps to discharge the pressing claims of creditors against the force. At the same time influential persons among his countrymen were urging him to resign. But when he arrived at Shanghai on the 8th August at 8 P.M., and learned that General Burgevine had left for Soochow with a large party of Foreigners in order to join the Tai-ping ranks, Gordon gave up his intention of resigning, and rode up to Quinsan that night in order to resume his command; because he did not think it creditable to leave the Imperialists when they were in so great a danger; because a change of command at such a crisis might have been most detrimental to the whole of the community at Shanghai; and also because he felt he had pledged himself to the Futai that Burgevine would not join the Rebels.

As this is the turning-point in Henry Andrea Burgevine's eventful history, it may be well to say a word as to his antecedents. Like Ward, he was one of those American adventurers, who, trained by the circumstances of their country to love fighting, could find no sufficient outlet for their restless energies before the great American war came to their relief. He was a Southerner by birth, and superior to Ward both in manners and education, though inferior in coolness and in the choice of means to an end. The latter filibuster had a nasty side-look, and a face which boded no good to any one in particular, unless it were himself; while the former had a pleasant expression on his dark countenance. The American papers say that he was born at Newbern, North Carolina, in 1836, his father having been a French officer under Napoleon; and that, though his early years were ill provided for, he was an accomplished student, and even in his youth entertained dreams of being some day able to build up a great empire in the East; and whether that be the case or not, he certainly entertained such a dream in China, where it was the cause of his misfortunes. A much-wandering man, he seems to have turned up in California of course, in Australia, the Sandwich Islands, India where he studied Hindustanee, Jiddah, London, and other places—being, in fact, one of those nautical gentlemen who combine a taste for literature with the power of navigating coasting vessels, and, would fate allow, of founding great empires. After that, finding a post-office clerkship and the editing of an American newspaper rather tame work for him, he found his way again to China, became Ward's second in command, and, as noted before, on the death of that worthy, was put in charge of the Ever-Victorious Army, quarrelled with the Futai, struck the patriotic merchant Ta Kee, was dismissed from his post, applied for redress at Peking, and was not reinstated.

These latter events had naturally irritated Burgevine's soul; and it is admitted, even by his friends, that, being weakened by an imperfectly healed wound, he was now in the habit of taking stimulants to an extent which at times disordered his brain, or at least that stimulants, whether taken in large quantities or not, had that effect upon him. There was a double motive for his action—revenge against the Imperialists, and his dream of seizing an empire in China; so he entered into com-

munication with the Moh Wang, now Tai-ping chief at
Soochow, and engaged about 150 Foreign rowdies at
Shanghai to enter with him into the service of the Great
Peace. This was a bold enterprise, for it was pretty well
known at this time that the Foreigners in the service of
the Tai-pings had no very delightful time of it; but
Burgevine was a persuasive person, his name had considerable power with the troops on both sides, and it
was believed, not without some grounds, that he could
command the services of many of the officers of Gordon's
army. As to himself, there is no doubt that his hope
and intention was to get a large body of foreign adventurers and disciplined natives into his own hands, then
to throw up the Tai-ping cause, and make an independent
filibustering movement across China in the direction of
Peking, in order to fulfil the dream of his youth. Considering the state of China at this time, wiser heads than
his might have been carried away by such an idea"; but
the Foreign Powers, having treaty-rights with that
country, would never have permitted the success of such
a movement; and even the Imperial Government would
have been roused to measures which would have defeated it. The time for such a project was before the
treaties of 1858.

This movement of Burgevine's was thus reported on
to Major - General Brown, commanding her Majesty's
forces in China, by Colonel Hough, on the 4th of
August :—

Burgevine has gone over to the Rebels with some Europeans
collected here; the number varies with the different reports from
100 to 1000, but 300 will probably be nearer the mark. From
Captain Strode's information Burgevine's terms with the Europeans are, service one month and money paid down; and other
information states unrestrained licence to pillage every town

they take, even Shanghai itself. The latter would be an idle
threat even under the present reduced state of the garrison, but
for the alarming defection of Major Gordon's force, who are all,
it is said, traitorously inclined to side with Burgevine. Names
of traitors are freely given, being those of Major Gordon's best
officers of the land forces, as well as those commanding steamers.
This, if true, would virtually be giving our siege-train, now with
Major Gordon, into the Rebels' hands, and to oppose which,
Captain Murray informs me, we have not a gun of equal force.
The Futai told Mr Markham yesterday evening that Burgevine
and 65 Europeans had seized the little steamer Ki-fow under
the walls of Sun-kiang, and taken her into Soochow, and had
been made a Wang of the second class and commander of all
the Rebel forces. The Futai also said that a report had reached
him, of Quang-san [Quinsan], Major Gordon's headquarters,
having been given up to the Rebels by its garrison. Should this
be true, the worst may be anticipated; Major Gordon a prisoner, the siege-train lost, and the speedy advent of the Rebels,
commanded by Burgevine, before this place; for it is idle to
suppose that they would respect the 30-mile radius when they
had no town outside with wealth enough to support their rabble
hordes, which exaggerated reports put down at 800,000, of which
they say 20,000 are disciplined by Frenchmen and Europeans
long resident in Soochow. In the present imperfect knowledge
of affairs, to move out would perhaps be to leave Shanghai open
to the Rebels, who can choose their own route, and whose advance would only be known by the country people flying before
them and the smoke of burning towns. I trust to hear from
Major Gordon to enable me to act decisively, of which I need
not say I will send you the earliest information.

This shows a very alarming state of matters, and that
Burgevine had not laid his plans without very considerable skill. Any one in Colonel Gordon's place must have
had serious thoughts on that solitary night-ride up to
Quinsan, seeing how much hung upon the disposition of
the officers whom he was to meet at dawn. On reaching
his headquarters no unsatisfactory signs appeared; but
the commander received reports during the day which

induced him to send reinforcements to Kahpoo, his most advanced post, and to return the principal part of his siege-ammunition to Shanghai. In the evening three men actually walked into his room and asked for Burgevine, saying they had been engaged by him, and had been told to wait at the "second station," which looked as if neither the Americo-Tai-ping nor his station could be very far off. This movement of Burgevine made Gordon's position an exceedingly difficult and dangerous one, for in addition to attacks from without he was also very liable to attacks from within. The ostensible cause of Burgevine's dismissal—namely, his assault on the banker Ta Kee, in order to get money for the force—had naturally left an impression on the minds of the men which was favourable to their late commander, and Colonel Gordon had reason to fear that some European emissary of the Rebels might find his way into the force, and stir it up to revolt. In case of such a result happening, the siege-train was sent back to Taitsan for safe keeping.

In the first part of August, the Tai-pings, reinforced by a number of the Europeans who had come up with Burgevine, made several strenuous but ineffectual attacks on Gordon's station at Kahpoo, which covered his position at Wokong. Indeed both of these places might easily have been captured had Burgevine acted energetically; for they were left in charge of Ching, the Imperialist general co-operating with the Ever-Victorious Army, and that commander was absent at Shanghai when the Rebels attacked, about 40,000 in number. The American adventurer, however, did not direct these operations, being occupied at Soochow, along with his lieutenant, Jones, a fellow-countryman, in trying to arrange about the formation of a Foreign Legion. At

this time Gordon was reinforced by a small Franco-
Chinese force, under Captain Bonnefoi, and by 200
Belooches of her Majesty's East India army, whom
General Brown stationed in Quinsan for the protection
of the heavy artillery.

For some weeks after this Gordon remained on the
defensive, but on the 29th September took Patachiao
without losing many men ; and immediately after, negotiations were opened with him by some of the Europeans
in the service of the Tai-pings. Behind the stockades
which he had taken there was a bridge, 350 yards in
length, with 53 arches, which had been partially cut
through, in order to let the Hyson pass into a lake near
it ; and this bridge was the scene of a curious incident
which occurred to Colonel Gordon. He was resting
upon its parapet one evening, smoking a cigar, when
first one rifle or musket bullet, and then a second,
struck the stone upon which he was sitting. These
shots came not from the enemy, but from his own camp,
where they had been fired accidentally. On the second
shot being fired, Colonel Gordon thought it necessary to
descend into his boat and go over to the camp in order
to inquire into this matter ; but he had hardly got
half-way across the creek below, when that part of the
bridge on which he had been sitting suddenly fell into
the water; so that the accidental shots which had endangered his life, probably saved it. Between the opposing forces there was another, a high bridge, which
became a kind of neutral ground where friendly intercourse took place between the European officers, many
of whom had formerly been comrades in arms, though
now serving on different sides. In the interviews which
took place on this bridge between the Foreigners on
both sides, it appeared that the Europeans and Ameri-

cans who had taken service with the Tai-pings were
by no means satisfied with their position. The result
was that Colonel Gordon had a private interview with
Burgevine himself, when that gentleman stated that he
was determined to leave the Rebels, but would not
do so unless his officers and men could obtain some
guarantee that they would not be held responsible for
the acts they had done when with the Tai-pings. On
this Colonel Gordon guaranteed that the authorities at
Shanghai would institute no further proceedings against
those men ; and offered to take as many of them as he
could into his own force, and to assist the remainder in
leaving the country. At another interview Burgevine
proposed to Gordon to unite with him, and together to
seize Soochow ; to keep both Rebels and Imperialists
out of it, and then to organise an army of 20,000 men,
with which to march on Peking. He said that in Soochow alone there was sufficient money to enable them
to carry out this plan ; but was at once informed that
Colonel Gordon would not entertain any such idea.
The situation was complicated by the fact that at this
moment General Ching was making attacks of his own
on the Tai-ping position, and also by the fear that these
proposals for surrender might only be a ruse to cover
secret tampering with the disciplined force. While these
interviews were taking place, severe fighting still went
on, and a desperate attempt of the Rebels to recapture
Wokong was repulsed with great loss on both sides.   In
the middle of October, however, Burgevine and the other
Europeans in Rebel employ sent information that they
intended, under pretence of making a sally, to throw
themselves on Gordon's protection. This accordingly
they did, rushing on board the steamer Hyson as if they
were capturing it, on which thousands of the Tai-ping

troops came out to their assistance, only to be driven back with volleys of shell and shot from the Hyson's artillery, while the steamer turned back and safely landed the deserters in the besieging camp. When these men were landed it was found that Burgevine himself and several other Europeans were not among them. Morton, their leader, made the excuse that the Moh Wang appeared to suspect their intention, and so he had thought it wisest to leave at once, without waiting for his commander. Fearing that Burgevine would be decapitated in consequence of this movement, Colonel Gordon at once sent a letter and presents to the Moh Wang, entreating him to spare Burgevine's life, and also returned all the Enfield rifles with which the deserters had been armed. It is highly honourable to the Taiping chief that after these events he sent Burgevine off in safety; and that worthy, after being received in Gordon's camp, was sent down to Shanghai. In this bloodless way the Tai-pings lost the greater number of the Europeans who were ranked on their side; and Colonel Gordon must have conducted the affair with boldness and skill, for the Imperialist authorities, aware of the negotiations that were going on, suspected even his loyalty, and he ran the risk of his own officers being enticed over to the enemy. The majority of the Foreigners who thus left the Tai-pings were seamen who had been taken from Soochow to Shanghai, with very little idea of their ultimate destination. Mr Mayers, the acting British Vice-Consul at Shanghai, who was sent to investigate this affair, states in an official letter,* that at one moment, while offering to surrender, Burgevine proposed to his Lieutenant, Jones, a plan for entrapping Gordon, but the more honest nature of his companion

* Blue-Book, China, No. 3 (1864), p. 169.

M

revolted against such treachery. The following extract from the statement of Mr Jones, regarding an occurrence which took place immediately before Burgevine's escape, will give a curious idea of the relationships which existed between these adventurers : " At noon I went to Burgevine, who was lying asleep on board a 32-pounder gunboat, and asked him whether I should assist him to get ashore, as many of our officers and men were making remarks on the condition he was in. On his demanding the names of those who had made remarks, I declined giving them, and shortly afterwards again attempted to remonstrate with him, in company with another officer. On my again declining to give up names, Burgevine drew out his four-barrelled pistol, which he cocked and discharged at my head from a distance of about nine inches. The bullet entered my left cheek and passed upwards. It has not yet been extracted. I exclaimed, 'You have shot your best friend!' His answer was, 'I know I have, and I wish to God I had killed you!'" The only reply which Burgevine made to this statement in a letter on the subject which he published in the Shanghai papers, is the following remarkably ingenuous one : " Captain Jones's account of the affair is substantially correct, and I feel great pleasure in bearing testimony to his veracity and candour, whenever any affair with which he is personally acquainted is concerned."

It may be well to notice here Burgevine's further proceedings and unfortunate fate. After his surrender at Soochow the Futai delivered him up to the American Consul, and at the request of Colonel Gordon, that latter functionary waived proceedings against him on condition that he would leave the country. For some time he remained residing quietly at Yokohama, in Japan, where the recalcitrant Daimio, Cho-shiu, who was fighting against the Tycoon, and who had heard of the absurd terror which Burgevine's name inspired in China, offered him an important post in his army.   While hesitating as to accepting this offer, the adventurer was prevailed upon to make a trip to Shanghai, early in 1865, in the steamer Fei-pang ; and from Shanghai he went down in another vessel to Amoy, near which place a remnant of the Tai-pings were still in arms.   His return to the coast of China seems to have been purely an accidental affair, though extremely improper and imprudent; and on the passage, when spoken to on the subject of joining the Rebels, a few of whom still made a stand at the city of Changchow in Fukien, he expressed his conviction that their game had been played out, and that neither honour nor profit were to be got from that quarter.   Unfortunately, when he reached Amoy, he fell into the hands of some Rebel sympathisers, and whilst in a state of intoxication, was induced to pledge himself to visit Changchow, and to give all the assistance in his power to the expiring Tai-ping cause.*   It was the duty of the American Consul at this port to have immediately arrested the misguided adventurer on his return to China ; but nothing of the kind was done, and so the Chinese authorities were com-pelled by the duty which they owed their country to take the matter into their own hands.

The movements of Burgevine were betrayed to these authorities by a black servant who accompanied him, and he was arrested on the 15th May, along with two companions, armed to the teeth, and proceeding to the Rebel lines.   Being confined in the Yamun of the dis-trict magistrate, the American Consul now demanded his rendition, and to avoid a dispute on this point he was secretly forwarded to Foochow, and there the Consul

* North China Herald, September 14, 1865.

also demanded his delivery ; but this request was positively refused, the chief magistrate stating that Burgevine would be sent on to Lí, Futai of Kiangsoo, under whose orders he had formerly acted.   Immediately on intelligence of this affair reaching Peking, Prince Kung wrote to the American Minister, informing him of the circumstances, and stating that Burgevine, having made himself amenable to the laws of China, would be judged by these laws, and might be executed as a felon, while three or four other Foreigners who had been taken along with him would be handed over to the jurisdiction of their respective Consuls.   Dr S. W. Williams, the acting American Minister at Peking, a gentleman of high character, and of almost unrivalled knowledge of China, seemed disposed to accede to this proposal, but requested his Highness to detain Burgevine in confinement for a few months, free from all insult and injury, whilst the Government at Washington was consulted on the subject.   In writing to Mr Seward on this case, Dr Williams said, " I am under the strong impression that this man's conduct has been a reproach to the fair name of all Western nations ; for all other Foreigners, so far as I know, who commanded the Imperialists, have acted honourably in this particular, leaving the service if they were dissatisfied, and not turning against it.   I am mortified that an American should have held this bad position." *   Dr Williams further pointed out that, while the Act of Congress of June 22, 1860, made rebellion against the Chinese Government a capital offence, and while there was no doubt whatever of Burgevine's guilt, the absence and death of important witnesses would render it extremely difficult to convict him in an American court.   At the same time, it was very desirable to

* American Diplomatic Correspondence for 1865, p. 454.

give every assurance to the Chinese Government that no efforts should be spared to prevent American citizens from joining the Rebels, or to punish them for so doing. The case was one of some difficulty, and the Chinese authorities consented to keep Burgevine a prisoner, but unharmed, until the Government at Washington decided what was to be done.

Meanwhile, as they were afraid to leave him on the sea-coast, lest an attempt at rescue should be made, he was sent from Foochow into the interior, to be forwarded overland to the charge of the Governor of Kiangsoo. What occurred to the unfortunate man after this is known only from Chinese statements. It was officially reported that he was drowned, along with ten Chinese, at Lanchi hien in Chekiang, by the capsizing of a ferry-boat, owing to a sudden flood in the river. Mr Lewis, the United States Deputy Consul-General, proceeded to the spot to investigate the circumstances; and though rumours of foul play were prevalent among the Foreign community, nothing was discovered to disprove the assertions of the Chinese. The adventurer's body was identified by a fracture which had been inflicted during his service in the Imperialist army; but it was too much decomposed to throw light on the manner of his death, which is said to have occurred on the 26th June 1865. The fact was proved of there having been a heavy flood at that time; but a certain amount of darkness must ever rest over the circumstances of his death. The Chinese authorities were under a very great temptation to get rid of him in some manner which would effectually preclude his giving further trouble, and which at the same time would not lead to any embroilment with the Government of the United States. Dr Williams says that the official correspondence on this subject gives

no idea of the alarm which filled the minds of the high
officers at Peking, when they heard of Burgevine's attempt to rejoin the Rebels.   Beyond this, and a rumour
of a piece of flayed skin having been noticed in his coffin,
I have no reason to suppose that their account of his
death was untrue; and if they did drown him purposely, they saved themselves and the American authorities a good deal of trouble.

CHAPTER XI.

THE FALL OF SOOCHOW, AND THE EXECUTION OF ITS WANGS.

THE INVESTMENT OF SOOCHOW — STORMING OF LEEKU — GORDON'S "MAGIC WAND"—DEATH OF CAPTAIN PERRY—DISPOSAL OF THE BESIEGING FORCES — THE FAITHFUL KING'S APPREHENSIONS— COMPLETE INVESTMENT OF SOOCHOW—PIRATING OF THE STEAMER FIREFLY—A DISASTROUS NIGHT-ATTACK—CAPTURE OF THE EAST GATE STOCKADES—NEGOTIATIONS FOR SURRENDER—MURDER OF THE MOH WANG — A CHARACTERISTIC LETTER FROM COLONEL GORDON—THE CAPITULATION OF SOOCHOW—GORDON'S PERILOUS POSITION—HIS GRIEF AND INDIGNATION—HIS SEARCH FOR GOVERNOR LI—EXECUTION OF THE WANGS—LI'S REASONS FOR THAT ACT — GORDON REFUSES TO ACT, AND REJECTS AN IMPERIAL DOUCEUR — IMPERIAL DECREE REGARDING THE FALL OF SOOCHOW.

WHILE the negotiations were going on for the desertion of Burgevine and his friends, the Faithful King came down to the relief of Soochow with a considerable army ; but, as was his invariable custom in similar circumstances, refused to trust himself within the walls of that city, and carried on his operations in its immediate neighbourhood. Colonel Gordon considered the Taipings to be so much weakened by the defection of their European allies, that he resolved to resume the offensive, and pushed on towards the South Gate of the city. Various stockades in that direction were soon taken, and

successfully defended against desperate attempts of the
Moh Wang to recapture them. In the fighting here, as
elsewhere, the steamer Hyson did good service. In one
engagement no less than 1300 prisoners were taken, and
as many more of the Tai-pings were drowned in their
efforts to escape. The taking of Wulungchiao and Patachiao rendered any sortie from Soochow to the south
impossible, and also enabled Gordon's force to operate to
the north, and thus form a junction with other Imperialist troops, under the Futai's brother, who had advanced
from Kongyin. The force which Gordon had under his
own immediate command was insufficient to enable him
to invest Soochow, yet he was enabled steadily to advance in the work of doing so, because the positions
which he took could be left in charge of the Futai's
other troops, as those of General Ching, or of the disciplined Chinese under Macartney and Bonnefoi. Thus the
Ever-Victorious Army gradually fought its way round
Soochow, and left a fortified circle held by its allies en-
compassing that city.

Among the engagements by which this operation was
performed was one on the 1st of November at Leeku, a
strong Rebel position five miles to the north of Soochow. This position was carried by storm by the 4th
and 2d Regiments, aided by some Franco-Chinese. In
almost all these engagements Colonel Gordon was very
much exposed, for he found it necessary, or at least expedient, to be constantly in the front, and often to lead
in person. Though brave men, the officers of his force
would sometimes hang back, and their commander had
occasionally to take one by the arm and lead him into
the thick of the fire. He himself seemed to bear a
charmed life, and never carried any arms, even when
foremost in the breach. His only weapon on these occa-

sions was a small cane with which he used to direct his troops, and in the Chinese imagination this cane soon became magnified into Gordon's "magic wand of victory." His Celestial followers, finding him almost invariably victorious and escaping unhurt, though more exposed than any other man in the force, naturally concluded, in accordance with their usual ideas, that the little wand he carried insured protection and success to its owner. Every one who knows the Chinese character will be aware that such an idea must have given great encouragement to the Ever-Victorious Army, and was of more service to its commander than could have been any amount of arms which he himself could possibly have carried. In this engagement at Leeku Colonel Gordon had a narrow escape; for one of his captains, Mr George Perry, was shot dead at his side under rather peculiar circumstances. Some days previously, Gordon found lying on the ground a letter in the handwriting of this officer to a Tai-ping sympathiser in Shanghai, giving information as to the intended movements of the force. On being shown this letter, Perry confessed that he had written it, but declared he thought the information of no importance, and had only intended to send it to Shanghai as a piece of gossip which might be interesting. On this his commander said to him, "Very good, Perry. I shall pass your fault over this time, on condition that, in order to show your loyalty, you undertake to lead the next forlorn-hope." This agreement had been forgotten by Colonel Gordon when, a few days after, they stood together on the edge of the ditch in front of the stockades at Leeku. They were both, in fact, leading a forlorn-hope; and while standing together, a ball struck Perry in the mouth, and he fell into Gordon's arms, where he almost immediately expired.

Shortly after, on the 10th November, another engagement occurred at Wanti, a place which was so well defended by massive mud-works that the shelling of all the artillery available scarcely made any impression upon it. When the place was surrounded by the disciplined Chinese, the Tai-pings inside rushed out and tried to escape, which led to much hand-to-hand fighting. The capture of Wanti nearly completed the investure of Soochow. The Taiho Lake was held by the steamers Hyson and Tsatlee, on board of which a force of 200 Imperialists was placed, and which cruised off Moodow, cutting off the communication between the lake and the Siaou Mun, or small West Gate of Soochow. The next great water outlet was closed to the Rebels by 1000 Imperialist soldiers stationed at Wulungchiao, off the Pan Mun, or South Gate. The main water and road communication with the south was also closed by 1500 Imperialists stockaded on the Grand Canal at Patachiao. A small creek leading from the South-East Gate was stopped by a fleet of Imperialist gunboats. General Ching's force, of about 4000 men, was encamped on the road to Quinsan, about two miles outside of the Loh Mun, or East Gate of Soochow. At Leeku and Wanti Colonel Gordon himself was stationed with a portion of his force, guarding the canal to Chanzu. The remainder of his army, together with 2500 Imperialist troops under Ching, and 400 of the Franco-Chinese, were moved about, and employed as occasion required. Altogether, 13,500 men were employed in November 1863 in the investment of Soochow, being arranged as follows :—

	Imperialists.	Gordon's Force.	French Force.
In stockades, . .	7,500	1000	...
For the field or siege, .	2,500	2100	400
	10,000	3100	400

In the neighbourhood, however, there were about

25,000 additional Imperialists under the Futai's brother, whose centre was at Fushan.   The Tai-pings had 40,000 men in Soochow and its suburbs; the city of Wusieh held some 20,000 more; and the Faithful King had 18,000 men stationed at Mahtanchiao, a place situated between Wusieh and Soochow, and from which he could assist either city, and also could attack on the flank any advance made by the Imperialists on the Grand Canal, the only great water and road line of communication left to the Tai-pings.

This able Tai-ping leader seems to have fully understood the perilous position of his cause, but was distracted between the danger to which Nanking was exposed, and the risk of losing Hangchow and Soochow. The following despatches from him, dated near Soochow, the 10th of November 1863, were intercepted by the Imperialists, and show how alive he was to the dangerous state of the Tai-ping cause at this period :—

To the Chow Wang.

The other day, on the return [from Nanking?] of the President Lí, I wrote you particulars of all he had to say, but have received no answer, and feel very anxious on this account. News arrived yesterday from Nanking that all the works in the neighbourhood of the Kao-chiao Gate and the Shang Fang Gate had been abandoned, and that the city is hard pressed in the extreme.   I am disturbed beyond measure by this intelligence; and, in view of all the President Lí has said, I earnestly hope that you will act in unison with the brethren, and give speedy thought to the general cause.   What is most earnestly to be wished is, that Nanking may be preserved from harm.   Only so long as the capital is held are our lives our own.

I look to you to act with the brethren, and not again to allow suspicions to arise.   If this is once cherished, the matter is at an end.

To the Hu Wang, commanding at Chanchu fu.

I write again, because on the 28th October I despatched

two letters by express messenger, with orders to deliver them within a certain time, in which I requested that, with the exception of those at Chanchu, all the forces might with all speed be brought together for a combined attack, in order that we might derive the benefit of conjoint action; but a length of time has elapsed, to my great anxiety, without the receipt of an answer. The news yesterday received from Nanking, to the effect that the works around the Kao-chiao Gate have been evacuated, has probably already reached you, as you are nearer to the spot. I was disturbed and grieved beyond measure by this intelligence, and at the same time I have no troops whom I can dispose. If you, together with the Wusieh troops, can come and make a combined effort, there will be reason to hope that the siege both of Nanking and of Soochow may be broken up. The beleaguerment of Nanking is, as you are doubtless fully aware, far different now from what it has been heretofore; and I am most anxious that you should consent to join with your forces, and also combine with the troops under She Wang. If all unite in sweeping away one division of the Imps., security will accrue on all sides; and the sooner we clear away this brood the sooner we shall be able to make a combined effort to relieve Nanking. If, however, Soochow and Hangchow are endangered, not only is it useless to talk of raising the siege of Nanking, but Chanchu and Wusieh will also be as good as lost, and it will be too late for repentance then. To yourself, who know this so well, it is not necessary that I should say more.

Gordon's aim now was to cut the Rebel line of communication, so that the Faithful King might be prevented from going to the aid of the Soochow garrison. The Imperialist officers co-operating with him were afraid of thus cutting the Rebels off from any possibility of retreat; but, with better knowledge of his enemy, he calculated that when completely surrounded, the Taipings at Soochow would be likely to surrender. One great reason for this conclusion was information he had received about dissensions among the Rebel Princes in Soochow. Of these, the Moh Wang, the most energetic and determined, had offended his companion Chiefs, though not much superior in ·rank to them, and the Imperialists had already begun to hold communication with some of the other Wangs. On hearing that the steamer Firefly had been captured near Shanghai by some European Tai-ping sympathisers, Colonel Gordon resolved to hurry the operations against Soochow, so as to cut the Grand Canal communication before the Rebels could make use of the steamer of which they had obtained possession.* This was done on the 19th November, at a village called Fusaikwan, where five stockades were captured without loss on the part of the assailants. After garrisoning this last post, which completed the investment of the doomed city, Gordon proceeded to the East Gate ; and being now in possession of all the exterior defences, he determined to make a vigorous attack on the north-east angle of the wall which surrounds Soochow.   In order to this, however, it was

* The Firefly was sent down to Shanghai under the charge of Captain Ludlam, who had strict orders to remain there only two hours, and to return then to Wanti. As General Brown, Commander of her Majesty's forces in China, wished to go up to see Colonel Gordon, the steamer was anchored at Shanghai for a night, during which Ludlam was detained at the General's quarters by wet weather, his place on board being taken by Captain Dolly, besides whom there were on board, of Europeans, Mr Martin, the mate, Mr Perry, the engineer, and Lieutenant Easton of the Artillery. At midnight the steamer was boarded by several Foreigners, headed by a man who calls himself "Lin Lee" (? Lindley), who were conducted on board by Captain Ludlam's Cantonese servant, and who, suddenly closing the hatches over Captain Dolly and his companions, took possession of the vessel. It was taken up to the Faithful King, who is said to have given £20,000 for it; and White, one of the men engaged in the capture, was condemned to two years' imprisonment for this, as an act of piracy, by the consular court of Shanghai, while his chief accomplice made his escape to England.   There was also some quarrel among the captors over their ill-gotten gains, which resulted in one of their number being shot by "Lin Lee" himself. The bodies of Dolly, Martin, Perry, and Easton were afterwards found at Wusich in a burned and mutilated state. Their captor "Lin Lee," after reaching England, published a book on the Tai-pings ; and my reasons for not noticing that work in the body of this history are given in Appendix V.

necessary to capture the inner line of the outside defences, which was very formidable. Accordingly, a night-attack was made on the 27th November, which resulted in the defeat of Gordon's force. The position to be attacked was a stockade situated on a mound about half a mile distant from the East Gate. The mound was covered with earthen fortifications, and its slope was well staked with short bamboos; while round it were three ditches from eight to nine feet deep, with their banks also well staked with sharp bamboos and iron spikes. Beyond these ditches there was also a long line of stockades. Gordon's plan was to surprise this place by a night-attack, and white turbans were served out to his troops in order that they might distinguish each other in the dark. About one o'clock in the morning the commander himself, accompanied by Majors Howard and Williams and two companies of his force, advanced to the outer stockade, leaving the remainder of his force already fallen in and under orders to advance at a given signal. Everything seemed quiet, and the Tai-ping guard gave no signs of being aware of this movement, so the remainder of the force received orders to proceed, while the advanced - guard succeeded in climbing inside the breastwork. The Moh Wang, however, was quite on the alert and prepared for this night-attack, having either received information that it was to be made, or having guessed that such was to be the case. Scarcely were all the troops up to the front, and a portion of them engaged in crossing a stockade in order to support their commander, when the Tai-pings opened a tremendous fire of grape and musketry on the whole force. The whole line of stockades held by the Rebels seemed one line of fire, while the Quinsan artillery were throwing rockets and shell into the Rebel works. The leading troops pushed gallantly on to the breastwork, headed by their leader; but the whole of the troops who had been detailed for service did not move up, and great confusion took place among them. Notwithstanding the efforts of the European officers, the Chinese soldiers showed a remarkable indisposition for fighting at night, so that Colonel Gordon had ultimately to retire, leaving numbers of killed and wounded on the field. Moh Wang, who was in the front stockade, without shoes or stockings, fought this night like a private soldier, and had about twenty Europeans with him. The Rebels must have lost tremendously from the fire of the twenty guns, which played upon them for about three hours with shot and shell; and the Ever-Victorious Army had 50 of its rank and file killed and 130 wounded, besides quite a large number of officers killed and wounded.

On the morning after the night-attack, General Ching told Gordon that he had had an interview with the Taiping Kung Wang, from which it appeared that all the Wangs in Soochow, with the exception of the Moh Wang, together with 35 Tien Chwangs, or expectant princes, with 30,000 men, were anxious to come over to the Imperialists. Notwithstanding their recent success, it was evident to these leaders that the capture of the city was only a question of time, and they proposed that if Gordon made another attack on the stockades at the East Gate, they would shut Moh Wang out of the city, and so be at liberty to make terms for their own surrender. Accordingly, Colonel Gordon determined to put forth all his powers to take the stockades, and on the morning of the 29th opened on them a tremendous fire from his heavy siege-guns and mortars. By this the Rebel works were so much battered that an advance

was ordered, and the stockades were taken by assault.
Ditches had to be swam across, breastworks had to be
mounted, and the Faithful King himself was engaged in
the defence, having arrived that morning, with his body-
guard of 400 men, by a small bridle-path which was still
open from Wusieh. During this attack, Colonel Gordon,
accompanied by only a few men, found himself cut off
from his force by a large party of the Tai-pings ; and
being unable to fall back, he deemed it the safest course
to press desperately onwards.   Finding the stockades
on his right almost vacated in the confusion, he pushed
through them, and seized the nearest stone fort.   Fortunately this movement was followed up by his force, who
occupied the stockades which he had passed through.
In this day's fighting also the loss was very heavy, and
among the officers killed in both attacks were, Lieutenant Jones of the Artillery, Captains Maule and
Wiley, and Lieutenant King of the 2d Regiment, Captains Christie and Agar of the 4th, Lieutenants Carrol,
Williams, and Glanceford, of the 5th, and Privates Up-
church, Foley, and Miller, of the Commander's European
body-guard. A great number were also wounded, among
whom was the Adjutant-General, Major Kirkham, whose
energetic services could ill be spared.*

* The following General Order was issued by Colonel Gordon at this
time :—

"Low Mun, Soochow, *November* 30, 1863.

"The commanding officer congratulates the officers and men of the force
on their gallant conduct of yesterday. The tenacity of the enemy, and the
great strength of their position, have unfortunately caused many casualties
and the loss of many valuable officers and men. The enemy, however, has
now felt our strength, and, although fully prepared and animated with the
presence of their most popular chiefs, have been driven out of a position
which surpasses in strength any yet taken from them. The loss of the
whole of the stockades on the east side of the city, up to the walls, has
already had its effect, and dissension is now rife in the garrison, who,
hemmed in on all sides, are already in fact negotiating defection.

"The commanding officer feels most deeply for the heavy loss, but is

As little more than 5500 men were available for attacking it, Soochow might have held out for some time longer, and its wall was surrounded by a ditch of appalling width, while to the north of the East Gate there were lines of stockades as far as the eye could reach ; but, as has been mentioned, the greater number of the Chiefs in Soochow were now anxious to surrender. Colonel Gordon and General Ching had an interview with three of them on the 1st December, and on the 2d the former officer had some conversation with the Na Wang. At these and other meetings the Na Wang stated his wish that Gordon would assault the city, in which case he and his troops, wearing white turbans, would not assist in its defence, on the condition that they should be protected on the entry of the Imperialists. On this Gordon replied, that if Soochow were taken by assault, it would be impossible to restrain an undisciplined force such as he commanded from plundering everywhere and every one. He added that, if the Wangs were sincere in their wish to surrender, they had better give over a gate as a guarantee of their good faith ; and if they could not do that, their best course would be to vacate the city, or to fight it out. Meanwhile he agreed to postpone any further attack, and left General Ching, who had been formerly a Tai-ping Chief, to arrange the terms of surrender.

The Moh Wang's suspicions were aroused by these negotiations, and he sent for the other Wangs to speak with them on the subject. After partaking of dinner, and offering up prayers, they arranged themselves in their robes and crowns, and adjourned into the recep-

convinced that the same will not be experienced again. The possession of the position of yesterday renders the occupation of the city by the Rebels untenable, and thus victualling the city is lost to them."

tion-hall, where Moh Wang seated himself at the head
of the table, which was on a raised dais. The discussion
between them then seemed to get animated, the Moh
Wang insisting that only Kwangsi and Kwangtung men
were to be trusted—a proposition naturally distasteful
to the other Wangs who belonged to other provinces.
As the discussion grew warmer, Kong Wang rose and
took off his robes; and on Moh Wang asking him the
meaning of this, he drew a small two-edged dagger and
stabbed the latter in the neck and back. Moh Wang
fell forward over the table, and was soon decapitated by
the other Wangs. This was a cowardly assassination of
a brave and intelligent man, who had never despaired in
the midst of his difficulties, and had always been good
to Foreigners, though cruel to his own countrymen.
When he was killed, some letters which Colonel Gordon
had written to him fell out on the floor, and were found
afterwards stained with blood. There is little doubt,
however, that if Na Wang and his associates had not
thus disposed of this chief, they would have run great
risk of being themselves decapitated by him, for he was
aware of their intended treachery: and it is not impossible that the Moh Wang himself meditated proposing terms of surrender; for a Frenchman, who was
present at the murder, mentions that this Wang had
directed him to write a letter to Gordon asking for an
interview, with the intention of being present at it in
disguise.

Colonel Gordon's characteristic letter to this chief
(relating to the release of the Europeans in Soochow,
of which mention has been made in the previous chapter) is of some interest, and reads as follows, so far
as I can make out through the blood with which it is
stained :—

To their Excellencies
  CHUNG WANG, MOH WANG.

STOCKADES, PATACHOW,
16th October 1863.

YOUR EXCELLENCIES,—You must be already aware that I
have on all occasions, when it lay in my power, been merciful
to your soldiers when taken prisoners, and not only been so
myself, but have used every endeavour to prevent the Imperial
authorities from practising any inhumanity.   Ask for the truth
of this statement any of the men who were taken at Wokong,
and who some of them must have returned to Soochow, as I
placed no restriction on them whatever.

Having stated the above, I now ask your Excellencies to
consider the case of Europeans in your service.   In every army
each soldier must be actuated with faithful feelings to fight well.
A man made to fight against his will is not only a bad soldier,
but he is a positive danger, causing anxiety to his leaders, and
absorbing a large force to prevent his defection.   If there are
many Europeans left in Soochow, I would ask your Excellencies
if it does not seem to you much better to let these men quietly
leave your service if they wish it ; you would thereby get rid of
a continual source of suspicion, gain the sympathy of the whole
of the Foreign nations, and feel that your difficulties are all from
without.   Your Excellencies may think that decapitation would
soon settle the matter, but you would then be guilty of a crime
which will bear its fruits sooner or later.   In this force officers
and men come and go at pleasure, and although it is incon-
venient at times, I am never apprehensive of treason from
within.   Your Excellencies may rely on what I say, that should
you behead the Europeans who are with you, or retain them
against their free will, you will eventually regret it.   The men
have committed no crime, they have done you good service, and
what they have tried to do—viz., escape—is nothing more than
any man, or even animal, will do when placed in a situation he
does not like.

The men could have done you great harm, as you will no
doubt allow ; they have not done so, and I consider that
your Excellencies have reaped great benefit from their assistance.

As far as I am personally concerned, it is a matter of indifference whether the men stay or leave; but as a man who wishes to save these unfortunate men, I intercede.

Your Excellencies may depend you will not suffer by letting these men go; you need not fear their communicating information. I knew your force, men and guns, long ago, and therefore care not to get that information from them. If my entreaties are unavailing for the men in . . . . yourself by sending down the wounded, and perform an action never to be regretted.

I write the above with my own hand, as I do not wish to intrust the matter to a linguist; and trusting you will accede to my request, I conclude, your Excellencies' obedient servant,

C. G. GORDON,
Major Commanding.

Immediately after the death of the Moh Wang there occurred certain important and painful events which made an immense noise at the time, which induced Colonel Gordon temporarily to resign his command, and which ultimately led to the withdrawal of her Majesty's Order in Council, which permitted him to serve under the Imperial Government. This officer, his coadjutor General Ching, and Lí, the Governor of the province, held towards each other somewhat indefinite positions. They all acted quite independently of each other at times, while on other occasions their functions were mixed up and confused. The Wangs in Soochow must have been rather at a loss to know to which of these three persons it was they were going to surrender. Gordon was the opponent whom they had most to fear, for it was he who had done almost all the fighting around their city, and, at the same time, he was the man on whose integrity and humanity they could place the greatest reliance. General Ching had also met them in the field, and being himself an old Rebel, had been the principal party engaged in carrying on the negotiations about their surrender. But behind these two there was

Lí, the Futai, close at hand, and holding a superior position. After the most careful examination of all the accounts available of the occurrence which now took place, it is difficult for me to determine to whom the Wangs did surrender. Surrender, however, they did, on which the following events occurred.

The North and East Gates of Soochow having been given up by the Rebels, and been occupied by the Imperialists on the 5th December, Colonel Gordon withdrew his troops a short way, being anxious to save them from the demoralisation that would ensue if they were allowed to plunder the city. And as almost all the fighting which led to the fall of Soochow had fallen upon his force, he went to the Futai and demanded two months' extra pay for his men as a reward for the services they had gone through, as a compensation for their abstaining from plunder, and as an inducement for them to push on with him and attack Wusieh, while the Rebels were dispirited by the fall of Soochow. On the Futai objecting to this proposal, Colonel Gordon said that unless it was agreed to he could not undertake to keep his troops in hand, and would lay down his own command by 3 o'clock P.M. Till that hour arrived he went into the city to the house of the Na Wang, where he met all the other princes, who informed him that everything in regard to their surrender was going on properly, and that they were quite satisfied. Colonel Gordon then went to the Moh Wang's palace, and tried to get the body of that chief buried, but none of the people near would touch it. Returning to his own force, he found General Ching with an offer from the Futai to give the Ever-Victorious Army one month's extra pay. On this the men made an attempt to march down upon the Futai; but this disturbance was soon quelled, Gordon determining to remain for the present in command, and, fearing to trust his force in the neighbourhood of Soochow, started it off next morning for Quinsan.

On the 5th, the day when Colonel Gordon went in to see the Wangs, General Ching informed him that the Futai had extended mercy to them all; and on the 6th the former officer again went into Soochow to the Na Wang's house, reaching it about half an hour before noon, when the Wangs were to go out to the Futai and the city was to be given over. At the interview which then took place Na Wang was in very good spirits. He said that everything had been satisfactorily arranged, and promised Colonel Gordon 1000 of his men for soldiers. The other Wangs, who seemed all unarmed, went out laughing and talking. Going down after this to the East Gate, Gordon saw a large force of Imperialists entering the city, yelling and firing off their muskets into the air, and remonstrated with them for this, as such conduct was likely to frighten the Rebels and cause some misunderstanding. Immediately after General Ching came into the gate, and on unexpectedly seeing his English ally, became much agitated, and looked very pale. On being asked as to the result of the interview between the Wangs and the Futai, Ching hesitated and equivocated so much that Colonel Gordon feared something had gone wrong, but could get no definite information on the subject. The latter then determined to go to the Na Wang's palace, in order to protect it and the family of that chief from the Imperialist soldiers who had begun to plunder. On arriving at the palace he found that it had been already gutted, and was accosted by the Na Wang's uncle, who asked him to come to his house and to conduct there the females of the Na Wang's family. Matters now began to look very threatening; and being unarmed, and accompanied only by his Chinese interpreter, Gordon hesitated; but the entreaties of the uncle were so great that he determined to escort the helpless females, and then to go out for some of his own troops in order to put a check on the Imperialist plunderers. When he got, however, down to the house of the Na Wang's uncle, he was surrounded by some five or six hundred armed Tai-pings, who closed upon him the doors of the courtyard which he had entered, and even refused to allow him to send his interpreter for assistance.

In order to understand the extraordinary and perilous position in which Colonel Gordon was thus placed, it must be borne in mind that by this time the Futai had executed the principal Wangs who had gone out to surrender to him, and had given up the city to be plundered by his troops. Thus, quite unintentionally, Gordon was made to act the part of a hostage for the safety of the Tai-ping Chiefs at the very moment they were being put to a violent death, and was left unarmed and alone in the midst of their infuriated followers when the conduct of the Imperialist soldiers betrayed to the Tai-pings in Soochow the true state of the case. I do not suppose that this result was intended by the Futai, who had some reason to suppose that before this Gordon would have left the city; but, as matters turned out, it is a wonder that the latter escaped a death of torture. He was kept, powerless, in the palace of the Na Wang's uncle from the afternoon of the 6th till the morning of the 7th, surrounded by Tai-pings, who knew that, contrary to agreement, the Imperialist soldiers were plundering and probably murdering in Soochow, and who must have suspected that some evil fate had befallen their Chiefs who had gone out to surrender to the Futai. It would have

been by no means extraordinary if, in these circumstances, they had put Colonel Gordon to death, and they
were probably prevented from doing so only by the
hope that his presence might afford them safety. At
two in the morning he persuaded them to allow his interpreter to take a letter to his boat, which was stationed
at the South Gate, to order the steamers of his force
to seize the Futai and to keep him prisoner until the
Wangs were given up, for at this time it was not known
by Gordon that these latter had been executed. About
3 A.M. a Rebel guide who had started with the interpreter to show the way, returned with the information
that a party of Imperialists had attacked the messenger,
had left him wounded, and had torn up the letters. After
this the Tai-pings allowed the prisoner to go out in
search of his interpreter, and so Colonel Gordon reached
the South Gate, where he was taken prisoner by some
Imperialist soldiers for being in the suspicious company
of the two long-haired Rebels who had accompanied
him to show the way. Escaping from these, he got
round to the East Gate at daybreak, where he found his
body-guard with Major Brookes, and sent them at once
to the palace of the Na Wang's uncle for the protection
of the Tai-pings assembled there. While waiting for
his steamers at this gate, he prevented the further
ingress of Imperialist soldiers, and despatched Captain
Bonnefoi, who came up with the Franco-Chinese, into the
city to prevent massacre. Shortly after General Ching
appeared and attempted to address him, but after what
had occurred Gordon refused to hold any intercourse
with him, and drove him away. A Major Bailey, an
artillery officer, who had been placed under Ching, then
came to explain matters; but even he seemed afraid to
mention what had actually occurred. When asked if

the Wangs had been executed or were still prisoners, he said that he did not know, but that he would bring the Na Wang's son, whom he had in his tent. This youth was the first to tell Gordon of the execution of the Wangs, on which the Colonel immediately crossed a creek and found on the other side eight of their headless bodies, together with the head of the Na Wang. The bodies were gashed in a frightful way, having been cut down the middle.

On witnessing this sight Colonel Gordon's grief and indignation knew no bounds. Though he had not actually guaranteed the safety of the Rebel Chiefs, yet he had assisted in inducing them to surrender, on the supposition that the Futai would treat them in an honourable and humane manner. His first impulse, when his two steamers came in sight, was to obtain hold of the Futai and inflict summary justice on that high official. General Ching, however, gave timely warning of Gordon's incensed state, and Lí very wisely hurried into the city, thus avoiding a meeting. For some days after this Gordon's anxiety to meet with the Futai was only equalled by that of the Futai to keep out of his way, and this was the only period of his campaign during which the Commander of the Ever-Victorious Army burdened himself with carrying arms. When he reached the Futai's boat, which he did very soon, he found it empty, and had to content himself with leaving a letter upbraiding Lí for his treachery. After this Colonel Gordon departed in his steamer for Quinsan, taking with him the Na Wang's son and the head of that unfortunate Chief. He had ordered up his force to assist him in seizing the Futai, but met them on the way down and brought them back to their quarters, where next morning he assembled the officers at headquarters and read to them with great agitation an account of what had occurred at Soochow, concluding with the statement that, as a British officer, he could not serve under the Futai any more unless the Peking Government should take steps to punish such treachery. At the same time he added that, as he did not wish the force to be suddenly disbanded, he would hand it over to the guidance of Major-General Brown, commanding H.B.M. troops in China.

We must now return to the fate of the Tai-ping Wangs, and to the reasons which induced the Futai to execute them as he did. On the first view, his conduct appears inexcusable, and he is specially to be reprobated for the use he seems to have made of Colonel Gordon in inducing the Chiefs to surrender, as also for the great danger to which he exposed that officer; but his action in the matter was not so bad as at first appeared, and can be palliated, if not entirely excused. Three vindications of the Futai have been put forward—one by himself; one by Prince Kung, the head of the Foreign Board at Peking; a third by a body of Chinese who called themselves "The Soochow Committee for the Protection of the Defenceless,"—and all these are interesting as illustrative of Chinese ideas. According to this side of the question, the Tai-ping Chiefs surrendered on the simple condition that their lives would be spared, and from the moment of their submission became subjects of the Empire amenable to all its laws. But when they came out to the Futai they had not yet shaved their heads; they still wore their arms, and their "general bearing was marked by extreme ferocity," being rather that of men who had terms to dictate than of penitent insurgents who had just been allowed to participate in an act of clemency. They insisted that the guardianship of Soochow should

be left in their hands, that all the soldiers then under
their command should be placed at their disposal, and
declared that, if these conditions were not complied with,
they would not return to their allegiance. They also refused to disband their followers ; stated their intention
of holding three of the city gates which were strongly
fortified positions, and demanded pay for their troops.
Such a menacing and intimidating attitude was wholly
unexpected, and could not be met by breaking off negotiations, or permitting the Wangs to return in safety to
the city. To have allowed them to do so, or even to
have given them the slightest warning of noncompliance
with their demands, would have resulted in an immediate
catastrophe. " If the Wangs," says Prince Kung, " had
not been promptly beheaded, not only would the Imperial
soldiers in the city have been slaughtered to a man, but
the enormous force under the command of these Chiefs
would still have remained within the Rebel ranks, and a
subsequent and much greater slaughter would have been
unavoidable ; and violence would thus have been done
to the beneficent principle of Heaven and Earth, which
delights to create, and is opposed to destruction."

There is something peculiarly Chinese in the argu-
ment that the Wangs, having once submitted, were
bound to be obedient to the Futai, and so were liable
to be put to death for their insolent rebellious conduct
towards him ; but, passing that, the other portion of
the excuse put forward seems sufficient if it could
only be satisfactorily proved that the Wangs really did
make the demands imputed to them. There is no
reason, however, to suppose that this portion of the
Futai's statement is untrue ; on the contrary, we may
assume the truth of it, because on no previous occasion
had he been guilty of treachery to Tai-ping Chiefs

who surrendered to him, and he might have turned
the Na Wang to very good use. Assuming, then, that
the Wangs acted as alleged, what was the Futai to
do ?   At Taitsan, as we have previously mentioned, the
Tai-pings had once already cheated the Futai, and managed to murder a number of his troops under cover
of a proposed surrender. Had he refused to comply
with their demands and allowed them to re-enter Soochow, the almost certain result would have been the
immediate massacre of the Imperialists who had entered
the city, together with an attack on his troops outside
the walls, who, scattered, unprepared, and unsupported
by Gordon's force, which had gone to Quinsan, would
have been easily cut up and dispersed. To have arrested
them and kept them in confinement would have been a
troublesome operation, which might have given the other
Chiefs warning of what was going on and allowed them
time to close the city gates, and so cut off the Imperialists inside the city from those who were without. Lí
was in a very difficult and critical position, which imper-
atively demanded sudden unpremeditated action ; and
though no doubt it would have been more honourable
for him to have made the Wangs prisoners, he cannot, in
the circumstances, be with justice severely censured for
having ordered the Tai-ping Chiefs who were in his power,
but who defied his authority, to be immediately killed. It
is also certain that Colonel Gordon need not have been in
a hurry to consider himself as at all responsible for this
almost necessary act, because in a letter to him (among
his correspondence relating to these affairs) from the
Futai, dated the 21st day of the 9th moon of the 2d year
of Tung-che, or the 2d November 1863, I find the following noteworthy passage, which shows that the Governor
did not wish Gordon to interfere at all in regard to the

capitulation of the Soochow Chiefs : " With respect to
Moh Wang and other Rebel leaders' proposal, I am
quite satisfied that you have determined in no way to
interfere. Let Ching look after their treacherous and
cunning management."

The Chiefs executed by Lí were the Wangs Na, Kong,
Sing, Pe ; and the Tien-chwangs Chang, Fan, Wan,
and Wong.

On the 11th December Major-General Brown came
up from Shanghai, saw the Futai, and explained to him
that Gordon's force would not act any more until the
above matter had been decided on at Peking. Gordon
in the meanwhile remained quiet with his force at
Quinsan, and on the 29th December Lí Adong came
to say that the Futai had received an Imperial decree
relating to Gordon, and wished to send a Mandarin to
him with it, and also with various presents. The presents Colonel Gordon indignantly refused, and he also
sent back 10,000 taels, or about .£3500, which the
Emperor proffered in acknowledgment of his services
before Soochow. The decree and the answer to it were
as follows :—

IMPERIAL DECREE.

On the 14th December 1863 the following decree was
issued to the Inner Council :—

Lí memorialises, announcing that, having led his forces to
the attack of Soochow, he has retaken the city. The perusal of
his report has afforded Us joy and satisfaction indeed !

Gordon, as a Tsung-Ping of the province of Kiangsoo, in
command of his auxiliary force, has displayed thorough strategy
and skill, and has put forth most distinguished exertions.

WE ordain that a medal of distinction of the highest class
be conferred upon him ; and further, that he receive a donation
of 10,000 taels, in token of Our approbation. Respect this !

On the same day the following private decree was issued :—

Li is enjoined to communicate Our decree of approval and praise to Gordon for the great bravery and exertions which attended the recapture of Soochow. The donation of 10,000 taels is to be provided and sent to him by Li. Foreign nations already possess orders of merit under the name of "stars." Let, therefore, the decoration of the first class which WE have conferred upon Gordon be arranged in accordance with this system. Respect this !

To this the following answer was returned :—

Major Gordon receives the approbation of his Majesty the Emperor with every gratification, but regrets most sincerely that, owing to the circumstances which occurred since the capture of Soochow, he is unable to receive any mark of his Majesty the Emperor's recognition, and therefore respectfully begs his Majesty to receive his thanks for his intended kindness, and to allow him to decline the same.

At Peking the capture of Soochow was heard of with great satisfaction, and the Emperor acknowledged in the following handsome decree the services of the various high officers engaged in that affair :—

The Grand Secretariat has received the following decree :— Li Hung-chang (Governor of Kiangsoo) reports that the army under his command has captured the city Soochow and exterminated [the Rebels within its walls]. The Rebels had been reduced to great extremity ; and those of them who were desirous of returning to their allegiance, together with the Imperial troops, entered the city, destroyed the Rebel army, and so recaptured the province of Kiangsoo.

The reading of this report has afforded his Majesty sincere delight and gratification.

Soochow, the capital of the province of Kiangsoo, was four years ago captured by the Rebels, and has remained in their hands ever since. The army, acting under orders from Li Hung-chang, captured in succession the lines of Rebel works outside four gates of the city, and [so] struck terror into the enemy in the city that urgent offers of returning to allegiance were made.

On the 30th November the Chung Wang, seeing that the attacks of the Imperial troops were daily becoming more vigorous, and that the Rebels in the city were in a state of disorganisation, fled under cover of night with more than 10,000 of his death-deserving adherents, handing over the city to the old Rebel Moh Wang (Tan Show-kuang), with orders to defend it to the death.

On the 3d and 4th of December the naval and military forces under Cheng Hsio-chi [General Ching], Lí Chow-pin, and Huang I-sheng attacked the different gates of the city, keeping up day and night an incessant attack, which became more vigorous the longer it lasted. Gordon also established himself close to the city walls and opened a cannonade against them.

On the 4th of December the Moh Wang ascended the walls to direct the defence; when at the head of his men, and in the act of issuing orders, a Rebel leader named Kao Ying-kuan, who with others had entered into a conspiracy with a Rebel officer named Wang Yu Wei against him, took him off his guard and stabbed him to death. After killing more than a thousand of Moh Wang's associates, they threw open the gates and came out to give in their allegiance. Cheng Hsio-chi, with the troops under his command, entered the city, and having posted his soldiers, searched out and killed above a thousand of the surviving Rebels. Lí Chow-pin attacked and killed great numbers who were escaping by the Pan Mun, and set at liberty several thousands of prisoners.

The recapture of the provincial capital was thus effected.

His Majesty directs Lí Hung-chang to take advantage of this victory to march with his troops upon Chanchu, which city having been captured, he will join his forces with those before Nanking, sweep that place clear of Rebels [lit., sweep the dens and take possession of the pools], and free the river of their presence.

His Majesty commands the Board of War to confer suitable honours on Tseng Kwo-fan, Minister of State and Governor-General of the Two Kiang, who sent a contingent to assist in the recapture of this noted city.

Lí Hung-chang, since he entered office as Governor of Kiangsoo, has displayed great prudence and calculation, and his skilful tactics have been completely successful; he has again and again captured cities and gained honours on the field of battle; and now the recapture of Soochow by his troops renders him still more worthy of praise; as a mark of his sincere approbation, his Majesty is pleased to confer upon him the honorary title of "Guardian of the Heir-Apparent," and to present him with a yellow robe.

Huang I-sheng and Li Chow-pin, in addition to receiving the hereditary rank of Yun chi Yu [a title with fourth-rank button attached], are recommended to the notice of the Board of War. Cheng Hsio-chi receives the same rank as the above, and in addition is presented with a yellow robe.

Gordon, specially appointed a General in the army of Kiangsoo, was in command of troops who assisted in these operations; his Majesty, in order to evince his approval of the profound skill and great zeal displayed by him, orders him to receive a military decoration of the first rank and a sum of 10,000 taels.

CHAPTER XII.

GORDON'S FURTHER OPERATIONS.

IMPERIALIST SUCCESSES—INACTIVITY OF THE EVER-VICTORIOUS ARMY
— GORDON'S REASONS FOR RETAKING THE FIELD — MR HART'S
REPORT ON THE SOOCHOW "MASSACRE"—SIR FREDERICK BRUCE
APPROVES OF THE RESUMPTION OF OPERATIONS—A LETTER FROM
HIM — GORDON RETAKES THE FIELD — STATE OF THE COUNTRY
OCCUPIED BY REBELS — EVACUATION OF YESING AND LIYANG —
SEVERE REPULSE AT KINTANG — COLONEL GORDON WOUNDED —
TAI-PING ADVANCE TOWARDS QUINSAN—GORDON SUFFERS A DISAS-
TROUS REPULSE AT WAISOO — FATE OF HIS CAPTURED OFFICERS
—IMPERIALIST SUCCESSES IN CHEKIANG — DEATH OF GENERAL
CHING—LI'S MEMORIAL OF HIM—TAKING OF HANGCHOW—CAP-
TURE OF WAISOO—CRUELTY OF THE VILLAGERS—THE REBELLION
NEAR ITS END—DEATH OF MAJOR TAPP—REPULSE AT CHANCHU
— A TAIPING LETTER — STORMING. OF CHANCHU — DEATH OF
THE HU WANG—CLOSE OF THE SERVICES OF THE E. V. A.

AFTER the taking of Soochow, the only cities in the province of Kiangsoo which remained in Rebel occupation
were Yesing, Liyang, Chanchu fu, Tayan, Chuyang, and
Kintang. The whole of the guns and munition captured at Soochow were given over to General Ching,
who had thus plenty of artillery under Major Bailey, one
of Gordon's old officers. The first use he made of his
strengthened force was to start with 8000 men to
attack a strong fort, which was still held by Rebels,
eighteen miles south of Soochow, and without difficulty
drove them out of it back on Kashing fu. Tan, the

O

Futai's brother, also carried on some successful operations to the north of Soochow, and managed to recover the steamer Firefly, which had been pirated at Shanghai.

Meanwhile the Ever-Victorious Army was lying idle in garrison at Quinsan. A great many of its officers and men were lying wounded, and various sums of money were to be paid as compensation to these victims of the recent campaign. About 20,000 taels were expended by the Futai in gifts to the wounded, besides the extra month's pay which he had promised on account of the taking of Soochow. The enforced rest, however, did not agree with the temper of this irregular force. "The officers," Colonel Schmidt writes, " did everything to honour Colonel Gordon, and show in how high esteem they held him ; but they were very jealous of each other, and during January quarrelled constantly with each other over the question as to who should succeed to the command in the event of his leaving." Though the fall of Soochow had given the Tai-pings a great blow, they were by no means completely vanquished even in the province of Kiangsoo ; and European rowdies began again to show themselves, perpetrating at this time several cruel murders. It was also rumoured that Foreigners were again joining the Tai-ping ranks ; Rebel sympathisers began to resume their work, and there was even danger that a portion of the Ever-Victorious Army, disgusted with inactivity, might transfer their allegiance to the Rebel cause.

On considering these facts, Colonel Gordon came to the conclusion that, in existing circumstances, it would be best for him to resume offensive operations. The nature of his force did not allow of its being kept inactive, and it could not be managed properly if only engaged in defending Shanghai. Its dissolution, in the unsettled state of the province, would have involved great cruelty to the people of Kiangsoo, who, on the faith of the protection which it afforded, had commenced to reoccupy their cities and resume the cultivation of their fields. Moreover, in the then condition of the Ever-Victorious Army, there was good hope that the province could be cleared of Rebels in two months, and reduced to a state of order and peace; whereas, if the army were dissolved or kept in a state of inactivity at Shanghai, a year would probably elapse before such a consummation could be arrived at. As to the conduct of the Futai, that officer had been warned to consult Colonel Gordon before ordering executions. Even if the Chinese Government had removed him, that would not have much mended matters, as his successor would probably have been quite as objectionable, if not more so, and a willing instrument in any plan for avenging his predecessor's disgrace. In fact, the removal of Lí from his high position at the dictation of Foreigners, was an event to be avoided, because it would have been a serious blow to the independence of the Chinese Empire, and would have caused Tseng Kwo-fan and other powerful Mandarins to disregard Imperial edicts. There was also the danger of the force being reconstituted by Lí, and placed under some other European, in which case the British Government would have had no control over it. Taking all these circumstances into consideration, Colonel Gordon resolved to sacrifice his own personal feelings, which urged him to retire; and his indignation at the massacre of the Wangs must have somewhat abated from its original intensity when he learned all the circumstances of the case.

This view of Gordon's duty was taken very strongly by Mr Robert Hart, the head of the Imperial Maritime

Customs, a gentleman who had then, and still retains,
the confidence and high respect both of the Chinese
Government and of the Foreign community. Mr Hart
made a full investigation into the circumstances of the
" Soochow Massacre,"* and found that " the taking of
the great city of Soochow had been followed by no more
bloodshed, and by no more questionable act, than the
beheading of about ten Rebel leaders." He came to the
conclusion that " there was no act of premeditated treachery," and that the Futai suddenly and unexpectedly
found himself placed in a dilemma, from which he saw
no other way of extricating himself with safety to general interests than by acting as he did. He also threw
doubt upon the supposition that it was any feeling of
confidence in Gordon which induced the Wangs to surrender, and noted several facts which went to prove that
it was the hopes held out by General Ching on which
alone they relied. On the general subject of Gordon's
position and prospects, Mr Hart wrote : "Disaffected
people—rowdy Foreigners and lawless Chinese—have
been immensely delighted with the inaction of the last
two months. Merchants fear to return to Soochow, not
knowing but that Gordon in his wrath may with his
men join the Rebels, and their continuance at Shanghai
is delightful to the owners of land and houses. The
Rebels themselves don't know what to make of the occurrence, and their expiring energies are again fanned into
a flame. His appearance in the field will have immediate results ; rowdies will commence to see that their
game is hopeless, and that they had better leave China ;
Chinese traders will again flock back to Soochow ; and
the Rebels will again lose heart. Chanchu fu will

* See his letter to Sir Frederick Bruce, Blue-Book, China, No. 7
(1864), p. 25.

soon fall, and that will be followed very probably by the
capitulation of Hangchow, Wuchu, and Keahing, and
the other two or three small cities still held by the
Tai-pings in this province and in Chekiang. Whether
a stand will be made or not at Nanking, Gordon
thinks very problematical, but he is rather of opinion
that it will not fight.* The destiny of China is at the
present moment in the hands of Gordon more than of
any other man, and if he is encouraged to act vigorously,
the knotty question of 'Tai-pingdom' versus 'Union in
the Cause of Law and Order,' † will be solved before the
end of May, and quiet will at length be restored to this
unfortunate and sorely-tried country. . . . Personally,
Gordon's wish is to leave the force as soon as he can.
Now that Soochow has fallen, there is nothing more that
he can do, whether to add to his own reputation, or to
retrieve that of British officers generally, tarnished by
Holland's defeat at Taitsan. He has little or nothing
personally to gain from future successes, and as he, has
himself to lead in all critical moments, and is constantly exposed to danger, he has before him the not
very improbable contingency of being hit sooner or later.
But he lays aside his personal feelings ; and seeing well
that, if he were now to leave the force, it would in all
probability go at once to the Rebels, or cause some other
disaster, he consents to remain with it for a time."

Some time before this it had been decided that the
policy of Britain in China was to support the Imperialist cause, and generally to favour the speediest possible
suppression of the Tai-pings. This was a wise and
humane policy, though it was foolishly accompanied by
absurd professions of neutrality, which sometimes misled

* As turned out to be the case.
† The title of the reigning Emperor.

the latter, and afforded Colonel Sykes and other Rebel sympathisers an appearance of legitimate grounds of complaint ; and it was adopted from an enlightened regard to our own interests, and not from any affection for the Imperialists or dislike to the Rebels.   In accordance with it Sir Frederick Bruce also gave his approval and support to Gordon in resuming operations.   He got the Chinese Government to promise that, when employing a Foreign officer, the rules of warfare as practised among Foreign nations would be strictly observed.   To Colonel Gordon he wrote on the 12th March 1864 :—

My concurrence in the step you have taken is founded in no small measure on my knowledge of the high motives which have guided you while in command of the Chinese force, of the disinterested conduct you have observed in pecuniary questions, and of the influence in favour of humanity you exercised in rescuing Burgevine and his misguided associates from Soochow. I am aware of the perseverance with which, in the face of serious obstacles and much discouragement, you have steadily pursued the pacification of the province of Kiangsoo ; in relieving it from being the battle-field of the insurrection, and in restoring to its suffering inhabitants the enjoyments of their homes and the uninterrupted exercise of their industry, you may console yourself with the assurance that you are rendering a service to true humanity, as well as to great material interests.   It would be a serious calamity, and addition to our embarrassments in China, were you compelled to leave your work incomplete, and were a sudden dissolution or dispersion of the Chinese force to lead to the recurrence of that state of danger and anxiety from which, during the last two years, Shanghai has suffered. . . . I approve of your not awaiting the result of the inquiry into the Futai's proceedings at Soochow, provided you take care that your efforts in favour of humanity are not in future defeated by the Chinese authorities.*

In a more private, but still semi-official letter, Sir Frederick entered into his reasons for pursuing this

* Blue-Book, China, No. 7 (1864), p. 22.

course ; and I give it here on account of the clear way in
which it describes the position, and also as a refutation of
the charges of laziness and of want of ability which have
sometimes been brought against this British Minister :—

PEKING, *March* 3, 1864.

MY DEAR MAJOR GORDON,—I only received yesterday your
letter telling me that you had again taken the field.   I have not
yet seen the Governor's proclamation, but I have obtained a
positive promise in writing from this Government that, in cases
of capitulations where you are present, nothing is to be done
without your consent; and I will inform the Prince of Kung
that it is upon the faith of this engagement that you are authorised to act.   If it is observed, scenes like that at Soochow will
not be repeated, and the interests of humanity will have the
benefit of you as a protector, instead of being committed to the
unchecked mercies of Chinese officials.

I did not ask for the Governor's dismissal ; I confined myself
in the first instance to asking for an inquiry, to which he was
entitled before being punished, and to supporting you in the
course you had taken.   If he has been generally successful as
Governor, it is not to be expected that this Government would
venture to remove him for an act with respect to which they
are more impressed by the extenuating circumstances than by
the treachery.   In the decree condemning Shung Pow to death,
one of the chief charges against him was that he had pardoned
some Rebel leaders who a year afterwards rose again in insurrection.   If it be true that the Chiefs of Soochow insisted upon
a quasi-independent command, which would virtually have left
Soochow in their power, and would have enabled them to take
advantage of any favourable circumstances to begin again their
career of pillage, I can understand that Governor Lí shrank
from the responsibility of granting such terms to them, and pre-
ferred treating them as contumacious, and setting the Government at defiance by their attitude and by their demands.   Such
a proceeding, though abhorrent to our ideas, can hardly be
termed a gross and deliberate act of treachery.

It is impossible for us to change suddenly the ideas and
conduct of the Chinese ; and the Taitsan affair showed that the
Tai-pings were not one whit more advanced in good faith than

the Imperialists. But the interests of trade and of the population of China demand the restoration of peace and tranquillity, and we do a good act in assisting the Government with that view. If this insurrection continues in force in the seaboard provinces, I see a great danger not far off arising from filibusters and corsairs.

Burgevine is a Southerner; the trading interests of America in China are Northern, and Burgevine attributes his treatment to the British authorities at Shanghai. It would not surprise me if he and the Alabama, &c., were to make common cause with the insurgents, and then, you may depend upon it, they would directly attack the Foreign settlements, where most plunder is to be had. You will do well to urge the Governor to take measures, either by steamers or by batteries, to prevent lorchas or armed vessels going up the Yangtsze river. It might be easy for a force of these adventurers to raise the siege of Nanking, and then advance again on the province of Kiangsoo. It will depend much on his future conduct, and on the readiness he shows to adopt good suggestions, how far I press the affair of Soochow. I am not implacable where offences are not repeated.

I beg you to do nothing rash under the pressure of excitement, and, above all, to avoid publishing in newspapers accounts of your differences with the Chinese authorities. We have supported this Government from motives of interest, not from sentiment; and as our interests remain the same, we must endeavour to get over our difficulties without taking any step which would neutralise all the results of the policy we have hitherto pursued, and which you have carried out so successfully. In the resolution you have now come to, you are acting wisely and rightly, and you may depend upon my lightening your responsibility by giving you the most cordial official support. Fortunately I have not committed myself with respect to Lí, so far as to make it difficult for me to be friends with him, provided he gives rise to no more scandals, and deals with Foreigners and Foreign interests so as not to give grounds for complaint. If you think it expedient you may hint this to him.

The objects we ought to keep in view are to restore order in Kiangsoo and Chekiang, to cut off the insurgents from communication with filibusters, and to reduce gradually the disciplined corps, so that it may not become a source of danger.

If the Chinese will put down piracy, and stop vessels not con-
forming to the regulations limiting arms, &c., I will direct the
gunboats to support them. But vessels under Foreign flags can
onlybe searched by a Chinese authority; and all we can do is
to support him if he is resisted in trying to search.—Yours
faithfully,

FREDERICK W. A. BRUCE.

When Colonel Gordon determined on retaking the field
there were two districts occupied by the Rebels—one to
the south of the Taiho Lake, including Hangchow, Kashing fu, and several other towns; the other to the north,
containing Nanking, Tayan, Kintang, and Chuying—the
two being about fifty miles distant from each other, and
communicating through Yesing and Liyang. Immediately after the fall of Soochow, the Tai-ping posts in its
vicinity—such as Wusieh and Pingwang in Kiangsoo, and
Pinghoo, Haiyuen, Kanshu, and Haining, in Chekiang—
were either evacuated or surrendered to the Futai, his
treatment of the Wangs having had apparently no effect
in preventing Rebel chiefs from submitting to his mercy.
Hence it appeared to Gordon that his best plan would
be to attack Yesing and Liyang, so as to separate the two
Rebel districts from each other, and leave those of the
south to be dealt with by Captain d'Aiguibelle, an officer
in the French service, who, with Franco-Chinese, was
associated with a Mandarin force; while in the north
Tseng Kwo-fan and his brothers could proceed, undisturbed, with the reduction of Nanking. In order to accomplish this work, he had to go a considerable distance
from Quinsan, the basis of his operations, and so found it
necessary to burden his force with commissariat supplies.

Leaving Colonel Morant and 200 men as a garrison at
Quinsan, he started with his whole force in bitterly cold
and snowy weather; but, delaying at Wusieh, did not

leave that place till the 27th. The country between
Wusieh and Yesing was almost destitute of people, and
the few to be found were in the last stages of starvation
—a fact which shows strikingly the result of Tai-ping
rule ; for since 1860 no Imperialists had been in that part
of the province, and no fighting had been carried on
there.   On advancing with a small party to reconnoitre
Yesing, Colonel Gordon found it was a small walled
city, two miles in circumference, with a broad ditch and
small lakes on its east and west sides.   The reconnoitring
party was driven away by a very accurate fire of a 12-
pounder gun at the North Gate.   The result was that he
resolved to cross the lake at the east side—from which
direction the Hyson was expected—to take possession of
the village at the south-east angle, and then, by taking
the stockades on the south side, to cut off communication with Liyang, the next Rebel city.   When this was
done, as it was without much difficulty, the village referred to was found full of the most miserable objects,
dead and alive, of both sexes and of all ages.   Those
who still remained in life had been driven to eat human
flesh, and the unburied bodies of the dead were in a condition which showed that much of this revolting food
had been consumed.   And this, it should be noted, was
under the walls of a city near which there had been no
Imperialists for more than four years.   After the stockades in front of the East Gate were taken, the mass of the
Rebels quitted Yesing by night, and it surrendered next
day.   As the troops were thus deprived of an opportunity of looting, and were rather dissatisfied at being
brought on a perilous march into the Tai-ping country
instead of being sent up to Nanking, they showed some
symptoms of insubordination, which had to be severely
repressed, one of their number being taken out and shot.

The starving villagers, however, were allowed to pillage in a small way, and so got enough rice to support them for some time.

Moving on against Liyang, he found the Rebel chiefs so much out of heart that they at once surrendered it to him. In that neighbourhood, also, nothing but misery and devastation prevailed; and even some of his own troops had to suffer from hunger for a few days, as no food could be obtained except what they had brought with them. "Hundreds of dead bodies," writes one of his officers, "were strewn along the roads—people who died from starvation; and even the few who were yet alive watched one of their comrades dying, so as to obtain some food off his dead body. Major Gordon gave as much food to these poor creatures as he could spare, but it was not sufficient to satisfy them all." Liyang was found to have a population of 20,000, and permission was given to all the Rebels who chose to do so, to leave the city with their effects. One thousand of the Tai-ping soldiers were enlisted into the Ever-Victorious Army, and were formed into a separate regiment. This city was three miles in circumference, with a formidable ditch, and a stronger system of stockades round it than any which Colonel Gordon had before met. It was well stocked with provisions, which were given to the starving people of the neighbourhood, who had not even rice for seed when the place was surrendered; but twenty-five gunboats were here taken and joined to Gordon's flotilla. When the commander was going into the town, he was called back by some Rebels to a large boat where the mother of the She Wang, or Attendant King, his wife, and his son, a child of seven years old, were kept prisoners. The Rebels wanted to kill them, because this King, who had originally been a butcher, had been cruel

to them in many ways, having shortly before burned a
man to death for meditating treachery, and had been
encouraged in his cruelty by his venerable mother, who
upon her capture behaved in a very violent and obstre-
perous manner. These people were all sent to Quinsan,
and from thence safely forwarded to the Attendant King.

After sending a letter to Kintang offering terms of
surrender, to which no answer was returned, Colonel
Gordon on the 15th March reconnoitred the route leading to that place, as the Hyson had been unable to find
any navigable route to it ; and next day, in spite of heavy
rains, he marched towards it with the 1st, 2d, and 5th
Regiments, and a large force of artillery mounted on
gunboats, leaving the newly-raised regiment and the remainder of his force for the protection of Liyang. On
the 17th he advanced personally within a mile of the
walls, and sent in a letter offering the garrison their lives
and property if they would surrender. About the same
time he received a letter from the Futai, announcing
that the steamer Tsatlee * had been seized by rowdies
at Shanghai, and taken up to the Rebels, and asking
him to come back to attack Chanchu fu, where the
Rebels had defeated the Imperialists, and had been
threatening an advance. The weather was so wet at
this time that the troops could only be moved with
great difficulty ; but on the 20th March they took up a
position at about 1200 yards from the walls of Kintang,
which were not surrounded by stockades, and which, contrary to the usual custom of the Tai-pings, were not

---

* The Foreigners who pirated this steamer were to have received £20,000
from the Rebels for doing so, but in their ignorance they ran her into the
possession of the Imperialist force under General Ching at Kashing fu.
The ringleaders were tried at Shanghai, and Morris, one of their number,
who had also been engaged in the capture of the Firefly, was sentenced to
ten years' penal servitude.

adorned with defiant flags. The want of flags, however, was a mere ruse on the part of the Tai-pings, who
were prepared to make, and did make, a most desperate
resistance. The north-east angle of the wall, on which
an enfilade fire could be brought, having been fixed on
as the best point of attack, the troops were moved up to
their several stations next day, and the heavy boats with
artillery were placed near the wall under cover of night.

At 9 A.M. on the 21st March everything was ready for
opening fire, when despatches were received from the
Futai, announcing that a large force of 7000 Rebels, commanded by Chung Wang's son, had left Chanchu fu,
turned the flank of the Imperialists, were threatening
Wusieh, had captured Fushan, and were besieging Chanzu, only thirty miles from Quinsan, the headquarters and
depot of the Ever-Victorious Army. This was startling
intelligence for Colonel Gordon ; but he thought that if
he retired without attacking Kintang the Rebels would
be much encouraged, whereas, if he took that place, he
could, by advancing on Chanchu, compel the Hu Wang,
who commanded there, to order back his expeditionary
force.

Fire was accordingly opened, and after three hours a
very fair breach was made in the walls, the Rebels not
showing much fight ; but whenever the storming-parties
for the assault appeared, and were pushed in boats across
the creek beneath the walls, the Tai-pings crowded to
the breach in a most determined manner, and swarmed
on the parapet, throwing powder-bags, stinkpots, and
every species of missile into the boats, which had in
consequence to retire and reland the troops. When the
artillery fire was reopened on the breach the defenders
disappeared, and the troops again being got into order,
were pushed over a stone bridge which was found stand-

ing in the neighbourhood. The second storming-party, however, was also repulsed, and Major Kirkham, who led it, was severely wounded. Colonel Gordon himself, who took part in the assault, was shot through the leg; but silencing one of his body-guard, who cried out that the commander was hit, he stood giving orders until he fainted from loss of blood, and was carried back to his boat. This was the first and only time that Gordon was wounded during his fourteen months of fighting; and the wonder only is, exposed as he constantly was, that he escaped so lightly. The sergeant-major of the 1st Regiment, which had come up the day before, mounted the breach with his regimental flag, but this was wrested from him. Notwithstanding the losses which the stormers had sustained, Major Brown, Colonel Gordon's aide-de-camp, and brother of the General commanding her Majesty's forces in China, headed a third assault, and bore his commander's flag up the breach; but the attack failed, and he too was wounded, and had to be carried back. On this Colonel Gordon, having no fresh regiments on hand with which to make a renewed effort, determined on withdrawing his force, which was effected without further loss, the troops resuming the positions they had occupied previous to the assault. During this unsuccessful affair not less than 100 of the rank-and-file of the assailants were killed and wounded; 15 officers were wounded, and 2 officers, Major Taite and Captain Banning, were killed.

During the night frequent attempts were made by the Rebels to set fire to the boats; they also came out and attacked sentries, and even crept up on their bellies and threw powder-bags, with slow matches attached, into the tents, which caused great confusion. The whole of the troops were glad when it became light enough to move

away, which was effected with order and without further
loss, though the Tai-pings made several attempts at
molestation.

On the 24th the whole force was again concentrated
at Liyang, where Colonel Gordon received further disastrous intelligence, being apprised that the Faithful King
was himself in possession of Fushan.   Immediately on
learning this, though unable to stand, owing to his wound,
he left the greater portion of his force in garrison at Liyang,
under General Lí Adong, and himself started for Wusieh,
along with the Light Artillery, the 4th Regiment, which
was only 400 strong, and 600 Liyang men, who a few
days before had been Tai-pings.   One scarcely knows
here whether most to admire the pluck, or to wonder
at the confidence, of the wounded commander.   However, on reaching Wusieh on the morning of the 25th, he
received despatches conveying the gratifying intelligence
that the enemy had been driven back from that place,
that though Fushan had been retaken, Chanzu continued
to hold out, and that the Imperialists still held the stockades at Chanchu.   Advancing the same day about ten
miles to the south-west of Kongyin, he drove parties of
Rebels before him, and cut off the retreat of the Chung
Wang's son, who had suffered a repulse at Chanzu, and
was attempting to return to Chanchu, by the way he had
gone.

Colonel Gordon's wound and weakness seemed only to
have increased his eagerness to be at the Rebels ; for
on the 26th he pushed on, with only his Light Artillery
and 400 of his Rifles, through a district where the houses
had been burned and the people butchered in every direction by the Tai-pings.   At dusk they drove a Rebel force
away from three burning villages, and then halted for
the night, which was spent in considerable anxiety, as

during nearly the whole of it the enemy were engaged in firing on the sentries, and trying to ride through the lines of the small disciplined force. The next morning Gordon, who had to direct operations reclining in his boat, drove the Rebels out of the village they held in front of his position, but had immediately to retire before a larger body of them which came down on his boats. Nearly 100 of these latter, however, were cut off from their companions, and bayoneted by the disciplined Chinese, while another body of them were forced over a bridge under fire of a howitzer. These operations brought Gordon's troops up to the foot of a range of hills near Chowchang, over which the Rebels were driven towards Waisoo; but finding that, if he continued to attack the Rebels in that direction, he would drive them into a new district of country which they had not visited, and on to Chanzu, he stopped to concentrate his troops, and determined to operate against the left of the Rebel line, so as to drive the enemy on Kongyin. In these rapid operations Gordon had a special object, which justified the risk he ran, and the exertions he demanded from his troops. The Tai-pings, who had issued out of Chanchu, had taken a bend towards the shore of the Yangtsze, with the hope of obtaining possession of Quinsan; and Gordon sought to compel them to abandon that design by attacking their line not at its extremities, but at its centre, so causing them to contract like a broken-backed snake. Finding their centre to be at Waisoo, he waited a day or two till reinforced by the Liyang men, and then advanced on Waisoo, being himself with the artillery in boats, whilst Colonels Howard and Rhode proceeded by land, being ordered to incline to the right before they reached the Rebel stockades, where they would join the boats.

Colonel Gordon and his artillery went on till they came close to the enemy's position, but there found neither the infantry nor any signs of their appearance. The consequence was that the boats were very nearly destroyed by the Tai-pings, who came out to the attack ; for the banks of the creek were too high to allow of the guns being used, and it was with great difficulty that a retreat was effected to the encampment from which he had set out. Arriving there, everything was found in confusion ; boats were leaving, men were fleeing, and naked persons were swimming the creek in their anxiety to escape from danger.

It turned out that his infantry had been repulsed, and had met with a very severe loss indeed. When they went out in the morning Colonel Rhode pushed on his regiment to the village of Waisoo, where there was a Tai-ping camp, strongly intrenched and stockaded. Instead of carrying this place at the point of the bayonet, he injudiciously halted before it for an hour, while he and Colonel Howard distributed their men by companies in several directions. This was perceived by the Tai-pings who swarmed among the neighbouring hills, from whence they could see how small a force was opposed to them, and in the valleys of which they had a considerable force of cavalry concealed. By degrees the Rebels worked down between Rhode and Howard. Soon they came rushing on in thousands, and the cavalry issued out of their hiding-places and attacked on both flanks. On seeing themselves thus hemmed in, the 6th, or newly-raised Liyang Regiment, was seized with panic, broke through the Rebel ranks behind, and threw themselves upon Colonel Howard's regiment, which was thus thrown into confusion, and began to retire gradually. The Tai-pings pressed on in thousands from every side, and their

P

horsemen charged into the disciplined Chinese, armed
with a sword in each hand, and cutting down their enemies right and left. The result was that the 4th, the
best regiment in the Ever-Victorious Army, and the
600 Liyang men took to flight. All attempts to rally
them were made in vain; it was a race for life over
three miles up to Lukachow, where the pursuers were
checked by the reserve at the camp. About 400 men
were either killed or taken prisoners, and the officers
suffered especially. Colonel Rhode, who was in front
of the whole affair, was fortunate enough to catch a
Rebel pony, otherwise he could hardly have managed to
escape. Captains Gibbon, Chirikoff, and Hughes, with
Lieutenants Polkson, Graves, Pratt, and Dowling, were
either killed in the fight, or taken prisoners and then
murdered. None of the bodies could be recovered at
the time, and great anxiety was felt as to the fate of
those who had been taken prisoners, but all their bodies
were afterwards found, decapitated and otherwise mutilated. It was not to be expected that the Tai-pings
would spare those taken in arms against them, when the
country villages around were full of young women and
children whose throats the Rebels had cut, and whose
bodies they had split open. This was by far the most
disastrous affair which had ever happened to Colonel
Gordon, and he was much incensed at the surviving
officers for not having kept proper reserves and looked
better after their flanks—which culpable neglect was the
main cause of their being surrounded and defeated by a
mere rabble, armed for the most part only with spears
and knives. The Liyang Regiment fought very bravely,
and so did the 4th, for some time. If the men had been
formed into square, which they knew well enough how
to do, they might easily have repulsed their assailants,

notwithstanding the determination and strategy which these latter showed ; but no attempt was made by the officers to form square until it was too late, and so the force was taken at a great disadvantage.

After this repulse Colonel Gordon withdrew his men on the 31st March to Siangchow, about thirteen miles north of Wusieh, and sent down his wounded to Quinsan.   He also ordered up the 3d Regiment, and occupied himself in bringing his demoralised troops again into order until the 3d April, when he went up and encamped about two miles from Waisoo, where he met the Futai, who had come from Soochow with 6000 Imperialists.

While these events were going on to the north of the Taiho Lake, General Ching had been operating at Kashing fu to the south ; and Tso, Chetai, along with the Franco-Chinese, had been engaged investing Hangchow. The former of these Imperialist generals carried the stockades in front of Kashing fu on the 17th March, after a sharp resistance, but found that the Rebels had constructed a series of small forts about 150 yards outside the walls of the city, which rendered further progress very difficult, though he got excellent information as to what was going on inside from spies whom he had previously sent to join the Rebels, and who were constantly coming out to him.   At night he carried two of these forts, and established batteries under the charge of Colonel Bailey, whom Gordon had given for instruction in the use of artillery.   On the 19th he stormed twice without success, and on the 20th the fire of the heavy guns was reopened and another assault given, when the Rebels gave way and the place was captured. On this occasion the Ting Wang and Yung Wang were killed—the one by a shell, and the other by the Imperialists. Ting Wang had walled up the gateways just previous to the attack, which prevented any of his men escaping, and led to a desperate resistance. Ching, the Imperial commander, was wounded in the head by a bullet (from the effects of which he died on the 15th April) as he was trying the depth of the water in the ditch just before the assault commenced; and this, together with the determined character of the resistance, led the Imperialist soldiers to give no mercy.

The death and previous services of this General were noticed at length in a report to the Emperor by Lí Hung-chang, dated 12th May 1864, and I give the following abridged translation of that document, because it is so strikingly illustrative of Chinese ideas and customs, and affords such a contrast to our own cold official way of acknowledging military services:—

Ching, the Tsung-Ping of Nanchang, was formerly presented with the hereditary rank of Shao-pei [Yun chi Wei]. He was subsequently made Patulu [a Manchu distinction]. Fiercely he attacked the city of Kashing, where he was wounded in the head by a ball which pierced his brain. He fainted, but was afterwards restored to consciousness and borne back [to Soochow] to be put under medical treatment. He himself knew that his wound was desperate, but he refused to take medicine. I over and over again exhorted him to submit to treatment, and I called in doctors who professed to cure both internal and external maladies, so that he at last consented to put himself in their hands. His mind and speech thus soon became clear. I left Soochow on the 7th April for the purpose of following up the Rebels, but at the moment of starting I visited him. He said that although the Rebels had been defeated, their strength was still not to be despised, and he told me to order the officers to be careful in battle. He also remarked that brave men were not easily obtained, and bitterly regretted his own fate, by which he was prevented from following up his duty to the country in exterminating the Rebels. He sobbed and sighed, and tears came into his eyes while he was speaking to

me. I, on the other hand, bade him be of good courage, and
told him that he would thus hasten his recovery, and that
it was not necessary for him to grieve and be anxious. When
I departed I left directions that the local Mandarins should
visit him from time to time. While I was at Kongyin attacking the Rebels there, a report suddenly reached me that Ching
was gradually sinking. His senses had not, however, deserted
him. On the 14th April he called his servant, and ordered
him to bring the Yellow Jacket presented to him by your
Majesty, and assist him to put it on. He then bowed his head
towards your Majesty's palace, and walked round his room.
Seeing tea on the table, he took up a cupful and attempted to
drink, but the fluid could not pass down his throat. By this
he was much moved, and wept. He ordered Han Chu, a Chi-
chao who had the superintendence of the camp, to mount a
horse and come to me, to beg that I would carefully follow
out my design of destroying the Rebels. He further said that
he knew he could not see me again in the provincial city.
There was not a particle of selfishness in his recommendations.
At the time when he felt death approaching, he bemoaned the
unfinished state of the work he had cut out for himself. He
felt that he had not returned the favours heaped on him by your
Majesty. The fluid of his brain continued to run out of the
wound, and on the 15th April, at twelve o'clock at night, he
died. I was excessively grieved. All the military officers cried
bitterly. Every one, whether belonging to Kiangsoo or to
Chekiang, whether Mandarins or scholars or common people,
lamented his death.

I then examined into Ching's previous history, and I discovered that he came from Tungchen hien, in the province
of Nganhwui, whence, during the Rebel troubles, he was taken
as a prisoner. The Four-Eyed Dog, Ying, placed great confidence in him. Ching, because he saw that the Rebels op-
pressed the people, at length made an attempt to get away
from them. The Rebels, however, managed to secure him again,
and shut him up so that he could not escape. In the fourth
month of the eleventh year of the Emperor, whose style was
Hien-fung, Tseng Kwo-tsun, the Futai of Chekiang, led his soldiers to Nganking. Ching, without mentioning the affair to
anybody, came over to the camp occupied by Tseng Chun-kan

[Tseng Kwo-tsun's brother], and surrendered himself. He was instantly recognised as a superior man, and one far above the general run of Rebel officers who had joined the camp, and was sent with the expedition which recovered Nganking, where his bravery was most conspicuous. The Governor-General, Tseng Kwo-fan, reported the affair to your Majesty, and pledged himself for Ching's worth. At the same time I myself was at Nganking, and constantly heard of Ching's exploits, as well as of his wisdom, daring, and varied ability. Shortly afterwards, when your Majesty ordered me to hurry to Shanghai, I begged Tseng Kwo-fan to allow me to carry with me Ching's two camps. . . .

When Soochow fell, Kow Ywen-kuan (who was the chief man amongst the Rebel Wangs who submitted to us), with eight others, proposed to divide the city into two parts. At this time these fellows had about 200,000 men under their command, and they thought that they could altogether neutralise any effort we might make. If this demand had been granted, and if, subsequently, the slightest opposition had been made to their wishes, they would have had " my head in chancery" in no time. But Ching told me, that as he had formerly been among the Rebels, he well knew their mode of thought, and that as their crimes had been outrageous, their punishment ought to be proportionately severe. " Cut off," said he, " the heads of their leaders, and their myriads of followers will instantly subside into insignificance. You will thus secure the tranquillity of the city." I therefore immediately ordered the execution of the Wangs, and restored tranquillity to their followers. Thus were the mighty difficulties which at first presented themselves at once solved. He was able to calculate beforehand, and he was also able to act with decision. Among the leaders of modern times there were few like him. When Gordon heard of his death he wept and groaned. He had seen with his own eyes how excellent he was as a general. Indeed, so highly did Gordon value him that he begged me to give him as a keepsake the two banners which Ching used to carry into battle, that he might bear them to his own country, and thus preserve the memory of one he loved so well. Ching possessed a mind of no ordinary depth and capacity. His plans and their subsequent execution were most clearly and minutely considered. His own countrymen and

Foreigners alike admired him; and had Heaven vouchsafed to him many years of life, it would have been seen that his labours were not finished at the period of his actual death. . . .

Now, since it was in the service of the country that he lost his life, is it not right that I should beg your Majesty to manifest your favour towards him in the manner due to a Ti-Tu who dies on the field of battle ? I also beg your Majesty to give him a posthumous rank, and to cause the story of his life to be inscribed on the records of this dynasty. Moreover, I would suggest that at Nganking fu, Soochow fu, and Kashing fu commemorative temples be raised to his exclusive honour, so as to celebrate his faithfulness. If your Majesty be pleased to do this, it will be a proof of your extraordinary favour.

I would further inform your Majesty that at the time of writing the above despatch, I received the Imperial edict, dated the 4th April, relative to the gifts to be presented to Ching, on account of the conquest of Kashing—viz., a white jade feather ornament, a white jade thumb-ring, a jade-handled knife, and a pair of pouches. I reverently ordered these presents to be carried to Soochow, and presented to Ching's family, to be placed before his coffin to solace his noble soul.

The Franco-Chinese, under D'Aiguïbelle, having arrived at Hangchow in February, made an attack, in combination with the Imperialists under Tso, on the Rebel stockades outside the city, and carried about a dozen of them early in March. After erecting a battery and breaching the South Gate, they assaulted on the 9th of the month, but were repulsed ; and also made another ineffectual attempt on the 12th March, when a number of their officers were wounded. The point of attack was badly chosen, because the gate was placed in bastions projecting from the rampart, so when the front wall was breached, there still remained another to be attacked behind. This place might have held out much longer had not Tsah, formerly a Tai-ping with the title of Wai Wang, threatened its communications, and led the Rebels to vacate it on the 21st. Lí, Futai, considered this eva-

cuation as a consequence of the taking of Kashing fu;
but not so did Tso, who, being Chetai of Chekiang, did
not much like General Ching, a Kiangsoo official, taking
a city in his province. Immediately after this the Rebels
evacuated Huhang, and fell back on Wuchu fu, close to
the south-west corner of the Taiho Lake. Thus they
were cleared almost entirely out of the district to the
south of that immense sheet of water; but small parties
of them took refuge in the uninhabited mountains which
formed the boundary between the provinces of Chekiang
and Nganhwui, and which run up by Kuanteche and
Liyang all the way from Hangchow to Nanking; for
the Imperialists did not care to follow them into the
fastnesses of those sterile hills, where starvation awaited
them.

We must now return to Colonel Gordon, who had
nearly recovered from his wound, and had put his
augmented force in movement in the neighbourhood
of Waisoo on the 6th April. The Tai-pings who had
so lately repulsed his force were in a rather dangerous
position; for behind them, on the north, beyond a range
of hills, was the river Yangtsze, held by Imperial fleets;
on the east was General Kwo Sung-ling, with a large
force of Imperialists; on the south-east, the disciplined
Chinese; on the south and west were also large Imperialist forces; while to the north-west Kongyin was
held by the Imperialists. Between the latter place
and the Rebel stockades at Waisoo the road to Tayan
passed; and now the Imperialists held no force upon
it, but had broken all its bridges past Kongyin, and
had arranged so that the Rebels would imagine this road
to be still open for retreat. As his men were rather
timid after their recent loss, Colonel Gordon advanced

with the greatest caution towards Waisoo on the 11th April, and found that town surrounded by strong stockades and breastworks. Having opened a fire from the 24-pounder howitzers, he moved the 4th Regiment and two mounted guns to the north of the Rebel position, which was its weakest side. This disconcerted the Tai-pings, who had expected to be attacked only from the south—the direction from which the howitzers were firing. The stockades on the north were taken with very little fighting; and on finding this, the Rebels suddenly vacated the town, and after a little desultory skirmishing began to retreat from the neighbourhood. Li's Imperialist soldiers then followed them up, and drove them in every direction over the country towards Tayan. Waisoo was found full of rice, which had been collected from the surrounding country. In it were discovered the bodies of upwards of 150 of the Liyang men who had been taken prisoners in the affair of the 31st March, and the mutilated corpses of the seven unfortunate European officers were buried with military honours.

Next day, when Colonel Gordon followed up the Rebels in the direction of Kongyin, the villagers of the country turned out to his assistance, armed with every sort of weapon, and showed no mercy to the Rebels, who suffered fearfully among the creeks which abounded, and whose parties were cut up in every direction. It would have been difficult even for a disciplined force to have withstood the attacks of these infuriated peasants, whose houses had been burnt, and whose relatives had been wantonly murdered, by the Tai-ping marauders. Several Chiefs and a great number of ponies were taken. All the Cantonese, Hupeh, and Kwangsi Rebels who were taken were immediately executed. Of the expeditionary force barely 1000 escaped back to Tayan and Chanchu.

Colonel Gordon then collected his entire force, which at this time numbered about 3000 men, and advanced to assist Futai Lí and the Imperialist troops who were engaged in besieging Chanchu fu. At this time the Rebellion was very near its last gasp ; for in Chekiang the Tai-pings held only the cities of Wuchu and Chang-ching ; in Kiangsoo they had only Nanking, Tayan, and Chanchu ; in Kiangsi their footing was confined to three towns held by the Che Wang ; and in the remainder of China they made no appearance at all. Hence it seemed practicable as well as important to prevent them making their escape from Chanchu to ravage fresh districts ; and Gordon pressed the importance of this upon the Futai, who was noways unwilling to invest the city on all sides, because the garrison, commanded by the Hu Wang and Tso Wang, were mostly Cantonese—desperate old Rebels to whom he was not disposed to show any mercy. The Futai was also very angry with his military Mandarins for having effected nothing against this place though they had been before it since January, and urged on matters by threatening to degrade them if they did not make sharp progress in the siege.

In the preliminary fighting among the stockades before Chanchu, Colonel Gordon lost his best artillery officer, and himself ran a great risk. About midnight on the 25th April, he, along with Major Tapp, was superintending a fatigue party of Imperialists engaged in constructing a battery, who were supported by a strong Imperialist picket on each side, and by a covering party in rear. This work was nearly completed, when suddenly, without any intelligible reason, the picket on the left fired into the battery. On this the covering

party fell back on a bank behind, and also opened fire
upon the battery, seeing which, the left picket again
fired into it.   Roused by this midnight disturbance, the
Tai-pings also directed their guns upon the same point ;
so the astonished party in the battery had to stand a
rear and flank fire from their own troops, and a front
one from the enemy.   Colonel Gordon, with his usual
good fortune, escaped untouched, and soon managed to
find a little shelter among some ruins ; but his companion
was shot in the stomach, and died in about ten minutes,
while of the handful of sappers in the battery there were
several killed and five wounded.   It is difficult to believe
that this affair was altogether an accident.   The troops
before Chanchu were not very eager to push on the siege,
because they knew that they would meet with a desperate resistance, and that the taking of that place would
end the campaign ; so it is not impossible that some of
them may have desired to try whether or not Gordon
actually bore a charmed life.

Major Tapp, who was thus killed, had been a warrant
officer in the Royal Navy, and was permitted to purchase
his discharge in order to enter the force in 1862.   He
was a singularly energetic as well as brave officer, and
had more influence over the men than any other of the
regimental commanders, so his loss was greatly felt.
Another fact worthy of notice in the preliminary fighting was, that a number of the Tai-pings who escaped to
the city wall when their stockades outside were taken
by the Imperialists, were drawn up by ropes to the top
of the parapet by their friends inside, and were there
and then decapitated *pour encourager les autres* who
might be meditating on the expediency of evacuating
any other stockades.

The Futai was very anxious to take Chanchu with

his unaided Chinese troops, and ordered Colonel Bailey, who was directing the late General Ching's artillery, to breach the wall between the South and West Gates on the 26th April. Gordon's artillery was then ordered to open fire on the town, in order to distract the attention of the garrison, and an assault was made by the Imperialists alone, who were repulsed with great loss. On the 27th Gordon had completed his batteries and opened fire on the south-east angle of the wall, laying under cover of this fire a pontoon bridge across the ditch, which was sixty feet broad and eight in depth. He had arranged that a fresh body of Imperialists should assault at the same time as he did at his point; and so at 1 P.M. he advanced two regiments as a storming party. On this the Rebels manned the walls in great numbers, and their leader, Hu Wang, was seen encouraging them in person. The resistance was so desperate that, though ten or twelve of the officers mounted the breach, they were driven back, and the column had to be recalled. It appeared that, owing to some mishap about their bridges, the Imperialists had not stormed at the time which had been agreed on, so the whole force of the Tai-pings had been at liberty to meet the disciplined Chinese; but the Futai sent round to Gordon asking him to renew the assault, and a combined movement was then made on the two points which had been breached. Again, however, both the Imperialists and the Ever-Victorious Army were repulsed; the Tai-pings inside being desperate, owing, doubtless, to Li's refusal to show mercy to the Kwangtung and Kwangsi men amongst them. Though Gordon's officers got up on this occasion to the crest of the breach—Colonels Cawte, Howard, and Chapman, and Captain Winstanley greatly distinguishing themselves—yet the men hung back; a retreat had to be ordered, and even the pontoons were abandoned. On this occasion the Tai-pings fought with the greatest determination, and were utterly regardless of their own lives. When they mounted the wall the artillery was played on them with shell and canister at a distance of only 120 yards; but no sooner was one party of them blown away from the breach than another replaced it, brandishing spears and shouting defiance. On the other hand, the disciplined Chinese were not very anxious to take the last town they were likely to have to attack; and though usually indifferent enough as to their own lives, yet, having got some plunder since leaving Quinsan, and not having had any opportunity of disposing of it, they did not like the idea of being shot before enjoying their little treasures. The loss among the officers, now much reduced in number by the affairs of Kintang and Waisoo, was very severe, nineteen being wounded, while there were killed, Colonel Morton, Captains Rhode, Hammond, Donald, and Smith, and Lieutenants Brown, Gibb, Chowrie, Robinson, and Williams.

Being unwilling to expose his officers to much more of such disastrous work, Colonel Gordon instructed the Futai's Mandarins how to approach the wall by trenches, and found that they readily took up the plan and executed it very well. While these were making, the Rebels in some stockades at the East Gate came over to the Imperialists and were pardoned. The Futai hung up proclamations large enough to be read from the walls, offering pardon to any one, except the Hu Wang, who might give up the city. This brought down deserters in dozens over the breaches every day, in spite of all their Chief's efforts to prevent them. The Cantonese Rebels in Chanchu were peculiarly obnoxious both to the authorities and to the people of the district, for they were purely marauders of the worst kind; while some of the other Tai-ping soldiers, and especially those drawn from Kiangsoo, were only unfortunate peasants compelled by threats of torture and death to fight under the banner of the Great Peace. To all such it was desired to show mercy; and on the 5th May the chiefs of one-half the garrison sent out a letter to Colonel Gordon, offering to give up the city if he would send his troops to the breach that night and make a false attack on two of the gates; but as there was much risk in this plan he declined to follow it, and these Rebels came over as they could escape, sometimes to the number of 300 daily.

The following is a translation of the letter which the Rebels sent to Gordon on this occasion; it is curiously illustrative of the existing state of matters, and of one of the means by which he made such rapid progress in clearing the country:—

We received your letter telling us to be on the look-out for you during the third watch on the night of the 27th.

Accordingly we procured strips of white cloth, made a fire in the city, threw fireballs and rockets from the wall; but up to the fourth watch saw nothing of you, neither was the floating bridge laid down.

Consequently we were in a great fright; and the white cloth being discovered, we were reported to Hwang, who would have beheaded us had not other officers interceded on our behalf.

In the event of your carrying out your plan, we shall be distinguished by wearing white bands, or by having the left arm out of the sleeves.

Should you intend coming to-night, hang up two lamps at the East Gate as a signal, then send troops to the North and West Gates to make false attacks, whilst another body lie in ambush near the South Gate, and also open fire on the new city. The Rebels will rush to defend the North and West Gates, and on our throwing two fireballs you should instantly scale the walls. Our party are on guard during the fifth watch, and will assist you, our cry being "Death to the Rebels!" Should you not come, hoist one lamp at the East Gate.

No future time [for your attack] need be fixed, as we can be guided by your signals. We are talked about as being traitors, and should anything be proved against us, 2000 of us would lose our lives. Our movements will be regulated by what is going on outside the city; and after the place falls we shall collect at the East Gate and await your Excellency.

You must have no misgivings as to our sincerity. May Heaven and Earth conspire against us if we be found liars! Pray keep our communications quiet, lest any one coming into the city betray us.

Futai Lí discovered that Chanchu had been taken by the Faithful King on the 11th May 1860, and determined to celebrate the anniversary of that day by a new attack, in which it was intended that the Victorious Army should have only a subordinate place. It is probable that the Rebels had become dispirited by this time, and they seem to have been taken by surprise, so no great resistance was made. The breaches had been planted with spikes and broken glass, but a heavy fire, bringing down masses of the wall, did much to cover these impediments; and the Imperialist soldiers of General Wang at one point, and of General Kwo Sung-lin at another, crossed the bridges over the ditch, and climbing up the ruins in perfect silence, soon crowned the rampart, where they met with a desperate resistance. The consequence was that Kwo Sung-lin's column began to give way in confusion; but at this critical moment Colonel Gordon himself, followed by his 1st Regiment and 200 volunteers from his other corps, rushed to its support over the bridges and up the breach. The Imperialists were rallied, the defenders of the breach were swept away at the point of the bayonet; and, Wang carrying his point about the same moment, the besieging soldiers began to swarm in thousands into the city. After this the struggle was short. "Cockeye," the Hu Wang, who did not seem to have expected the attack, came up in hot haste with a large body of troops, but they were thrown into confusion, and he himself was taken prisoner, resisting to the last. The other chiefs also made rallies, and at one moment a panic seized the Imperialists, but soon the place was entered on all sides, and resistance entirely ceased.

The garrison of Chanchu fu was found to number about 20,000, and of these only 1500 were killed at the capture. All the Cantonese among the prisoners were executed, including the famous "Cockeye." This Wang, who had ravaged Soochow some years before, and who refused to make submission to Lí when brought before that Futai, was simply beheaded, as he well deserved to be. He was a native of Kwangsi, a very early adherent of the Tien Wang, and in personal appearance was strongly made, but with rather small features. The city proved to be in a very impoverished, dilapidated state, but contained rice sufficient to have supported its defenders for two years; and very little plunder was found in it, either for the Imperialist soldiers or for the Ever-Victorious Army,—which had now taken its last city, had fought its last battle, and was to be dissolved, owing partly to the withdrawal of that Order of her Majesty in Council which permitted British officers to take service under the Chinese Government.

CHAPTER XIII.

THE DISSOLUTION OF GORDON'S FORCE, AND A REVIEW OF ITS RESULTS.

THE causes which now led to the dissolution of the Ever-Victorious Army were twofold—one set relating to the very success which it had achieved, and the other to a change in the position of British officers serving the Chinese Government. After the taking of Chanchu fu little more remained for it to accomplish except at Nan-king, where it was not wanted either by the General-

issimo, Tseng Kwo-fan, or by his Lieutenant, Tseng
Kwo-tsun.   Kintang had surrendered a few days previously, and Tanyan was given up on the 13th May by
a portion of its garrison who murdered their leader.
The Rebels held only the city of Wuchu to the south of
the Taiho Lake, and Nanking far to the north of it,
where they were closely besieged.   In Kiangnan the
Tai-ping movement was almost at an end, and the
ordinary troops of the Futai, provided as they were with
39,000 stand of European arms, with heavy artillery,
and with a large supply of ammunition, were quite able
to prevent its again making head, or threatening the
consular port of Shanghai.   In these circumstances it
became a serious question to Governor Lí, whether, in
the impoverished state of his revenue, he ought to continue in existence so expensive a force as that which
Gordon commanded.   It had done its work admirably
indeed, but with the completion of that work its *raison
d'être* had ceased.   At the same time the withdrawal
of Colonel Gordon from his command afforded another
set of reasons for the dissolution of the force.   The great
outcry raised by Tai-ping sympathisers, both in China
and at home, regarding the execution of the Soochow
Wangs had not been without effect on her Majesty's
Government and on public opinion in this country.
False reports had been industriously disseminated of
there having been a general massacre of the Rebels who
surrendered in that city; and the facts were not known,
which, as I have pointed out, had partially justified the
execution of nine persons which actually took place.
Hence it is no wonder that the British Government
should have decided on recalling, as it did on the 1st of
1864, the Order in Council which permitted Colonel
Gordon to take service under the Chinese Government,

and that the War Office determined to withdraw ex-
plicitly from that officer all leave and licence to serve
the Emperor as he had been doing.   There was, in my
opinion, no necessity for such action, and the consequences might have been seriously hurtful both to the
people of China and to our interests there, had Gordon
not resumed active operations in March, or had he not
assailed the Tai-pings with so much swiftness and success; but, as it providentially turned out, his work had
just been accomplished at the moment· when he was
called upon to retire from the field of his victories.

A new responsibility now devolved on the Commander
of the Ever-Victorious Army, for the Futai requested
him to decide on what should be done with that force,
intimating at the same time that he had difficulty in
meeting the heavy monthly expenditure which it involved, and that he entertained fears of the ability of
the Mandarins to deal with it should Colonel Gordon
leave.   To disband the force was so important a step
that, could the opinion of the British Minister and of the
General commanding in China have been soon obtained,
Colonel Gordon would have waited to consult them; but
considering the time that must have necessarily elapsed
before he could have heard from these authorities, he
determined to act on his own responsibility, as he had
previously done in resuming operations.   On maturely
considering the whole subject, it appeared to him to be
highly dangerous to leave the Ever-Victorious Army in
existence; because a force constituted as it was might,
under some other leadership, turn against the Imperial
authorities at any moment and join the Rebels, or become the nucleus of a third party in China.   It clearly
had been Burgevine's wish to form such a party, of
which he himself might be the head; and if the dis-

ciplined force happened to pass into the hands of such a
chief, it would very likely be employed for a like purpose.

Having determined that it would be best to dissolve
his force, Colonel Gordon judged that no time should be
lost in doing so. The last arduous campaign of three
months, with its severe losses, had somewhat dispirited
the men, and the officers were ready to leave if they
received gratuities; whereas, if they were kept on in
inactivity for some weeks, they would probably have
been anxious again to take the field. On this being
represented to him, the Futai agreed to pay a gratuity to
the officers and men, and intimated through Commissioner Hart his wish to reward the labours of Colonel
Gordon by a large sum of money. This the latter
thought proper to decline, as he had done the 10,000
taels previously awarded him by the Imperial Government, and this self-denial was not without good effect on
the minds of the Chinese authorities. Up to this time
they had found the Foreigners with whom they came in
contact eagerly seeking after money whether services
had been rendered or not, and they had naturally come
to the conclusion that personal aggrandisement, in the
shape of dollars, was the ruling motive with all our
countrymen. In Gordon, however, they discerned a
man of quite a different stamp. Confining his personal
expenditure to the smallest limits, he had spent all his
pay and even some of his own private funds in promot-
ing the efficiency of his force; he had spared himself no
labour or trouble, had shirked no danger, and yet refused
any monetary reward. Latterly the Futai showed that
he was capable of understanding and appreciating this
disinterested conduct, and so Colonel Gordon experienced no difficulty in obtaining the sum which he

thought necessary as a reward to his troops before dis-
banding them, and the whole details of the arrangement
were left entirely in his hands.

Colonels of regiments and the wounded officers of the
force received each 4000 Mexican dollars, or about £900;
and other officers sums in proportion. Captain Shamroffel, a Prussian, who had lost both his eyes before Soochow, got £1600; while the unwounded men of the rank-
and-file received, in addition to a month's pay, a small
sum proportionate to the distance they had to travel to
their homes. As the whole force had been paid at a
very high rate throughout its career, this could not be
considered illiberal on the part of a Government so
deeply involved in debt as the Chinese then was.

The force arrived at Quinsan on the 16th May, and
by the 1st of June its Commander had paid off all the
officers and men, and sent the former to Shanghai, the
latter to their respective homes, returning, at the same
time, all arms and ammunition to the Imperial stores.
He left, however, a few officers of artillery and some men
with the Futai, to strengthen him in that branch, and
recommended that a camp of instruction should be
formed at some place near Shanghai where native troops
might be drilled by British officers. Great caution was
necessary in every step of these proceedings; and before
the work was effected some mutinous disposition was
shown, which might have become serious under a less
determined officer. It now only remained for Colonel
Gordon to take leave of Futai Lí previous to his departure. The latter received him with the highest marks of
respect and regard, and expressed himself in a manner
which proved that his intercourse with an officer of so
chivalrous a spirit had had much effect in inclining him
to look upon Foreigners with respect. The Peking

Government also departed in a remarkable manner from its old traditions in acknowledging his services. It publicly admitted that it was under great obligations to this Foreigner, conferred upon him the rank of Ti-Tu, and presented to him a banner and the Order of the Star, along with the distinction of the Yellow Jacket, which, in the estimation of the Chinese, is one of the highest marks of Imperial favour. The following correspondence will also show that the Emperor specially recommended Colonel Gordon to the British Government :—

HONGKONG, *July* 12, 1864.

MY LORD,—I enclose translation of a despatch from Prince Kung, containing the decree published by the Emperor, acknowledging the services of Lieutenant-Colonel Gordon, Royal Engineers, and requesting that her Majesty's Government be pleased to recognise them. This step has been spontaneously taken.

Lieutenant-Colonel Gordon well deserves her Majesty's favour; for, independently of the skill and courage he has shown, his disinterestedness has elevated our national character in the eyes of the Chinese. Not only has he refused any pecuniary reward, but he has spent more than his pay in contributing to the comfort of the officers who served under him, and in assuaging the distress of the starving population whom he relieved from the yoke of their oppressors. Indeed, the feeling that impelled him to resume operations after the fall of Soochow was one of the purest humanity. He sought to save the people of the districts that had been recovered from a repetition of the misery entailed upon them by this cruel civil war.—I have, &c.

FREDERICK W. A. BRUCE.

The EARL RUSSELL, K.G.

The Prince of Kung makes a communication to Sir Frederick W. A. Bruce :—

Some time has elapsed since his Excellency the British Minister, profoundly animated by the feeling of friendliness towards China entertained by the British Government, did, in view of the fact that rebellion was still rife in Kiangsoo, authorise Gordon and other officers of the British army to co-operate heart and hand with the Forces of the Chinese Government against the Rebels.

On the 11th of the 5th moon of the 3d year of Tung-che [14th June 1864], Li, the Governor of Kiangsoo, in a memorial reporting a series of distinguished services rendered in action by Gordon now a Tsung-Ping, with the title of Ti-Tu, together with the particulars of his conduct and discipline of the Ever-Victorious Army, requested his Majesty the Emperor to be pleased to commend him; and on the same day the Grand Secretariat had the honour to receive the following decree:—

"On the occasion of the recovery of Chanchu WE issued a decree conferring on Gordon, Provisional General of Division of the Army of Kiangsoo, for his co-operation with the force he commanded, the title of Ti-Tu [Commander-in-Chief of a provincial army]; and WE further presented him with banners and decorations of honour. This was to distinguish his extraordinary merit, and Li Hung-chang was to address Us again whenever he [Gordon] should have brought the Ever-Victorious Battalions under his command into a satisfactory state of drill and discipline, and to request Us to signify Our approval of his conduct in laudatory terms. Li Hung-chang now writes to say that, both as regards its movements and its discipline, the Ever-Victorious Battalion under Gordon is in a very satisfactory state, and to request Us to signify Our pleasure accordingly.

"Since the spring of last year Gordon has distinguished himself in a series of actions with the Ever-Victorious Force under his command; he has co-operated with the Forces of Government [with such effect that] Fushan has been recovered, the siege of Chanzu has been raised, and the sub-prefectural city of Taitsan, with the district cities of Quinsan and Wokong, have also been retaken, as well as the provincial capital of Soochow. This year he has retaken Ihing and Liyang; he has driven off the Rebels who had worked their way to Yangshê, and he has recaptured Chanchu. He has now brought the Ever-Victorious Force to such a degree of improvement that it will prove a body of enduring utility. Not only has he shown himself throughout both brave and energetic, but his thorough appreciation of that important question, a friendly understanding between China and Foreign nations, is also deserving of the highest praise.

" WE command that Gordon be rewarded with a yellow riding-jacket * to be worn on his person, and a peacock's feather to be carried on his cap; also that there be bestowed on him four suits of the uniform proper to his rank of Ti-Tu, in token of Our favour and desire to do him honour. Respect this."

A copy of the above having been reverently made and forwarded to the Tsung-li Yamun, the Prince and the Ministers, members of it, have to observe that General Gordon, ever since he began to co-operate with the Forces of the Chinese Government against the Rebels, has been alike remarkable for his courage and intelligence, and displayed extraordinary energy. But the fact that he was further able to improve the drill and discipline of the Ever-Victorious Force shows him to be in very eminent degree both able and respectable, while his success in supporting the friendly policy of the British Government, whose subject he is, entitles him to the admission that he has not shown himself unworthy of the language ever held by the British Minister regarding him.

In respectful obedience to the will of his Imperial Majesty, the Yamun is preparing the uniforms and other articles for transmission to him. The banners and decorations will be cared for by Lí, the Governor of Kiangsoo.

Meanwhile it becomes the duty of the Prince to address the British Minister, that his Excellency may bring these things to the notice of her Majesty the Queen of England, in evidence of the desire of the Chinese Government, by its consideration of [Colonel Gordon's] merits, and its bestowal of rewards, to strengthen the *entente cordiale*.

General Gordon's title, Ti-Tu, gives him the highest rank in the Chinese Army; but the Prince trusts that if, on his return home, it be possible for the British Government to bestow promotion or reward on General Gordon, the British Minister will bring the matter forward, that all may know that his achievements and his character are equally deserving of praise.

June 16, 1864.

The dissolution of the Ever-Victorious Army was viewed with some concern by Sir Harry Parkes, who

---

* The Yellow Jacket is a high distinction conferred only rarely on Chinese officers.

thought that he, as Consul at Shanghai, or at least that
the British Minister, ought to have been consulted on
the subject.   Accordingly he wrote somewhat sharply
to Lí, Futai, upon the subject, complaining that Shanghai
might be again exposed to Tai-ping assaults, and received from Lí a letter dated the 23d May 1864, from
which I make the following extracts, without changing
the rather peculiar English of the native Chinese interpreter who penned it, as they serve to illustrate the
Futai's own view of his share in the victories of the
preceding year ; and this view, whether correct or not,
should be taken into account before commenting on the
general subject of Gordon's achievements :—

When the force was first raised by Colonel Ward it numbered less than 1000 men, which number was gradually added
to till it reached several thousand. It went on like this till
1862, when, in consequence of the failure of the Nanking expedition, and the defection of Burgevine, I settled that it should
be weeded out, and 3000 only retained. The command then
passed into the hands of Holland and Gordon, who being willing to consult me, the force, with the co-operation of some tens
of thousands of the Imperial army, kept the field for a year or
so, and finally achieved the glorious capture of Soochow.

During this time a large number of the old soldiers deserted,
tired by their long service, and the bravest of the force were disabled by death or wounds ; and as the vacancies have been supplied in many cases by Rebels who had newly come over, the
force could not be expected to perform as well in future, should
it be necessary to employ it. Colonel Gordon, accordingly, desiring to return to England, proposed that the force should be
disbanded, that the revenues may be relieved of the expenses of
its support, and his future reputation be secured.

The measure being a felicitous idea of Colonel Gordon's, and
not an underhand project of mine. However, as the force has
been a long time in the field, I am unwilling to disband it without notice, and I propose to retain the artillery corps, numbering
600, 300 picked men of infantry, and the complement of the

Hyson, being one-third of the whole force. I also give the Foreign officers I dismiss considerable gratifications, in consideration of their service; and I shall similarly see the privates properly rewarded. The measures, therefore, which have been quietly considered by Colonel Gordon and myself on the spot, would appear sound, and the reduction practicable, as far as the force itself is concerned.

You refer in your letter to the three attacks on Shanghai before 1861, which occurred before my arrival at Shanghai; but, though not present, I think you must have heard of the progress of the campaign since 1862—how at the commencement of the summer of which year I arrived in Shanghai with 6000 infantry only, the whole country, save some three miles E. and W. of the river, being infested with Rebel armies 100,000 strong. Army replaced army. Kading and Tsipoo, which had been recovered, were lost; and although we were most fortunate in the protection afforded the place, and great assistance was given by your officers and men, it was not till I took the field in person, and by my victories slaughtered some 10,000 of the Rebels, and abated their pride, that Shanghai could spread out, or even be considered safe itself. Reinforcements then coming down, and my army having been at length brought up to some strength, I divided my force, and despatched it E. and W.—the eastern division, under General Ching, numbering 20,000 men, acting with Gordon's force, and capturing Wokong, Chanzu, Taitsan, and Quinsan, and clearing the way to Soochow; the western division, under Generals Lí Lin and Kwo, numbering some 20,000, proceeding west, and capturing Kongyin, Wusieh, clearing the way to Chanchu. A third army, under Pau, Futai, after clearing out Nanhui, Kinsan, and Pootung generally, eventually recovered Pingwang, Pinghui, and Chapu.

This year General Ching recovered the prefectural city of Kashing; and I, in person, with some 40,000 men, with Gordon's assistance, recovered Chanchu, and Colonel Gordon, an eyewitness, can testify to the bravery of both. Such is the brief history of the campaign—how the Imperial army, sometimes co-operating with Gordon's force, sometimes acting by itself, has achieved complete success.

I have entered thus into the details that the position may be clear to you.

Again, as although the Rebels are now twice as formidable as they were in 1854—though they fight desperately, whether in attack or when defending themselves—my troops have been a match for them, they [*i. e.*, "my troops"] should not be named in the same day with the old Imperial forces. I would point out that even when Burgevine's tribe gave them [the Rebels] every aid in their power, when they purchased steamers at exorbitant rates, my troops burnt the first at Kachiao, the second at Penmin, and the third at Kashing, besides capturing innumerable Foreign muskets and guns in every victory, whereas now the Rebels are reduced to the depths of poverty, and it is not expecting too much to look forward to the speedy capture of Nankin and Hoochow [Wuchu], to assist in reducing which I am sending a considerable force.

The eastern frontier—Pingwang, the Taiho Lake, and Kashing—[being] held by 10,000 odd men, there is no fear of the Hoochow Rebels breaking out; and the western frontier—Changchow, Tinghu, Chinshan, Piao Yang, and Kiu Yang—being held by 30,000 odd men, an eruption of the Nanking Rebels is not to be apprehended. At Soochow, again, my own force, amounting, between soldiers and marines, to 10,000 odd men, is stationed ready to march at a moment's notice, and there is not a single spot left open, not an inch uncovered. Shanghai, therefore, as it is a long way behind all these, and its approaches are guarded by victorious troops, can repose calmly; and when you consider that, although in 1862 I had but the one city of Shanghai and some three miles round, I was able to make head against the Rebels, till now Soochow and Chanchu are clear of them, and they possess two places, only both many hundred *li* from Shanghai, and the country is held by first-class troops, you will have, I think, little cause for apprehension; and it certainly appears to me that the measures you say in your letter should be taken to secure the future peace and tranquillity of Shanghai may be seen in operation, and it would be taking a very one-sided view to say that Gordon's force is the only one on which reliance could be placed, and that the tens of thousands of tried Imperial troops are not sufficient. I refer you, however, to Gordon, who is well acquainted with the matter from having been present with the army, while I repeat, I do not intend to disband the force entirely, but I shall retain a certain number for the sake of their name and reputation.

Again, I saw in the newspaper of the 1st day of the 3d moon that the Queen of England had ordered her decree of 1862 to be cancelled, and prohibited her officers, whether naval or military, drilling or commanding troops for the Chinese Government. If this (as I suppose it is) be so, I presume it would be impossible for your high authorities, military or civil, whether at Peking or Shanghai, to act in defiance of it; and, if Gordon wishes to reduce the force, it is impossible for me to insist on retaining it, and force British officers to command it.

I have given the greatest attention to the various considerations now urged by you, as my responsibility is very great, and I have no one to share it with me. I desire greatly that we should act together and co-operate in anything that may occur. I certainly would not run into danger by obstinate adherence to my own views; but, knowing both the state of the force and the position of the Rebellion, it is well to take advantage of Colonel Gordon's retirement to arrange the reduction of the force, and I trust you will calmly review the matter.

One other important document regarding Colonel Gordon deserves a place in these pages. The Foreign community in Shanghai was a good deal divided as to the expediency of giving aid to the Imperialists and of putting down the Rebellion ; but there was only one opinion among them as to the admirable manner in which the young British officer who had taken command of the Ever-Victorious Army had performed his share of that work ; and on his departure from China, towards the end of 1864, they presented him with the following expression of their opinions and feelings on the subject :—

To Lieut.-Colonel GORDON, R.E.,
     &c.   &c.   &c.

SHANGHAI, *Nov.* 24, 1864.

SIR,—On the eve of your departure for your native country, we the undersigned, mostly fellow-countrymen of your own, but also representing various other nationalities, desire to express to you our earnest wishes for a successful voyage and happy return to your friends and the land of your birth. Your career during the last two years of your residence in the East has been, so far as we know, without a parallel in the history of the intercourse of foreign nations with China; and, without entering at all upon the political bearings of the great question with which your name must ever remain so intimately connected, we feel that we should be alike wanting towards you and towards ourselves were we to pass by this opportunity without expressing our appreciation and admiration of the line of conduct which you personally have pursued. In a position of unequalled difficulty, and surrounded by complications of every possible nature, you have succeeded in offering to the eyes of the Chinese nation, no less by your loyal and, throughout, disinterested line of action, than by your conspicuous gallantry and talent for organisation and command, the example of a foreign officer serving the Government of this country with honourable fidelity and undeviating self-respect. It is by such examples that we may trust to see many of the prejudices which warp the Chinese mind as regards foreigners removed, and from such experience that we may look forward with hope to the day when, not only in the art of war, but in the more peaceful occupations of commerce and civilisation, the Chinese Government may see fit to level the barriers hitherto existing, and to identify itself more and more with that progressive course of action which, though springing from the West, must prove ultimately of equal benefit to the countries of the East. Once more wishing you a prosperous voyage and a long career of usefulness and success, we remain, Sir, your obedient servants,

(Signed)   JARDINE, MATHESON, & Co.
DENT & Co.
RUSSELL & Co.
SMITH, KENNEDY, & Co.

And about fifty other firms or private individuals.

To Messrs JARDINE, MATHESON, & Co., DENT & Co., RUSSELL
    & Co., SMITH, KENNEDY, & Co., AUG. HEARD & Co.,
    LINDSAY & Co., &c. &c. &c.

SHANGHAI, *Nov.* 25, 1864.

GENTLEMEN,—I have the honour to acknowledge the receipt
of your handsome letter of this day's date, and to express to you
the great satisfaction which I feel at the honourable mention
you have made therein of my services in China. It will always
be a matter of gratification to me to have received your approval;
and, deeply impressed with the honour you have paid me, I have
the honour to be, Gentlemen, yours obediently,

C. G. GORDON,
Capt. R.E., and Brevet Lieut.-Colonel.

Before dismissing the subject of the Ever-Victorious
Army, I may be allowed to make a few observations
upon the military results which it actually effected, and
upon its political relationships; for a right understanding of these matters is absolutely essential to a general
knowledge of the history of the suppression of the Tai-
ping Rebellion, and more especially to correct the erroneous supposition that the Chinese Government was in any
very great need of our assistance to that end.

As to the military question, it is impossible to consider
Colonel Gordon's operations without admiration of his
energy and genius. On assuming command of the force,
he found it defeated, disheartened, and in a chaotic condition. Almost the entire province of Kiangsoo, with a
considerable portion of Chekiang—an enormous district
of country with vast tea and silk districts—was in the
hands of the Tai-pings, who had not only procured arms
in abundance from Shanghai and Ningpo, but were also
engaging Foreign rowdies to fight for them. Moreover, the disciplined force, of which he assumed command, was almost as ready to take one side as the other;
and its officers were in a state of disaffection, owing to

the supercession of their former leader, Burgevine, by
a British officer, and to the limits within which their
plundering propensities were soon confined.   Yet on
these men Colonel Gordon was obliged to rely for assistance in carrying out his plans; and he had often to
place in them a dangerous confidence.   Difficulty after
difficulty arose between him and his own troops, all of
which had to be conquered by his almost unaided tact
and judgment.   On the other hand, the Chinese authorities caused at first a great deal of unnecessary
trouble; and in some very critical moments he was
quite uncertain whether the course he pursued would
receive the approval of his own Government.   Finally,
the country in which he had to operate was unknown
to him: it was peculiarly unsuited for military movements, owing to an absence of roads and to the manner
in which it was intersected by canals, streams, and
creeks of most varied dimensions; and, being fright-
fully devastated, it could afford no commissariat supplies, while during part of the year it was extremely
unhealthy, with its moist fields and stagnant waters
steaming under a blazing sun.

Notwithstanding these disadvantages, Colonel Gordon fought for more than a year with not far from uninterrupted success.   Both his officers and men became
devoted to him, and conducted themselves with a regularity and propriety which were quite astonishing, considering the perils to which they were exposed and the
temptations which they had to resist.   By leading in
person in critical moments he shamed the more back-
ward of them, and endeared himself to all by the unselfish
manner in which he laboured for their benefit, not neglecting to look after the most minute details connected with
their comfort.   Even his enemy, the Tai-pings, who found

in him so formidable an adversary, could not but admire the humanity he displayed in all his dealings with them, and which led him to run many risks in protecting those who surrendered, and in trying to prevent useless fighting. During the latter months of his command, the body-guard which he had for his own protection, and in whose power he often completely lay, separated from his force, was almost entirely composed of Tai-ping soldiers who had surrendered to him. Quite as remarkable were his sleepless activity, the manner in which he obtained information though himself ignorant of Chinese, his habit of reconnoitring the country by night almost unattended, and the rapidity with which he moved his troops from point to point. " By his activity and genius," says an article in the ' Cornhill Magazine ' of November 1864, written by a gentleman who had personal opportunities of judging, though unconnected with his army, " the three thousand men composing his force seemed multiplied tenfold ; and those who, in China, followed the daily accounts of his movements were astounded with the rapidity with which, in a difficult country, under a scorching sun, and with every obstacle that absence of commissariat or an organised transport system could throw in his way, he circled from east to west, from north to south, of the devoted city ; now suddenly swooping down upon a line of external fortifications, now falling upon and utterly routing a relieving army of enormous numbers brought up to attack him in rear, and at another time forcing his steamers through all impediments under the very walls of Soochow, and seizing a position which, if properly defended, might have withstood an army with success." " Never," said the London ' Times,' when reviewing his career in China, " did soldier of fortune deport himself with a nicer sense of military honour, with more gallantry against the resisting, and with more mercy towards the vanquished, with more disinterested neglect of opportunities of personal advantage, or with more entire devotion to the objects and desires of his own Government, than this officer, who, after all his victories, has just laid down his sword. A history of operations among cities of uncouth names, and in provinces the geography of which is unknown except to special students, would be tedious and uninstructive. The result of Colonel Gordon's operations, however, is this : He found the richest and most fertile districts of China in the hands of the most savage brigands. The silk districts were the scenes of their cruelty and riot, and the great historical cities of Hangchow and Soochow were rapidly following the fate of Nanking, and were becoming desolate ruins in their possession. Gordon has cut the Rebellion in half, has recovered the great cities, has isolated and utterly discouraged the fragments of the brigand power, and has left the marauders nothing but a few tracts of devastated country and their stronghold at Nanking. All this he has effected, first by the power of his arms, and afterwards still more rapidly by the terror of his name."*

I have said so much, against Colonel Gordon's own wishes, because so much has been said on the subject and must be repeated here in order to explain the actual course of recent events in China ; but when we come to look carefully at the sweeping statement that it was Colonel Gordon who put an end to the Tai-ping Rebellion, truth compels me to pause. Though perhaps Li, Futai, in the despatch quoted above, takes a good deal too much credit to himself for his share in the operations

* Leading article in the 'Times' of 5th August 1864.

in Kiangsoo, yet there is no doubt that Gordon and his
force, unaided, could not have cleared the province.
While the brunt of the fighting fell upon him, he
required Imperialists to hold the places which he took ;
and their forces, under General Ching and others, fought
along with him so as greatly to contribute to his success.
And it must be remembered, which is of far more importance, that it was the Imperialist victories of Tseng
Kwo-fan and his generals which drove the Tai-pings
into the seaboard districts of Kiangsoo and Chekiang.
The Imperialists appear to have calculated upon the
Allies preserving for them the cities of Shanghai and
Ningpo. Had they not done so, they would probably
have adopted a different course. Our countrymen,
alarmed at the proximity of the Rebels to their rich
trading settlements, seemed to have imagined that this
betokened a general triumph of the Tai-ping cause in
China, but nothing could have been further from the
real state of the case. There is no doubt that, had the
Tai-pings been allowed to take Shanghai and Ningpo,
and so to obtain Foreign steamers, arms, and recruits to
almost an indefinite extent, they would have given an
immense deal more trouble than they did to the Chinese
Government ; but to have allowed them to do so, would
have been to ignore our own treaty obligations to that
Government. Hence the Imperialists had a twofold
reason for making no great efforts to prevent the
advance of the Rebels towards these two consular ports.
They calculated that both our interests and our duty
would lead us to hold these ports against the Tai-pings,
and they calculated rightly. What they might have
done in other circumstances is a matter of speculation ;
but it is quite clear, judged both by the situation and
by the results, that their allowing the Tai-pings to

advance as these did was no proof whatever of their
inability to deal with the Rebellion effectually in their
own slow and systematic way.

Turning to the political aspect of Colonel Gordon's
action, the question arises, whether it was not giving the
Imperialists aid on too easy terms, and was not calculated to foster some of the vices of their administration?
This point is of the more importance, because at the
same period a vigorous attempt was being made by
Mr H. N. Lay and Captain Osborn to provide the
Chinese Government with a European-manned naval
force on terms which they thought would work a beneficial revolution in the state of the empire ; and it is
necessary to refer briefly to that subject, because of an
erroneous supposition which has been entertained, that
Colonel Gordon's service with the Chinese was a main
cause of the failure of that scheme.

The Imperial maritime customs and the Lay-Osborn
fleet form a distinct chapter in the recent history of
China, but one closely connected with the main subject
of this book. Partly from the corrupt tendencies of
Mandarins, and partly from the bullying propensities of
Foreign merchants, the Chinese Government found great
difficulty in levying its maritime customs. To remedy
the evils which thus arose, a Foreign Inspectorate was
established at Shanghai, about twenty years ago, for the
purpose of arresting, as Lord Elgin phrased it, " a system
of irregularity and fraud in the collection of duties at
that port, which was introducing confusion into all business transactions there, and converting the payment of
duties into a gambling speculation, in which the violent
and unscrupulous carried off all the prizes." Out of this
there arose a customs service, chiefly composed of Englishmen, Frenchmen, and Americans, paid by the Chinese

Government, to collect its maritime revenue. The object
of such an arrangement was very obvious. Respectable
Foreign merchants in China greatly prefer a fixed rate of
duty, rigidly enforced by their own countrymen, to slid-
ing duties, the amount of which depends on the weakness
and venality of local Mandarins, and the unscrupulousness of competitors in trade.

In 1859 and 1860 the inspectorship of this service
was in the hands of Mr Horatio Nelson Lay, a gentleman
who had previously been an interpreter in the consular
service, having gone out to China at an early age.
When Mr Lay returned to England on a visit in 1861,
his place of inspector was taken conjointly by Mr Fitz-
roy and Mr Robert Hart, but practically by the latter
gentleman, who had also been in the consular service,
and was well acquainted with Chinese. The change thus
made was exceedingly acceptable to the Foreign community in China; and at the invitation of Sir Frederick
Bruce, Mr Hart was invited up to Peking, where, as Sir
Frederick says in an official despatch, " by his tact, good
sense, and modesty, he obtained access to the Prince of
Kung, and turned to useful account the favourable impression he made upon his Royal Highness and his
advisers." One of the results of this visit was, that Mr
Hart persuaded the Imperial Government to sanction the
purchase on its account in England of some war-vessels,
to be used for the protection of its revenue, for the suppression of piracy, or even, if expedient, against the
Rebels at Nanking. On a general authorisation to effect
this being sent to Mr Lay, that gentleman seems to have
conceived a magnificent scheme for regenerating China
and exalting himself. It is difficult to understand how
any person of ordinary common sense could have supposed that the Imperial Government would agree to the

project on which Mr Lay entered ; but he himself seems to
have foreseen no difficulties in the way. Having simply
received orders to purchase some steam-vessels for the
Chinese Government, and to make the arrangements for
the employment in them of a certain number of European officers and men, he, a subordinate official, arranged
that Captain Osborn, the commander of the squadron,
should receive no orders except directly from the Emperor, that these orders should only be conveyed through
Mr Lay, and that Mr Lay should only convey such of
them as he thought proper. Thus he would have placed
himself in a position not only independent of the Emperor's viceroys, but practically independent of the Emperor
himself, and also of the British Government.*

On this singular understanding seven expensive vessels were actually fitted out and despatched to China
under the command of the well-known Captain Sherard
Osborn, C.B., of the Royal Navy; but, of course, when Mr
Lay and the fleet reached Shanghai, the Imperial Government refused to ratify the arrangement. Still entirely
misunderstanding his own position, and over-estimating
his influence, Mr Lay went up to Peking, demanded a

---

* The thing is so incredible that it is necessary to quote the precise words
of the agreement, as given in the Blue-Book, China, No. 2 (1864), p. 7 :—

" Osborn undertakes to act upon all orders of the Emperor which may be
conveyed direct to Lay, and Osborn engages not to attend to any orders
conveyed through any other channel.

" Lay, upon his part, engages to refuse to be the medium of any orders
of the reasonableness of which he is not satisfied.

. . . .

" In the event of the death of either Lay or Osborn, these conditions,
which are entered into with the authority of the Emperor of China, are not,
it is understood, in either case to be departed from."

This last stipulation is really comical ; for the death of Lay would have
left Osborn still bound to receive orders from no one else, and consequently
would have obliged him to cast anchor and remain where he happened to
be at the time, until he himself or the four years of the engagement expired.

palace to reside in such as the Emperor allows to princes
of the blood, and insisted on the arrangement he made
being carried out.   Prince Kung, however, refused to
have an interview with him, and the members of the
Foreign Board who admitted him to their presence
would not give him what he considered satisfaction.
The result was, that the vessels were sent back to this
country to be sold on account of the Chinese Government;
and all the monetary obligations entered into with the
officers of the fleet were honourably fulfilled.   The whole
affair cost the Chinese about half a million sterling, and
would have cost them more had not Sir Frederick Bruce,
ashamed of the transaction, and of the way in which her
Majesty's Government had been mixed up with it, agreed
to repay the expenses of the fleet returning home out of
the indemnity-money which was being paid, by China to
Great Britain on account of the last war, out of the Imperial customs.   This arrangement was almost incum-
bent upon Sir Frederick, because he had objected on
political grounds to so powerful a squadron being left in
the hands of the Chinese, and it received the sanction of
the home Government.

After this *fiasco* Mr Lay seems to have gone down to
Shanghai, still labouring under the impression that he
was a dutiful servant and invaluable agent of the Chinese
Government, but was soon undeceived by a despatch
from the Prince of Kung, dismissing him from the post
of Inspector-General of Customs, and directing him to
hand over all his accounts to Mr Hart.   The Prince
observed on this occasion, that if Mr Lay had been a
Chinese subject, he would have been punished for his conduct in uselessly wasting public money; but, despite that,
he was treated very leniently, for the Government allowed
him £1000 a-month for the expenses of his establishment

at Peking ; they continued his salary at the rate of
£8000 a-year for several months beyond the period which
he required to make up his accounts, and they also gave
him a gratification of £2000 to pay his expenses to England, though it had been expressly understood from the
outset that he held his appointment only at the will of
the Government, and might at any moment be dismissed
without reason given or pension allowed.

Sir Frederick Bruce wrote home a very able despatch on this subject,* in which he said, "The Chinese
Government comprehended the scope and bearing of
this scheme, and look upon it as an insidious attempt
to take the administration out of their hands. They
are profoundly irritated, not only because of the embarrassments in which they are involved by his [Lay's]
having exceeded his authority, but on account of the
position he thus sought to create for himself. They
attribute his conduct to personal motives, and their
confidence in the good faith of Foreign agents has been
most seriously shaken." In answer to this and other
observations, Mr Lay published a pamphlet in the end
of 1864, misentitled 'Our Interests in China,' in which
he violently attacked the British Minister, and garnished
his pages with amusing quotations from some letters
which Sir Frederick had written in the confidence of
private intercourse. The pamphlet, however, makes no
alteration in the case as I have stated it above, and
there can hardly be a question, except perhaps in the
mind of Mr Lay himself, that Lay's scheme failed from
its own prodigiousness, and could only have been accepted by a government which was prepared to abdicate
altogether,—which was very far indeed from being the
position of that of China. Perhaps never was there a

* Blue-Book, China, No. 2 (1864), p. 22.

finer repetition of the old fable of the fly which had
settled on the axletree of a carriage, exclaiming, "Behold
what a dust I make!" The course of events had exalted
Mr Lay into a position for which he had no very special
qualifications, and he seems to have supposed that he
had done it all, and was the pivot round which everything in China turned. Had there been no Colonel
Gordon in the world, and had the Chinese Government
been in circumstances a hundred times more alarming
than those which existed at this period—when it had
made peace with Foreign nations, and the Emperor's
viceroys had swept the Tai-pings out of the Yangtsze
valley—it would scarcely have dreamed of accepting
the degradation which this scheme implied.

At the same time, there was something of importance
in the ideas which Mr Lay thus abused. The possession
of a small efficient force, well drilled in the European
fashion, and provided with European artillery and small
arms, would have enabled the Chinese Government to
have dealt much more effectually than it had hitherto
been doing with rebellion in all parts of its domain.
Such a force could only have been obtained by employing European officers of good character, and these
would not have entered such a service without sufficient guarantees as to the period and the manner of
their employment. Hence it may very reasonably be
asked, whether Colonel Gordon, giving his valuable services in the generous way he did to the Chinese Government, did not spoil a great opportunity of inducing it
to establish such a force, and lead the Chinese to imagine
that if ever they fell into similar difficulties by their
own mismanagement, they could calculate on receiving
Foreign aid on their own terms? This is not a subject
to dogmatise upon; but it seems to me that his action

had no evil effects in that respect : because, firstly, the Peking Government was not in such straits as to stand greatly in need of Foreign aid ; secondly, it was not prepared to carry out any great reform in its military system ; thirdly, it was not in a position to make so great a change in the customs of the country ; and, fourthly, it would hardly have been decent in us to have taken advantage of its temporary distress to force upon it such a measure.

On the first of these heads enough has been already said to show that though the Peking Government was willing to accept Foreign aid for a special purpose, it had got the upper hand, and without that aid would have put down the Rebellion sooner or later. As to the second, all our officials who have been thrown into contact with the higher Mandarins of late years, will acknowledge that there never was any abasement in the demeanour of these officers, and that we frequently offered assistance before it was asked for. Though the Chinese Government was rapidly increasing in knowledge of Foreign affairs, and gradually adapting itself to changed circumstances, yet it had never displayed any wish to advance beyond the point of having a certain number of its troops accustomed to Foreign drill and the use of Foreign arms. And even if the Government had been exceedingly desirous to make a change in its military system, by establishing a small efficient army which it could employ in any part of the empire, it could not have done so in face of the opposition of Tseng Kwo-fan and the other generals who for many years had been successfully opposed to the Rebels. I daresay the Tartar section of Peking officialdom would have been not averse to a military reform which might have been a formidable counterbalance to the growing influence

and power of Tseng Kwo-fan, Tseng Kwo-tsung, Lí, and
other purely Chinese Mandarins in the south and centre
of the country; but these latter would have had the
support of the people in their opposition to such an innovation. Any departure from the old time-honoured
system of leaving the government of every district very
much in its own hands is opposed to Chinese sentiment,
and a rash introduction of much additional interference
from Peking would have been viewed by the masses of
China as an interference with their rights of self-government, and, in point of fact, as something very like that
intolerable Tartar domination which Sir Frederick Bruce
and Colonel Gordon have been so erroneously accused of
upholding.   Lastly, it may be asked, with what face
could we, after our treatment of China, and when the
Rebels were drawing their chief strength from a section
of our traders, have taken advantage of a temporary distress on the part of the Government to gain its consent
to measures to which it was averse ? It may be said, that
we might have done nothing, that it was our duty to
observe strict neutrality ; but to have really done this,
and to have acted up to treaty obligations, it would have
been necessary to have undertaken the almost impossible
task of preventing British subjects from joining the Tai-
pings, and from supplying them with munitions of war.

CHAPTER XIV.

THE MEDICAL ARRANGEMENTS OF GORDON'S FORCE.

RUDIMENTARY STATE OF MEDICAL SCIENCE IN CHINA — ASSISTANT-
SURGEON MOFFITT'S SERVICES TO GORDON'S FORCE — CAPACITY OF
THE CHINESE AS SOLDIERS — MALARIA — ORGANISATION OF THE
MEDICAL DEPARTMENT—HOSPITAL TABLES OF DISEASE—EFFECTS
AND CURE OF OPIUM-SMOKING—DYSENTERY—TABLE OF WOUNDS
RECEIVED IN ACTION—CASES OF WOUNDS.

IT was a matter of great importance to introduce European medical arrangements into the force of disciplined
Chinese which Colonel Gordon commanded. The Imperial army was not less defective in that respect than it
was as regards drill or the use of arms; and medical
science among the Chinese is still in a very rudimentary
state. Surgery especially may be said to be almost entirely unknown amongst them in all its branches, owing
to their prejudice against dissection of the dead; and
their ideas as to the interior of the human body are of
the most fanciful kind. It is also not usual for Chinese
armies to trouble themselves much about soldiers who
are seriously disabled; and the story goes that when,
after the Convention of Peking, the Mandarins were
offered back the wounded prisoners who had been taken
by our troops, they showed a disposition to refuse the

offer, saying in effect, "Keep them; what should we do with them?"

In setting to the Chinese an example in regard to this important matter, the commander of the Ever-Victorious Army found an able and zealous coadjutor in Mr A. Moffitt, an assistant-surgeon of H.M. 67th Regiment, who was made his principal medical officer. In noticing the services of this gentleman, the 'Lancet' of the 11th August 1866 said that "it is impossible to over-estimate the good done by Dr Moffitt, not only to the force in which he served with so much distinction, but to the reputation of his profession and country." Colonel Gordon also has always been ready to testify that the confidence felt by all ranks of his force in the surgical skill of the principal medical officer was of signal service in nerving their minds for any enterprise, however hazardous. One result of Mr Moffitt's fame as an operator was that he was called in to treat Yang, a Ti-Tu or native general, who was wounded in the chest, and given up for lost by his own countrymen; and his success in this case being brought to the notice of the Governor of the province, was specially reported to the Imperial Government, and Lí himself immediately sought to obtain the medical services of Dr Wong Fung, a Chinese who had taken a medical degree in the University of Edinburgh. It may also be noted that, besides having frequently to be under fire, Mr Moffitt did good service on some occasions in leading the troops. He has reported so fully on the medical aspects of the force in which he served, that I have little more to do than to condense his remarks.

As the Chinese would be less expensive, and not less efficient, than English soldiers for service in India, it is of importance to note their physical characteristics. The

old notion is pretty well got rid of, that they are at all a
cowardly people when properly paid and efficiently led ;
while the regularity and order of their habits, which
dispose them to peace in ordinary times, give place to
a daring bordering upon recklessness in time of war.
Their intelligence and capacity for remembering facts
make them well fitted for use in modern warfare, as do
also the coolness and calmness of their disposition. Phy-
sically they are on an average not so strong as Europeans, but considerably more so than most of the other
races of the East ; and on a cheap diet of rice, vegetables,
salt fish, and pork, they can go through a vast amount
of fatigue, whether in a temperate climate or in a tropical one, where Europeans are ill-fitted for exertion.
Their wants are few ; they have no caste prejudices,
and hardly any appetite for intoxicating liquors. Being
of a lymphatic or lymphatic-bilious temperament, they
enjoy a remarkable immunity from inflammatory disease,
and the tubercular diathesis is little known amongst
them. The portion of Kiangsoo in which Colonel Gordon's force operated is rather malarious, being a flat
which would now be a vast swamp and marsh, growing
reeds and aquatic plants, were it not for the labours of
a most thrifty people, who have rendered it capable of
supporting a dense population. Through the summer
months a vast evaporating surface is exposed to the
sun, and the consequent decomposition of vegetable
matter becomes a fertile source of miasmatic disease.
Mr Moffitt seems to think that the houses of Kiangnan,
being situated on the plain, and having dark unventi-
lated rooms with low ground-floors, are peculiarly unsuited for a malarious district ; but this view I am disposed to question. The miasma from the paddy-fields,
which is so destructive to human life, rolls upwards, but

never descends, and the Chinese guard themselves against
it by having their houses on the same level as the rice-
fields, or, if higher up, carefully protected by walls, trees,
and bamboos.   During hot weather the European in
China naturally prefers the highest and most airy position he can find to sleep in ; but, while thus avoiding
the discomfort of stewing in a close apartment below,
he is borne on a poisonous air into the other world, or
awakes to find his constitution impaired for life.

At the time of Colonel Gordon's taking command of
the disciplined Chinese, the medical department was
scarcely entitled to that name, and Mr Moffitt, assisted
by two other medical officers, proceeded to organise a
stationary hospital and a field establishment.   The
former was first placed in Sungkiang ; but on the capture of Quinsan, was transferred to and retained there,
being placed in a situation where the wounded could be
conveyed to it by boats.   Bed-frames found in the city,
with bottoms worked of cocoa-nut fibre, were found sufficient for the invalids without the use of mattresses,
and the staff of attendants was managed by a young
Chinaman who had received a European education.
Of this ward-master Mr Moffitt remarks, curiously
enough, "From his knowledge of the Classics he soon
became a most expert compounder of medicines, in
which capacity he was invaluable."   The field establishment consisted of one Chinese non-commissioned
officer and six coolie orderlies, who had to attend to
the medical officers on the field, together with one commissioned officer and eight men from each regiment,
whose sole duty was to carry back the wounded of
their respective regiments to the hospital tent or boat—
an arrangement which caused a kind of rivalry to spring
up between the different corps, it being considered dis-

honourable if the wounded of a regiment were not quickly carried back. Two large covered boats usually constituted the field hospital, and from these the wounded were sent easily and comfortably to Quinsan in Chinese gunboats from thirty to forty feet long, and covered with a canvass awning. Thus they were landed very quickly at the stationary hospital, nothing the worse of the journey, so that, suppuration not having had time to set in, the first dressing did not require removal until the patients were quiet and settled in their beds.

The annual average strength of the force was 3000 Chinese and 120 Foreigners. Among the former the admissions from all diseases and from wounds not received in action were 4166, and the deaths 87, for the year commencing 1st April 1863, as the following table shows :—

Diseases.	Admissions.	Deaths.	Diseases.	Admissions.	Deaths.
Ophthalmia, . . .	6	0	Scabies, ...	66	0
Dysenteria, . . .	54	7	Mania, ...	1	0
Diarrhœa, . . .	690	9	Bronchitis, . . .	25	0
Cholera, ...	2	2	Dyspepsia, . . .	6	1
Febris inter., . .	1755	8	Hæmorhois, . .	3	0
,, remit.,.. .	1247	48	Pleg. and ulcus. .	99	2
,, cont., . .	67	8	Contusio, .	87	2
Rheumat. ac., . .	1	0	Not received in action. { Vulnus incis.	40	0
Syph. prim., . .	6	0	Combustio,	11	0
			Totals, . . .	4166	87

From this and other tables it appears that six-sevenths of the whole admissions, and over eleven-twelfths of the whole deaths, arose from miasmatic diseases ; while the immunity from tuberculous and hepatic, with other constitutional and local affections, was greater than is usual in any other country. Intermittent and remittent fevers were by far the most fatal diseases ; but it is remarkable that in the crowded cities of China, where there is almost no drainage and no supervision of the removal of filth, epidemics should be so rare. The intermittent fever often yielded easily to antiperiodic remedies, but when it passed into the remittent form it frequently became fatal. At the commencement its most prominent symptom was a burning gastric pain, followed by vomiting and total loss of appetite. In cases about to terminate fatally headache and vertigo became violent, forbidding the use of quinine, and the disease assumed a typhoid character. Purgatives were always found to give relief, and the other medicines which proved most useful in these cases were calomel, combined with jalap or Dover's and James's powders. The diarrhœa which was so common had three distinct varieties, connected respectively with indigestion, fever, and the use of opium. The first of these arose chiefly from improper food and want of occupation; the second was merely fever in course of elimination through the mucous membrane of the bowels; and the third afflicted those whose constitutions had been debilitated by the excessive use of opium. The latter form of diarrhœa usually appears only in the hot season, and sooner or later attacks those who give themselves up to a regular practice of smoking opium. There was no pain or fever with it, but general debility, wasting of tissue, loathing of food, and depression of spirits. It was found very difficult to induce the patients to give up opium-smoking, the craving for it being often beyond control, and it was necessary to administer the drug for some time in another way. Dover's powders and tonics were of much use; but I believe, from the experience of German missionaries in the south of China, that camphor is of still more. Contrary to Indian experience, ipecacuanha was not found of great value in the treatment of dysentery, which was for the most part of sub-acute character; and its subjects were usually debilitated by previous fever or diarrhœa : but here, again, my own experience and observation in China induce me to question the results arrived at in regard to the use of this medicine, which I consider to be the most valuable of all for treatment of dysentery whether acute or chronic.

The following table classifies the wounds received in action, for the fourteen months from 1st April 1863 to 1st May 1864, by the 3000 Chinese and 120 Foreigners who on an average constituted the force; but of course this does not include the number of those killed in action :—

REGION OF BODY WOUNDED.	CHINESE.		FOREIGNERS.	
	Total Wounds admitted into Hospital.	Deaths from Wounds and Operations.	Total Wounds admitted into Hospital.	Deaths from Wounds and Operations.
Wounds of the head, . . .	92	8	9	1
,, ,, face, . . .	73	5	3	0
,, ,, neck, . . .	55	6	2	1
,, ,, chest, . . .	39	12	7	2
,, ,, abdomen, . .	23	4	1	1
,, ,, back and spine,	17	4	2	0
,, ,, peritoneum and genital organs, and pelvis,	26	1	1	0
,, ,, shoulder, . .	69	1	2	0
,, ,, arm, . . .	70	5	3	0
,, ,, forearm, . .	32	1	4	0
,, ,, hand, . . .	73	2	7	0
,, ,, fingers, . . .	12	0	4	0
,, ,, thigh, . . .	40	7	17	3
,, ,, leg, . . .	120	5	8	0
,, ,, foot, . . .	123	4	0	0
Wounds opening large joints,	0	0	2	2
,, injuring large arteries,	0	0	1	1
Total, ...	864	65	73	11

The proportion of soldiers rendered unfit for service was very small as compared with the number of those

S

disabled in European warfare, because, owing to the nature of the firearms used by the Tai-pings, the bullets went at a low velocity, and seldom caused much laceration or disorganisation of the parts struck. In cases where the wounds were caused by European arms, it usually happened that when a limb was struck the missile passed completely through it, leaving a large track, lacerating and destroying the muscles and shattering the bones; while the bullets from Chinese matchlocks and gingalls, going with a low velocity, passed very often between the muscles, leaving only a small track with scarcely any destruction of tissue, and either lodged against the bone or glanced aside from it without causing fracture.

Among the more interesting cases of wounds the following may be mentioned :—

In the assault on the city Taitsan, Private Wong Ta-sin received a matchlock-bullet on the forehead, which inflicted a large scalp-wound and caused a fissured fracture of the bone in the shape of the letter V, with a slight depression of the apex ; but he was so busily engaged in collecting loot in the captured city that he did not report himself wounded until the second day after receiving the injury, and though then ordered to remain in bed, he returned to duty in the afternoon and marched with his regiment for three successive days. This wound healed without a bad symptom, greatly to the gratification of the patient, who took no small amount of credit to himself for his foresight.

At the night-attack on the intrenchments before Soochow on the 29th September 1863, Major Kirkham was struck by a bullet over the anterior part of the left parietal bone, about two inches from the sagittal suture, so that the bone was fractured with quite a perceptible

depression. For four days he remained in a half-stupe-
fied, sleepy state, without any pain or suffering, and
after recovering from this, could not speak, owing to
partial paralysis of the right side of his face. When
consciousness returned he made signs for a pencil and
paper, and succeeded in writing what he wanted, but
left out several words in the sentence and letters in the
words. At the same time the pain of his wound began
to make itself felt ; but under ordinary treatment the
paralysis completely disappeared, and at the end of six
weeks he was able to resume his duties, with only a
slight hesitation of speech and a little excitability of
temper. The same officer was struck at Kintang by a
musket-bullet, which entered his chest about its centre,
and, passing upwards, fractured the upper margin of the
scapula and lodged under the skin on the back of the
shoulder, but without injuring the lung or being attended
with fatal consequences.

Captain Martin was struck on the head by a bullet
at the assault of Chanchu, which caused a comminuted
fracture of the occipital bone and depressed the fragments. When brought to the hospital two days after
the injury, he was in a comatose state ; and an incision
being made through the scalp - wound, and all fragments of bone being removed by means of an elevator
and forceps, the dura mater rose and seemed uninjured.
During the operation the patient manifested little sense
of pain, but when the wound was washed he suddenly
recovered his senses, and began vociferating furiously.
By simply dressing with lint and water, and slightly
touching his mouth with calomel, he was able to resume
duty on the twenty-first day after the operation, with the
wound almost closed.

Captain Shamroffel, a young Prussian, received a small

bullet in the face, which entered immediately behind the orbital margin of the external junction of the frontal and malar bones, and, passing through the globes of both eyes, completely destroying them, made its exit at a corresponding point on the other side of his face. No time was lost in getting the patient under the influence of mercury, and the inflammation was confined to the membranes of his eyes. The brain was not affected ; and in spite of the extensive course taken by the bullet, no important part was injured except the eyeballs, which, as the inflammation subsided, gradually receded within the orbits, so as to be covered by the eyelids. On the breaking up of the force this man was compensated by the Chinese Government with £1600. Another European was struck by a bullet on the face, which entered at the angle of the inferior maxilla, and went out about the position of the mental foramen on the other side, shattering in its course the whole of the horizontal ramus and mental process of the maxilla. Of course he could not swallow anything for several days ; but when the wound took on a healthy action, hard tissue was thrown out to replace the bone which had been removed ; and a gutta percha mould being used to give the parts a proper shape, the patient made a good recovery, with very little deformity.

One Chinese private, when lying on his stomach watching the enemy over a mound, received a bullet, which entered the face on the right side of the nose, penetrated the palate near the centre, passed through the base of the tongue, and finally lodged under the skin of the back close to the second dorsal vertebra, where it was extracted ; but no bad symptoms followed this extensive wound, and it healed without difficulty or deformity, except leaving a small opening in the palate. I remember myself once seeing a Chinaman who had received a bullet in his right eye, which came out under the left jaw, shattering his palate considerably; and yet when the splinters of bone were picked out he did not even wink, nor was it necessary for any one to hold his head during the operation.

In the case of General Yang, which has already been alluded to, the bullet had entered the side of the chest between the second and third ribs, and, passing through the lungs, had lodged in the muscles forming the posterior fold of the axilla. The removal of the bullet by incision greatly delighted the patient and his friends, for Chinese doctors never venture on such an operation; and the effusion which took place into the cavity of the chest was relieved after a fortnight by a copious expectoration of a pinkish-coloured pus which lasted for two days. At the end of four weeks he was able to walk about, and some time afterwards resumed his command, and was also married.

PART IV.

THE END OF THE TAI-PINGS

CHAPTER XV.

A VISIT TO TSENG KWO-FAN—SKETCHES OF NATIVE AND ENGLISH OFFICIALS IN CHINA.

In June 1864, after the dissolution of his force, Colonel Gordon paid a visit to Tseng Kwo-fan at Nganking, and had some interesting and important conversation with him regarding military matters in China. On reaching Nanking on his way up the Yangtsze, the Colonel first met with the great man's brother, Tseng Kwo-tsun, the Governor of Chekiang, who commanded all the troops round the Rebel capital, and who was residing on one of the hills behind Porcelain Tower Hill. This Mandarin was about forty years of age, pleasant and active, and was at the time particularly engaged in

mining operations.   Few of his troops were armed with
muskets ; and when asked why he did not get more of
these weapons from Futai Lí, he said his men did not
know how to use them, and that he soon would be able
to take the city by famine, for the Rebels were very
badly off, and some months before had sent out 3000
women and children, whom he had taken charge of and
lodged in a stockade, allowing the country people to take
any of the females as wives who were willing to go.   On
examining the works round Nanking, Colonel Gordon was
struck by the extraordinary perseverance which the Imperialists must have exercised.   One very large stone fort
had been taken by constructing stockades and breastworks all round it, thus isolating it, and causing the
Rebels such annoyance that they had to evacuate.
From the summit of the hill above the Porcelain Tower
a fine view of Nanking was obtained, and its palaces
were plainly distinguishable.   Inside the walls were
large empty spaces and no stockades.   For miles the
rampart was deserted, with only here and there a single
man visible, miles from any support ; not a flag was seen
flying, and a deathlike stillness seemed to overhang the
city.   The wall was about forty feet in height, and about
thirty in thickness ; and in some places the Imperial
stockades were within a hundred yards of it.   Half-a-
dozen Tai-pings were observed to be lowered from the
wall by a rope, and immediately began gathering a species of lentil which grew outside, without being molested
when doing so by the Imperialist soldiers, who were not
more than eighty yards distant.   From this hill the Imperial lines also were seen stretching for miles, consisting
of a double line of breastworks connecting round mud-
forts, of which there were one hundred and forty, at a
distance of about 600 yards from each other, and each

of which contained 500 men. In some places the forts
were much closer together, and the breastwork was of
triple or even quadruple construction. The stockades
were surrounded with the shops of small sutlers ; no men
appeared to be on the look-out, and a free-and-easy picnic
style pervaded the whole force. One of their mines, being
constructed to lead under the wall, was fifteen feet below
the surface of the ground, and 150 yards in length.

Proceeding up to Nganking, Colonel Gordon was received by Tseng Kwo-fan, whom he found to be a man
of low stature, with a black straggling beard and mustache, a careless dress, and a very ancient hat. The conversation soon turned on the inefficient manner in which
the Imperial troops at Nanking were armed, and Colonel
Gordon went on to make some representations which he
thought it expedient for the good of China to be laid
before the Generalissimo. After explaining the reasons
which had induced him to dissolve the Ever-Victorious
Army, he pointed out the importance of the Imperialists
avoiding the employment of the low class of Foreigners
whom they had hitherto used for strengthening their
military force, and also of getting rid of the presence of
European troops at the open ports. He urged the creation of an Imperial Force, which could be moved anywhere within the Empire ; the regular payment of the
men who composed it, and their instruction in their own
language, under native officers, in the use of foreign
arms. Ten thousand men so trained would suffice for
a very large district of country, and the existence of
such a force would prevent rebellion springing up. He
strongly recommended that some steps in that direction
should be taken at once ; that men and officers should
be carefully selected for the purpose ; and that the latter
should be made to understand that they should suffer

extreme penalties if they did not properly attend to their duty, while they should receive every encouragement if they made themselves efficient.

Tseng Kwo-fan listened very attentively while these remarks were being translated to him, and took with a certain degree of interest a memorandum in which they were embodied. He seemed a man who did not commit himself to opinions without a considerable amount of thought. He was surprised to hear that the Japanese were almost as far advanced in knowledge of artillery as are the Western nations, and asked several questions about Japan with some concern. His own position, however, was one of no small difficulty as regarded military reform. There were forty Ti-Tus, or provincial generals, at Nanking, who did not wish any change, and he could not do much in defiance of all these. One result of this interview was, that Tseng was so far gained over as to give his support in the matter of military reform to Futai Lí, who at this time was in the habit of nightly studying military Foreign works, and was preparing for Peking a treatise on European artillery.

On his way down the river, Colonel Gordon met Paou Chiaou, an Imperialist General of high reputation, who pursued the Faithful King in 1861, and also Tseng Kwo-fan's right-hand man, Ping Lu-lin, a very high Mandarin, who was Secretary to the Board of War. Paou had a floating flower-garden alongside of his boat, and both these Generals seemed well aware of the capabilities which the Ever-Victorious Army had displayed. From what he learned on this visit, Gordon was convinced that Nanking would fall very soon, and that, though the Tai-pings there might escape from it by a vigorous sally, there was no place of safety for them to go to. He was also convinced that Paou Chiaou, with his army, would soon be able to surround and dispose of the Rebel remnant still left at that time in Kwangsi. He thought a longer time would be necessary to reduce the cities of Wuchu and Changching in Chekiang, which were still held by the Tai-pings, but that there was no fear of their giving any trouble in that neighbourhood beyond the walls of those cities. In Nganwhui he could learn of only one town, Kuante, which still held out against the Imperialists; and the whole aspect of affairs seemed to indicate that the final suppression of the Great Rebellion was exceedingly close at hand.

Perhaps it may not be out of place to give a short account, in connection with this visit, of some of the great Celestial officers who, during recent years, have been brought prominently in contact with Foreigners. The word "Mandarin" is not Chinese, being from the Portuguese *mandar*, to command, and is used by us to denote a class of persons in China which includes civil officials, military officers, literati, and, in general, what may be considered the nobility of the Empire. Though the reigning family are Manchu Tartars, and the members of that family are ennobled by birth, and when at all fit are readily advanced to high posts, yet the great bulk of Celestial officialdom is composed of native Chinese, taken by competitive examination from all ranks of the people excepting those of barbers and play-actors. Hereditary titles are conferred on distinguished members of this service, but the honorary rank which these denote is not very highly esteemed in China when there is no connection with the Imperial family. To be in the "Middle Kingdom," what we call a "Mandarin," is to reach a position which gives the command of intellectual

fame, of wealth, and of political power.   The Chinese, in
theory at least, and in practice to a greater extent than
the people of any other nation, are exceedingly averse to
any separation between these three kinds of eminence.
They hold that none but able men are entitled to possess
wealth or political power, or to be otherwise elevated
above the toiling millions of mankind.   It must not be
supposed, however, that admission into the governing
classes depends in China on a "system of competitive
examination" anything like what is suggested to us in
England by such a phrase.   The Chinese would regard
our competitive examinations, with their minute details
of learning, as ill fitted to aid in the selection of eminent
men, and suitable only for testing ordinary schoolmasters.
They lay stress almost entirely upon acquaintance with
first principles, moral and political, especially as developed
in the Classics, holding that a power of dealing with these
marks the man who is best fitted, when the occasion
comes, for dealing with all the problems of life ; but in
advancing men from the lower to the higher ranks of
officialdom, judgment is chiefly based upon the tact and
success which has been displayed in practical matters.

There is a Red-book published periodically at Peking,
giving the rank and occupations of all the Mandarins,
who are divided, with reference to the latter point, into
literary, civil, and military.   This arrangement, however,
does not affect their rank.   As regards that there are
nine classes, of which the first two have red buttons of
different descriptions, the next two blue ones, and the
remainder glass or gilt ones, in the lowest class of all
there being a subdivision who bear the title of "Not yet
entered the stream."   If we applied this system to England, it may be roughly said that the Premier, the Lord
Chancellor, the Foreign Secretary, and the Commander-

in-Chief, would be found wearing ruby buttons of the first class, the other Cabinet Ministers would have red coral ones, and on the caps of the Under-Secretaries of State would be seen sapphires.

It is not necessary for me to touch on the character-istics of Commissioner Lin, Muh Chan-gah, and other Mandarins who appeared in connection with the Opium war and the treaty of Nanking; but Ki Ying, who was noted at that period, reappeared in the time of Lord Elgin's Embassy, and comes in for notice. Perhaps never Chinese official had a more checkered career; for from 1817, when he became junior Vice-President of the Board of Revenue, to 1859, when he was condemned to strangulate himself, he was incessantly being either advanced to very high posts or degraded to very low ones, and to the latter sometimes at his own request. In August 1842 he concluded, as chief representative of his Government, the first treaty of China with England, and for some years afterwards held the post at Canton of Imperial Commissioner for Foreign Affairs. Being replaced by Yeh Ming-chin, he returned to Peking in 1848, having composed an ode to the officials, literati, and gentry of the "City of Rams," of which the following is the concluding stanza :—

During all these revolutions of the stars, and descents of the night-dews, silken [*i. e.*, grey] hairs have encroached upon my brow.
When I rein in my horse upon the mountain-path, I fear and tremble exceedingly ;
My thoughts are anxiously busied about my plants, the people ; I would wrap my cloak round them.
I have served till I am grey, yet how dare I pluck out the sign of office from my cap ?
No! though profitless as the stubble, I am still ready to put forward my counsels for securing peace to this realm.

Though valueless as the mallow-flower, I cannot forget the gratitude I owe to the State.

After holding some high offices at Peking, and being occasionally reproved, Ki Ying had a terrible fall in 1850 on the death of the Emperor Tao-kwang, and the accession of Hien-fung, when, for reasons not very intelligible, he was suddenly degraded from the Presidentship of the Civil Board and the Commandant-ship of the Peking gendarmerie to the condition of a simple Bannerman, or full private in the Imperial stand-ing Tartar army. One of the reasons assigned for this tremendous descent was an alleged favourable tendency towards Foreigners, and an assumed connection with Christians. This latter supposition gave rise to a curious literary forgery, perpetrated at Foochow in 1850, where a work was published purporting to be a collection of Ki Ying's writings, and containing a prayer to the God of the Christians. There is an engraving of him in Dr Williams's 'Middle Kingdom,' which correctly represents his very curious head and face ; but Mr Wade says, that in his demeanour " there was a combination of dignity and courtesy which more than balanced the deficiencies of a by no means attractive exterior."

Though Ki Ying was far in advance of the Mandarins of his time, he entertained some amusing ideas as to the means which should be employed for " soothing and bridling the Barbarians." He thought that they should be treated with a mixture of patronage and conciliation. When Canton was taken in the end of 1857 by our troops, a memorial to the Emperor on this subject by Ki Ying was found among Commissioner Yeh's archives, in which he analysed the character of Foreigners, and complained especially of their incessant restlessness, for which, he argued, allowance ought to be made. " Bred and born," he wrote, "in the Foreign regions beyond, there is much in the administration of the Celestial Dynasty that is not perfectly comprehensible to the Barbarians, and they are continually putting forced constructions on things of which it is difficult to explain to them the real nature." In proceeding to characterise us as uncivilised, blindly unintelligent in the styles and modes of address, and incapable of appreciating forms of communication which duly place the superior above and the inferior below, it is evident that he is expressing his own feelings as well as those of every Chinaman, except persons of the lowest classes, who comes in contact with us; and perhaps something might be said in favour of that Celestial view of British bluntness and unceremoniousness. Ki Ying further explains to the Emperor that we must be judiciously directed, but without explanation of the "reason why," as evidently, in his opinion, we are not quite capable of entering into such matters. He also notes our habit of combining feasting with business. "The meal," he remarks, "which the Barbarians eat together, they call *Ta tsan* [great dinner]. It is a practice they delight in to assemble a number of people at a great entertainment, at which they eat and drink together. When your slave has conferred favour upon [has given a dinner to] the Barbarians at the Bogue or Macao, their Chiefs or leaders have come to the number of twenty or thirty; and when, in process of time, your slave has chanced to go to Barbarian residences or Barbarian ships, they have in their turn seated themselves round him in attendance upon him, striving who should be foremost in offering him meat and drink. To gain their good-will he could not do otherwise than share their cup and spoon."

After his fall in 1850, this Mandarin lived mostly in

T

retirement until 1858, when, being appointed an Imperial Commissioner, he was sent down to Tientsin, with the expectation that he might be able to induce Lord Elgin to give up demanding some of the most important stipulations in the proposed new treaty between England and China. At this time there was something pathetic both in his appearance and in his position. Much broken by his seventy-two years of age, very blind, and scarcely able to walk or even stand, he was placed in a most unfortunate dilemma, between the firmness of the British Plenipotentiary and the obstinacy of the Chinese Government. It was evident that some heavy penalty hung over him in the event of his being unable to make Lord Elgin give way. With tears in his eyes he spoke of himself as the "friend of two generations" of Chinese and Foreigners, and complained much of what he had undergone as a suspected traitor in Foreign interests. For his devotion to these his sons had been imprisoned, he had contemplated suicide; and he had been sent down to Tientsin because his name had been mentioned in a recent despatch of Lord Elgin's. The contemptuous manner in which this poor old man was treated by Lord Elgin and Mr Lay at this time may have been a necessity of the position, for Ki Ying's business there was evidently to procrastinate and delude; but it is much to be regretted that her Majesty's representative, whose career in China was otherwise so unexceptionable, should have found it or thought it necessary to act towards him as he did. Probably had he shown for him more respect and nominal deference in the presence of Kweiliang and Hwashana, the two other Commissioners, the Chinese authorities would not have been so cruel to Ki Ying as they were on his return, unsuccessful, to Peking. They probably concluded that he had vastly overrated his influence with Englishmen; and the consequence was that the "friend of two generations," though a member of the Imperial family, had "the silken cord" sent to him, and ended his checkered but brilliant career by private strangulation in a dungeon.

The next high Mandarin who was brought prominently before the notice of this country was Yeh Ming-chin, the son of a village apothecary, who was Governor-General of the Two Kwang, and Imperial Commissioner for Foreign Affairs at Canton at the outbreak of the lorcha Arrow affair, which led to the war with China in 1857-58, and to the treaty of Tientsin. Yeh's resemblance to Henry the Eighth of England, and his conversation on his passage to Calcutta, where he died a prisoner in 1859, were fully reported to the British public by Mr Wingrove Cooke of the 'Times.' It is not known, however, in this country, that when his body was brought back to Canton it was received with extraordinary marks of respect and affection, both by the officials and the people of that city. They owed him special gratitude for the decisive manner in which he had acted against the Rebels in 1856, which cleared the Province of these dreadful marauders, and which has been unreasonably held up only as a proof of his brutality and cruelty. The times in which he lived, and the position in which he was placed, required him to act with stern determination; and it is difficult to see how he could have done otherwise than he did, in resisting our demands in 1856-57. The temper of the Peking Government and of the people of Kwangtung was such, that to have ceded these demands would have been for Yeh to have sealed his own destruction. Moreover, it must be remembered that the British House of Commons, after a long debate, homologated Yeh's interpretation of the treaty of Nanking; and that at the very time we made war on China, nominally because of his violating two unimportant and very doubtful stipulations in the treaty, we were openly and unquestionably violating it on more important points, by carrying and forcing on the opium traffic, and by engaging in trade at other ports than those which the treaty opened.

On the capture of Canton and its occupation by our troops, Englishmen were brought into close intercourse with Pih Kwei, the Governor of Kwangtung, who was conjoined with the French and English Commissioners in the government of the provincial city. Kweiliang, and Hwashana, who negotiated with Lord Elgin the treaty of Tientsin, were both Manchus of high standing; the former being one of the four Chief Secretaries of State, and the latter President of the Civil Board, the most important tribunal of the empire. Mr Oliphant has described Kweiliang as a venerable man of placid and benevolent expression, with a countenance full of intelligence, with manners polished and dignified, and with the bearing of a perfect gentleman. Dr Rennie,* however, states that notwithstanding these characteristics, this eminent statesman was treated with much discourtesy at Tientsin in 1858 by Mr H. N. Lay, who was then interpreter to Lord Elgin's Embassy, and that this was the chief cause of Sankolinsin's aversion to carrying out the treaty of that year.

Rather unpleasant recollections are connected with the next high Chinese officials who were brought prominently in contact with foreign affairs. Sankolinsin, the Mongol Prince, whose history I have elsewhere noticed,† was the most influential person in delaying the ratification of

---

* 'Peking and the Pekingese,' vol. ii. p. 288.
† See *ante*, p. 51.

the Tientsin treaty.   He commanded the Chinese troops during our most disastrous attack upon the Taku forts in 1859, when these forts were taken in 1860, and when Sir Harry Parkes and others were taken prisoners during Lord Elgin's advance upon Peking.   This prince was an honourable and patriotic soldier, much respected by the Chinese, and not disliked by Foreigners, despite the painful circumstances connected with the murder of the prisoners.   When this subject was inquired into, he distinctly denied knowing anything whatever about them or about their fate beyond having ordered some of them to be sent into the capital.   Nearly three years ago he himself was murdered, though Generalissimo of all the Imperial forces, when operating against the Nien-fei Rebels in Shantung.   These plunderers were very active horsemen, and, at a critical moment, Sankolinsin's troops falling back and deserting him, he was seized by the enemy, and immediately cut into minute pieces.   In his opposition to Foreigners this soldier was strongly supported by the Prince of I, a member of the Imperial family, and President of the Imperial Clan-Court ; by the Prince of Ching, Commandant of Peking and President of the Astronomical Board ; and by Su Shu-en, a junior Chief Secretary of State—an ambitious Mandarin, who acquired great power and influence during the last years of the reign of Hien-fung.   These men had that Emperor very much in their hands ; they were chiefly responsible for his opposition to Foreign demands ; and on his death in 1861 they forged a decree, purporting to be from him, appointing themselves regents over the new boy-Emperor. Their power, however, was overthrown by Prince Kung's *coup d'état* of the 2d November, the two princes being strangulated in private, and Su Shu-en being publicly decapitated, "giving forth sounds to the last which were

not obedient," as an indignant witness of his conduct remarked.   More fortunate for a time was their supporter,
General Shung Pow, a warrior given to poetry and wine ;
for after their death he was continued in his command.
There is now no doubt that this man was responsible for
the decapitation of Captain Brabazon and of the Abbé
de Luc, as they were put to death by his soldiers when
retreating on the 21st of September 1860.   Eventually,
however, Shung Pow came also to a bad end, being
condemned to strangulate himself, for, among other
reasons, having introduced concubines into his camp,
the Chinese apparently being stricter on that point than
the War Offices of either France or England.

After the conclusion of the Convention of Peking, and
the establishment of Sir Frederick Bruce as Resident
Minister at the capital, our relationships with high Chinese officials were of a much more friendly and satisfactory
kind.   The Prince of Kung in particular, as President of
the Foreign Board, was brought much in contact with
our representatives, and favourably impressed them by
his candour, and his enlightened views in regard to other
nations.   He is still almost a young man, of distinctly
Tartar but agreeable and intellectual countenance, and
his chief fault is an aversion to much business.   It has
been complained of him that in one respect he shows too
great a tendency to follow the evil practices of Charles II.
of England ; and about two years ago he fell into temporary disgrace, and was severely reproved for want of
proper respect in private to the two Dowager-Empresses.
It is indeed almost impossible to say where the chief
power lies in China at any given time.   Now one prominent personage, now another, is popularly spoken of as
having everything in his hands, but the next moment we
hear of his being degraded or censured.   One year it is

Sankolinsin, the next Prince Kung, and then Tseng Kwo-fān, who is considered to be in a position to make himself Emperor; but there is a power behind which can pull such men down as well as raise them up. So far as I can judge, this power seems to be the *consensus* of the higher officialdom of China, and of the members of the Imperial family. Any one who seeks to raise himself above that tribunal is brought down very sharply; and even Prince Kung, notwithstanding his *coup d'état* and his being uncle of the Emperor, has been handled quite unceremoniously. After this Prince, the prominent states-man best known to the British Legation at Peking is Wan See-ang, the senior Secretary of State, or Premier of the Empire. He is a Manchu by birth, and now only fifty years of age, having taken high literary honours when he was quite a youth, and worked his way from office to office. Of low stature, slightly built and gen-tlemanly in appearance, he has also an astute, states-manlike countenance, and has shown remarkable ability in "harmonising" Imperial and Foreign interests.

The immense trade of Shanghai, and the proximity to it of the Tai-ping capital Nanking, has made it a very important point of contact between Foreigners and Chinese officials. Setting aside Ho Kwei-tsin, General Ching, and many other officers, civil and military, whose names might be introduced in this connection, I pass at once to the two great Mandarins, Lí Hung-chang and Tseng Kwo-fan, who had most to do with the suppres-sion of the Tai-ping rebellion. The former of them has been often mentioned as Futai of Kiangsoo, in connec-tion with the Ever-Victorious Army; and his counte-nance strikes one by its intelligence and quiet energy.

He is a native of Seuchew in the Hohfei district of the province of Nganhwui, and is now between forty

and fifty, having passed the Han-li College in 1849.
Immediately after, on the Rebels invading Nganhwui,
he took command of a small militia force, and then went
as a secretary into Tseng Kwo-fan's army. We next
find him with the title of a provincial judge in the
province of Chekiang, but also acting as commander of
a body of troops. In 1861, the first year of the present
Emperor, Lí first rose to high position, being, on Tseng
Kwo-fan's report, made acting Futai or Governor of
Kiangsoo. This brought him into contact with Foreigners; for Soochow, the capital of the province, was in
the hands of the Rebels, and so he had to make Shanghai his headquarters. Taking the field with his troops,
and often leading in person, he defeated them at various
places; but as they were pressed down in great masses
by Tseng Kwo-fan in his direction, he did not make
much head against them till he employed the services
of the disciplined Chinese of the Ever-Victorious Army.
After Colonel Gordon took command of that auxiliary
force, Lí Hung-chang made rapid progress in clearing
Kiangsoo of the Tai-pings. Soochow, the capital, was
taken in the end of 1863; and for his services there he
was confirmed in his Futaiship, received the decoration
of the Yellow Jacket, and was created temporary Junior
Guardian to the Emperor. For his services at the close
of the Rebellion in entirely clearing Kiangsoo of Tai-
pings, and for operating with a fleet before Nanking, he
received a double-eyed peacock's feather, and was created
a hereditary first-class noble of the Peh or third rank.
When, in 1866, Tseng Kwo-fan became Generalissimo of
all the Imperial armies, Lí was made Governor-General
of the two provinces Kiangsi and Kiangsoo. A few
months ago he was engaged in operating against the
Nien-fei in Shantung, and was said to have perilled his

position by allowing a large body of them to escape
through his intrenchments; but in the end of last year
he destroyed them altogether, and is now about to be
sent against the Mohammedan rebels.

Tseng Kwo-fan, to whom reference has frequently
been made in preceding pages, is even a greater Mandarin than Lí, and is at present the most distinguished
and influential person in the Empire not of royal blood;
while even of the royal family itself there are none to
compare with him in influence, unless it be the youthful
Emperor himself, the Dowager Empresses, and the Emperor's uncle, the Prince of Kung, who is President of
the Tsung-li Yamun or the Foreign Board.* He is now
a man of about sixty—stout, dark, with a Chinese resemblance to Oliver Cromwell—and entered the ranks of
Celestial officialdom by passing the examination of the
Han-li College in 1838, the eighteenth year of the Emperor Tao-kwang, and was soon afterwards made a
member of the Board of Ceremonies. In 1852, the
fourth year of the Emperor Hien-fung, he retired from
office, owing to the death of his mother; and whilst at
home at his native town, Hseang-siang, in the province
of Honan, he raised a river-fleet, and undertook the
management of a body of militia which were employed
against the Tai-pings, who had taken several cities in
the province. Being made an Imperial Commander, he
recaptured several of these cities, and destroyed a great
portion of the Rebel flotilla. Immediately after this, in

* The Luh Pe, or Six Boards at Peking, are—the Civil Office, the
Revenue Office, the Office of Rites, the War Office, the Office of Punishments, and the Foreign Office. At the head of each are two presidents
and four vice-presidents; and in each are three subordinate grades of
officers—directors, under-secretaries, and controllers—besides a host of
clerks. There are also several separate bureaus in each board; and the
Tsung-li Yamun, or Foreign Office, has lately been extended and remodelled.

conjunction with other Imperialist forces, he entered the neighbouring province of Hupeh, and retook its capital, Woochang, along with other towns. Thus the two Hu were cleared of Tai-pings very much through his patriotic exertions. For this Tseng received a second-class button, and was made a member of the Board of War. In 1853 he moved down the Yangtsze, and attacked Kiukiang ; but, owing to losing part of his fleet, he was repulsed. During the next three years he took part, along with his brother, in various operations against the Rebels on the Yangtsze and in its neighbourhood, and aided in rescuing the capital of Kiangsi from their grasp.

The death of Tseng Kwo-fan's father in 1857 led, as is usual in such cases, to his retirement from public employment for a nominal term of three years; but in 1859 he was made Commander-in-Chief in the province of Kiangsi, and raised to a higher position in the Board of War. On taking the field this energetic Mandarin soon cleared Kiangsi of Tai-pings, and was in consequence made Imperial Commissioner and Chetai, or Governor-General of the Two Kiang*—that is to say, of the rich and important provinces of Nganhwui, Kiangsi, and Kiangsoo —which is one of the highest appointments that the Chinese Crown has it in its power to give. About the same time, in 1860, he was made Commander-in-Chief in the four provinces of Kiangsi, Kiangsoo, Nganhwui, and Chekiang; so he was thus placed in supreme command of all the operations against the Tai-pings, a position which he occupied for four years, until the fall of Nanking and

---

* This phrase, the "Two Kiang," though still often used, is apt to mislead, for it arose previous to the division of Kiangnan into the two provinces of Kiangsoo and Nganhwui. The "Two Kiang" are properly Kiangsi, "west of the river," and Kiangnan, "south of the river;" the latter including both Kiangsoo and Nganhwui.

the suppression of the Rebellion.   In 1861, the first year
of the present Emperor Tung-che, he became a Cabinet
Minister, but continued to direct in person the military
operations against the Tai-pings.   Next year, with aid
of his brother Tseng Kwo-tsun and other lieutenants, he
cleared the Yangtsze valley of the Rebels, with the exception of Nanking, which they still held.   The appointment, on his proposal, of Lí as Governor of Kiangsoo, and
the employment of Gordon's force, led to the expulsion of
the Tai-pings from that province, and, on the fall of their
capital, to the final suppression of the Tai-pings in 1864.
Tseng Kwo-fan received a double-eyed feather, and was
made Senior Guardian to the Emperor and a first-class
noble of the rank of How—or Marquis, as it might most
correctly be rendered in English.   After the death of
Prince Sankolinsin in 1865, Tseng acted successfully
against the Nien-fei Rebels ; and, being succeeded in his
Chetaiship by his *protégé* Lí Hung-chang, succeeded
Sankolinsin as Generalissimo of all the Imperial forces in
China.   Whenever in late years there has been any difference, or rumour of difference, between this great Mandarin and the Peking Government, popular report has
assumed that he would proceed to the capital and ascend
the dragon throne, or else found a southern empire ;
but he has shown no intention of making any such
attempt ; and if he did, it would not likely be successful,
as, in such a case, the Imperial Government would probably receive the assistance of Lí and others of his *pro-
tégés*, on whom he would have in great part to rely.
Tseng Kwo-fan, besides, is more of a soldier than of a
statesman ; his public life has been spent in fighting on
the banks of the Yangtsze—not in exercising his wits
among the bureaucracy of Peking ; and he resembles the
late Duke of Wellington in being strongly inclined to-

wards the Conservative party of his country. By Hong-kong *quidnuncs* he has been described as reactionary in sentiment, and as opposed to intercourse with Foreigners ; but in his practice, at least so far as it is known to us, he has shown no such disposition.

As this is a somewhat personal chapter, it may not be amiss to give sketches of the chief British officials who have been brought in contact with the Chinese during recent eventful years. What may be termed the modern period commences with Sir John Bowring, who succeeded to Sir George Bonham, after a long service at the Canton Consulate, as Governor of Hongkong and Minister-Pleni-potentiary to China, only to become one of the best-abused men of the day, both at home and in the Far East. A philosopher and linguist of some ability, but with a partly self-conferred reputation much beyond his real merits and acquirements, Sir John has displayed neither the scholar's devotion to ideas nor the statesman's grasp of practical principles, but has rather sunk into the scholar when he should have been a statesman, and has striven to be a man of the world when he had better have continued a philosopher. A certain jocular Mandarin understood this Minister very well, when, in answer to a complaint as to the use of the term *I*, or " Barbarian," in his despatches, he replied, that it was not for him, an insignificant one, to enter on linguistic discussions with so great a scholar. But Bowring exercised hardly any personal influence on our relations with China; he scarcely deserved the abuse which was heaped upon him in Par-liament for his connection with the lorcha Arrow affair, and not even the angel Gabriel could win golden opinions in the position of Governor of Hongkong. When he was made Minister to China matters were in such a state that a conflict was almost unavoidable. The British mer-

chants in that country had long resolved on obtaining
a great extension of the privileges of trade ; they had
been profoundly irritated by the cruel murder of six of
their young men at Hwang-chu-kee, near Canton ; and
though the Chinese could plead treaty-rights in favour
of the conservative position which they held, yet certain
higher considerations forbade that their Empire should be
isolated any longer.   Had Sir John Bowring been a man
better fitted for his position, he would in these circumstances have advised his Government to approach the
Chinese authorities in an open and candid manner, stating what were the arrangements which the new time required ; but instead of doing so he made himself a willing tool in the hypocritical and injurious policy of pick-
ing a quarrel with the Celestials on some dubious point
of an existing treaty.   I have been told on high authority that, previous to the Arrow affair, Sir John Bowring
had received private instructions from the Foreign Office
on no account to let any opportunity pass of commencing
a quarrel with the Chinese Government ; and this explains
the pertinacity with which Lord Palmerston afterwards
supported his subordinate, even appealing from the House
of Commons to the country on that subject.   Neither
the lorcha case nor the alleged right of entry to Canton
were points upon which a very conscientious plenipotentiary could have had recourse to arms; and Nemesis soon
overtook Sir John in shape of the obloquy which he had
to endure, and in his unexpected supercession by Lord
Elgin as Plenipotentiary in China.   Thus, if Bowring
had any pleasant vision of figuring in Peking as a greater
successor of Macartney and Amherst it was cruelly disappointed ; and from being the holder of plenipotentiary
powers in regard to four nations—Annam, China, Siam,
and Japan—he found himself suddenly and unexpectedly

reduced to the humble and almost intolerable position of Governor of the islet of Hongkong and of its adjacent waters.

After hostilities with China had commenced, and we were determined to obtain a new treaty, the appointment of Lord Elgin as the new Plenipotentiary to China was a fortunate event. Of an historical family, descended from Scottish royalty, and connected with the proudest traditions of his country, this nobleman, along with his two brothers, General Bruce and Sir Frederick Bruce, had devoted himself from his early years to the public service. As Governor in Jamaica, where he subdued the disorders consequent on the Emancipation Act, and as Governor-General in Canada, where he opposed the various factions, and brought the mass of the people from a state of chronic disaffection into one of permanent loyalty, Lord Elgin had shown a disposition to protect weaker races from the unreasonable violence of the unthinking portion of our countrymen, while at the same time he had pursued Imperial interests with distinguished tact and success. As with all the Bruces, not excepting King Robert, the great founder of the family, there was more of the Englishman than of the Scot in his physique and temperament ; but to great clearness of mind, and to a strong sense of the practical requirements which, in his various positions, he knew so well how to subserve, there was added a speculative ability and power of appreciating general considerations which belong more distinctively to the Northern intellect, and particularly fitted him for grasping the problems which arise from the conflict of great opposing races. His personal appearance, " venerable beyond his years," and a placidity of aspect and demeanour which partially concealed a keenness of eye that bordered on the disagreeable, were specially calculated to impress with confidence and respect a calm-tempered people like the Chinese, of whom Du Halde so truly said, that they would not hear in a month what a Frenchman would speak in an hour. Moreover, being raised above the temptations to which men of less fortunate circumstances struggling with the world are subject, he was not actuated so much by personal ambition as by a deep sense of duty ; and, on going out to China, his sincere resolve was—"No human power shall induce me to accept the office of oppression of the people." *

To the Chinese it will probably appear absurd that such a species of praise should be ascribed to Lord Elgin, for they knew him almost solely in his unpleasant function of pressing upon them changes to which they were at the time averse ; and they can scarcely know what was the pressure he had to resist against doing so to excess, at a period when our knowledge and understanding of China were at the lowest ebb, and what was the dissatisfaction which his moderation caused among a section of our countrymen there. While seeing that the time had come when the whole relationship of the Celestial Empire towards Great Britain required to be changed, he firmly set his face against demanding any changes which would only serve the interests of individuals ; and I well remember observing, on going out to China in 1858, the strength of the secret animosity which this determination had caused among what might be called the "Old Canton" party of our countrymen, who had discovered, to their ineffable disgust and secret rage, that, in calling in the aid of the arms of Great Britain, they had

* See an interesting article on Lord Elgin's last days, attributed to the Dean of Westminster, in the 'North British Review' of May 1864.

subordinated their own petty aims to Imperial interests, and had to do with a Plenipotentiary who neither sought their favour nor feared their frown. The mistakes which Lord Elgin made arose chiefly from the defects of the agents he had to employ—as from the timidity of Mr Wade and the overbearing presumption of Mr Lay. The frank decision with which he pressed his demands on the Chinese, and which led the French officers in the Peking Expedition to speak of him as being capable of being *un officier de dragons*, was, in the circumstances, as some of the leading Mandarins now admit, the greatest kindness he could have shown towards them. Even the burning of the Emperor's Summer Palace was quite justifiable, and was well calculated to promote a good end without inflicting painful injury, though it is deeply to be regretted that, when ordering the conflagration, Lord Elgin did not take steps to insure the preservation of the oldest library in the world.

When Sir Frederick Bruce went up to Peking as Resident Minister in November 1860, and established his mission in the capital in March 1861, it was scarcely anticipated that he would show distinguished ability in his new position. He had seen service enough: in Washington, where he was attached to Lord Ashburton's special Mission in 1842; in Hongkong, where he had been Colonial Secretary from 1844 to 1846; in Newfoundland as Lieutenant-Governor; in several of the South American Republics; as Consul-General in Egypt from 1853 to 1856; as attached to Lord Elgin's Mission to China in 1857; and as Envoy Extraordinary and Minister Plenipotentiary to the Emperor of China in 1859, when he refused to go to Peking except up the Peiho river; but in none of these positions had he had

opportunity of attaining eminence. Perhaps an easy
off-hand manner, and facility in making himself agreeable, had tended to conceal his real abilities. Those
who knew him superficially were apt to suppose that he
would sacrifice anything to comfort and the pleasures of
good companionship; while a closer acquaintanceship
with him dispelled this illusion, and disclosed a man of
very firm character and sound judgment, who allowed
others to trifle with him as they pleased, not because he
was afraid to cause them annoyance when duty required,
or in any degree to incur their resentment, but simply
because he felt that he could rely on his own strength.
During his service at Peking, this fact made itself very
apparent. Taller and handsomer than his brother, Lord
Elgin, with a commanding presence and agreeable manners, Sir Frederick exhibited a demeanour at once dignified and suave, whether towards the Imperial Mandarins
or his own countrymen; but any attempt to interfere
with his direction of the interests of his country was
very promptly checked when it could not be set aside
in a lighter way. By a portion of the mercantile community he was accused of indolent neglect of their
interests; but his despatches clearly show that he had
fully weighed their complaints, and was prepared, had
he deemed it advisable, to answer these complaints
very fully.

The position in which Sir Frederick Bruce was placed
at Peking was exceedingly difficult, between the unreasonable expectations of the British merchants, who
imagined that the new treaty was to produce a commercial millennium, and the timid suspicions of the Mandarins, who were inclined to look upon every Foreign
proposal as hurtful to their own interests and destructive
to China. A fussy, meddling man might in his place

have done irretrievable injury by inclining injudiciously to either side. To have ignored just Foreign demands would have confirmed the Chinese Government in its worst mistakes, and to have urged that Government beyond the limits of its own judgment would have had a very similar effect. It required no small degree of moral courage, even for a man who understood the position, to act in it so calmly and satisfactorily as Sir Frederick did. He was not afraid even to rebuke her Majesty's Foreign Secretary, Earl Russell, for acting on the Lay-Osborn agreement; and Lord Palmerston, the then Premier, when referring to this matter in Parliament, seemed rather to chuckle over the boldness of his subordinate. An attentive perusal of Sir Frederick Bruce's despatches from Peking, and of a number of his private letters, has left upon me a very high impression of his great ability and honesty of purpose. It is quite true that in 1863 he hesitated a good deal, and so for a short period his policy assumed an appearance of feebleness and vacillation. The cause of hesitation lay, not in his own character, but in the extreme difficulty of the question which he had to decide. Desiring, for the sake of our mercantile interests and of the people of China, to aid in strengthening the Imperial Government and in putting down the Rebellion, he felt bound to give the full weight of his support to Colonel Gordon and any other British officers who chose to enter the Imperial service. At the same time he had to see that the assistance so given should not confirm the Chinese Government in its old inefficient style of dealing with rebellion. It is no wonder that he hesitated in these circumstances, for even now it is difficult to say whether he might not with advantage have inclined a little more to one side or the other; but no one can aver with even

the slightest show of truth, that having once made up
his mind as to the course to be pursued, he did not
pursue that course in a persistent manner, or shrunk
from responsibility, or failed to acknowledge in a generous manner the services of his coadjutors. It may also
be noted that he was eminently successful in leading the
other Foreign Ministers at Peking to act along with him,
so as to present an undivided front to the Mandarins;
and there can be little doubt that this was one of the
chief reasons which led to his promotion to the still
more difficult post of Minister at Washington, where he
also acted with rare tact and discretion, almost up to
the very day of his sudden and lamented death,—a death
which, as the President of the United States remarked,*
revealed to Americans the fact that the friendship which
they had cherished for him " had even acquired the intensity of fraternal affection."

It is not necessary to say much about Sir Rutherford
Alcock, the successor of Sir Frederick Bruce as British
Minister at Peking.   In ordinary times the Chinese
need not expect that we should always be represented
by distinguished or able men, or that our Foreign Office
should overlook the claims which long service in the Far
East may confer on a mere *routinier*. It is greatly to
Sir R. Alcock's credit that nothing particular has to
be said against his conduct of the mission to China ;
for both as Consul at Shanghai and as Minister to Japan
his previous career had given indications of considerable
want of judgment. One or two of his earlier reports to
his own Government on the state of China, and on our
relationships with that country, are really valuable documents, characterised by sound knowledge and great

* In his address to Mr Thornton, the successor of Sir F. Bruce as British
Minister at Washington.

moderation of tone; but as Consul at Shanghai he did
not always act on the principles he had propounded,
and especially in threatening, on account of some dubious
dispute with the Imperialist authorities in his neighbourhood, to lay an embargo on the sea-going supply of
grain to Peking.   In Japan the conduct of Sir Rutherford Alcock was productive of more serious consequences,
and a good deal of our difficulties with that newly-
opened country may be fairly charged against him.
Towards the Japanese he was both overbearing and
timid.   He greatly weakened his position as her Majesty's representative by, at an early period of his mission, threatening them with war on insufficient grounds
and without sufficient authority, an offence for which he
was severely reproved by Earl Russell, then Foreign Secretary; and yet when the Japanese Government, pursuing
its policy of intimidation towards Foreigners, warned
him that it could not protect the Legation at Yedo, he
had the weakness to remove his flag to Yokohama, while
Mr Harris, the American Minister, continued to reside
in safety at the secular capital.   Towards his own countrymen in Japan also Sir Rutherford Alcock behaved
very injudiciously, trying to control and thwart them in
regard to matters in which they were perfectly in the
right,—such as preferring Yokohama to Kanagawa as a
place for a commercial settlement, and travelling in the
country, with the connivance of Japanese authorities,
beyond the limits allowed them by treaty.

In our connection with China a great deal depends
on the character of certain British officials who are well
acquainted with the Celestial language, but who do not
come prominently before the notice of the British public.
Of these by far the most important of late years has
been Mr Thomas Wade, who acted for long as Chinese

Secretary to the Legation, and filled at one time the post of *Chargé d'Affaires* at Peking. Having gone out to China as a subaltern in one of her Majesty's regiments during the period of the Opium War, Mr Wade's linguistic proclivities led him to acquire a knowledge of the Chinese tongue, and his first civil employment was in the somewhat humble position of interpreter to the Supreme Court of Hongkong. Neither well skilled, nor professing to be well skilled, in the use of colloquial Chinese (a defect which he shares, along with the American, Dr S. W. Williams, one of the most eminent of living Sinologues), Mr Wade has, nevertheless, enormous knowledge of the Chinese language and literature, and has done good service by his translations, published or only privately printed, of Chinese State-Papers. His irritable repellant air, as of an ill-used and over-worked man, has not been fitted to inspire the confidence of a calm-tempered people like the Chinese, and he has been not altogether unjustly accused of a fondness for working in the dark in circumstances where the interests of the two countries would have been much better furthered by greater frankness and publicity. In brief, Mr Wade's great fault is, that in a position of great power and responsibility he has failed to rise above the subservience and caution which are the characteristics of subordinate officials in small colonies such as Hongkong.

Sir Harry Parkes and Mr H. N. Lay come to be noticed together, as both belonging, *longo intervallo*, to the same school. They both went out to China at a very early age, and had the misfortune of being pupils of the late Dr Gutzlaff, a man of somewhat unscrupulous character. I have noticed that Europeans who have been brought up from childhood or from early youth in India or China, and have at the same time

made early acquaintance with Eastern languages, are
disposed to treat the natives of these countries with
greater rudeness, or, as some would call it, energy, than
is usual among other Englishmen in the East of similar
social standing.   The real cause of this I believe to
be partial arrestment of moral development at the bois-
terous schoolboy stage, owing to a too early acquirement of power among people of a different moral code
from that of their own countrymen ; but it may plausi-
bly, however erroneously, be argued that it proceeds
only from appreciation of the best means of dealing with
Asiatics.   Be that as it may, both the gentlemen now
referred to acquired a reputation among the Chinese for
this characteristic.   Of Mr Lay enough has been said
already,* and I have no wish otherwise to compare Sir
Harry Parkes with him; but the latter also has certainly
been affected by early Eastern training, both as regards
a habit of *driving* the Chinese, and as regards a quality
which may be called subtlety.   When he was engaged
with Sir John Bowring in obtaining our treaty with
Siam, the officials of that country said that he combined
the energy of a European with the *finesse* of a Chinese
Mandarin ; and a similar suggestion is made by the
contrast between his brilliant forehead and manly open
countenance and his stereotyped hollow smile, so indi-
cative of oblique design.   Though that affair passed very
soon out of his hands, yet a certain responsibility for
the Arrow difficulty rests upon him ; and I have heard
more than one impartial observer speak of his treatment
of Chinese officials on certain occasions as having been
something " quite frightful." †

* See *ante*, p. 260 *et seq.*

† On this subject generally, Dr Rennie makes the following remark,
which is worthy of note, in his ' Peking and the Pekingese,' vol. ii. p. 290 :
" Wang a small Mandarin, who has often complained bitterly of his

When Sir Harry Parkes fell into the hands of the Chinese in 1860, no one expected that he would ever reappear in any other shape than that of "minute pieces;" but his unshaken courage and firmness had something to do, as well as his good fortune, in preserving him from the fate of his companions; and his estimable personal qualities, as well as his value as a public servant, made his release unharmed a matter of rejoicing to all his countrymen in China. Being still little past Dante's *mezzo del cammin di nostra vita*, his success in life has been somewhat remarkable; but it has been well earned by his singular activity and his devotion to the interests of the British merchants in China. I believe it was the intention of Lord Elgin, when he superseded Sir John Bowring, to have sent Sir Harry, then Mr Parkes, back to his unimportant consulate at Amoy, as having proved himself of rather too active a disposition; but the services of the latter were found indispensable, and on our occupying Canton he was made British Commissioner for the Government of that city, fulfilling the multifarious duties which devolved on him, with an ardour which knew no rest, and a personal fearlessness which despised even common prudence. His captivity at Peking, and services about that period, were rewarded with the title of K.C.B.; and from the Shanghai Consulship he was advanced to be our Minister in Japan, a position which will probably lead to his obtaining the Peking mission.

treatment by Sir H. Parkes, when he went over to the north fort, at Taku, in August 1860, to deliver a letter to Lord Elgin from the Governor-General of Chili] attributes a great deal of the troubles of the British Government with China to the overbearing conduct of our interpreters, who, he remarks, lose themselves completely as soon as they have learned the Chinese language, and try to carry everything by bullying, and what they call 'knowing how to manage the Chinese;' an observation that my own experience inclines me very much to endorse, from what I have on several occasions myself witnessed."

312 SKETCHES OF OFFICIALS IN CHINA.

This, in a public service like that of Great Britain, is a splendid career for so young a man, aided by no special interest, and distinguished rather by ordinary parts in a high state of activity, than by the qualities of what Confucius was wont to call "the superior man."

Mr Thomas Taylor Meadows is a remarkable contrast to Sir H. Parkes: his Northumbrian stature and solidity indicate a man of slow adaptability, not easily moved from any opinion he once takes up; and his early education at a German University has given him a tendency to theorising somewhat in excess of the actual grasp of his mind. He has been connected in an important manner with the Tai-ping movement, because from an early period of its existence he took a great interest in it, and industriously availed himself of his position in the Consular Service to collect information regarding that movement. In his most valuable and interesting work, 'The Chinese and their Rebellions,' and in his long reports to Government, he always took a very favourable view of the Tai-pings. Mr Meadows has the credit of having been the first among our modern Sinologues to comprehend the vital principles of the Chinese State, and the pretensions of the Rebellion in relation to these principles; and his great knowledge of the Chinese has been gathered not only by hard and intelligent study (for there is such a thing as industrious unintelligent study) of their language and literature, but also by frequently travelling among them as one of themselves, in circumstances which exposed him to very great danger. He is not for a moment to be confounded with the rut of Tai-ping sympathisers in China, or with Colonel Sykes *et hoc omne genus* at home; but, owing to the interest which the Rebellion excited in him from its resemblance to earlier revolutionary movements in China, and to

the foolish character of many of the objections brought
against it, he greatly exaggerated its merits, and lost sight
of the deterioration which took place in the character
and in the practices of its leaders. It was of importance, however, for a competent person among our officials in China to take the side of the Tai-pings and say
all that could be said in their favour. While doing so
Mr Meadows has always shown himself a scholar and a
gentleman, and he has thrown much light on collateral
subjects of interest and importance. It is greatly to be
regretted that some differences with Sir Frederick Bruce
when Mr Meadows was Acting Consul at Shanghai, and
his own love of studious retirement, should have prevented him from taking a much higher place than he has
done in Anglo-Chinese officialdom. At his own request
he was banished to the unimportant consulship of Newchwang in Manchuria some years ago, and as he has never
shown any disposition to be released from that post, we
can only hope that he may soon lay before the public
the result of his researches in Manchu language and
history.

So far as I can judge in regard to a subject which
seems purposely kept as much in the dark as possible,
Admiral Sir James Hope was the British officer in China
who took the most active part in bringing about a change
in our relationships towards the Tai-pings; but I have
no means of determining whether this was done from a
serious view of the position, or simply from the natural
tendency of naval officers to cut out work for themselves
and for those under their command. There can be no
doubt that the Taku disaster of 1859 was one which
would have been fatal to the prospects of any British
admiral not backed up either by great interest or by
much popularity in the service. Both these causes, com-

bined with his own personal gallantry, have served to
throw a veil over Admiral Hope's management on that
occasion ; and it may also be said, that previous to the
disaster our experience of Chinese warfare had not war-
ranted any expectation of such serious resistance as Sankolinsin made at the mouth of the Peiho in 1859.   In
determining on the clearance of a thirty-mile radius
round Shanghai, in the operations which effected that
end, and in his support of the course of conduct followed
by Captain Dew in Chekiang, Admiral Hope did valuable service to the cause of order and peace in China ;
but it was by the support he gave to General Ward, and
to the establishment of the Ever-Victorious Army on the
footing of a respectable force, that he dealt his most
effectual blow against the Tai-pings.   Of his subordinate,
Captain Roderick Dew, it is not necessary to repeat here
what has already been said in the commencement and
the end of Chapter VII.   The valley of the Wye has
reason to be proud of so dashing and distinguished a
naval officer.

Both the chief of the present Abyssinian Expedition
and his second have served in China.   Sir Robert Napier
held a divisional command under Sir Hope Grant on
the Peking Expedition, and directed the capture of the
North Fort at Taku, impressing on his troops a high idea
of his ability, and on observers like myself, of his geni-
ality of disposition.   Major-General Sir Charles W. Staveley went through a good deal of service in the Crimea,
having been in the battles of Alma and Balaclava, and
in command of the 44th Regiment at the fall of Sebastopol.   In the China campaign of 1860 he commanded a
brigade, and, in April and May 1862, was in command
of the force employed against the Tai-pings in the neighbourhood of Shanghai, when the fortified town of Najow

was taken, the walled cities of Kading, Tsipoo, and
Cholin, and several intrenched camps. He has the reputation of being very active and kind-hearted, but cau-
tious, and more inclined to fulfil the duties of a second
in command than for assuming the initiative and the
responsibility required of a chief. His appointment of
a British officer to command the Ever-Victorious Army
was an event forced upon him by circumstances rather
than of his own seeking, and his bearing towards the
Chinese was dignified, reserved, and guarded; but at
the same time he was very polite towards them, and they
thought very highly of him. His successor, Major-General W. G. Brown, on the contrary, was not at all afraid
of incurring responsibility, and was apt to be a little high-
handed with the Chinese. The acquaintance of this
officer with active service had been drawn chiefly from
the Punjaub campaign, he having been wounded at the
battle of Chillianwallah, and commanded the 29th Regiment at the battle of Goojerat. Like many other officers
who have seen much service in India, he was disposed to
deal with the Chinese as we do with the natives of India,
which the Celestials do not at all appreciate; but any un-
pleasantness arising from that cause was amply compensated to them by the hearty and effective support which
he gave to Colonel Gordon, and, in general, to the Imperialist cause, regardless of the outcries of Tai-ping
sympathisers, and fearless of the responsibility which he
incurred.

In the persons of Colonel Gordon and of Mr Robert
Hart the Chinese have, at a very critical period of their
history, been happily brought in contact with two Foreigners of a higher tone of mind and character than
their previous experience had made them much acquainted
with. Of the former officer I have thought it necessary

already to say much more than is agreeable to himself, and shall only add here a very few words. A great deal of what has been mentioned to his credit I should never have learned from himself; and the reader who has gone through the details of fighting and bloodshed with which his name is associated, might be surprised on finding him to be a man still young, of quiet manners and disposition, and of varied culture. Deeply religious in sentiment, and a soldier of the Havelock and Stonewall Jackson type, Colonel Gordon presents few of the characteristics usually associated with the common notion of the dashing leader of an irregular force. Great pleasure in activity, a self-sacrificing disposition, and a sense of duty, have been evidently the mainsprings of his conduct; and the results, whatever others may think, have been too pleasant and satisfactory to himself, and, as he thinks, too undeserved, to allow of his glorying in them.

Mr Hart, the Inspector-General of the Chinese Imperial Maritime Customs, was in the British Consular Service in China before he entered that of which he became the head on the dismissal of Mr Lay in 1863, and brought much previous culture to assist him in acquiring a knowledge of the Chinese language and people. While fully alive to the defects of the Celestial Government, he has shown great tact and wisdom in leading it along the path of progress; at the same time he has commanded the respect of his own countrymen in the somewhat invidious position of Inspector-General of Customs. His lucid memorandums on the trade and the condition of China are well worthy the consideration of those who desire to see gradual and pacific improvement in that country. Of late he has almost entirely taken up his residence at Peking, and has become the confidential adviser of the Peking Government in all that refers to

its Foreign relationships.   To the effects of the confidence
which he has inspired may be ascribed the appointment
of the Laou-yeh Pin to proceed to Europe in 1866 as
a Commissioner from the Imperial Government, the
establishment of a College at Peking for the study of
European languages and science, and the appointment
of Mr Burlinghame as Minister from China to the Treaty
Powers.   In character, and, to a less extent, in manner,
Mr Hart reminds one of an Indian civilian of the higher
class, and especially of that school of Indian civilians of
which Sir Bartle Frere is *facile princeps*.   The pleasant
demeanour of an Irishman has been useful to him at
Peking, as it was, many years before, to Earl Macartney.
He is more inclined to lead than to drive the Chinese,
and has established himself as a power in the country ;
but it may be well for him to keep in mind the deserved fate of Mr Lay, and not to lose sight of the fact
that, though he has used them well, he has had great
opportunities provided to his hand.   Hitherto his course
has been favoured by that of events ; and while he has
himself reaped a large share of the resultant rewards,
perhaps the most arduous portion of the task of adjust-
ing our international relationships with China has fallen
upon those who have received no remuneration or
even acknowledgment for their unselfish but invidious
labours.   Now that he is able in some degree to command
events similar to those by which he has been guided,
and of which he has so wisely availed himself, it remains
to be seen how far he will be equal to the high respon-
sibilty and grand opportunities of a very powerful
position between England and China.

CHAPTER XVI.

THE FALL OF NANKING AND THE LAST STRUGGLES OF THE TAI-PINGS.

THE TIEN-WANG'S INDIFFERENCE AND SECLUSION—SWEET DEW—HIS WISDOM AND GOOD FORTUNE—COMPLETE INVESTMENT OF NANKING — DESPAIR OF THE FAITHFUL KING — LAST DAYS OF HUNG SEW-TSUEN—HIS DEATH AND BURIAL—HIS SON FU-TIEN ASCENDS THE THRONE—THE FALL OF NANKING—CAPTURE OF THE FAITHFUL KING — HIS CHARACTER AND AUTOBIOGRAPHY—HIS EXECUTION—FATE OF THE SHIELD KING AND OF THE YOUNG MONARCH — STATE OF NANKING WHEN CAPTURED — REPORT ON ITS CONDITION BY VICE-CONSUL ADKINS — RECEPTION OF THE NEWS AT PEKING—IMPERIAL DECREE—THE FALL OF WUCHU — EXPERIENCES OF PATRICK NELLIS — RETREAT OF THE TAI-PING REMNANT THROUGH KIANGSI INTO FUKIEN—THEY APPEAR AT CHANGCHOW, NEAR AMOY — MANIFESTO OF THE ATTENDANT KING—THEIR DISPERSION AND FINAL DISAPPEARANCE—FATE OF THE I WANG.

WHILE Soochow was in course of being taken in 1863, Tseng Kwo-tsun, the Imperialist General, was engaged with large forces in closely investing Nanking. He intrenched himself so closely and strongly round that city as to be able to cut off all supply of provisions, and easily to defeat the attempts of the Faithful King to bring it relief. That latter prince, however, managed himself to gain admission to the Rebel capital, and besought the Tien Wang to make his escape and give up the city, as it could no longer be held, and was defi-

cient in the necessaries of life ; but the monarch, according to the Faithful King's Autobiography, was highly
displeased at this proposal, and indignantly exclaimed,
" I have received the commands of Shangte [God] and of
Jesus to come down upon the earth and rule the empire.
I am the sole Lord of ten thousand nations, and what
should I fear ? You are not asked your opinion upon
anything, and the Government does not require your
supervision. You can please yourself as to whether
you wish to leave the capital or to remain. I hold the
empire, hills, and streams with an iron grasp, and if
you do not support me there are those who will. You
say, 'There are no soldiers !' But my troops are more
numerous than the streams. What fear have I of the
demon Tseng ? If you are afraid of death then you
will die." It was in this way only that the Heavenly
Monarch would look at practical matters. Burying
himself in the depths of his palace, and engrossed with
religious exercises and the society of his women, he
gave himself no concern about either the approach of
his enemies or the terrible state of his people. When
any one memorialised him on internal affairs, or made
suggestions pertinent to the preservation of the kingdom,
he would invariably silence them with remarks on heaven
and earth, which, as the Chung Wang complains, were
" totally irrelevant to the main point in view." When
it was mentioned to him that only the very wealthy
people in Nanking had any food to eat, he issued a
decree that the remainder should support themselves
upon " sweet dew," and illustrated his meaning by ordering some herbs from the palace garden to be prepared
for his own dinner. His subordinates in the Government were allowed to do as they liked so long as they
professed implicit submission to his decrees ; but their

chief was very particular with them in regard to points of theological phraseology, and threatened to draw any one asunder between five horses who omitted a due use of the term "Heavenly" in all official documents.

It should not be supposed, however, that such conduct on the part of Hung Sew-tsuen was altogether insane, for it was in great part by following such a course that he had created Tai-pingdom and maintained his supremacy over it. At no period had he personally interfered much in the details of government or in the management of fighting. Even when blaming him for his inactivity, the Faithful King admits that "the Tien Wang had been inwardly conscious for some time past of an impending crisis and of the insecurity of the capital; but, being of an elevated mind, he did not care to review the past or speculate on the future." And it is very questionable whether he would have gained anything by admitting the serious nature of the circumstances by which he was now surrounded, for one of the greatest supports of his position was his lofty reliance on the favour of Heaven. It would have been exceedingly dangerous for him to have shown any signs of failing or of apprehension; and his extraordinary past career afforded at least some show of reason for his confidence in Heaven, and his disregard of prudential considerations and of merely human advice. Certainly he had enjoyed the smiles of Fortune for a very long period, and that without any great exertions of his own. He had survived all his colleagues who had issued with him from Kwangsi. Of the four leading Kings who started with him on his journeys, two, those of the South and of the West, did not live to reach Nanking; while the Eastern and the Northern Kings had been put to death for conspiring against his authority. More than

once before he had been in apparently desperate circumstances, and been relieved not so much by any efforts of
his own or of his subordinates as by a fortunate turn in
the course of affairs.   Hence it was not altogether bad
policy of him to refrain from reviewing the past or
speculating on the future with his elevated mind.

The Faithful King was well aware of the desperate
state into which matters were falling, but no thought of
faithlessness to his Lord seems to have crossed his mind;
and it is to his honour that he largely expended his
own means in assisting the starving people of Nanking.
In the commencement of 1864 Nanking was closely invested on all sides, so that the only road from it open
was that to Tayan.   The Imperialists had a large flotilla on the Yangtsze.   From this river their double, and
at some places even treble, intrenchments ran above
Nanking to Porcelain Tower Hill, which commanded
the city ; and on the north extended down from the
Tsao-hia creek almost to the hills above the Ming
tombs, where the Rebels still held a strong position.
The forts below the capital had also been captured by
the Imperialists, and when the Faithful King returned
to it in January 1864 he lost about 100,000 of his men
merely from having no rations to give them all, and no
spot on which to camp them.

When the Ever-Victorious Army was dissolved in
June 1864, the capture of Nanking and the final suppression of the Tai-ping Rebellion were events which
appeared evidently close at hand.   On the 1st of June
the investment of the Rebel capital was completed sufficiently to prevent its receiving any further supplies.
The Imperialists had exploded several mines at different
places beneath the walls, so compelling the garrison
to be continually on the watch.   The Imperialist lines

around the city were about thirty miles in length, consisting of strong forts, stockades, and deep ditches. These fortifications were so constructed as to protect the besiegers, who were about 80,000 in number, from any attack from the outside ; and though the pay of some of these troops was considerably in arrear, they were well fed and contented. The besieging army was about to be reinforced by Colonel Gordon's late corps of artillery under Colonel Doyle, and also by Bailey's artillery, which had operated under the late General Ching; while Gordon himself took occasion of a flying visit to select the best point for attack, choosing the north-east angle of the wall, which in most parts of its circuit was about 40 feet high and 50 feet thick.

Before matters had got quite to this pass, some of the Tai-ping leaders escaped with their troops and fled into Kiangsi ; but the poor Faithful King remained true to his name and to the Tai-ping cause. He had lost heart, however, and regarded the Rebel movement as virtually defunct. Even then the Heavenly Monarch would not listen to his advice, and trusted the management of affairs to the Shield King alone. He still continued his policy of ignoring the actual state of things, and of discoursing grandiloquently on the mysteries of heaven and earth. Inside the doomed city matters were daily becoming worse and worse. The Faithful King says that starving men and women were constantly clinging round him, beseeching relief which was no longer in his power to afford. As the Tien Wang refused to allow any of the famished people to leave the city, the Faithful King issued secret orders enabling them to do so ; and so about 3000 women and children were allowed to go out to the Imperialist General, Tseng Kwo-tsun, who had established a provident fund for their relief. On

the other hand, the Cantonese soldiers of the Shield
King plundered and murdered as they chose, so that
complete anarchy and confusion reigned in the beleaguered capital of the Great Peace.   "Thieves and
robbers," says the Chung Wang, "sprang up in the
city.   The nights were disturbed with incessant can-
nonading within the walls, and murders and pillages
of whole families took place.   These were fatal omens,
and indications of coming destruction."   As dangers
gathered round him, Hung Sew-tsuen, the Heavenly
Monarch, became more cruel in his edicts, and ordered
any of his people who might be found communicating
with the enemy to be flayed alive or pounded to death ;
but even he could no longer conceal from himself the
fact that the days of his reign and of his life had drawn
to a close.   It would be interesting to know what were
the last thoughts of this extraordinary man when he
found himself in these circumstances.   Did he still believe that he was a favourite of heaven, and authorised
representative of Deity on earth, or had he in his last
hours some glimpse of the true nature of the terrible
and cruel destiny which he had had to fulfil?   Surely
as his thoughts reverted to the simple Hakka village of
his youth, he must have known that his path over the
once peaceful and happy Flowery Land could be traced
by flames and rapine and bloodshed, involving a sum
of human wretchedness such as had never before lain to
the account of the most ferocious scourge of mankind.
Where there had been busy cities, he had left ruinous
heaps ; where fruitful fields, a desolate wilderness ; " wild
beasts, descending from their fastnesses in the mountains, roamed at large over the land, and made their dens
in the ruins of deserted towns ; the cry of the pheasant
usurped the place of the hum of busy populations ; no

hands were left to till the soil, and noxious weeds covered the ground once tilled with patient industry." Even, as has been remarked, the very physical features of the country, owing to neglect of the embankment of great rivers, had been largely changed by his destructive career. And, after all this ruin and misery, what had the Tai-ping movement come to at last but the restoration of Imperial rule in China, while a cloud of fear and wrath hung over the doomed city in which the king and priest and prophet of the Great Peace anticipated death in the midst of his trembling women and the remnant of his ferocious soldiery ?

It is a dreadful story, but chiefly interesting and solely valuable to us from the warning it gives as to the disorganisation and ruin which may swiftly overtake the human race, when it tries to avoid the constantly recurring necessity of facing the exigencies of its position ; and as to the danger of allowing a man of powerful imaginative mind to become mad in the fire of his own repressed energy, and under a sense of his own sufferings and wrongs. Men like Rousseau and Hung Sew-tsuen are not to be held personally accountable for their destructive effect on the society in which they grow up. "They made themselves a fearful monument ;" but in order to its being made, society must have become ripe for ruin—the tree must be ready to fall ; and there is no surer indication of such rottenness in any civilisation, than its inability or its unwillingness to find a fitting place for men of so remarkable powers. In the case of the Tai-ping chief, over-population, nominal submission to Tartar dominion, and unlooked-for contact with a different civilisation, at least as powerful as its own, had brought China to a condition in which it required a great purifying punishment. A

striking indication of this fact was the sale of civil offices
for money, because there was nothing on which the
Chinese had so justly prided themselves, and in which
they were so superior to other nations, as their committal
of both power and wealth to men of regal qualities.
" Virtue," says the commentator in the ' Great Learning,'
" is the root, wealth is the result ; " and so long as the
Chinese acted on this principle their empire flourished ;
when they departed from it, trouble came, as it has
always come, and always will come, upon nations who
value this result more than its root, and having first
allowed the exercise of low qualities to determine the
possession of wealth, proceed to the almost necessary
consequence of allowing wealth to wield the chief power.
It really required some such terrible affliction as the Tai-
ping Rebellion to save China from the state of corruption
and imbecility into which it was sinking ; and when
that rebellion had served its purpose, it too came to an
end, and fell like a tree prepared to fall.   In all this
there was nothing but that benevolence of Heaven to
which Confucius refers, terrible as its working may seem
to human eyes ; and so it becomes intelligible how the
nation which required this punishment had not the
privilege of meting out justice and inflicting retribution
on the instrument of it.

Those who were in intercourse with him at this period
gave no indication as to Hung Sew-tsuen's state of mind.
His son, the "Young Lord," only states that on the
" 24th May 1864 the Tien Wang succumbed to sickness ;" but the Faithful King more probably relates that,
terrified by the bursting of mines which the Imperialists
had sprung round the East Gate, the Rebel Monarch fell
into such anxiety and trouble of mind that on the 30th
June he poisoned himself.   His corpse was buried by

one of his wives in the garden behind his palace, where it was afterwards dug up by the Imperialists, and was found draped in yellow silk, the head being bald and the mustache grey.

After the death of this monarch, his eldest son, Hung Fu-tien, a youth of sixteen years old, ascended the nominal throne; but he had been brought up in ignorance of state matters and of military operations. The city was still more closely beleaguered, and on the 8th July the Faithful King made a sortie, but was driven back after a severe fight. As it was plain to him that the city could not be held much longer, he was now anxious to surrender, but was so closely watched by his colleagues that he could not get away, and an attempt he made to escape nearly cost him his life, through the drunken loquacity of one of his adherents. On the 19th of this month the Imperialists fired an enormous mine, said to contain over 40,000 lb. of gunpowder, which blew a long breach clean through the wall, and through this the Imperialists poured into the city, while at the same time false attacks were made on all sides. On seeing this, the garrisons of Chung-kuan, and of the few other forts which remained to the Tai-pings outside, either surrendered or were killed when running away; but inside the city the Faithful King rallied his troops, and repulsed the assailants near the Tien Wang's palace, which he held till midnight, protecting the Monarch's weeping family. As the Imperialists thronged into the city, however, he found he could no longer make a stand, and, having set fire to the palace, along with his own residence, retreated towards the South-west Gate. Here Hung Fu-tien and two other sons of the Rebel Monarch claimed his assistance, and, as a last instance of his wonderful and unselfish faithfulness, he mounted the Young

Lord on his own war-horse, and contented himself with a weak, useless animal. "Though the Tien Wang's days," he writes, " had been fulfilled, the nation injured, through others baffling and deceiving him, and the state lost, still, as I had received his favours, I could not do otherwise than evince my faithfulness by endeavouring to save his son."

In the confusion which followed the capture of Nanking, the Faithful King, the Shield King, and the Young Lord, with about 1000 of their followers, did manage to escape out of the city and through the Imperialist lines, but were immediately followed by a body of Tseng Kwo-tsun's cavalry. The first of these Wangs soon got separated from the others, but finding that the wretched pony which he rode was unable to carry him, he soon took refuge in a ruined temple on the Huang Hill. On learning that he was the Chung Wang, some country people who discovered him there, knelt down before him and gave way to tears. They besought him to shave his head and assume disguise ; but to this he answered, " I am a great minister of a nation now extinct, and of a sovereign now no more. Had I not escaped, but been taken by the Imperialists, I should not now be in life ; and even though I now live, it will not be fair to my men who have fallen if I submit myself to have my head shaved." On being pressed, however, the Faithful King gave way to the proposal, but before his further escape was contrived, another party came up who recognised him to be a high Tai-ping Chief, from his being in possession of some seals made of precious stone, and who accordingly insisted on his being delivered up to the pursuing cavalry of General Tseng.

On the further fate of Li Seu-cheng, the Chung Wang or Faithful King, it is painful to dwell. He was executed by simple decapitation, without any previous torture ; but during his whole connection with the Rebellion he had behaved in so humane a manner, that his life might well have been spared ; and the constancy he had displayed to the Tai-ping cause, even when suspected and ill-treated by his monarch, was a sufficient guarantee that, having once submitted to the Imperialists, he would not again have taken up arms against them. His last act of fidelity, that of giving his horse to the young Tien Wang, was a noble trait in his character, for had he not done so, he might very likely have himself escaped. Among the Tai-pings generally he was very much beloved, and the country people always spoke well of him, and distinguished him favourably from other Rebel leaders. On various occasions during his career he sacrificed his own property to relieve the distress of cities which some of his colleagues had misgoverned, and the people of Soochow had erected a monument to commemorate one of these his humane efforts. All this, however, did not avail to preserve his life. The Imperial Commissioner, Tseng Kwo-fan, referred his case to Peking; and during the respite thus afforded, the Chung Wang occupied himself in writing his autobiography, which he completed in eight days, at the extraordinary rate, considering the nature of the Chinese language, of about 7000 characters daily. This *apologia pro vita sua*, though written in these curious circumstances, to show cause why he should not be put to death, is a masterly production, being an exceedingly clear and condensed sketch of the history of the Rebellion, and displaying very graphic powers of description in those parts which relate to the author's own experience. Of its truthfulness there need be no question, because it is accurate on points where it can be checked, and it is tinged throughout with a fine colouring of philosophic melancholy, suitable to the circumstances in which it was produced.

On second thoughts Tseng Kwo-fan did not wait for Imperial directions as to the disposal of this Tai-ping Chief. It occurred to him that, if sent up to Peking, the Faithful King might either escape on the road and cause new misfortunes, or else avoid a public execution by starving himself to death; so he suddenly took upon himself the responsibility of ordering his decapitation, which took place on the 7th of August 1864, and his head was sent round to various cities "in order to gratify the public mind." So far the Faithful King was actually fortunate, for an Imperial decree which arrived soon after condemned him to a "slow and ignominious death;" but his execution in any way must be condemned. Even as a matter of policy it was inexpedient, for he had offered to secure the allegiance of the Rebels in Hoopeh and Kiangsi as a ransom for his life. There can be no doubt that he had sufficient influence with the remaining Tai-pings to secure this result; and had his offer been accepted, the people in various districts in China, where the Rebellion still lingered for more than a year, might have been saved from a good deal of misery.

Hung Jen-kan, the Kan Wang or Shield King, a near relative of the Tai-ping monarch, was also taken prisoner when fleeing from Nanking, and executed along with the Faithful King. This man has a prominent place in Tai-ping history, but not one of a very attractive kind. He was born about the year 1820, and at one period of his life had lived in Hongkong, and so made acquaintance with Foreigners. During that period he professed to be a Christian, and was either employed by, or was in other intimate relationships with, some of our mis-

sionaries. In 1851 and in 1854 he made ineffectual
attempts to join his Heavenly relative, but did not do
so until 1859, when he reached Nanking, received a
title of nobility, and was soon after created a prince,
and made Generalissimo of the Tai-ping armies. Dr
Dickson, lately of Canton, who met the Kan Wang
during one of the attempts the latter was making to
reach Nanking, informs me that he was a tall, dark
man, of rather coolie-like appearance; but he must have
possessed a good deal of intelligence and education, for
on that occasion he was acting as tutor in a wealthy
Chinese family. Hung Jen-kan's knowledge of Foreigners led him to understand how important it would be for
the Tai-pings to establish themselves at Shanghai and
Ningpo, but he does not seem to have otherwise been
any accession to the Rebel cause. When the Rev. Mr
Roberts, the American missionary, who had been the
Tien Wang's first Christian instructor, was residing in
Nanking in 1860, it was this Chief with whom he came
most in contact, and who drove him away from the
rebel capital by striking him on the face, and murdering
one of his servants before his eyes.* And it does not
seem that the Shield King was any milder in his demeanour towards the Tai-pings themselves. Very seldom taking the field himself or exposing his person, he
was cruel in his treatment of those subject to his sway,
and was hated by the people of Soochow and of other
cities which had reason to feel his presence. As it was
customary with the Tai-pings to keep up titles so far as
possible, there are some obscure notices of another Kan
Wang existing among the remnants of the Rebellion in
1865, but that was a different person from Hung Jen-
kan, the Heavenly Monarch's Prime Minister from 1860

---

* See Blue-book, China, presented to His Majesty, April 8th, 1862, p. 142.

to 1864. The latter was executed immediately after the fall of Nanking; and before doing so he wrote a short biography of himself, at the conclusion of which he says, "Three years back, little did I think, when holding such a high position at the capital, and endowed with such vast power as I then had, that affairs would come to such a pass at the present day, and that an ignominious death would await me."

Though the Faithful King gave his war-horse to Hung Fu-tien, the second Heavenly Monarch, the latter did not long escape his Imperialist pursuers. Roused by the fall of Nanking from his easy life and the society of his young queens, he was ill fitted to meet adverse circumstances. In the course of his flight he got separated from the Kan Wang and his other companions, and concealed himself among some hills, where he suffered so much from starvation that he actually wished for death. Being relieved by some country-people, the unfortunate youth continued his wanderings for some weeks, when he fell into the hands of Imperialist braves, and being delivered up to General Shung Pow, was quickly executed at the provincial city of Kiangsi, apparently not expecting such a fate; for in his declaration made after capture, he repudiated all ambitious designs, and expressed a hope that he might be sent to Hoonan "to read for a literary degree."

When the city of Nanking was captured, it was found to be in a very deplorable state; grass was growing luxuriously in the streets, and most of the houses were in ruins. Judging from various statements, there could not have been more than 20,000 fighting men within the walls; of these about 1500 escaped, and about 7000 were put to death. This is not in accordance with Imperialist statements, which speak of 100,000 men having

been killed, which is merely an indefinite phrase used
by the Chinese when they cannot conveniently compute
numbers. There is more probability in Tseng Kwo-tsun's
statement, that during the last two years' siege 10,000 of
the Imperialist soldiers fell victims to sickness, and 8000
or 9000 of them were killed in fight. The fire which
the Faithful King had kindled raged for three days
before it was got under and arrangements were made
for restoring order. After this the Rebel palaces were
found to be only heaps of ashes, and the strictest search
could discover no treasure, though it had been rumoured
that the Rebel Monarch's wealth was " vast as the sea."
Tseng Kwo-fan seems to have been a little disappointed
at this result, and complains that even Soochow had
more wealth in it than Nanking had. He acknowledges,
in his despatch on this subject to the Imperial Government, that some of his soldiers took a good deal of money
from individual Tai-pings, but he did not think fit to
interfere with their privileges in that respect. He only
required that any buried treasure which might be discovered should be handed over to the public funds ; and
none such being forthcoming, he philosophically observes,
" To capture the great stronghold of the Rebels, and to
find no wealth whatever, certainly surpasses your humble
servant's calculations, and is a thing of rare occurrence."

A very few days after the fall of Nanking, a visit was
paid to that city by Mr Adkins, the Acting British Consul at Chinkiang ; and he describes what he then saw
in the following extract, from a despatch to Earl Russell,
dated the 29th July 1864 :—

I have the honour to inform you that the city of Nankin, so
long the centre of disaffection in China, and the point from
which so many bands of ruthless plunderers have started on
their raids upon the peaceful and wealthy cities of Central

China, has been captured by the Imperialist Army under the command of Tseng-kwo-chuen, the Governor of Chekiang, and brother of the Viceroy of the provinces of Kiang Nan and Kiang Su.

The city was stormed on the 19th of this month, through a breach caused by a mine sprung under the wall near the east gate. Rumours of its capture reached me on the day following the assault, but I paid no attention to them, having been so often deceived by reports of Chinese victories. On the 24th of this month, however, I obtained a copy of the Memorial to the Throne formally announcing the capture.

On the following day I started for Nankin in her Majesty's ship Slaney, intending to congratulate the Chinese Commander-in-Chief on the auspicious termination of his two years' siege. I found his Excellency at his camp outside the south gate of the city.

When the Imperialists made good their entrance into the city, they found that the palace of the Tien Wang, the leader of the Rebellion, and the claimant for many years past of divine honours and attributes, had been burnt to the ground. It is said that the impostor and his immediate attendants lie buried in its ruins. I am inclined to credit the rumour, for the city has been closely blockaded since January last, and I think that nothing but a desperate sortie would have enabled him to get clear.

But the most important fact of all is the capture of Chung Wang. This person has for many years been the most restless and determined of all the desperadoes Tai-pingdom has sent forth. He it was who threatened Shanghai in 1860; he was Admiral Hope's antagonist in his operations near Shanghai; he fought against Colonel Gordon at Soochow. He tried to introduce the foreign element into his levies, and was said by Rebel sympathisers to be the main hope of the Tai-ping cause in its declining days. After the assault, he managed to leave the city with a few followers, but he was captured three days subsequently by a party of cavalry. I was much pressed to visit the Chung Wang in his confinement, but declined, as I had no personal acquaintance with him.

On the day following my interview with the Commander-in-Chief, I rode into the city and visited the breach. Words cannot describe the utter desolation of everything within the walls

The main thoroughfares traversed by me were the streets between the south-west and east gates, and those between the south-west and south gates. On either hand, the houses left standing had the appearance of having been tenantless for years, while the gaudy gateways, denoting the residences of the wangs or princes, opened in most instances on to courts full of brickbats and charred timbers. As for the side streets, they were, many of them, overgrown with jungle four feet high.

During my ride through the city I saw a great number of unburied bodies, and in many places the smell was so offensive that both myself and Lieutenant Lee, who accompanied me, were almost overpowered. But on the whole I came to the conclusion that the Rebel force in the city at the time of its capture could not have been very large. The Imperialists, according to their own account, spared very few able-bodied males, so that the dead lying in the streets would be a fair criterion of the strength of the garrison. I estimate it at 10,000 men, against 50,000 under the Imperialist commanders.

I think a ride through the streets of Nankin, as they are at present, would satisfy the most ardent advocate of the Rebel cause of the dreadful hollowness of the system they support. Some eleven years ago the Tai-pings took Nankin, then one of the finest cities in China. Ever since its capture it has been their headquarters. In it the chiefs of the movement built their tawdry houses, and from it they despatched plundering bands in all directions. Meanwhile the works of civil government and social organisation are entirely neglected, and when the city is retaken it is found to be a wilderness of empty houses.

The Imperial Government was greatly elated at this victory, the news of which reached it in six days, and made Tseng Kwo-fan a Marquess, or noble of the second grade, and senior guardian of the youthful Emperor, and his brother, Tseng Kwo-tsun, a noble of the third grade, and junior guardian of the Emperor. The other officers who distinguished themselves in the siege were also suitably rewarded; and the Prince of Shun was appointed to proceed to the Shrine of Glorious Happiness, the resting-place of the coffin of the Emperor Hien-fung, to announce the victorious news to that departed monarch. "This," says the Imperial decree announcing the fall of Nanking—"this was indeed a special dispensation in OUR favour, for which we are grateful to Heaven and OUR sacred Ancestors. The Empresses Dowager are agreed in their feelings of gratitude for the peace and order which have been granted to Us. They knew how to choose fit persons (to whom to intrust this great undertaking), so that everywhere there was the greatest unanimity; and both civil and military officials girded themselves for the task set before them, which has now been fully accomplished. OUR Imperial Father, now enthroned in Heaven, will congratulate himself on the turn affairs have taken; while the inhabitants of the world, from the highest to the lowest, will be grateful. We acknowledge that virtue lies not in ourselves; how, then, could WE bring about these successes? WE look back on the deceased Emperor, who never desisted from the pursuit of that purpose of his (the extermination of the Rebels). It continually grieves Us to think that HE did not survive to see his designs carried out. Since this Rebel Hung first created confusion in Kiangsi fifteen years have elapsed, and since he settled himself in Nanking twelve years have dragged slowly on. The Insurgents have trampled more than ten provinces under foot, and overthrown several hundred cities, which have gradually been won back. Now, however, that the originator of all this mischief has met his fate, those great warriors who, during the pacification of the country, were exposed to every blast of heaven, and were drenched with rain, tasting every danger and difficulty, are indeed entitled to most unmistakable marks of OUR favour and gratitude."

So rare is it for people in this country to follow closely the course of events in China, that for long after the fall of Nanking it was supposed by many that the Tai-ping Rebellion was still in existence ; and even at the present day the question is sometimes put, whether it has really been extinguished or not. No one acquainted with the subject has any doubt that Tai-pingdom has long been extinct ; but it is easy to understand why such questions are raised. A portion of the Foreign community in China was exceedingly anxious for a continuance, and afterwards for a revival, of the Rebellion, because a state of confusion and misery in China served their own petty interests, and they have spared no pains in sending home letters and telegrams calculated to convey a false impression. They have also been assisted to this end by the facts of the case. China is an immense country, having, according to the last census accessible, a population of 450 millions, or nearly double that of Europe. Among this enormous mass of human beings, having varieties of religion, language, and blood, it is hardly to be expected that perfect order and tranquillity should always prevail. If we consider the enormous wars of Europe during this century, and the gigantic conflict which has recently convulsed the United States of America, it may be seen how absurd it is to presume that China, to be in a satisfactory state, must be absolutely free from all internal disorder. Nevertheless, that is the ridiculous assumption on which we are incessantly asked to judge the affairs of the Celestial Empire. If in some out-of-the-way corner of China any unusually large band of robbers manage to make their appearance, it is immediately telegraphed to England that rebellion has again broken out in Fukien or Kwangsi. Since the suppression of the Tai-ping Rebellion there have been several disorderly movements in China of more or less note, and all these are apt to be accepted, not merely as political movements, but as remnants of Tai-pingdom. We have heard of Nien-fei, and of Tu-fei, and of " Honan Filchers," and Hakkas, and Mohammedan rebels, until it has very naturally been supposed that the whole Empire must be in confusion and rebellion. In point of fact, we are too apt to judge of that great country, just as a Chinaman might do, who, reading in English newspapers of Fenians and Reformers, of Confederates and Northerners, of Danes and Prussians, of Romanists and Garibaldians, and of French and Austrians, came to the conclusion that the people of the West were living in a state of endless dissatisfaction and strife.

I shall speak presently of the Nien-fei and other bodies of men who have recently disturbed some portions of China ; but before doing so let me note, that after the fall of Nanking the Tai-ping Rebellion became insignificant, and within two years was entirely extinguished. It would serve no good purpose to follow minutely the fate of the different bands of Tai-pings, and it will be quite sufficient to note the points at which they made anything like a serious stand previous to their final disappearance altogether. After the fall of Nanking the Governor of Kiangsoo had still some fighting with the Tai-pings in his province and its neighbourhood, but none of any importance, except at the city of Wu-chu, or Hoo-chow, in Chekiang, a strongly-fortified place, where the Tow Wang, or Yellow Tiger, made a desperate stand, and where at first he defeated some of the Imperialist forces sent against him. Li's troops, however, among which were Colonel Bailey's Artillery and the army formerly commanded by General Ching, formed a combination with forces which came up from the South under the

orders of Tso, the Governor-General of Chekiang, and
which included 1800 Franco-Chinese under MM. D'Aiguibelle and Giquel, besides 800 disciplined Chinese, commanded by an Englishman called Reynolds, who was
killed in the fighting which then took place. The jealousy which existed between Tso and Lí caused some
bungling at first, of which the Yellow Tiger availed himself very smartly ; but he soon found his position untenable, evacuated the town in the end of August, and
retreated towards Kiangsi, with the intention of there
joining the She Wang, or Attendant King, who had
escaped from Nanking some time before its capture.

There were about a dozen Europeans, who had fallen
accidentally into the clutches of the Tai-pings, fighting
along with the Yellow Tiger in Wuchu. One of these,
Patrick Nellis, formerly in the Royal Engineers and in
Gordon's Artillery, made a statement of his experiences,
when, after many adventures, he contrived to reach
Shanghai. This man, being seized by the Tai-pings when
convoying silk, was forced to serve with them, and gives
an appalling account of the state of matters which existed in Wuchu. "All offences," he said, "received one
punishment—death. I saw 160 men beheaded, as I understood, for absence from parade ; two boys were beheaded for smoking ; all prisoners of war were beheaded ;
spies, or people accused of being so, were tied with their
hands behind their backs to a stake, and brushwood put
around them, and they were then burned to death. In
spite of the orders against smoking, the Chiefs were in-
veterate smokers." Nellis mentions, that when he was at
this place a certain "Kang Wang" arrived from Nanking
with an escort, and spoke to him in English very slowly,
from whence arose a rumour that Hung Jen-kan, the
Kan Wang, or Shield King, was not really executed at

Nanking; but there is good reason to believe that this new Kan Wang was a young fellow who could only speak very little English, and who had a title resembling that of the Shield King. This same leader afterwards turned up at Changchow, near Amoy, and an American, named Baffey, who served under him there, describes him as only thirty-five years of age. Had he really been the Prime Minister of the Rebel Monarch, the fact would have been notorious, and he would not have been in a subordinate position to the Attendant King.

After the loss of Wuchu the Rebels retreated along the base of the mountain-ranges of Chekiang into Kiangsi, where they threatened the city of Kwangsin, but were defeated with great loss. Having formed a combination with the forces of Li Siu-shien, the Attendant or Protecting King, they came down and occupied Changchow-fu, in the province of Fukien, near the consular port of Amoy. The Kang Wang was at this time with them, but the Attendant King was the principal Chief, and issued a manifesto in the beginning of 1865, addressed to the Representatives of England, France, and America, asking their assistance, and offering to divide with them the Celestial Empire. " If," he modestly proposed in this curious document, " your various nations, relying in the omnipotence of our Heavenly Father and Jesus Christ, and acting upon the doctrine of Christianity, will come to terms with us for destroying the Tsing dynasty; if you command your naval armies, and attack those places near the water, whatever cities, districts, ports, and passes you will have taken and conquered by your force, you will be at liberty, without the least opposition on my part, to keep; and whatever treasures and food found therein you will be at liberty to appropriate; and so I will attack on land, and whatever cities, districts, and

passes I conquer, and whatever treasures and food I find,
I will divide, giving one half to you; and all the distant
cities and marts will be surrendered to you." The only
result of this invitation was to induce about a dozen
Foreigners of loose character and in desperate circumstances to join the Rebels. Among these were Rhode,
Williams, and Baffey, who had formerly been officers in
Gordon's force, but who at this time were out of employment; and Burgevine, as I have already mentioned,
made an effort to join them, which resulted in his being
seized by the Imperialists, and drowned, according to report, by the accidental upsetting of a boat.

The local militia of Fukien were unable to do much
against these Tai-pings, but the Government, roused to a
sense of danger, sent down 8000 troops, disciplined at
the Tung-wang Shan camps, under the command of Kwo
Sung-ling, and accompanied by Colonel Kirkham. On
this force making its appearance the Rebels evacuated
Changchow by night on the 16th April 1865, and retreated towards the town of Tungshan. Pressed on all
sides by Imperialist forces, and in the midst of a hostile
population, they were soon broken up into small parties,
and retreated into the mountainous region which sepa-
rates the three provinces of Fukien, Kwangtung, and
Kiangsi, where they may be said to have disappeared.

The last accounts we have of the Tai-pings in this retreat is derived from a statement made at the British
Consulate at Canton in 1865 by George Baffey,* who,
as before mentioned, had been in the Imperial service,
but had been induced by Rhode and others to join the
Rebels. This man states, that eleven days after the
evacuation of Changchow the Attendant King's division
became disorganised near Yingting, on the Han river,

* See Appendix IV.

and that he then joined the Kang Wang, who pushed into the province of Kwangtung with 15,000 fighting men. Almost all his Foreign companions were murdered at different times, and none received the fulfilment of the promises by which they had been enticed over. In the middle of July Baffey managed to escape, being horrified by the cruelties which the Tai-pings perpetrated—such as burning two Mandarins alive, and slaughtering in cold blood 1600 local militia, who had surrendered on the promise of their lives being spared. When he left the Rebels they were talking of returning to Kiangsi; and apparently they did so, for soon after the 'Peking Gazette' announced that the city of Kanchow had been taken from them, and the province of Kiangsi finally cleared of their presence. Since nothing more has been heard of them, we may conclude that a portion of them perished miserably among the sterile mountains of that region of China, while the remainder may perhaps still haunt these mountains as small bands of banditti. It only remains to be added, that Rhode, who did such good service as a military instructor in Gordon's army, was at first reported to have met with a fate similar to that of Burgevine. After the evacuation of Changchow, he and a man named Mansfield delivered themselves up to the Mandarins, who handed the latter over to the British authorities, but reported that Rhode, their former servant, had been accidentally drowned by the upsetting of a boat; he turned up, however, at Canton, and is now living at Shanghai. The only other Tai-pings of which there is any rumour after this date, are the remnants of the force which went into the distant western province of Szechuen, under the leadership of Shih Ta-kai, the I Wang, or Assistant King, who broke off from allegiance to the Heavenly Monarch, and set up his own standard in 1861. After that Chief was captured by an Imperialist colonel in 1863, he was executed by order of the Governor-General of Szechuen, and a portion of his whilom followers are rumoured to have escaped into the province of Kansuh, and to have been amalgamated with the Mohammedan Rebels in the extreme north of China.

CHAPTER XVII.

NIEN-FEI AND MOHAMMEDAN REBELS.

DURING the last two years a great deal has been heard
about the Nien-fei Rebels, and in some quarters it has
been supposed that these constitute a political party in
China. Some wiseacres have also told us of Tu-fei, and
of other Fei, all which the ingenuous British reader is
asked to believe betoken the dissolution of the Chinese
Empire. Now the fact is, that words of this kind are
used to designate thieves and banditti in general; and to
use them with a political signification, or even as denoting separate varieties of marauders, is about as sensible
as to talk of England being convulsed by Thieves and
Prigs. The term Nien-fei is merely a local name for
marauders prevalent among the inhabitants of the
southern part of the province Chili, the western part

of Shantung, and the northern part of Honan.   Through
this district flows the great Ho-ang Ho, or Yellow River,
which the Chinese, from the earliest historical times, have
had great difficulty in keeping within its embankments.
In many places the bed of the river is considerably
higher than the surrounding country, and it is only
by constant and careful labour on the embankments
that it is prevented from overflowing these districts.
Of course, whenever the works on this river are much
neglected, as sometimes happens when the Government
is greatly out of funds, the water breaks through,
and floods immense tracts of land.   Now, one of the
results of the Tai-ping Rebellion has been to diminish
the funds at the disposal of the Chinese Government to
such an extent, that for many years the embankments of
the Yellow River have been so neglected, that the people
in considerable stretches of country have been deprived
of the means of subsistence.   Moreover, the march of
the Tai-pings towards Peking in 1853 through these
very districts caused an amount of destitution from
which they have scarcely yet recovered.   Hence, in the
three provinces just mentioned there has been for some
time a good deal of brigandage—the usual Chinese way
of levying a benevolent fund for the relief of washed-out
agriculturists, who are not very particular when collecting
the tax in person.   The number of these Nien-fei must
not be judged by the extent of country over which they
roam.   Mr Gibson, lately H.M. Acting Consul at Tientsin, who came into rather unpleasant contact with them
in 1863, estimated their numbers as under 10,000, exclusive of women and children.   They move about in
large parties, covering a track as large as two or three
English parishes.   The women and the carts usually follow the public roads, while the men scatter about over

the country, but retreat to their waggons when danger appears. They are all pretty well mounted on good ponies, and can move when necessary at the rate of sixty miles a-day. Captain Coney, of H.M. 67th Regiment, who went out against them from Tien-tsin with some disciplined Chinese in 1863, never saw Nien-fei till the Nien-fei concentrated and attacked him; and when they found that they were getting the worst of it, they were out of range again in a few minutes. Extremely ill armed, with spears, rusty swords, gingalls, and a few cannon, they are very bad shots. They take good care, however, to send patrols out before them, and are chary of going in directions where they are likely to meet with serious resistance. Almost anything in the way of plunder they can carry or consume is acceptable to them. They loot young women, boys, gold, silver, silk, cotton, rice, wheat, and clothes of all kinds, but seldom wantonly destroy life. The necessity which knows no law before that of self-preservation, has created these robber-bands, but of course they have attracted to them many idle and disreputable fellows, inclined for all kinds of mischief, and such bands necessarily grow by what they feed on. The well-to-do people whose houses they plunder become themselves Nien-fei, in order to avoid starvation; and so a band increases rapidly, until it attains such dimensions that Imperialist troops are directed against it.

The theory of the Chinese Government, that each village, district, department, province, and viceroyship, should harmonise itself or settle its own affairs, is consonant to the genius of the people, and acts admirably in ordinary circumstances, but it is quite inadequate as a basis for preserving order during the great convulsions to which nations are sometimes exposed, and when large districts of country are suffering from the want of means of subsistence. In such circumstances the weakness of the central government, and its dependence upon moral force, are disastrously felt; for on the one hand, it is not till the very existence of the Government is threatened that it will rouse itself to check rebellion effectually; and on the other, sufficient efforts are not made to prevent famine in afflicted districts by throwing into them supplies of food from the rest of the Empire. The state of local disorganisation which thus arises is greatly aggravated by the difficulties of transit in China as regards the conveyance both of troops and of provisions. Occupied by its foreign war and the great Tai-ping Rebellion, the Chinese Government allowed the Nien-fei, or the marauders of the North-eastern provinces of China, to continue their depredations, until they became rather formidable bands, threatening at times to advance on Tientsin, and cut the communication between Peking and the sea. Parties of them also pushed to the south, and appeared in the Yangtsze valley, co-operating with the Tai-pings in the end of 1860, but in the following year were soon disposed of by the Imperialist forces. In the North-east they gave much more trouble, and extended their ravages beyond their usual limits into the provinces of Shantung on the one side, and Hoopeh on the other. In the year 1865 their numbers had increased to a formidable extent, but by that time the Imperial Government was able to deal with them more effectually than it had hitherto done, having been released from the incubus of the Tai-ping insurrection. Operations were directed against them, not only by Prince Sankolinsin from the North, but also by Tseng Kwo-fan from the South. These two great Chinese officers had never met, and were very jealous of each other's power and influence. The first represented the Tartar element in the Chinese Government, while the latter was the acknowledged head of the native Chinese Mandarins. The opposition between these two great parties in the Chinese state has not of late years been of a serious kind—not any more so than that between the Conservatives and Liberals in England—but it has been sufficient to affect the course of events. Sankolinsin and Tseng Kwo-fan were both warriors rather than statesmen, and perhaps specially on that account took the lead of their respective parties ; for the recent course of events in the Flowery Land has had the effect of giving military Mandarins a higher position than that which they usually hold. In one important respect the Chinaman had an advantage over the Tartar, having to do with the Tai-pings, who could be suppressed, while the latter had to deal with the demands of Foreign nations, which the whole power of China would have been unable to resist. So, while Tseng was reaping glory in 1860 by his operations on the Yangtsze, the Tartar prince had to face defeat at the hands of the allies, and never quite recovered his former cheerfulness and prestige. He was always afraid that the Southern leader was attaining a height of glory which would overshadow the power and influence of the Imperial house, and even went so far as to procure the issue of an edict from Peking which degraded Tseng Kwo-tsung, the military commandant at Nanking, and ordered Tseng Kwo-fan himself to proceed to the capital to explain his conduct. This edict, however, was openly disregarded, and any further conflict between the two great fighting men of China was put an end to by the death of Sankolinsin in 1865, and by the want of success in his operations. The Peking Government were not inclined to say much more on the subject to Tseng Kwo-fan, who had despatched a body of his picked troops to the north of Nganhwui, to protect that province and Hoopeh from invasion. Indeed, the Peking Government, sinking all minor points of difference, at once ordered Tseng Kwo-fan and Lí Futai to move all their available forces upon the Nien-fei, who were now commanded by leaders of some note—namely, Shung, a son of concubine-loving Shung Pow, who had been compelled to strangle himself the year before; Miao, who, when a Tai-ping, had made peace with the Imperialists by betraying to them the Heroic King; and Chang, a son of the notorious Chang Lo-hing.

The position of affairs demanded prompt action, for in Shantung they had advanced to Kiachow; in Chili they were not far from Powting, where the Tai-pings had been arrested in 1853, and even Chiu fu in Shantung, the birthplace of Confucius, had fallen into their hands, and they had there destroyed the temple of the sage, which was considered the most sacred and magnificent in China. After the death of Sankolinsin, his son, the Pao Wang, defended the city of Tsinan with 30,000 Mongol cavalry, and there awaited the arrival of the experienced troops of Tseng Kwo-fan, who had been appointed Generalissimo of all the Imperial troops in China. The movement of the Nien-fei, however, collapsed at this moment without much necessity for fighting. They evacuated the entire province of Shantung, and proceeding into Shansi, a large body of them were swept away by a sudden inundation of the Yellow River, while the remainder retreated through Shensi to join the Mohammedan Rebels in Kansuh. The parties of the Nien-fei who had entered Chili were now easily cut up by the Tartar cavalry, and a new outbreak which took place in the end of this year was easily suppressed by a

portion of the garrison at Nanking, with European
drilled artillery which were ordered to proceed against
them.   Early in the year 1866, marauders again made
their appearance on the banks of the Yellow River, and
established themselves for a time in some districts to the
north of that stream.   In the south of Shantung also
they reappeared, but were put down there by a Mandarin called Puan, who had served along with Colonel
Gordon.   In the spring some of them pushed down
south into Kiangsoo by forced marches, and a circuitous
route along the seaboard, where there were no troops to
oppose them, and assembled in imposing numbers at
Tungtai.   Tseng Kwo-fan, who advanced against them
at this place, concentrated his troops round them very
carefully, but the brigands managed to give him the
slip.   During the same year marauders of a similar kind
threatened Hankow in the very centre of China, having
been joined by some Imperialist regiments, whose pay
was in arrear ; but these latter were easily brought back
to allegiance, on which the Rebels dispersed and returned to their homes.   In the beginning of 1867,
Nien-fei were again reported to be ravaging the country
between the Yangtsze and the Yellow River, while
others of them had reappeared on the confines of Shantung and Honan, where they managed to slip out of the
toils of our old friend Governor Lí, now a Chetai.   It
requires, however, a close scrutiny of such reports, and
of the sources through which they come, to know what
value to attach to them.   Contrary to a usually received
opinion, Mr Wade, who of all Europeans is probably
best acquainted with such papers, has said that, for
some reason known only to Chinamen, the reports on
contemporary affairs in the ' Peking Gazette ' always set
out the worst view of the case, without any conceal-

ment, and it is possible to get at the true story of events in China, when we have these documents, or when the intelligence comes through Foreigners of sufficient intelligence and knowledge of the country to enable them to discriminate ; but without such aids, it is impossible to know what value to attach to the innumerable reports which come every mail from that country, some of which are the pure invention of unscrupulous persons, while others are the joint handiwork of young Foreigners who enliven their exile by abundant gossip, and of their Chinese hangers-on, who take a peculiar pleasure in stuffing them with startling stories. A very few months ago Lí contrvied to hem them up in the Shantung peninsula, and crushed them almost entirely. Still it may be assumed without rashness, that there are yet a good many Nien-fei or robber bands left in existence in China, and that they will continue to give trouble for some years.

Of perhaps still more importance than the Nien-fei, are the Mohammedan Rebels of the north-west of China ; for they really aim at something like political separation, and gave a good deal of trouble to the Celestial Empire in the year 1862. The relationship between China and Mohammedanism began at a very early period ; for so early as the reign of the Kalif Walid, about 708, an embassy was sent to China by way of Kashgar, and on a tablet in the Mohammedan Hiang Fang, or "Echoing Tomb," at Canton, it is stated that there were disciples of the Prophet settled in Shensi in the reign of the Emperor Wu-tsung, 842. In one Chinese native work, the statistics of Kwangchau, it is even stated that Mohammed himself sent a maternal uncle to trade with China in the sixth year of the Hegira. Be that as it may, we know that in the ninth century Wahab and

Abuzaid, the Arabian travellers, wrote an account of the Flowery Land; and about 1330, Ibn Batuta found wealthy Moslem merchants in all the great Chinese cities. The Arabs do not seem to have had any difficulty in getting on with the easy-going Celestials, and it was not till Mohammedanism got some hold over the rough tribes of the north-west frontier, that it began to cause trouble. As that frontier of the empire now expanded, now contracted, according to the vigour and good fortune of the Government, the Mohammedans in that region were naturally left in some dubiety as to how far it was necessary or expedient to acknowledge the Emperor. Hence they have every now and then shown a disposition to rise, and in 1827 Jehangir caused the Government some anxiety by his insurrectionary movement.

There are small communities of Mohammedans at Canton, Tientsin, Peking, and scattered elsewhere over China; but most of these have become Celestialised, though not to the same extent as the Jews who established themselves in the Empire many centuries ago, and who, while retaining a few rules of the Pentateuch, have lost all the other peculiarities of their race and faith. In the recent disordered state of the Flowery Land, and weakened condition of the Imperial Government, it was to be expected that the adherents of a creed so cruel, proselytising, and uncompromising as that of El-Islam, would try to assert themselves and to throw off the rule of a Government which, while it tolerates all forms of religion, will allow no interference with the Celestial Emperor's sacred function in matters of the state. The wonder is that so fanatical a set should for so long have held in complete abeyance the command of their Prophet, that those who will not accept the faith should be put to death by the sword. It was after a very long interval of quiet, and perhaps instigated by Russian emissaries, that they broke into insurrection in 1862 in the mountainous province of Shensi. Though that province is only separated from the deserts of Mongolia by the Great Wall, it is the most ancient part of China ; and its capital Signan is dear to the Chinese as having been the seat of the Tang dynasty, and of the great Emperor Tai-tsung, who established the system of literary examinations, drew up the Celestial code, pacified the whole country, and extended his sway, so that westward it was only limited by a line stretching from Behar in India to the Caspian Sea. The greater part of the inhabitants of Shensi are Mohammedans, so the Rebels had little difficulty in taking the capital and slaughtering many of the Emperor's adherents ; but the revolt was soon put down, partly by force, partly by arrangement, as a similar one was managed in last century by Kien Lung.

In 1855 certain other circumstances occurred to rouse the Mohammedans. Behind Shensi there is the immense province of Kansuh, or " Voluntary Reverence," for the most part a howling wilderness of sand and snow, extending over about 400,000 square miles beyond the Yellow River and the Great Wall, and inhabited chiefly by Buddhists. Behind this, again, still to the north-west and near the " Roof of the World," there is the kingdom of Ili, surrounded by savage deserts and mountains covered with perpetual snow, and inhabited by Mohammedans proud of their isolation and devoted to their faith. These Turkestanes are quite out of the way of Chinese government ; but a century and a half ago, the principal cities of the district being in perpetual feud, their chiefs besought the Chinese to put an end to these disturbances. After much hesitation the Celestials granted this request so far as to assume military command of Ili, leaving the entire civil administration in the hands of the native authorities.* By position, race, and religion, this wild high-lying country has naturally as little to do with China as it has with India ; and when the pressure of the Tai-ping Rebellion weakened the power of the Chinese Government to suppress the feuds of its Turkestani tributaries, it was only to be expected that the latter would throw off the Foreign military government to which they had voluntarily subjected themselves. The connection of China with this and similar dependencies about the " Roof of the World" was only a source of weakness to the Imperial Government, and continued simply because the inhabitants of these regions were solicitous for it. When the Mohammedans there severed the connection, no objection was made by the Celestial Government ; but it was a different matter in regard to the more properly Chinese provinces of Shensi and Kansuh. When the Mohammedans who populate the former of these heard of the excitement among their co-religionists in Turkestan, they made a renewed outbreak in 1866, but with so little success that, instead of advancing eastward in the direction of Peking, they were pressed back by the Imperialists out of their own peculiar province into Kansuh, which, as has been remarked, is inhabited chiefly by Buddhists, who consequently are not favourable to their pretensions. This caused a good deal of suffering to the people of Kansuh, whose capital was taken and burnt by the Rebels ; but instead of being an indication that the Mohammedans are making any real progress in the north-west of China,

* See Vambéry's 'Travels in Central Asia,' and William's ' Middle Kingdom,' vol. i. chap. iv.

Z

it only shows that they have been beaten back from their own proper ground into a thinly populated, half-desert country, where it could not be expected that any efficient obstacle could be opposed to them, until an Imperial army, sent for the purpose, has time to come up from the south-east. The establishment of a Mohammedan state up in that little-known part of the world is not likely to cause any one much anxiety; and if formed, it will likely be soon dealt with by Russia.

There are other disorderly sections of people in China, who are occasionally raised to the rank of Rebels, and sometimes even identified with the extinct Tai-pings. Among these the most prominent are the Miaou-tsz, or supposed aborigines of the country, who have remained distinct from the Chinese for ages, and are even mentioned as such in some of the earliest chapters of the 'Historical Classic,' relating to a period of about 2000 years B.C. The progress of Chinese civilisation drove these savages into the more inaccessible mountains of Yunnan and other south-western provinces, where they still linger, resembling a good deal the aboriginal hill-tribes of India, and sometimes living in peace with their more cultivated neighbours, sometimes descending for the purposes of plunder. The Hakkas, also, in the south of China, keep up a great deal of local conflict, with which the Mandarins rarely interfere, and which is accepted by the people almost as one of their amusements. At the other end of the Celestial Empire, in Manchuria, there have been of late some roving bands of mounted banditti, one of which lately threatened the open port of Newchwang. Wherever, also, village braves are allowed to gather together in large numbers, or Imperialist troops are kept very long without pay, disturbances are apt to arise. These usually involve destruction of life and property, but none within the last two years have assumed formidable dimensions. The Central Government is still unwilling, and probably still too weak, to interfere promptly with cases of local disturbance; but it does not allow matters to go beyond a certain point, and of late has exercised more control and power of this kind over China than it could put forth during the years of the Great Rebellion.

CHAPTER XVIII.

THE PRESENT AND FUTURE OF CHINA.

CHINA EMERGING FROM A PERIOD OF DISTURBANCE AND TRANSITION
—CAUSES OF SUCH PERIODS—OVER-POPULATION — FALSEHOODS
REGARDING THE PREVALENCE OF INFANTICIDE—DANGERS OF
PROSPERITY—CHINA'S PRESENT FAVOURABLE POSITION—CRUSH-
ING OF THE NIEN-FEI REBELS — DEGRADATION OF LI HUNG-
CHANG—EUROPEAN GUNBOATS AND ARTILLERY EMPLOYED BY
THE GOVERNMENT—MILITARY REFORM—SERVICES OF A BRITISH
OFFICER REQUIRED—CHINA'S FOREIGN RELATIONSHIPS—FOREIGN-
ERS HAVE PROVOKED HOSTILITY—SPANIARDS AND PORTUGUESE
—OPIUM *versus* TEA—ENGLISH MERCHANTS IN CHINA—THE EAST
INDIA COMPANY—OPENING OF THE FIVE PORTS—REMARKABLE
SUCCESS OF OUR MERCHANTS—THEIR DISSATISFACTION—THE
TREATY OF TIENTSIN — THEY ARE RUINED BY THE OPENING
OF CHINA — OVERTRADING—TEA SOLD CHEAPER IN LONDON
THAN IN CHINA—COMPLAINTS AS TO EXACTIONS ON THE TRAN-
SIT OF GOODS—MEMORIALS OF THE ANGLO-CHINESE CHAMBERS
OF COMMERCE — JARDINE, MATHESON, AND CO. ON THE OPIUM
TRAFFIC, AND ON ACCESS TO THE INTERIOR OF CHINA—NET
RESULTS OF AN AGGRESSIVE POLICY—A PROPHECY BY WAN SEE-
ANG—DANGER OF OUR TRADE PASSING INTO CHINESE HANDS.

THERE is a remarkable contrast between China as described by the older European travellers, from Marco
Polo to the mission of Macartney, and the China of
to-day, or of the last twenty years. The prevailing
impression left by the former vision is one of ease, order,
peace, luxury, silks, and sumptuousness, such as war-

ranted a use of the words "Flowery" and "Celestial;"
while our more recent notion of China is a good deal
associated with poverty, squalor, and almost unlimited
bloodshed. No doubt one cause of this difference is,
that the Occidental ideas of what constitute comfort and
splendour have changed a good deal from what they
were a century or two ago; and another is, that in late
years our judgment of the country has been somewhat
vitiated by the representations of persons who either
cannot appreciate it, or suppose they have a distinct
interest in representing it in the blackest colours.
"'Spose," said to me, in "Pidjin English," * a young
Chinaman whom I once proposed taking to England—
" 'Spose I no catchee lice (rice), I makee die." And just
as this youth could not conceive of comfortable or even
of possible existence in England without his accustomed bowls of *fan*, so a large class of narrow-minded
Foreigners in China (unknown there, or almost so, in
former years) regard it as an uncomfortable country
simply because of the strangeness of its aspects to themselves, and have done something to impress their own
outraged feelings on the mind of Europe.

But making due allowance for such elements of
opinion, there still remain in China itself broad grounds
for our changed idea of that country. We, of the present generation, have seen it only in one of those periods
of transition and disturbance with which it is afflicted at
intervals of a few centuries, and from which its recu-
perative force enables it to recover with remarkable
rapidity. The Chinese people stand unsurpassed, and
indeed almost unequalled, in regard to the possession of

---

* "Pidjin" is a corruption, in the Chinese mouth, of our word "busi-
ness," and has nothing to do with pigeons, or with pigeon-holes, as Colonel
Fisher, in his otherwise excellent and interesting work on our last war with
China, seems to suppose.

freedom and self-government. Their social and political system is the result of the transmitted experience of many centuries in regard to what human life is, and to how it may best be controlled ; but in periods of great excitement, and especially when brought in contact with the disintegrating influence of foreign nations, it fails in ability to suppress the uprisal of the dangerous classes. Moreover, deeply seated in the national mind there are certain ideas in regard to progeny which have a powerful effect in producing over-population in China, and so leading every now and then to a great national catastrophe. No competent political economist nowadays is disposed to dispute substantially the Malthusian law, whatever differences of opinion may exist as to the action which it calls for. The tendency of population to increase in a much greater ratio than the increase of food is an established fact, and this tendency comes into play in China in a specially terrible manner. The neighbouring Japanese are practically almost as good Malthusians as the French, and their custom of placing in the "tea-houses," for a term of years, a large number of the young women of the middle and lower classes, has enabled them to check the growth of their population without exercising any ascetic self-denial. But in China we have all the circumstances which go to favour over-population in the old countries of Europe, together with certain peculiarities of its own. It is an old country, where every foot of ground is cultivated which can profitably be so, and no scrap of manure is allowed to be wasted. The feelings of the people are opposed to colonisation, and so also were the laws of the country up to a very few years ago. It is true that a considerable Chinese emigration has gone into Malaya, America, and Australia, but that has only been in recent years ; it is

really very inconsiderable when compared with the population of China itself, and it has been composed chiefly
of persons who were either worthless in character or
desperate in circumstances.   And while there is thus
no sufficient outlet for the ever-increasing population of
China, either in the country itself or in opportunities for
emigration, the Celestials are governed by ideas which
lead them to regard an increase of progeny with more
favour than do any other people on earth, unless it be
some of the nomadic tribes of Central Asia.   On this
subject some confusion has arisen from notions which
have got abroad in Europe as regards infanticide in
China.   Some of the statements of Gutzlaff and men of
that stamp, with Barrow's invention about carts going
round the streets of Peking of a morning in order to
pick up the bodies of exposed children, have but too
pointedly illustrated Talleyrand's lie, that if a lie gets
only an hour's start it will never be overtaken.   I
have heard Englishmen, whose acquaintance with China
was entirely drawn from Hongkong, Macao, and the fac-
tories of Canton, speak as if it were impossible to take
a walk in the Celestial Empire without seeing a dead
child lying under every bush ; but in all my wanderings
among the Chinese I never came across any indication
of a single case of infanticide, and found abundance of
proof that they regard their children, both male and
female, with great affection, and set a high value upon
the possession of them.   Indeed, there is nothing which
a Chinaman dreads so much as to die childless.   In the
popular imagination, the spirits of those who so die wander
about in the air discontented, miserable, and malignant,
because there is no one on earth to care for them ; and
so strong are the Celestial notions on this point, so much
is the malignancy of these friendless spirits dreaded,

that in most districts there is yearly what is called a
" Universal Rescue," to provide offerings of food, clothes,
&c., to propitiate and soothe these spirits. Every Chinaman likes to have as large a family as possible, and is as
proud of its size as English Hodge is told to be of the
thirteen children whom he has brought up without parish
aid. Among the great masses of the population the
labour of female children is so useful to a father that in
circumstances of ordinary comfort it is an object to him
to have as many of them as possible. Of course, when
districts of country are ravaged by famine, or by rapa-
cious and cruel rebels, infanticide becomes not uncom-
mon, and in such circumstances female children are the
first to be sacrificed ; but the infanticide of China, so far
from arising from any tendency among the Chinese to
destroy infants, whether male or female, is caused, so far
as it exists, by the desire of the people to have as many
children as possible, and by the over-population which is
thus produced.

It consequently follows that the more China is in a
state of peace and prosperity, the more danger is it in
of a great catastrophe ; for when in such a state its
population expands so immensely, that a foreign war, an
internal rebellion, or a great inundation, cannot fail to
deprive vast masses of the people of the means of subsistence, and even the natural expansion of the population tends to produce such a result. But the very ease
and luxury which prepare the way for such catastro-
phes have a demoralising effect upon the Government,
making it both weak and corrupt ; so when a great
check occurs, there is no power in the nation prepared to
meet the difficulties which arise. Thus the very peace
and prosperity which China had enjoyed for nearly
three hundred years before, peculiarly unfitted it for

meeting the events which overtook it during the last quarter of a century, and assisted in plunging it into the painful and almost desperate circumstances with which we have seen it struggle. At several points in the ten years, between 1853 and 1863, it looked as if only a very little additional weight were required to throw the country into a complete state of disorder and anarchy; but always, and usually from unexpected quarters, something intervened to prevent that result. Now it was quarrels among the Tai-pings themselves, then the energy of Yeh Ming-chin, next a sudden change in the policy of Great Britain, then Colonel Gordon's advent on the scene, and the rise to power of such able mandarins as Tseng Kwo-fan and Lí Hung-chang, that unexpectedly came to the assistance of the Chinese State, and enabled it to float over floods which threatened to sweep it away and strand it on the shore where the wrecks of so many states and nations lie.

There is no doubt that China has at present reached a very favourable position. The Tai-ping Rebellion has been so completely crushed that for almost three years it has given no signs of even the smallest local exist-ence; the Nien-fei and other rebels have been so far subdued that their destroying influence is no longer of much importance, and there is no prospect of any seri-ous disturbance from the Foreign relationships of the Empire; but the two latter points may seem to require a little more extended remark, before I allude to what is the subject of most importance as regards the future of China.

Lí Hung-chang, to whom was committed, two years ago, the task of dealing with the Nien-fei rebels, found that his heavy artillery and foot-soldiers, disciplined after the European method, which had been found so effectual against the Tai-pings who fortified themselves in cities, could not effectually be brought to bear against the Nien-fei, who scamper about on their ponies over the rolling plains of the north-east of China.   Accordingly he fell back on the old Chinese tactic of hemming them into corners by long lines of Imperial troops; and as parties of them occasionally broke through and escaped from these lines, and as all such events were faithfully recorded in the official 'Peking Gazette,' and recorded in the Anglo-Chinese papers, it looked, to superficial observers, as if he were making no progress in his task, while in reality he was gradually disposing of the rebels. Towards the middle of last year he succeeded, at great expense, and with an army said to be 200,000 in number, in hemming them up into the extreme north-east corner of Shantung; but a force of 30,000 of them managed at that time to escape through his lines (which are marked in my map of the Tai-ping routes), and again began devastating a district of country which had been restored to order.   It was half expected that the Peking Government would degrade Lí on that account, it having supplied him very liberally with funds; but probably he was too powerful to be interfered with then; and after dispersing the band which had escaped, he continued his intricate and serpentine operations, striving to keep the rebels within the narrowest compass.   The result was, that in the beginning of this year Chetai Lí succeeded in his darling project of closing round them, so that he could effectually attack them with the main body of his army.   Having got them pressed back into the Shantung peninsula, and shut in there by a strong series of forts extending across that peninsula from Laichow to Kiachow, he defeated them in a series of engagements, and drove them eastward on another

Imperial army. Between these two forces the Nien-fei
were crushed, and their chief, who at first managed to
escape along with his wife (who was one of the ablest of
his lieutenants), was also soon after killed; for his spouse,
when reconnoitering, having been drowned in fording
a canal, he insisted on going to the spot in order to
recover the body, and, venturing too near an Imperial
camp, was taken prisoner.

According, however, to the latest news received from
China, it appears that some parties of the Nien-fei had
escaped through Lí's lines into the province of Chili,
and had there combined with a party of Mohammedan
rebels who had made an unexpected excursion from
the north-west. It was also reported that on this
account Lí himself had been degraded by the Peking
Government, and deprived both of his yellow jacket and
of the two-eyed peacock's feather, the mark of his nobility; but this requires confirmation: and even if true, as
the Chetai continued to follow up the rebels, it is possible he may feel himself strong enough to set at nought
any decree degrading him, or to get it revoked.

The present state of internal affairs in China is not to
be judged of merely by the fact that there is now very
little rebellion in the country; the more important point
is, that the Government has shown a capacity and will-
ingness to employ means for preserving order, which
should make rebellion much more difficult in the future
than it has been in the past, and indeed almost impossible so long as the Government is tolerably just and
active. The camps for disciplining Chinese troops after
the European manner at several places in the country,
the arsenal at Nanking,* under the charge of Mr Mac-

* This arsenal was first established at Soochow, but was removed in
1866 to Nanking, being erected close to the site of the ruined Porcelain

artney, for the construction of European artillery and munitions of war, the number of steamboats and even of steam gunboats which have been procured for the Imperial service in its various branches, the readiness and celerity with which Chinese troops are moved from one province to another as circumstances may require, and the extensive powers which are now committed to high officers, such as the Prince of Kung, Tseng Kwo-fan, and Lí Hung-chang, all go to constitute a new state of matters highly unfavourable to the rise, and almost destructive to the progress, of insurrection in China. Were, for instance, anything like the Tai-ping rebellion in its genesis again to break out, the Imperial Government, with its steamers, artillery, disciplined troops, and competent commanders, could easily crush the movement in the bud, long before it obtained formidable dimensions, swollen by the crowds it might ruin ; and the practice has already been inaugurated of not leaving such movements to be dealt with locally until they become formidable.

At the same time it must be admitted that military progress in China has not during the last few years been anything like what it might easily have been, and what it might have been expected to be after the lessons of the years 1862-64. A very small efficient force, with flying-artillery, a few fast gunboats, and a certain number of competent European officers conjoined with Chinese ones, might at very small expense be made more serviceable in the preservation of peace and order in the Celestial Empire than any force yet established in China, and immensely more so than the expensive, exhausting, and all but useless local levies which each

Tower, and almost entirely from the bricks of that edifice, while the woodwork was taken from the ruins of the Tien Wang's palace, so that likely, before long, it will be the only memorial of these two famous structures.

province frequently counts by hundreds of thousands. Sooner or later the Celestials must come to depend entirely on European science in matters of war, and they can never learn to do so without the aid of European officers ; but their jealousy and fear of us is not a matter of surprise, when they consider the career of the *Si Yang Jen,* or "Western Men," in other parts of Asia. Moreover, there is the great difficulty as to what party in China should have command of so formidable a force thus constituted. If it were established from Peking, the provincial Governors, together with the great mass of the officials and people of China, would regard its formation with jealousy and distrust, as threatening complete Tartar domination in the Flowery Land ; while if it were formed by the great Chinese Mandarins, such as Tseng and Lí, the Court party at Peking would regard its own rights, and even the dynasty itself, as endangered. With such difficulties in the way, and no great pressure of circumstances requiring military reform, we need not look very sanguinely for much immediate improvement in that respect in China. Such affairs have already advanced greatly from their position during many centuries back, and the Chinese are not a people so eager of new things as to change their organisation, except under pressure of some kind or other. It strikes me, however, that if Mr Hart exercised fully his influence, or if there were an able British Minister at Peking who enjoyed the confidence of the Imperial Government, it would not be very difficult to prevail on the Chinese to form their military power in a manner which would completely secure the preservation of order, and at the same time relieve the country from the great burden of its provincial levies, which themselves, being so often and of necessity left unpaid, have been a fruitful source

of disorder and rebellion.   To such an end nothing could
be so useful, so well fitted to allay local jealousies, and
to secure provision against dangers lying in the future,
as the employment of the services of a British officer
of high character, and of talent for organisation.   If the
Mandarins could only be assured that he would not
employ his power except as a servant of the Chinese
State, they would be glad to accept his services ; and the
best guarantee for that, as well as an assurance against
his employment in any manner repugnant to Western
civilisation, would be his continuance in the service of
her Majesty the Queen while he was employed by the
Emperor of China.   It may be said, that for us to con-
solidate the military power of China, would be to put
arms into the hands of very probable enemies ; but this
is a weak objection.   The prestige of British arms would
be vastly increased, not decreased, in the Middle Kingdom, by the fact of the Celestial troops having been
trained by British officers ; in the event of a war these
troops would be ready to come over to us in large numbers ; and even if China's power of foreign resistance
were greatly increased by the training we had given to
it, that would be a positive advantage to Britain in any
war with China, because it would present us with a
point of resistance which could be easily crushed, like
Magdala, so as effectually to overawe the country.

In the present state of the world, the foreign relationships of China are even of more importance than are its
internal affairs ; for the latter can be settled on principles
which are assented to by the people of the country,
while the former demand the harmonising of very formidable opposing forces.   The Middle Kingdom can no

longer be secluded from the rest of the world by the God
of Hurricanes on the south and east, and by its deserts
and lofty mountain-ranges on the north and west. At
this day the China Sea, instead of being sparsely dotted
by a few junks, Arab *buglahs*, and barnacle-covered
caravels, is veiled with the smoke of European steamers,
and fanciful speculators in the West even speak of pushing railways from Burmah into Szechuen.

It is frequently complained of the Chinese, that for
the last two centuries, and more especially during the
last twenty years, they have laboured unnecessarily and
injudiciously to raise obstacles against the entrance of
their country into the comity of nations; but to do
them justice on this point, and practically to understand
the question which arises, it is necessary to bear in mind
the position which Foreigners have taken up towards
them. So to speak, there has been no *innate* objection
on the part of the Chinese to intercourse and interchange
with Foreign nations. The first Europeans who went to
China were received very hospitably; but when the relationship changed into the simple fact, as it did too soon,
of naval commanders like Simon Andrade and Mendez
Pinto ravaging the coast, plundering towns and villages,
and carrying off young women and boys to be sold as
slaves, it must be admitted that it was difficult for the
Chinese to appreciate the great advantages which were
to be derived from a connection with the nations of the
West. So, when the emissaries sent from France by
Louis XIV., with Jesuit and other Roman Catholic missionaries, began instructing the Celestials in astronomical and other scientific truths (which, by a curious
inconsistency, the Romish Church itself denied and de-
nounced), the Chinese were not only willing to receive
the new knowledge, but also conferred upon those who

conveyed it an amount of respect and practical recognition which priests of science rarely receive.   It was only when the Roman Catholic agents were found to be aiming at the possession of supreme power in the country, that the Chinese turned against them and sought to shut up the country; because the Mandarins soon saw, and only too clearly, that these Europeans were threatening to establish in China what they had failed to do in Europe, a political and intellectual despotism, which is equally opposed to the generous freedom of Confucian ideas, and to the loftiest instincts of the human race.

After the Spanish and Portuguese adventurers ceased to vex the coast of China, and the Roman Catholic missionaries were excluded, there came an interval of about two centuries to the Flowery Land, when it was almost entirely undisturbed by Foreign influences; but with the mercantile and political progress of Great Britain in the East there came an entirely new state of matters.   Up to very recently, however, the relationships thus opened have not been of a kind calculated to inspire the Chinese with confidence.   I am afraid the two words, Opium and Tea, express the two sides of it only too correctly.   We have got the Chinese to supply us with a very beneficial article called tea, which has increased our pleasures without doing harm, and has ameliorated our manners; while, in return, we have forced them to accept a highly dangerous, if not deleterious, substance, which they did not want, and which both the officials and the people had agreed to exclude from China.   I am no opponent, however, of the opium traffic; and this point of our mercantile relationship to the Chinese requires a little special elucidation.

The mercantile life of England has been a sort of midway career, partaking on the one side of the ferocity and cruelty, the chivalry and adventure of Spaniards and Portuguese, while on the other it has borne no little resemblance to the heavy plodding, the meanness, and the dull unscrupulousness of the Dutch. The poet drew a very accurate picture when he wrote—

> " To trade the Dutch incline ; the Swiss to arms ;
> Music and verse are soft Italia's charms ;
> Britannia justly glories to have found
> Lands unexplored, and sailed the world around."

Though the English have always had a very strong warm appreciation of the advantages of merchandise, merely considered as such, yet they have always, or at least until very lately, associated it with something better, and been ready to sacrifice it to many things higher. Thus the merchants of the East India Company could not stoop, like the Dutch at Nagasaki, to sacrifice their personal dignity to immediate commercial crumbs ; and whenever they got a chance they were eager and prepared to exchange their place of traders for that of enlightened rulers of the numerous millions of India. It may be said as a rule, our mercantile effort has gone in directions where there was something more than mere mercantile gains to lure on the young and adventurous spirits of the country who found no sufficient outlet for their energies at home. The consequence was, that our outlying mercantile history had much in it that was really noble and romantic. The mere exchange of pigs for poultry in a quiet market is apt to develop only the lower tendencies of human nature, and merchandise on the most extensive scale, the traffic even of " merchant princes "—so called—is little better when it refers only to questions of gain. But, at least up to a very recent period, the commercial enterprise of Britain has been connected with many things besides mere commercial gain ; and so has both commanded external respect and nourished internal strength.

In this department of our history the China merchants occupy an important section, and it would be interesting for a competent historian to depict them in the three great phases of their career. From the archives of the East India Company it would be easy to disinter many details which would afford a graphic idea of our relations with China previous to 1839, and of the life led in old times by the Company's agents at Canton before the existence of treaties between China and Britain. During that early period matters went on very smoothly, and commerce brought great gains on both sides. The dangers of piracy gave a sort of romance to the passage of the Chinese Sea and of the Straits of Malacca ; but on the Celestial seaboard difficulties rarely arose, because the exchange of commodities was severely regulated by the Mandarins on the one side and by competent officers of the East India Company on the other.

This state of matters, however, could not continue after the independent commercial enterprise of Britain broke into Eastern seas, and the Opium war provided an entirely new state of matters, of which the principal feature was the establishment of five ports for the residence of Foreigners, and open to the Foreign trade on the coast of China. The consequence of this " opening of China " was, that several energetic English communities were established on the seaboard of that country, and under no jurisdiction or guidance further than what was supplied by the Supreme Court of the nominal colony of Hongkong, by the action of the consuls appointed by the Foreign Office of Great Britain to the open ports in China, and by the natural tendency of British communities to control the actions of their own members. Shortly after the opening of the five ports in China, over-trading was carried on by the English merchants to a considerable extent, and so, on a lesser scale, there arose a state of matters resembling that which has existed for the last few years in our commercial relationships with the Chinese.

It was expected that the opening of the five ports would give a much greater impetus to British trade with China than it actually did for a long period, and the consequence was that the opening of these ports was at first followed by overtrading, and considerable losses on the part of the Foreign merchants. In time, how-ever, the position began to be understood, and the China merchants entered on a period of wonderful prosperity. In no part of the world, before and after the year 1850, did commerce bring so large returns with such ease and certainty as in China. It was understood that one of the How-kwas possessed a fortune equivalent to about fifteen millions sterling, when the Imperial Government came down upon him with a "squeeze," thinking that sum rather too ample a reward for dealing successfully in tea and opium; and most of the Foreign merchants on the coast of Cathay enriched themselves largely. Almost the entire trade was carried on by word of mouth; and though Chinese agents were intrusted with immense sums for the purchase of tea in the interior of the country, and were often absent for months on such errands, they were never known to fail in fulfilling their engagement.

The very ease with which they made money, and their otiose, luxurious style of life, however, brought the Foreign merchants into a condition like that of Jeshurun when he waxed fat and kicked. The repelling attitude of the

Celestials at Canton, the Hwang-chu-kee murders, the
expansion of commerce in other parts of the world, and,
above all, vague but glowing hopes connected with a
proposed opening of the Yangtsze river, and of the interior of the country in general, threw the Foreign community in China into a feverish state of dissatisfaction
with the past, and disgust with the then present, and of
boundless anticipations of the future.   It must have
been a great relief to their minds when Sir Harry Parkes
picked up the bone of the lorcha Arrow, and Sir Michael
Seymour suddenly remembered that we had a right, or
something like a right, to enter the gates of Canton.
Still the insertion of the small end of the wedge was
provokingly imperilled and delayed.   The Chinese question got mixed up with Earl Russell's and Mr Glad-
stone's quarrel with Lord Palmerston ; it was also contrary to the principles of these and other statesmen to
support our demands on China, and the movement for
coercion in that country was defeated in the Parliament of Great Britain.   Then, when the country had
reversed that decision, in order to support its favourite
Minister, and troops were on their way to Hongkong,
the red light of the Indian Mutiny arose in the Eastern
horizon, and operations against Canton had to be delayed for a year.   When that city was taken it began to
dawn disagreeably on the mind of the mercantile community, that something more than the seclusion of China
was being broken into ; that most old things were to
pass away, including many of their former privileges,
and a portion of their former power.   The heads of
great houses found their position not so commanding as
it had been before, and the smaller merchants kicked
violently against being refused permission to make their
own bargain with the Chinese Customs.   At Shanghai

a great number of rowdies made their appearance and associated themselves with the interests of the Tai-pings. Foreign arms and Tai-ping rebellion shook the Chinese Empire to its foundations; loud were the cries that it was doomed, and Mr Lay and Captain Osborn hastened out to regenerate it, and to divide it between themselves, being unaware that, if they did not immediately succeed, Sir Frederick Bruce was prepared to assist them back again.

After the events to an account of which this volume is chiefly devoted, the Foreign community in China entered on a phase of matters very different from what it had fondly anticipated. Judged by Chinese Custom-house returns, our trade was very largely increased, but it is impossible to say how far this was an increase in the trade itself and not simply in the regular and notified payment of customs dues. It soon became painfully clear that the opening of a large number of new ports, the influx to China of an increased number of Foreigners, and a wild tendency among them to competition and overtrading, which was taken advantage of by combined action among the native merchants, were producing a period of commercial distress and ruin. First the small merchants, then one after another of the large houses, fell into difficulties or failure; and lastly the great house of Dent and Company, which a few years before stood as high in reputation as the Bank of England, came with a crash to the ground, paying only half-a-crown in the pound in instalments over a term of years, and causing much suffering to military officers and to Foreigners who, after spending their best days in the East, had intrusted it with the use of their savings. So far has the spirit of overtrading been carried, that tea, which is by far the most important article in our trade with China, and is

now imported into this country to the value of over
£10,000,000 annually, has been purchased in China, as a
rule, for several years, *at higher prices than those for
which it is sold in London,* and, which is of more importance to consumers in Britain, *its quality has gone on
steadily decreasing, while its price (without the duty
in this country) has greatly increased.* This highly
objectionable state of matters has been caused by the
largely increased demand for tea in England, consequent
on reduction of duty and other causes, and the great

---

* These extraordinary facts require the authority of the following extract from the Circular of the 7th January 1868, issued by Messrs Benyon,
Harding, & Co., the well-known tea-brokers of Mincing Lane :—"Referring to the importation of tea from China as a source of profit, it appears
to us highly improbable that the day will ever arrive when that result can
be looked forward to as a rule and loss the exception. For many years
past the average result has been loss, and though in a few instances large
profits have been made, it has generally been attributable to some unforeseen
and unexpected occurrence, which even those who have benefited by it have
never calculated upon. Notwithstanding the falling-off in quality, prices
in China are fifty to sixty per cent higher than they were when tea was
so much better, though now we are close to the producing districts, and the
expense of transit to Canton and Shanghai is saved to the Chinamen. As
a rule, prices in China are above home rates, and tea is bought under the
idea that something favourable will turn up before it comes upon the
market. In the season of 1852-53, the finest ever known, the first crop
black leafs were bought at Canton at 23 to 26 taels, and paid the Chinamen handsomely. At Shanghai in the same season they ruled 3 or 4 taels
lower. So superior were the teas of those days to those of the present
that the third and fourth grades, which were laid down in London to cost
1s. 3d. to 1s. 4d. per lb., were equal if not superior to the finest first crop
teas of the present season, or any other since 1860-61. Such being the case,
it is quite clear that the price has been continually forced up by competition among buyers, while the quality has persistently declined ; the quantity taken has doubled itself, the quality is infinitely worse, and the price
has advanced fifty, sixty, and even seventy per cent. It is next to impossible that importing tea can pay, with a quality always getting worse, and
an extravagantly high price ruling. On this side the price paid by dealers
is high considering the quality, but in China it is enormous, and until
some very great change comes either in the price or in the quality, importing tea can never be relied upon as a source of profit to those engaged
in it."

competition among Foreign purchasers in China. The
latter cause enables the Celestial to sell his inferior teas
at the same price as his fine ones ; and, not having done
much of late in the way of making new plantations, he
has met the increased demand by plucking the old trees
much too freely, and so deteriorating the quality of the
leaf which they produce.   A very good authority on this
subjects asserts to me that, quality considered, tea, less
duty, is now fifty per cent dearer than it was before
Hankow was opened in accordance with the Treaty of
Tientsin.

The prospects of the China merchants have considerably brightened this year, but the facts just alluded to
strongly suggest that their trade is in an unsatisfactory
state, because of their own faults quite as much as on
account of any obstacles which they meet with in the
Chinese Empire.   With the exception of a few of the
more intelligent of them, their cry has ever been that
their trade is fettered by want of access to the interior
of the country, by the illegal exactions levied on the
transit of goods by local authorities, and by customs
arrangements unfavourable to commerce.   It is vain to
point out to them the great fact that our trade with
China is conditioned by the demand in Foreign countries
for Chinese products, that the Celestials are so thoroughly
organised, self-controlled, and economical, that, managing
the matter in one way or another, they will not consent
to pay for articles from abroad except out of the profits
which accrue from the sale of their own products.

Their fixed idea is that China is not opened, and that
commerce will expand immensely and immediately if
only they can get further access to the interior of the
country.   In the memorials addressed by the Chambers
of Commerce in China to the British Minister at Peking

in regard to the revision of the Treaty of Tientsin, which should come on this year, the one great subject of complaint on which almost all the Chambers agree is the alleged obstacle to commerce arising from illegal transit-dues in the interior of China. Now, before the Treaty of Tientsin was framed, this statement was advanced with more reason than it can be now, but it was partly disproved by the low prices at which Lord Elgin's expedition up the Yangtsze found English goods selling at Hankow in the centre of China, and Mr Wingrove Cooke discussed the subject pretty fully in the 'Times.' Since then China has been " opened; " there are a large number of new ports, and Foreign travellers have permission to go through the country, and protection in doing so, yet it seems that the high duties charged at internal custom-houses in China are still the great cause why our commerce with China does not increase more rapidly. There is some truth in this view, but its importance is exaggerated. In Hongkong itself, a British colony and a free port, articles exported from Europe are hardly at all purchased by the Chinese residents for their own use ; and I have no doubt that the coolies who carried the members of the Hongkong Chamber of Commerce to their meeting denouncing inland transit-dues were all clothed in cotton stuffs of Chinese manufacture. In a country such as China, where irregular transit dues are levied, that often tends to protect commerce rather than to hamper it; the extent to which that is done is probably greatly exaggerated, there being nothing but strong vague assertions to prove it ; and it is very questionable whether all the exactions on trade in China, legal and illegal, amount to such a sum as is levied on the China trade by our own taxation. The recklessness with which such subjects are discussed in the East may be judged of from the following passage in the memorial of the Shanghai Chamber of Commerce: "Your memorialists beg to illustrate their views by putting the question of what would have been said if, immediately after the conclusion of the Cobden Treaty with France, the French Government had proceeded to make a tax, not upon English goods, but upon those who traded in them ; or what would have been thought if, in the British Parliament, a poll-tax had been voted upon all persons who dealt in French wines? It is scarcely to be imagined that such ill faith would have been tolerated, and yet it is what we are submitting to in China." Here it is entirely overlooked that such a "poll-tax" does exist in Britain on the vendors of French wine, while there are *octroi* duties in France ; and that, in forming their treaty, neither country dreamed for a moment of relinquishing its right of levying its internal revenue to the extent and in the manner it deems best.

At once the ablest and most reasonable of the memorials referred to is that which the great house of Jardine, Matheson, & Co. has sent in on its own account,*

* The bold manner in which this house defends the opium traffic is amusing, and worthy of note. "Since 1860," say these much-misrepresented philanthropists, "it has been rendered abundantly clear that the use of opium is not a curse, but a comfort and a benefit, to the hard-working Chinese. As well say that malt is a curse to the English labourer, or tobacco one to the world at large. Misuse is one thing, use another. If to a few the opium-pipe has proved a fatal snare, to many scores of thousands, on the other hand, has it been productive of healthful sustentation and enjoyment." There is a great deal of truth in this view of the subject. Most Chinese who use opium do so in moderation, just as we do wine and beer, and often with positive advantage to themselves; but if the people were polled, they would exclude the drug from China by an almost unanimous vote : and we forced the introduction of it against their wishes—first, by, contrary to treaty, giving the opium-receiving ships on the coast the protection of our flag, so forming a basis of operations for smugglers on a line of coast which it was impossible for government officials to watch sufficiently ;

and the point on which it lays most stress is, the right of residence in China by British subjects at other places than the ports opened by treaty. Undoubtedly this is an important matter, but it is not true, as some other of the memorialists allege, that residence in the interior of the country is impossible at present. A very large number of Roman Catholic, and a smaller number of German Protestant, missionaries do at present reside, and for many years have resided, in the interior of the country, away from the open ports, holding houses and lands on their own account. The mercantile community have never displayed any particular readiness to undertake the trouble and undergo the risks necessarily attendant upon residence among a people such as the Chinese. What they too much want, in point of fact, is, that the imperial power of Great Britain should be employed in enabling them to sit down anywhere they choose in the vast empire of China, without being at the least trouble in adapting themselves to Chinese habits or institutions, and in greater safety and comfort than they ever enjoyed in London. This is not the style of thing in which Britannia justly glories, nor is this the spirit which created our commerce and founded our empire in the East.

It is beyond my plan to enter fully into a discussion of our mercantile relationships with China, so I must remark on the subject only curtly, and therefore apparently *ex cathedrâ*. When Messrs Jardine, Matheson, & Co. assert that the alleged inland transit dues in China " are deadly foes of the English artisan, for they make teas and silks dear, as well as impede the distribu-

and secondly, by making the result thus obtained an excuse for insisting, *vi et armis*, that the admission of opium at a fixed and low rate of duty should be legalised by an article in the Treaty of Tientsin.

tion amongst millions of buyers of the various productions of his handicraft," they leave entirely out of sight certain responsibilities which attach to the British merchants in China. What have been the net results of the aggressive policy they have supported during the last twelve years? Since the lorcha war gave such an impetus to the Rebellion in China as to disorganise the Government and ruin large districts, we have paid on an average about a pound sterling per chest of 100 lb. dearer for tea than we should otherwise have done, and about ten shillings extra on every pound weight of raw silk, even making allowance for the failure of the European crop; in war expenditure on account of China we (including the British artisan) have laid out about fifteen millions sterling, _minus_ two or three repaid back as indemnity money; our soldiers and sailors have been buried in Celestial soil by thousands, while the impetus we gave to the Rebellion has caused the Chinese to be buried untimely by tens of millions; half the English mercantile houses in China have gone down; and, in return, a few new ports have been uselessly opened, Sir Rutherford Alcock resides at Peking, and the whilom Mr Consul Parkes has been made a K.C.B. Any further progress effected in China during late years has been due to the natural unforced expansion of trade,* which the Chinese value as much as we do ourselves; to the assistance which Colonel Gordon and others have given to the Government in restoring order; and to the legitimate influence which has been exercised by Foreigners such as Sir Frederick Bruce, Mr Burlinghame, and Mr Hart.

* The latest reliable returns which I have on the trade of China are in the Blue-book on that country presented to Parliament by her Majesty in February of this year, from which it appears that, in the year 1866, the

We may, however, confidently hope that the China
merchants will not be disappointed in regard to the
further progress which they desiderate, and especially as
regards the right of Foreigners to reside in the interior;
the introduction of steam carriage on land, with its
further introduction on water ; and the development of
the mineral resources of the country. Already steamboats are freely used in China by the Government as well
as by the mercantile classes ; the local Viceroys possess
steam gunboats. Docks have been constructed, and at
least one arsenal is worked successfully. A college has
been established at Peking for the study of European
languages and science ; a Chinese Commissioner has
visited Europe ; and the Celestials have appointed a
representative, albeit he is a Foreigner, to the Courts of
Europe. Further changes, however, are still urgently
required. After the questions of over-population and the
military organisation of China, there comes the position
of the Mandarins. At present they have nothing to fall

estimated value of the trade of China with Foreign countries and coastwise
was as follows :—

	Imports.	Re-exports.	Exports.	Total.
Great Britain, British Possessions & Colonies,	£22,723,128	...	£14,769,295	£37,492,423
Japan, ...	928,646	£607,043	235,041	1,770,730
United States of America,	91,780	...	2,000,111	2,091,891
Sundry countries, . .	617,858	...	780,127	1,397,985
Chinese open ports or coastwise, ...	30,251,596	13,520,849	14,807,721	58,580,167
Total,	£54,613,008	...	£32,592,295	£101,333,196

This may appear to contradict my statement that the Chinese will not
pay for articles from abroad, " except out of the profits which accrue from
the sale of their own products." One explanation is, that the Chinese do
make profits to speak of on their side of the trade ; they do not sell tea at
less than it costs themselves or otherwise, try to force a trade.

back upon, in the event of unsuccess in the discharge of their duties, except concealed funds which they may have levied illegally when in office. The highest among them, as well as the lowest, stand in danger of being degraded to intolerable positions simply for want of success; and, consequently, they seek to lay up private funds when in office, regardless of the general interests of their class and of their country. The evils thus arising could easily be obviated by a reconstruction of the Civil Service of China on a footing, in this respect, resembling that of India; and such a change would be the most efficient means of putting an end to any illegal transit-dues which may at present be levied.

What it seems to me we have to dread is, not China hanging back but going too quickly for our own interests and comfort. Wan See-ang is reported to have said some time ago to Mr Hart, " Foreigners complain at present that China is changing too slowly, but fifty years after this you will make war upon us for going too fast." This astute Mandarin was not speaking thoughtlessly. It takes a considerable time to wheel round a very populous and democratic people like the Chinese to an unaccustomed stand-point, but once get them round and their action from it comes to be something tremendous. In Japan, a feudal country, any individual Daimio who takes it into his head may introduce a European improvement, such as the use of steam; but in China the mass of the people must be to a certain extent prepared for the innovation before it can be introduced. Hence progress in some respects is very slow in that country; but what will be the state of the case when the people of China have got fairly turned round to the point of accepting and using the practical appliances of Western civilisation? I doubt whether then there will be any great English mercantile houses on the coast of Cathay. It is to be feared that the native Chinese merchants will very quickly take their maritime commerce into their own hands, and try to dictate prices in London as they are already doing at Hankow and Shanghai. Already the Anglo-Saxons of Australia have had recourse, and not very effectively, to a heavy capitation-tax in order to keep down the competition of Chinese emigration, which is nothing compared with what it is capable of becoming. Without doubt we shall open up the Flowery Land effectively enough ; but the results of that opening promise to be somewhat different from our fond anticipations. At all events, any change for the better in our position with reference to that country must come from England outwards. In order that Great Britain may extend, or even continue to hold, its once grand position in the East, it must be more worthy of doing so than it is at present, and there must be a return to some tolerable connection between its higher intelligence and the wielding of its power : otherwise, Britannia will soon share the fate of Carthage and Venice, of Spain and Holland ; while *delenda est*, or the *capta* of the Arch of Titus, enscrolled after its name, will afford another instance of the Confucian benevolence of Heaven towards trees which are prepared to fall.

APPENDICES.

LIST of CHINESE TITLES, CIVIL and MILITARY.

Civil.

Chinese Title.	English.	Rank.	Button.
Che-tai, or Tsung-tú	Governor-General	1	Red
Fu-tai, or Hsiun-fu	Governor	2	Do.
Fan-tai, or Pu-cheng-sze	Superintendent of Finances	2	Do.
Nie-tai, or An-cha-sze	Provincial Judge	3	Transparent blue
Yen-tai, or Yen-yuen-sze	Collector of Salt by Gabel	3	Do.
Leang-tow, or Leang-chu-tow	Grain Collector	4	Opaque blue
Taou-tai, or Show-siun-taou	Intendant of Circuit	4	Do.
Che-foo	Prefect of Department	4	Do.
Chih-le-che-chou	Do. Inferior do.	5	Uncoloured glass
Tung-che	Sub-Prefect	5	Do.
Chih-le-tung-che	Independent do.	5	Do.
Tung-pan	Deputy Sub-Prefect	6	White
Che-chow	District Magistrate	5	Uncoloured glass
Che-shien	Do. do.	7	Plain gilt
Tso-tang, or Hsien-cheng	Assistant do.	8	Gilt

Military.

Ti-tú,*	. .	General.
Tsung-ping,	. .	General of Division.
Tu-tsi-ang,	. .	Brigadier.
Tsan-tsi-ang,	. .	Colonel.
Yú-kí,	. .	Lieutenant-Colonel.
Tu-sze,	. .	Major.
Shau-pí,	. .	Captain.
Tsien-tsung,	. .	Lieutenant.
Pa-tsung,	. .	Ensign.
Wai-wei,	. .	Sergeant.

* In China proper, or the "Middle Kingdom," which contains eighteen provinces, there are eighteen Ti-tus only employed in times of peace, but in time of war this rule is departed from, and other Ti-tus, sometimes in all to the number of 200, are employed under the Governors, or Futais of each province, in command of distinct levies raised for a specific purpose. Legitimately there could no more be two Ti-tus in a province than two Futais. Colonel Gordon's force was one of those raised for a specific purpose—the suppression of rebellion, and so was General Ching's. The Ti-tu of a province is Commander-in-Chief of its naval as well as of its military forces.

LIST of OFFICERS and other EUROPEANS KILLED and WOUNDED during COLONEL GORDON'S CAMPAIGN in 1863 and 1864.

Rank.	Names.	At what Place.	Killed or Wounded.
Captain	Belcher	Fushan	Dead
Lieutenant	Baffy	Taitsan	Wounded
Colonel (Capt.)	Williams	Do.	Do.
Captain	Robertson	Do.	Do.
Do.	Chidzwick	Do.	Do.
Do.	Bannon	Do.	Killed
Do.	Ludlam	Do.	Wounded
Captain (Col.)	Chapman	Do.	Do.
Major	Murant	Do.	Do.
Lieutenant	Murdock	Wokong	Do.
Captain	Baffy	Do.	Do.
Do.	M'Guiness	Patachiao	Do.
Lieut.-Colonel	Rhode	Do.	Do.
Captain	Chapman	Do.	Do.
Do.	Perry	Leeku	Killed
Do.	Gibb	Wanti	Do.
Do.	Parker	Do.	Wounded
Private	Nicholson	Do.	Do.
Do.	Friday	Do.	Do.
Major	Kirkham	Soochow	Do.
Captain	Wiley	Do.	Killed
Lieutenant	King	Do.	Do.
Captain	Maule	Do.	Do.
Lieutenant	Polkson	Do.	Wounded
Captain	Hartney	Do.	Do.
Do.	Christie	Do.	Killed
Lieutenant	Agar	Do.	Do.
Do.	Carrol	Do.	Do.
Do.	Williams	Do.	Do.
Do.	Glanceford	Do.	Do.
Colonel	Brennan	Do.	Wounded
Do.	Tapp	Do.	Do.
Lieutenant	Rhodes	Do.	Do.
Captain	Baffey	Do.	Do.
Lieutenant	Jones	Do.	Killed
Do.	Shamroffel	Do.	Wounded
Captain	Wilson	Do.	Do.

Rank.	Names.	At what Place.	Killed or Wounded.
Private	Upchurch	Soochow	Killed
Do.	Miller	Do.	Do.
Do.	Rodgers	Do.	Wounded
Do.	Ryan	Do.	Do.
Do.	Hallick	Do.	Do.
Corporal	Brown	Do.	Do.
Private	M'Clean	Do.	Do.
Do.	Clark	Do.	Do.
Lieutenant	Herzog	Yeshing	Do.
Commander	Gordon	Kintang	Do.
Major	Brown	Do.	Do.
Colonel	Kirkham	Do.	Do.
Do.	Tumblety	Do.	Do.
Captain	Cramer	Do.	Do.
Colonel	Williams	Do.	Do.
Captain	Banning	Do.	Killed
Major	Taite	Do.	Do.
Lieutenant	Williams	Do.	Wounded
Captain	Wilson	Do.	Do.
Lieutenant	Rudimare	Do.	Do.
Do.	Bertrand	Do.	Do.
Captain	M'Mahon	Do.	Do.
Do.	Mansell	Do.	Do.
Lieutenant	Polkson	Waissoo	Killed
Captain	Chirikoff	Do.	Do.
Do.	Hughes	Do.	Do.
Do.	Graves	Do.	Do.
Do.	Gibbon	Do.	Do.
Lieutenant	Pratt	Do.	Do.
Do.	Dowling	Do.	Do.
Colonel	Taylor	Do.	Wounded
Do.	Tapp	Chanchu	Killed
Lieutenant	Chowne	Do.	Do.
Captain	Everest	Do.	Wounded
Do.	Hendrickson	Do.	Do.
Lieutenant	Maloney	Do.	Do.
Do.	John	Do.	Do.
Captain	Donald	Do.	Killed
Lieutenant	Greenlaw	Do.	Do.
Do.	Donelly	Do.	Wounded
Captain	Smith	Do.	Killed
Do.	Reynolds	Do.	Wounded
Major	Morton	Do.	Killed
Captain	Hammond	Do.	Wounded

Rank.	Names.	At what Place.	Killed or Wounded.
Lieutenant	Robinson	Chanchu	Killed
Do.	Mitchel	Do.	Wounded
Colonel	Rhode	Do.	Do.
Captain	Graham	Do.	Do.
Colonel	Howard	Do.	Do.
Major	Coats	Do.	Do.
Captain	Carr	Do.	Do.
Lieutenant	Jones	Do.	Do.
Do.	Williams	Do.	Killed
Captain	Bailey	Do.	Wounded
Colonel	Doyle	Do.	Do.
Captain	Rhodes	Do.	Killed
Lieutenant	Brown	Do.	Do.
Captain	Dunn	Do.	Wounded
Do.	Murphy	Do.	Killed
Colonel	Chapman	Do.	Wounded
Lieutenant	Gibb	Do.	Killed
Do.	Greenlaw	Do.	Do.

OFFICERS WHO DISTINGUISHED THEMSELVES.

The following Officers particularly distinguished themselves under Colonel Gordon's command, being frequently in front and very much exposed:—

THROUGHOUT THE CAMPAIGN—

Major Brown, . *Staff.*
Colonel Kirkham, ...
Doctor Moffitt, . *P.M.O.*
T. Thorpe and C. Draper, *Orderlies.*
Colonel Brooks, . *Provost Marshal.*
Mr Hobson, . . *European Interpreter.*
Captain Davidson, . *Steamer Hyson.*
Colonel Doyle.
Colonel Baily.

AT CAPTURE OF TAITSAN—

Captain Williams, . 2d Regiment.
Captain Tchirikoff, . 5th do.
Major Brennan, . 5th do.
Captain Howard, . 5th do.
Captain Brooks, . 2d do.

At Capture of Quinsan—

Captain Howard,   .   5th Regiment.
Captain Cawte,   .   5th do.

At Capture of Wokong—

Captain Cawte,   .   5th Regiment.
European Sergeant-Major Smith.

At Patachiaou—

Major Tumblety,   .   1st Regiment.
Captain Williams,   .   2d do.
Captain Chapman,   .   5th do.

At Leeku—

Major Howard,   .   4th Regiment.

At Wanti—

Captain Gibb,   .   1st Regiment.

Soochow—

Captain Cawte,   .   5th Regiment.
Captain Williams,   .   2d do.
Captain Tuite,   .   2d do.
Captain Chapman,   .   5th do.
Lieutenant Henrickson,   4th do.
Lieutenant Bremler,   4th do.
Captain Maule,   .   2d do.
Captain Wilson,   .   2d do.
Major Howard,   .   4th do.

At Chanchu—

Colonel Cawte,   .   4th Regiment.
Colonel Howard,   .   4th do.
Captain Winstanley,   5th do.
Colonel Chapman,   .   5th do.
Lieutenant Cane,   .   4th do.
Captain Bremler,   .   3d do.
Captain Henrickson,   4th do.

At Kintang—

Colonel Kirkham,   .   Staff.
Colonel Brooks,   .   Staff.
Major Brown,   .   Staff.
Colonel Williams,   .   2d Regiment.
Colonel Tumblety,   .   1st do.

ARRANGEMENTS for placing the EVER-VICTORIOUS ARMY under the joint command of Chinese and Foreign Officers, appointed by his Excellency the Futai and General Staveley, C.B.

1. The Force shall be placed temporarily under the joint command of Captain Holland, and Captain Gordon shall be recommended to Pekin as joint commander, and to regularly enter the Chinese service. The Futai appoints Futsiang Le Heng Sing to the joint command.

2. No expedition shall be undertaken beyond the thirty miles without previous reference to the Allies (England and France), but in reference to sudden expeditions within those limits their consent shall not be required.

3. A Chinese officer, of the 4th or 5th grade, shall be placed under the orders of the joint commanders as provost-marshal, to carry out such punishments as they shall order, who shall always be on the spot ; another officer, of equal rank, shall be appointed under their order to superintend the commissariat and pay of the Force, who shall always be on the spot. A third officer shall be appointed to take charge of military stores, who shall report from time to time to the Futai.

4. Three good linguists shall be appointed permanently to the Force.

5. The discipline and internal economy of the Force shall be in the hands of the joint commanders, and they shall be both present in person, or by deputy, at all issues of pay or of rations to the Force.

6. Orders on the Harguan Bank for six months' pay shall be issued every year, payable as due monthly, the amount to be settled when the standing of the Force is arranged.

7. The strength of the Force shall be 3000, but if the custom-house receipts should fail, this number may be eventually reduced.

8. No foreign officer of the Force shall be dismissed without a mixed court of inquiry, the sentence of which must be confirmed by the Futai, and which sentence cannot be reversed without the concurrence of the British General. No officer shall be appointed to the Force by the Chinese Commander without the concurrence of his British colleague.

9. The commanders shall not interfere with civil jurisdiction of Sung-Kiang and its suburbs.

10. The civil authorities shall carry out the wishes of the joint commanders in all matters connected with the defence of the city, but no public works shall be undertaken without their consent.

11. No purchases of arms, ammunition, or military stores of any kind, shall be made without the written consent of the Futai.

12. The British commander shall rank as equal with a Chêntai or Taoutai, and shall be given a proper Chinese designation corresponding thereto, but shall be under the orders of the Futai.

13. The British commander is only to leave the Force (if at his own request) with the consent of the British Commander-in-Chief, obtained and signified through the Consul. If the Chinese are dissatisfied with

the commander they shall not dismiss him without a judicial inquiry (in which the Consul shall take part), and due notice must be given.

All subordinate officers are to be appointed at the discretion of the joint commanders, due regard being paid to the 8th Article.

14. That the number of coolies employed by the Force shall be reduced, 100 per 1000 soldiers only being allowed, and their pay put on the footing of those employed in the Futai's camp—viz., 3 dols. per mensem.

15. That the hospital expenses be reduced. The Force to be put, as regards sickness, wounds, &c., on the same footing as other Chinese troops.

16. That the Foreign officers of the force shall receive certain pay, but no extra allowance.

"TI-PING TIEN-KWOH."

In a note to page 189, giving an account of the capture of the steamer Firefly, it is mentioned that the leader of the men who perpetrated that act escaped to England, and under the name of "Lin Lee" published a book, entitled 'Ti-ping Tien-Kwoh.' My reasons for taking no notice of that book in the body of my history are various and sufficient. It is not necessary to go beyond the author's own admissions in order to find ground for receiving his statements with caution. Though he does not mention the name of the Firefly, he admits (Chap. XXIII.) having been engaged in heading the capture of a steamer at Shanghai, in circumstances which leave no doubt that the Firefly is referred to; he actually complains (Chap. XXIV.) that for being engaged in that act one of his accomplices, a man called White, was condemned to three years' imprisonment by the British Consular Court of Shanghai; and he ingenuously adds, "Besides the fact that my medical adviser ordered a change of climate, directly I became aware of my lieutenant's fate I determined to take a trip to England."

These are not recommendations, for they involve a direct admission that he committed what the laws of his country condemned as an act of piracy; but many a worthy man has fought in a bad cause, and I should not have refused to notice Mr "Lin-Lee's" statements on those grounds alone. More remains behind. He admits having made prisoner on board this captured steamer four Europeans (the same whose names I have mentioned in the note to page 189), and that he promised to endeavour to pass them into Gordon's lines as prisoners of war, though he does not say that this was the condition on which they surrendered to him. How this promise was fulfilled can now only be judged from "Lin-Lee's" own statements, and from the fact that when Colonel Gordon occupied Wusieh he found there the bodies of the four men—Dolly, Martin, Perry, and Easton—in a burned and mutilated state, which proved, in the judgment of his medical officers, that they had been deliberately tortured before death. In one sentence, "Lin-Lee" suggests that this was done by the Imperialists, and in another that it was committed by the Tai-pings in revenge for the execution of the Soochow Wangs; but before determining the value of his evidence I should like to have some more light on this dark subject than either his statements or his suggestions.

But even this is not all. According to his own account (Chap. XXIV.), Lin-Lee shot dead Hart, an Englishman, one of his four foreign associates in the capture of the Firefly, as they were all returning from Soochow to Shanghai with the price which they had received for that steamer. At the same time he drove away, and "nearly frightened out of life," Thompson, an American, the second of his associates; and on reaching Shanghai, White, the third, was "betrayed" to the British authorities and cast into prison, while only the virtuous "Lin-Lee" [? Lindley] escaped unscathed with his prey to England. Of course all this was forced on "Lin-Lee." Hart and Thompson tried to murder him and White for the sake of the prize-money; and it was the dastardly Thompson who betrayed White at Shanghai. The Chinese have another version of the story, but then they are Asiatics, and of course liars.

Further, what actually was this man's connection with the Rebels? There is no doubt about his taking the Firefly to Soochow, and then coming down with the price and escaping to England; but he also gives a long account of previous adventures which he had among the Rebels. These may be perfectly true; but unfortunately he has entirely mistranslated a Tai-ping pass in Chinese, of which he gives a fac-simile in the commencement of his work, and has so mistranslated it as to make it an evidence of his previous connection with these Rebels, and to make it cover operations of war. I here give in parallel columns "Lin-Lee's" version of this document, as he divides it into pargraphs, and a true translation prepared by one competent Chinese scholar and revised by another :—

LIN-LEE'S VERSION.	TRUE TRANSLATION.
The General of the Chin-chung (truly faithful) Army, Chung-wang Le (The "Faithful Prince" Le).	Lí, the Faithful King of the True and Faithful Army, issues a certificate [or passport].
Hereby certifies that the undermentioned Foreign Brother, Lin-le, aforetime traversed the country between Shanghai, Ningpo, &c., conducting and managing military affairs (or ships of war).	The Foreign Brother Ling-li, being now about to proceed to Shanghai and Ningpo to obtain vessels [or a vessel] of war,
He has traversed the whole country, and from time to time has been actively engaged, and has collected commissariat (or military) stores, neither sparing pains nor valuing difficulties, but directly managing the affairs.	The places through which he shall pass are directed to furnish him sufficiently with rice, oil, salt, and firewood, so that he shall not want anything necessary.
After this he proceeds to Kia-hing (or Cha-shing) Prefecture to conduct operations (with regard to organising an auxiliary force, &c.), and to receive and use, from Ting Wang, certain moneys for affairs in which he succeeded (or may succeed).	When he shall have obtained [what he proceeds to obtain], he shall take the same to the Prefecture of Kia-hing, and deliver [the same] to the Ting Wang, who will pay the price.
We therefore hereby command those in charge of the military posts on the frontier to examine this closely, and to allow him to pass to and fro without let or hindrance.	And farther, the military in charge of the Customs Stations on the route are directed to "release upon examination," and to permit him to come and go without hindrance.
This is an Express Commission ! Dated, The Celestial Kingdom of Ti-ping, 13th year, 10th month, 26th day.	This pass is given 13th year of the Celestial Kingdom of our Heavenly Father, Elder Brother and King, and the 26th day of the 10th month.

From the above it will be seen that this document is merely a pass authorising the bearer to go thorough the Tai-ping lines, and to receive payment from the Ting Wang, in the event of his bringing a vessel of war, whereas "Lin-Lee" makes it out to be a certificate of his having previously engaged in military operations for the Tai-pings, and an authorisation to conduct such affairs in future. Without such mistranslation, he produces not even the mockery of Tai-ping authority for his capture of the Firefly, and delivery to the Tai-pings of the Europeans on board. If he has not been misled as to the meaning of the Chinese document, the audacity of giving a fac-simile of it is something stupendous, but is not out of keeping with his acknowledged exploits, and may have served a purpose with certain readers.

One would think that the force of nature could not go much further than this, but there is even something more. "Lin-Lee," on returning to England for the benefit of his health, &c., is not content with availing himself of his success, but must place himself in prominent contrast with Colonel Gordon. The latter officer is supposed by almost all who know him, either personally or by report, to be not a bad specimen of the Christian gentleman. His officers and soldiers idolised him; Chinese of all classes regarded him with high respect; when in their power his enemies offered him no injury, and their troops came over to him in large numbers; always foremost in moments of danger, no coolie of his force cared less for personal comfort; the Foreign merchants admired him, and he returned from China a poorer man than he went out, with little more than the honorary acknowledgments of his own and of the Chinese Governments. But it seems we are all under a mistake. The real hero is "Lin-Lee," whose exploits, so far as he adduces testimony, are the midnight capture of a small steamer lying off a peaceful settlement; the delivery, for money, of it and of the Europeans on board to cruel Tai-pings; the killing of one of his associates; and a secret flight to England!

So far 'Ti-Ping Tien-Kwoh' is a curiosity in literature; but otherwise I cannot recommend a perusal of it to any one seeking a knowledge of China; it is not interesting or amusing, and I regret much feeling myself called on to take even this notice of it. As regards Colonel Gordon's action in China, the statement of facts so far as it goes does not differ much from my own. The chief difference is in the gloss which is put upon these facts —a gloss which, I had believed, there was only one mind in the world pessimist and poisonous enough to have exuded.

STATEMENT OF GEORGE BAFFEY, A PRISONER SENT TO
H.B.M. CONSULATE, CANTON, BY THE CHINESE AUTHORITIES.

George Baffey states, I am aged twenty-two, was born at St Paul's,
Minnesota, and am a citizen of the United States.

I joined the rebels at Changchow about the 18th March. I went up
from Amoy to join them. When the rebels evacuated Changchow, I
came with them into this province, and stayed with them until the 14th
July, when I deserted them in disgust. The name of the Chief I joined
at Changchow was the Tze (She) Wang, and it was with his party to
the number of 20,000 that I left Changchow. There were thirteen
Europeans with them at that time. Eleven days after leaving Changchow the Tze Wang's division became disorganised near Yingting on a
branch of the Han River, and I joined the Kan Wang. It was with
the latter that I entered this province. The Kan Wang numbers his
force at 100,000, but he has not more than 15,000 fighting men, who,
however, are well armed. I got disgusted with them at last; the
slaughter was dreadful : at the city of Chênping they took 1600
Imperial braves prisoners, who surrendered on the promise of their
lives, but the same night they beheaded the whole number, and I saw
the creek run with blood for four hours. On the night of the 14th
July I took advantage of my being with a party at a point some sixty
li in advance of the city of Chênping to desert by floating down the
river on a plank, and the next day I took to the mountains. I wished
to avoid the troops, as I knew I should be put to death if taken prisoner
by them, so I made inquiries previously to my flight from the country
people within the rebel lines respecting the direction of Kia-ying-chow,
and at length I gave myself up to a village mandarin. Previously to
this I was seized by some boatmen belonging to the village, who bound
me hands and feet, and were about to behead me when a respectable old
man induced them to desist, and led me to the mandarin. The latter
sent me to Kia-ying-chow, where I was confined in an office belonging
to the magistrate, and treated well by the officials, but very badly by
the people. I only had rice and water. I was then sent down to Can
ton by boat in charge of a small mandarin, who treated me kindly. I
arrived at Canton the night before last, and was taken in a chair into
the city, where I was lodged in a yamên, and last night was examined
before two magistrates. It was at a Chinese prison; a linguist inter-
preted, but so badly that I could understand nothing.

To go back. I was originally employed in Colonel Gordon's force as
Captain of Artillery, and on its being broken up I served under the
Futai Li for three months as drill instructor, and then, wages being reduced from 211 dols. to 150 dols. a month, I went to Foochow and took
service under Baron de Meritens, who put me under the orders of a
Frenchman at Amoy, with whom I disagreed ; and, in consequence of
this, I went to Shanghai and endeavoured to get employed in the

2 C

Customs. I had previously endeavoured to get employment at Amoy and Ningpo, but had been refused everywhere; and so at length, having been unemployed for seven months, and receiving offers from Rhode and others who had joined the rebels, I went to Amoy and joined them.

Rhode was one of the thirteen who left Changchow with the rebels; of these only three besides myself are now alive. They are Williams, an American; McAuliffe (who made the mortars and shells, &c., at Changchow), an Irishman; and Rhode. Williams was very ill with dysentery when I left. The remainder, I believe, were all murdered at different times.

While with the Tze Wang after leaving Changchow I was four days without food; but the Kan Wang had been well supplied by pillage. When I left, the rebels were talking of retreating towards Kiangsi. The rebels have great confidence in the Kan Wang; the latter is an exceedingly clever man, very fond of European ideas, but very distrustful of foreigners. None of the Europeans were allowed to hold any authority, and none ever received the fulfilment of the promises by which we were enticed over. The Baron de Meritens sent Gerard and others into Changchow with letters and passes, endeavouring to get the Europeans over; but Gerard having previously cheated the Tze Wang out of 3000 dols., the latter seized and beheaded him.

The greatest number of Europeans ever at Changchow was sixteen. I attempted to escape out of Changchow, but was prevented by information given against me by a German. The cause of my wishing to desert was seeing two Chinese mandarins burnt alive by the rebels in the city of Changchow. For every tail of a mandarin soldier produced the Kan Wang gives 6 dols. reward. The Kan Wang is about thirty-five years of age. He is the principal rebel chief at the present moment. I have never heard the rebels speak of coming near Canton, but they are very anxious to get to the coast so as to obtain arms. There is very little money among the rebels, and this province is not productive enough to support them. They threw up fourteen fine stockades around the city of Chênping, very different from the wretched ones erected by the Imperial troops.

The country people are very hostile. They had cut down the unripe paddy around Chênping to prevent its falling into the hands of the Kan Wang. The latter, unlike the Tze Wang, does not allow useless devastation among the villages.

(Signed)   GEORGE BAFFEY.

Statement taken by me,

(Signed)   W. F. MAYERS.

August 5, 1865.

LIST of the CHINESE NAMES of PLACES near SHANGHAI.

In the text of this work, and in the "Sketch-Map of the Operations against the Rebels in 1862-64," many of the names of places are given as they were pronounced in the local dialect, and written down in English sometimes by persons ignorant of Chinese. For the benefit of travellers who may visit that part of China, now that it can be traversed with tolerable safety, I give the following list of some of the principal places, with their names as represented in the Mandarin or Peking dialect, and with their rank occasionally added. As a key to the meaning of many Chinese names, it may be well to mention that *kiang* signifies a river, and *shan* a mountain.

Sketch-Map.	Peking Dialect.	Sketch-Map.	Peking Dialect.
Chanchu fu	Changchow fu.	Najow	Nankiao.
Chinkiang	Chingkiang.	Poashan	Pooshen hien.
Chuenza	Chuensha.	Quinsan	Kwenshan.
Fusiquan	Kwangfu.	Seedong	Pasiao.
Haiyuen	Haiyen hien.	Semen	Shihmun hien.
Kading	Kiating hien.	Siangchow	Siyangkiao.
Kashing fu	Kiahing fu.	Taitsan	Taitsang chow.
Kashur	Kiashan hien.	Vongnai	Tunghien hien.
Kinsaiwai	Kinshan hien.	Wokong	Wukiang hien.
Kongyin	Kiangyin hien.	Wuchu fu	Hoochow fu.
Naiwai	Nanhwei hien.	Yesing	Yeshang.
Naizean	Nansiang.		

THE END.